earliest times to the present day documents how the invisible has become visible. They posit the idea that the visible global dimension of action provides us with an unprecedented opportunity in world history to use knowledge and creativity to construct a better, more open world."

Donald Fisher, Co-Director, Centre for Policy Studies in Higher Education and Training (CHET), University of British Columbia, Canada

"*Global Creation* is a path-breaking, magisterial treatment of the global knowledge economy in all of its detail and complexity. Thanks to Marginson, Murphy and Peters we discover what they call 'the K-economy,' a unique space for innovative public and private partnerships, constant networking as well as a global market for millions of students. Rich in ideas, they provide us with an unforgettable picture of the new dynamics of power, the fascinating world of state strategies and the cultural categories of creativity in the new global information economy. Critically, their research also establishes the structural limits of these markets. In a word, indispensable, provocative and challenging."

Daniel Drache, Professor of Political Science and Associate Director of the Robarts Centre for Canadian Studies, York University, Toronto, Canada

"This book opens fresh perspectives on the phenomena of globalization and knowledge economy. The authors not only broaden our historical understanding but also open new insights into creativity and its relationship with higher education institutions, the potential sources of innovation in global knowledge economies. The authors claim that we enjoy an enlarged freedom to create in a global knowledge economy. Our main challenge is, however, whether we use our growing freedoms for production of meaning, for originality in creativity and design, for ideas that open up our condition and our fate. This excellent and thought-provoking book may be recommended to everyone interested in understanding the nature of creativity and higher education in global knowledge societies."

Jussi Välimaa, Professor of Higher Education, University of Jyväskylä, Finland

"Global creation—what does that mean? From one perspective globalization processes have shown us the inescapable and imminent creativity of humans in this world. It seems that the historical creativity—set on form in art by e.g. modern aesthetics, from Baumgarten to Adorno, art as such—however brilliant, almost succumbs to the quotidian creativity at large in globalization processes. From another perspective such a view is naive. Global creation is creation under certain terms and taking place in certain confines and contexts—it is under the constraint of form. This volume attempts to follow creation at large but under the constraint of form: to map globalization as if it was creation proper, yet under the constraint of a particular topic—reflection, knowledge, science. The book is mapping crucial and strategic relations between 'the protean and the global' in an intense set of texts focusing on the formation of knowledge as global creation proper. First, it maps the conditions for the emergence of organized knowledge within the pre-modern and modern network of portal urban linkages circumspanning the oceans of the world. Then, it deals with the formation of the ensuing and enduring institutional forms, the modern research universities, as a field where all the prospects and constraints of modern global creativity are playing out. Finally, in the third set of texts, it presents a breathtaking overture of open knowledge and creativity set loose as novel form—complicit with global networks and civil societies and possible new roles for the modern institution of the university. Here we see the agenda of this highly learned work: the fascination of knowledge as a system turning in upon itself and discovering what it means to take command over its own form of creativity, e.g. in the self-reflective process now known as open source—that is, the importance of free, creative and self-reflective intellectual work. Few books have the persistent courage of the present volume: to argue that knowledge is neither primarily of something, nor a constructivist or merely political zero sum game, but in itself a world shaping creative magma and as such shaping a global world where there are fewer areas to discover outside our own enigmatic and human creativity."

Anders Michelsen, Associate Professor and Director of Studies, Department of Arts and Cultural Studies, University of Copenhagen, Denmark

"This is the best attempt so far to interrogate the global dimension of higher education. The book deserves to be widely read by anyone involved and interested in the global context. It is thought-provoking and is directed to the key points, with an air of enchantment."

Rui Yang, Director, Comparative Education Research Centre, University of Hong Kong

"This is a timely and welcome addition to understanding the effects of globalization on knowledge creation and change, and how the emergence of new and global forms and systems are reconstituting the conditions of creating and institutionalising the processes of knowledge production. More than anything else, this book gives us insight into how the rise of a new global dimension transforms not just culture and communication, but also science and intellectual production, work and the future, and how indeed our core identities as 'learning' and 'knowing' beings are being transformed as well. A rich book, pregnant with insight, and warmly welcomed."

Mark Olssen, Professor of Political Theory and Education, University of Surrey, United Kingdom; Author of Toward A Global Thin Community: Nietzsche, Foucault, and the Cosmopolitan Commitment

"As policy makers turn increasingly to issues of creativity and innovation in seeking the sources of value in the global knowledge society, this superb book provides fertile ground for thinkers of all kinds. It excitingly discusses the various dilemmas, paradoxes, antinomies and enigmas that underlie the conditions for creativity and provide the liquid environments that so frequently source the new and durable patterns and abstractions of true innovation. Moreover, it does so within that wide appreciation of historical, cultural, aesthetic, economic and educational skeins that sustains integrated multi-disciplinary work at its very best. The specific of the global, its dialectics of openness and closure, the centrality of universities in global processes, the continuing relevance of older theories within the swirl of the new, and the relevance of loose ties for creativity are key themes that are handled in exhilarating yet meticulous style. This lucid book will be read and re-read for its agenda-setting and research-shaping importance."

Roger King, Visiting Research Professor, Centre for Higher Education Research and Information, Open University, United Kingdom

Global Creation

PETER LANG
New York • Washington, D.C./Baltimore • Bern
Frankfurt am Main • Berlin • Brussels • Vienna • Oxford

Simon Marginson, Peter Murphy,
and Michael A. Peters

Global Creation

Space, Mobility and Synchrony in the Age of the Knowledge Economy

PETER LANG
New York • Washington, D.C./Baltimore • Bern
Frankfurt am Main • Berlin • Brussels • Vienna • Oxford

Library of Congress Cataloging-in-Publication Data

Global creation: space, mobility and synchrony in the age of the knowledge economy /
[edited by] Simon Marginson, Peter Murphy, Michael A. Peters.
p. cm.
Includes bibliographical references and index.
1. Education, Higher. 2. Creative ability. 3. Globalization—Economic aspects.
I. Marginson, Simon. II. Murphy, Peter. III. Peters, Michael A.
LB2325.G53   378—dc22   2009034448
ISBN 978-1-4331-0526-5 (hardcover)
ISBN 978-1-4331-0527-2 (paperback)

Bibliographic information published by **Die Deutsche Nationalbibliothek**.
Die Deutsche Nationalbibliothek lists this publication in the "Deutsche
Nationalbibliografie"; detailed bibliographic data is available
on the Internet at http://dnb.d-nb.de/.

Cover design by Sophie Boorsch Appel
Cover photo by Simon Marginson

The paper in this book meets the guidelines for permanence and durability
of the Committee on Production Guidelines for Book Longevity
of the Council of Library Resources.

© 2010 Peter Lang Publishing, Inc., New York
29 Broadway, 18th floor, New York, NY 10006
www.peterlang.com

Printed in the United States of America

Contents

Preface

In this the second of three books on creativity in the age of the knowledge economy, we focus on the global dimension. In Book 1, *Creativity and the Global Knowledge Economy*, released in early 2009, we interrogated the knowledge economy historically and conceptually. We traced the emerging society of ideas-driven production and of design that is reshaping the nature of creativity and the potentials of higher education, pushing against the more restricted neo-liberal mode of thinking and working that seeks to control knowledge production and dissemination as Intellectual Property. Book 3 on *Imagination* will bring readers closer to the new aesthetics of sciences and arts and of productive economy and nation in this period. This book *Global Creation: Space, Mobility and Synchrony in the Age of the Knowledge Economy* explores the two-sided transformation of global creativity.

First, the book describes how openness and networking, place-shifting, cross-border people movements and flows of capital and knowledge, portal cities and littoral zones, and new and audacious systems with worldwide reach, are changing the conditions of imagining and producing and sharing of creative work in different spheres. And how this is reaching back into the remaking of the core structures of our social world. Second, the book talks about the creation of the global dimension of action itself, in terms of its communications and culture, its fecund knowledge and science, its bounding, lurching economy and its under-developed government; and above all the acts of imagining, initiative-taking and strategy-making that are entailed in making the global.

In the middle of the worldwide recession and the attempts to solve it, not to mention the larger ecological crisis that is coming on with a rush from behind the recession, it is not hard to demonstrate global interdependence and convergence. Still, the forms of planetary integration, always incomplete but ever more potent, outstripping every intention of nation states, keep on spreading and mutating and surprising us.

We are staggered by the pace of change. Every time we look the global knowledge economy is bigger. Consider: the number of Internet users rose from zero to 1.5 billion between December 1988 and December 2008.[1] In 2006 broadband access was at 25 per cent in the OECD countries and broadband and blogs were growing exponentially.[2] Consider: from 1990 to 2005 the participation rate of school leavers in tertiary education in China, a nation of 1.3 billion people, rose from 4 to 23 per cent.

Not only is the global dimension the zone where the future is disseminated, increasingly the future is also being incubated there. *Global Creation* traces the implications of globalization for science and knowledge systems, for power and hierarchy, for American hegemony and for the rise of Asia, and for the institutions of education and research that seem ever more central to human endeavour (and seem also to be always problematic!). Despite reflex moves to national protection, the recession has accelerated remaking projects in which ecological and social interdependence are at the front. Global governance, which has lagged behind cultural and linguistic integration and the roll-out of world markets, is moving into the spotlight. Something more fundamental than a new political economy is involved in these transformations. The open collaborative systems of the Internet age, voluntary and loosely coupled, are opening a vast new space for creative potentials. This is filling a void that was long identified by fiction and mysticism, that of the universal mind; though it is a mind that seems also postmodern, fragmented and incomplete, and exhibits a diversity of cultural forms. The changes of the next two decades will be more extraordinary than those of the last.

Each of us is acting as lead author for one of the books of the trilogy. It has been a delight to share *Global Creation* with Michael and Peter, to be stimulated by their many ideas and instructed by their marvellous scholarship. Production of the trilogy has created fecund interfusions (joint and several) between philosophy, cultural studies, social science, and educational studies. It seems that we often do our best work in collaborations of this kind, in teams of the differently like-minded, in which older projects are reworked and transformed and turned into something new, and with ongoing effects in other work. I would also like to thank Glyn Davis, Johannah Fahey, and Brian Pusser, who provided helpful suggestions in relation to the Introduction and Chapter 5.

The deep and grateful thanks of all three of us go to Chris Myers, Bernadette Shade, Sophie Boorsch Appel who prepared the cover designs, and the rest of the team at Peter Lang, for all their work on the trilogy. It is a pleasure to share the project with such a fine publisher. We also thank our colleagues who generously read Books 1 or 2 in advance and provided commentary: Bill Cope, Peter Roberts, Eduardo de la Fuente, Edward A. Kolodziej, Nicholas C. Burbules, Bob Lingard, Glyn Davis, Bill Tierney, Fazal Rizvi, Don Fisher, Daniel Drache, Jussi Valimaa, Anders Michelsen, Rui Yang, Mark Olssen and Roger King.

Simon Marginson
Melbourne, May 2009

Endnotes

1. Internetworldstats, 2009.
2. OECD, 2008, 55–62.

References

Internetworldstats (2009). Accessed 3 May 2009 at: http://www.internetworldstats.com/

Organisation for Economic Cooperation and Development, OECD (2008). *Trends Shaping Education: 2008 Edition*. Paris: OECD.

Acknowledgments

Parts of Chapter 7, 'Higher Education as a Global Field,' were originally published in Simon Marginson, 'Global Field and Global Imagining: Bourdieu and Relations of Power in Worldwide Higher Education,' *British Journal of Sociology of Education*, 29 (3), 2008, pp. 303–316.

'The Rise of Global Science and the Emerging Political Economy of International Research Collaborations' by Michael A. Peters was originally published in *The European Journal of Education*, 'Special Issue: 'The European University: Between Governance, Discipline and Network,' (Eds.), Martin Lawn & Edwin Keiner, 41 (2), 2006: 225–244. Reprinted with permission.

Part of Chapter 10 , 'Hospitality, the Gift and the Politics of Friendship,' draws on material taken from Michael A. Peters & Gert Biesta, *Derrida, Politics and Pedagogy: Deconstructing the Humanities*. New York, Peter Lang, 2009.

CHAPTER I

Introduction

The Protean and the Global

◻ Simon Marginson

A blaze of creativity in Vienna

In less than three years between February 1784 and December 1786, when he was between 28 and 30 years of age, the Austrian composer and musician Wolfgang Amadeus Mozart created and performed 12 new concertos for the pianoforte. These works, each of which were written in three movements and about 25 minutes in length, were interspersed between many others, but for a time seemed to constitute the backbone of Mozart's oeuvre, the chief medium though which his ideas emerged. He found that the structural forms of the classical concerto in sonata form developed by Joseph Haydn could be extended and made ever more complex; and the new instrument of the pianoforte, in conjunction with strings and winds, enabled him to make many innovations in tonal colouring. In 1784–1786 the piano concertos were also central to his household accounts. Mozart's solo performances of the concertos in public in his adopted city of Vienna enabled him to exploit his own skills as a musician to the maximum possible advantage. They occupy a pivotal position in his career-long progression from paid court musician bound to Salzburg, to impresario of the largest mass audience available to him, the opera with its greater financial risks, its larger division of labour and its European reach.

The concertos issued in those years were unique in conceptual form, novel in changing instrumentation and utterly startling in their emotional and expressive range. They moved in masterly fashion between development and repetition. More than the output of any other composer they shaped the concerto as a musical form, with its oscillation between individual and chorus, agent and condition, voice and existence. Perhaps music is more essential to us than is speech, and the bearer of a larger set of codes and ideas. Mozart's piano concertos bristle with ideas. They retain the power to reach, to disturb and to illuminate. They have found their way to the centre of the Western mentality; they are played all over the world; and some of their themes abstracted from the rest have become too familiar. No doubt the impact on the innocent audiences of Vienna at first hearing of each concerto, at a time when the old order was trembling, was much greater. How are we to understand creative work of this kind?

The series evolved with great rapidity and repeatedly took wholly unpredictable turns. Consider the concertos numbered 20 to 24. We have the operatic dramas of number 20 in D Minor, its opening movement like the closing scene of *Don Giovanni*, anticipating Schubert fifty years in the future, and the romantic composers that followed. Concerto 21 in C Major follows less than a month later. The vital optimism and pace of its first movement, like a fast carriage journey through the spring countryside, is followed by the slow beautiful *andante* with its *pizzicato* strings that is unlike anything else Mozart wrote. The surviving notes from the time suggest that the composer worked on these two contrasting concertos simultaneously. The *andante* from concerto 21 was used to carry the love scenes in *Elvira Madigan*, the 1967 Swedish film directed by Bo Widerberg, based on the tragedy of the Danish tightrope dancer Hedvig Jensen. Seven years later Neil Diamond liked the main theme of the *andante* so much that he transposed it into his 1974 hit *Song Sung Blue*, which was not Mozart to be sure, but reminds us that great creations have an inexhaustible life as prototypes!

Then there is piano concerto number 22 in E flat Major. Again, it is very different to its predecessor. Out go the oboes and in come the clarinets. The first movement begins unhurried, queenly in dignity, the trumpets have the feel of the baroque. A quieter, less imperial, more restrained version of Handel perhaps. But slowly it becomes apparent that the music is full of unsolvable mysteries. Amid the fluid and swirling piano solos, more circular than serial with their bottomless depths, the soloist interrogates reality in the linear mode, and interrogates the linear mode at the same time, breaks off and returns, again and again. Every attempt to reach a final closing statement is followed effortlessly by the reopening of thought. The old certainties are dissolving and Mozart finds the questions have no end. There is no solution to the problems posed here except the finitude of life. Eventually the *allegro* stops and is succeeded by a sombre, funereal *andante*. This movement affected its first listeners, a select private audience, so strongly that it had to be repeated on the spot. Mozart's piano concerto number 22 is utterly contemporary. It speaks to us as we are, as penetrating a rendition of the paradoxes of modernization (and hence of globalization) as any devised in words.

In turn the E flat Major gives way to the open lyrical beauties of concerto 23 in A Major, where the intellectual power and fluency and clarity of the *allegro* are followed by an *adagio* which sinks into desolation with the stark simplicity of one of the composer's piano sonatas with its single line of notes. The winds breathe quietly and the strings descend gently behind the solo piano. Such is the spare communicative intensity of this music that its few bars carry a lifetime of sorrow, as if the whole Argentine tango tradition was distilled into one final song; only there is no love of melancholy at the end, no reconciliation with god or fate, nothing of the Bach andante with its final acceptance and gratitude for life. Sadness and nothing else. And after that extraordinary statement of pure human feeling in Christian Europe, after that cry into the night in a world without god, three years before the Bastille fell and everything was remade, Mozart turns round again and produces piano concerto number 24. Concerto 24 in C Minor is an even more powerful rendition of operatic grandeur and Sophoclean heroism and tragedy than was number 20 in D Minor. Some people consider 24 in C Minor to be the finest of all works ever written in the concerto form. It makes us shiver with exhilaration.

Leaving aside Mozart's exceptional mastery of technique, whose foundations had been laid before he was five years old; and without knowledge of Mozart's own agency freedom, his will to produce; what was happening in and around Mozart that made his amazing creative journey possible? We cannot isolate lines of direct causation for each specific concerto between on one hand the ecology, the circumstances of the compositions, and on the other the concertos themselves. We cannot explain these works in terms of the economic drivers of their commission; because while their purpose was to trigger a flow of capital, these were works that Mozart wrote for himself, artistically as well as economically. At this time the composer was under intensified pressure to produce more and more novel works. At the same time, by then his reputation was such that he was strong enough in the market to make his own rules about content and to vary them as he saw fit. The circumstances of today's scholar-professor are not very different (even though the achievements are mostly less exciting!). Each research scholar operates with an established form and with the potential for variation and innovation. More rarely, there are 'breaks' in the form itself. Nevertheless, though we cannot explain Mozart's concertos in direct terms we can speculate about the interplay of influences. Mozart's vocational journey as a composer was also a journey from the aristocratic world of pre-given status, donated privileges and preferment, to the world of the Viennese bourgeoisie in which merit and money could make their mark. Mozart was a cosmopolitan modernist soaked in the Enlightenment; impatient with the old religion and its claimants; curious about cultural distinctions, European-wide in his sensibilities and interested in the Ottoman; more open than most to novel ideas about gender; drawn to both science and the occult; in touch with many of the intellectuals and political players of his day. He was fascinated by the continuous innovations in economy and ideas. He crossed borders freely, which did not always endear him to the powers-that-were, for whom a creative talent was something to be owned, displayed and disposed of at a whim. He had a profound sense of his own project and the aesthetic value of his work. He knew a 'public.' He was the quintessential communicator.

In many respects Mozart's world is our world. We see it in the incessant modernization in his urban environments, the fecundity of markets, the flourishing of often very diverse talents, the gathering authority of civil society and public opinion, the pushing through (not always successful) against social closure, Mozart's own free associations, and his mobility of body and mind, and the way in which he and his friends seemed to relish the undermining of certainty. In pre-Bastille Vienna, as in 1960s America and as in many of our settings today, far from being chronologically aligned and opposed to each other, the modern and the post-modern were simultaneous, supporting Lyotard's notion of the post-modern as the nascent moment of the modern: 'a work can become modern only if it is first postmodern, for postmodernism is not modernism at its end but in its nascent state, that is, at the moment it attempts to present the unpresentable, and this state is constant.'[1] There were many such post-modern moments in Mozart's piano concertos. Their flow would not stop. We can imagine the consternation that was provoked by those pristine moments in audiences and musicians alike.

Yet there are also differences between Mozart's world and our own. These differences take us closer to what is distinctive about the knowledge economy, its institutions and agents. In many respects the differences lie in the enhanced role of the global in this era. In its subtitle *Space, Mobility and Synchrony,' Global Creation* attempts to capture those differences.

In the world of Mozart there were no electronic networks. Sociability was vectored entirely by face-to-face meetings, written communications and the doubtful transmission of gossip. Something of today's dialectic between grounded locality and loosely coupled external association was present, but there was little of the incredible transparency and visibility that we have quickly come to take for granted (though it is without precedent, and would have amazed Mozart, while circulating his work and building his reputation far more rapidly). Late eighteenth century Vienna was less dependent on the visual imaging now so central to our statements of identity except in painting, architecture and interior design. In place of photos, film, Internet and the cultivation of the face and body there were performing music, opera, letters and the cultivation of the soul. The Mozart of today might be a software designer.

For Mozart and his contemporaries the constraints of space were often more compelling than the strategic possibilities it offered. Mobility was a means to freedom but this was a mobility without airports and Internet portals. Land travel was fraught and expensive. The distances between capitals could be bridged but it took time, and in contrast with today the journey itself was long enough to be turned into an alternate kind of life, in which fashions changed and favourites rose and fell within the ranks of touring parties. Significantly, the social sites that were situated at the cultural cutting edge were often mobile localities such as travellers in passage and courts that moved between cities and palaces. The mobile existence contrasted sharply with the peasants who were bound to the soil, and the villages and towns such as Salzburg that Mozart had escaped; but even the mobile settings were *sui generis*, bounded in ways no longer possible. Life was lived more locally than we can ever know.

Mozart's world was Europe, and the historical opposite of the Austro-Hungarian Empire, long ranged alongside it and against it, the Ottoman Empire. The mixed populations of the Balkans broadened Viennese cosmopolitanism in ways familiar to us. But Asia beyond the Ottomans, and sub-Saharan Africa, were little known. The pre-Columbians in America had never been understood. The Pacific was invisible. Though the earth was round there was only a vague sense of it as a single entity. Mozart's contemporaries often went abroad for their education. They were multi-lingual and were adroit with national and regional differences. But they had none of our huge range of options for imaginative spatial organization: e-institutions, world-wide conferencing, international mergers and consortia, cross-border production, and the like. Space was everything outside the self;[2] it was large and inchoate. Space was not the game-zone that we can readily fly over and encompass, that we can imagine, calculate or possess. 1780s Vienna was not informed by the pictures of earth from space that have framed globalization visually for us. We can see the edge of the world. They could not.

In short, for Mozart and his contemporaries space was not global space. The only world projects were the longstanding claims to universalism, doomed to fall short of their ambition, if only because they rested on 'othering' the pagans and barbarians beyond their borders, the Catholic church, and an imperialism dating back to Rome held in place by military force.

Mozart's fellows had Latin as a common intellectual language and wanted to join with each other across boundaries in a republic of ideas. But there were no global libraries at their finger-tips, no Internet to compel them into instant conjunctions. They were not constantly crowded by communications from everywhere, the crowding that creative people today can only overcome temporarily and by acts of will. Mozart just had words on paper with which to find the way to distant fellowship. Letters ran deep, they enabled a cross-border community in which complex thoughts could evolve, the harbinger of teams of scholars and researchers today, but letters were much slower than the mental flickering of face-to-face and electronic conversations, especially in the dispatch. Letters permitted global sympathy at the edges of daily life, but not global synchrony. A corresponding association was a fragile connectivity. Wars and other follies could temporarily suspended postal networks. Government was partly relativized by the old global Church and the new global enlightened intellect but continued to control its territory. It could shut the world out, reasserting the horizon of the nation.

The stronger European nation-states, the superintendents of modernization in Mozart's time, formed what Hegel called an 'enclosure,' 'an enclosing surface which separates off a single whole space.' Heidegger called it 'insideness.'[3] Hegel described space as the unity of two moments, discreteness and continuity.[4] In the late eighteenth century the state fell short of its universalist pretensions, and its instruments of surveillance were less complete in coverage than those of today, but it could expand the scope for 'discreteness.' Nation-states no longer have this power. World system and connectivity are uppermost. The nation-state remains the seat of government. But it no longer constitutes itself as the final arbiter of the possible.

Time was also felt differently. It was in a world that was still the world of Mozart that Hegel wrote half a century later that time is negation. Things do not change 'in' time, time itself is change. In the passage of time everything is transformed. Yet, he remarked in one lecture, 'if everything stood still, even in imagination, then we should endure, there would be no time.'[5] Perhaps we need to imagine this more often than Hegel. 'Only something which endures can be altered,' stated Heidegger in *The Essence of Human Freedom* (2002/1930).[6] But what endures? In the age of the global knowledge economy, change quickens and the time of passage is reduced, intensifying modernization. Space-time compression brings us closer to the paradox. As time as duration becomes pressed into an ever smaller compass, the negation is reduced. Along with the shrinking of duration, regardless of the quickening of the pace of change there comes a point when the scope for change itself begins to disappear. 'Indeed, we are reduced almost to infinity' says Voss in Patrick White's novel of the same name.[7] Living always in the moment, we find ourselves approaching not just infinity but eternity.[8]

And it seems that this is what we want. Consider the alterations in the political culture. Government has shifted from planning society a generation ahead to spinning the media. The latest opinion poll on party preferences, short-term equity prices, trends in the morning housing market, the last university ranking. This kind of indicator now determines ready value in the political economy. This is what the activist wants. The farsighted planner stays in the picture, not instrumentally but as a simulacrum, as a politically sexy image created for the President or Prime Minister by the marketing department. The future might have to be factored back in to politics. Parties crave not government but victory. Victory is eternal.

We yearn for the sublime moment, in which the capacity for memory disappears, and the potential for iterative creativity is jettisoned with it. The American political system creates an imperial president, 'the most powerful person on earth,' but for eight years, not forever. Unlike the Romans, Americans do not worship their former presidents as gods. The winner of *American Idol*, the queen of the beauty pageant, the gold medallist at the Olympics: these hold court in our minds for just a few months. For a few hours, anyone with $500 can be an aristocrat, for this is the price of a five star restaurant or hotel. Our existence culminated in seconds. Prior to the 2008 Beijing Olympics a group of Australian athletes was asked to choose between winning an Olympic gold medal and dying young, or failing to win the medal and living a full life. Most opted without hesitation for the eternal moment. 'What endures is esteemed higher than what perishes, but all bloom, all beautiful vitality, dies early' (Hegel).[9] It seems that this is enough for us. Though perhaps it is not. We rummage through the pre-modern. Archaeology fascinates us. The West cultivates nostalgia for hierarchy and installs cultural categories as determinants of status (securing the comforts of order without locking in to genetics or the divine right of monarchs). In the East scholars soaked in modernization search for a Confucian ancestry. But for Mozart, as for Adam Smith in the *Theory of Moral Sentiments* and *The Wealth of Nations*,[10] aristocratic tradition was an old skin to be discarded. Time was felt more simply. Memory was ever present, and records were maintained. Forward evolution was expected. The future held more promise than the past.

Mozart's Viennese piano concertos are one of the great glories of the artistic canon. There was more at work than 'innovation' as we have come to understand the term. Innovation has become synonymous with all forms of novelty, from sales pitches to products to path-breaking ideas. Mozart was a creator, an originator. He was the source. It takes autonomy to be an innovator. It takes independence to be an originator, and something more. Innovation policy is focused on predictable business applications. It tends to blur the distinction between creation and application and downplays the domain of original ideas in which most 'innovations' are ultimately sourced. Something in Mozart, together with something in his setting, enabled him to be a source, an originator whose ideas are still fresh 220 years later. These are the peaks of creativity. It is the standard by which we should measure the present age, and any age.

Western Europe at the crest of the Enlightenment, culmination of the Renaissance, harbinger of modernity, on the brink of the promise of the French revolution that was when the hold of clericism on knowledge was broken and all things were possible (or so it seemed). 'Bliss was it in that dawn to be alive,' Wordsworth later said. The right period, we might think, for this highpoint in sonata form. Something special was needed to hold an audience. Ideas were in the air. If there is no direct line between environments and creative excellence some settings are more favourable to creativity than others. They provide a stimulus, or take off the brakes.

Today our cultural forms are in a greater turmoil than in Mozart's time. The ecology is unraveling, the economy is down, and regulatory systems are up for grabs. It comes at a time when human association and productive forms have been suddenly widened. New forms of information and knowledge are exploding into life. The potential for civil society has been greatly advanced, especially at the global level, and national supervision of populations is wearing thin.[11] The political economy faces as great a challenge as did the *ancien regime* in Europe, albeit a very different kind of challenge. As in late eighteenth century Europe, the changes that are recreating the social order are manifest in a process of modernization that touches every sector: new urban precincts, new social and individual freedoms, and new and seemingly insoluble gaps between haves and have nots. Is this a time of fluorescent creativity? Maybe. Is it stimulating extraordinary inventions? Yes. But how are they being used? Are we gathering great new concepts, deeper ideas, extraordinary breakthrough in form? Have the intellectual brakes really come off? Or is this a revolution in quantity rather than quality?

Perhaps it is a highly creative (certainly an inventive) time in some sectors and locations, but not all sectors; and not in the countries shut out of the global centres of power. In contrast with the 1780s much of the creativity is taking place in the global dimension, and the sectors such as communications and knowledge most closely implicated in the creation of the global.

The global dimension

So what is it that marks our time as a distinctive zone in which creation takes place? We have emphasized that it is a more 'global' time. We will now explore more closely what this means.

Global Creation rests on a sense of the *specificity* of the global dimension of action. We do not see the global sphere as a universal 'Everything' that contains within it any and every other dimension of life. (Perhaps the term 'worldwide' will serve for that awesome notion of a container with 'everything' known and unknown in it). Here the term 'global' refers to phenomena at the *world or planetary level*, such as the interdependent ecosystem, the flows of scientific knowledge across the world, and the evolving systems of international law and trade. These global phenomena are at one and the same time political, cultural, economic and social. And they exist alongside other activities that we can tag as 'local' and 'regional' and 'national.'

The local is the immediate horizon of our senses and of institutional sites within a short travelling distance. It is an irreducible part of our lives. The 'imagined community' of the nation, to recall the words of Benedict Anderson,[12] also remains a potent force. Predictions by 1990s theorists of globalization that the nation would fade to obsolescence were premature.[13] At the same time the once inviolable nation-state has been relativized by global comparisons and systems and by the free movement of information, ideas, and often people across borders, and both sub-national and meta-national regions seem to be gathering a growing weight. The human world is a mosaic of different ways of imagining, horizons of being and spheres of action with the differences vectored by spatiality. The local, national, regional and global dimensions are mutually constitutive. No one dimension wholly subsumes the others.

From the world religions that emerged between 700 BCE and 700 CE, to European science and the trade and conquer empires of the sixteenth to eighteenth centuries, global ways of seeing and doing have long been important. Typically it was the globally-inflected empires, nations, cities and trading zones that led human creativity. The long historical experience of creativity has much to tell us about the motors of our own age. For most of human history the global dimension of action was readily isolated from nation-states and local life, but in the nineteenth century it became harder to ignore, with the telegraph and telephone. After World War II mass air travel began, and its cost progressively reduced. Then in the 1990s the Internet installed global communicative association at the heart of our lives. Perhaps the creation of global communications and transport since the industrial revolution constitute the greatest change in human affairs since the advent of agriculture, the social surplus and the shaping of nature in the Neolithic revolution. It is here we differ most radically from the world of Mozart. The global dimension can no longer be marginalized. For us it has become inescapable.

Each year the global dimension is larger, visible in a greater clarity and detail. We imagine the planet as a single global eco-system. Likewise, we can imagine a single global knowledge economy in research, higher education and innovation in industry and government. This capacity to see the global as a whole has not always been part of human society. It began in Copernicus' astronomy and the first circumnavigation of the world in the sixteenth century (see also Chapter 5) and was powerfully advanced again in the first pictures of the earth from space beamed back by the astronauts and cosmonauts of the 1960s. This visualization of the global as a single bounded space for exploration and strategy has been further advanced since the 1960s by on one hand satellite mapping and location technologies, and on the other the Internet, which allows us to observe in virtual form every place and every organization that has its own web-page and through Google Earth large parts of the planet, including our own homes as they look from space. In our minds we can readily see the global knowledge economy as an ever-growing set of networked sites within a common system of financial exchange and part of the reason is our earth-from-space visual imagination. Phones and radios allowed people to talk at a distance but it was not until satellites and computing that we could share the image of the world as a single sphere, one integrated site or 'field' in Pierre Bourdieu's sense.[14] This is both a powerful simplification, and a means by which greater complexity is placed within our reach.

At the same time, when it is understood as a set of practices and relationships in the knowledge economy, that is as a social organism, the global dimension or 'field' is less singular and coherent than is suggested by that crisp blue-green image of the planet turning against the black background of space. The global knowledge economy contains fragments, gaps and closures. It is vectored by hierarchies and some of them are steep. There are vastly uneven concentrations of resources and authority and a third of the people of the world (people this book cannot reach and who cannot reach this book) live on less than a dollar a day. Even in higher education the unevenness is marked. The Internet renders every university visible to every other but global inclusion does not constitute global equivalence. There are profound differences in presence and capacity between k-economy sites in the developed world and those in emerging nations and cities. There is still greater inequality between sites within the global circuit and those that lie outside it, still existing in the time before communicative globalization had taken hold. Above all the knowledge economy is dominated by leading zones such as California, the Boston corridor, Texas, Seattle, London, the Netherlands, Tokyo, Eastern China and so on; and by a small number of dominant research universities. As Chapter 7 will discuss in more detail, in the global dimension of higher education, universities located in the US play a dominant role on the world scale. For example, in 2005 Indonesia, a nation of 223 million people, produced 205 science and technology papers as classified by the National Science Board in the US. The United States, a nation of just over 300 million people, which is just one third larger than Indonesia in population, produced 205,320 science and technology papers. This is one thousand times as many.[15]

The global field or dimension of the knowledge economy is also in constant motion; and the patterns of mobility are complex, uneven and unpredictable. There are few certainties. Global patterns are constantly changing, not only in small localized ways but in large ways. For example, there is potential for new entrants at the peak of the knowledge system, as the rapid rise of science-based research in China, Korea and Singapore is demonstrating. The global dimension of research, education and innovation is the site of bold strategies for re-imagining space and identity and numerous projects designed to form, manage and exploit global connectivity (see Chapter 6). Some such projects are grounded in the political economy of business and budgets. Some want to generate university status or knowledge for its own sake. Many projects feed into deep desires for synchrony with the global other. Others are still on the drawing boards awaiting their opportunity. All of them are potentially transformative.

Like the nation-state was in its heyday the global dimension of action is shaped by the dialectic of sameness and difference[16]: the antinomies of homogeneity and heterogeneity. Global systems such as finance and knowledge are normalizing. Indeed that is the chief benefit of such systems. They standardize. This has a downside. Much is lost from view and eventually eliminated from existence. Yet paradoxically global systems also bring us into encounters with diverse localities and organizational forms and cultural sets. Global creation, especially in open source form, has the potential to sustain and augment diversity in our methods of valuation. There are powerful actors pulling us in the directions of unity, of diversity and of unity-in-diversity. Which tendency is uppermost is a case-by-case question.

'Powerful actors.' Often it is a new kind of power. Until recently global relations were centred on nation-states and their bilateral or multilateral relations—'international' relations. But in the formation of the new global systems most of the actors are non-government actors. In global space forming there is an 'invisible hand' at work. Not so much the invisible hand of market coordination—though that is present—but the invisible hand (or many invisible hands) of communicative association and global civil society. The global dimension of the k-economy is a largely non-governmental zone that is becoming extraordinarily fecund in the creation of both private and public goods and relations. In part this global dimension is formed through the 'invisible colleges' of intellectuals and researchers with their myriad of linkages; in part through the transactions of the cross-border student market[17] and knowledge-intensive industries; and in part formalized and regulated through corporate agreements and official university forays into partnerships, networks and offshore sites of production. In the knowledge economy, national government, which is always handicapped by the spatial limits on its mandate even while it pushes against those limits,[18] is more often follower than leader, though at the same time all governments want to structure global systems in their favour if they can. On the whole EU policy has been more advanced than the official strategies of global formation elsewhere, though its effectiveness is confined to the fashioning of Europe and its global presence. In part the EU is relatively effective because it embodies a pronounced element of voluntarism and informal synchrony atypical of nation-states. Nevertheless state investments remain highly influential in global knowledge economy formation, especially investments in basic research and universities. In the strong knowledge zones such as the USA, China and Western Europe the global forays of knowledge producing institutions are seen to have foreign policy implications. In an informal but real sense the independent US universities, including the Ivy League private sector, function as arms of imperial policy.

A large part of global formation takes place in the interplay between agents in civil society, nation-states, and worldwide policymakers such as the OECD and World Bank. It is unsurprising that institutions such as research universities and communications companies, which tend to be located somewhere on the border between 'public' and 'private' sectors in their nations—and also the private media companies which have become central in constituting the public civil space—are all playing a prominent role in the creation of the global dimension.

The longer term issue posed here is that of the future role of orthodox systems of government. Globalization embodies an alternative modernist reflexivity to that of the nation-state. The peak of ambition for the nation-states is the perfect formation of 'its' population and the ultimate triumph of itself. For Hegel the nation-state was the higher mode of organization than civil association.[19] But global formation as global civil society has fundamentally overturned that sequencing, and poses for the first time in concrete form the possibility of the withering away of the existing state-based forms of regulation. At the same time the global dimension also poses the unresolved, scarcely tackled issue of global governance, the associated problem of global rights, and how to tackle globally vectored inequalities.

The long view

These are large issues; coming on with a rush; and it is urgent that we address them, because they are the starting point for much else. At the same time, and paradoxically, the conscious evolution of the global dimension of action requires us to take the long view. To learn from our history in order to make our history. To nurture the institutions and ways of seeing that enable us to take the long view. In that respect it is no accident that the knowledge sectors are central to the frame. It is in the institutions of higher education, scholarship and research; and the sites in the associated sectors of publishing, design, science and artistic creativity; that we have the capacity to consciously imagine the future in terms of sequence and duration, which is essential to us. Provided, of course, those institutions and sites have the autonomy they need to do so. A free iterative creativity that continually builds on past achievements and goes ever deeper is not in conflict with engagement, responsiveness and powerful social communication, as the career of Mozart shows. But a free iterative creativity does require a distinct long view temporality. Our enemy here is hyper-modernity, the end of thought, the tyranny of the eternal present: when in the words of the white rabbit in *Alice in Wonderland*, there is 'no time to stop.' Like all readings of time, hyper-modernity is in the mind. It is not compulsory for us. But it has secured a purchase, in intellectual work along with everywhere else, and we must work hard to lodge a different temporality. The long view is a central theme of *Global Creation*.

The long view opens us to the diversity in space and time that is our greatest resource. Consider Mozart's extended tour of Italy between 1769 and 1771, which began when he was just 13 years old. Italy was the home of opera. During the tour Mozart wrote and adapted operatic compositions to much acclaim. But above all he was exposed intensively to the past and present of the great creations in the genre. This material, percolating inside him for years, was the foundation for his own operas of the 1780s in Vienna, where he shifted the language from Italian to German, bringing the great stories to all who could pay the price of admission, and leaving us with the works that are constantly performed around the world today. Consider Johann Sebastian Bach, who, seventy years before Mozart went to Italy, sent for the violin concertos of his Italian contemporary Antonio Vivaldi whom he greatly admired. Bach transposed Vivaldi's concertos and then began to compose his own. And something happened to Bach when he got closer to the inventive forms used by Vivaldi, with his open-ended, almost post-modern structure, disjunctive and surprising, so different from the certainties of Bach. When the German master completed his violin concertos he found he had married his own deep and perfect form to solos whose soaring beauty and protean clarity were secured with Italian grace. In the double violin concerto in D Minor, in the *adagio* of the concerto in E, and in the ascending and descending cycles of the slow movement in the A Minor concerto which is the sum of life, Bach's synchrony with Vivaldi brought the instrument to levels that have not been surpassed since. Yet in our time there are more resources and more diverse resources available to us. What heights might we not scale, if we permit ourselves the time to borrow and learn, and think, and build, and push ourselves to the highest point that we can?

In the global knowledge economy we enjoy an enlarged freedom to create. Whether we use our growing freedoms as well as did our eighteenth and nineteenth century predecessors is less clear. The challenge is to use the incredible opportunity provided by more democratic forms in information and knowledge to widen also the potentials for production of meaning, for originality in creativity and design, for ideas that open up our condition and our fate.

The chapters

This introduction has sought to open some of the issues rather than close them. What follows in *Global Creation* approaches the question of global creativity from three different vantage points, all antipodean in origin and now located in the USA and Australia, multiple in the communities with which they correct and in the place/times that excite their enthusiasm here.

In Chapters 2–4, Peter Murphy begins by stepping back from the present day to explore the antecedents of global creativity. Murphy assays the long history of cross-border connections and passages, and the evolution of knowledge hubs and long-distance cultural flows over time to illuminate the distinctive social structure, geographical location, cultural presuppositions, and historical dynamics of knowledge-intensive societies. These chapters describe the structural origins of the global knowledge economy today and its key institutions and the leading role that the maritime world circumference plays, and has long played, in this formation. The research-based cities and organizations, and arts-and-science driven economies, of the world circumference, notably maritime Europe and America, East Asia, and Australasia, are discussed, along with their underlying mentalities. Murphy ruminates on the peculiar social, military, and civil power that this circumference projects via the medium of its global connectivity and its knowledge productivity.

In Chapter 2, 'The Enigma of Distance,' Murphy examines portal societies with long-distance global reach. He hypothesizes about the enigmatic cultures, cognitive ethics, and high-level knowledge-generating capabilities that emerge in such locations. Drawing on multiple examples from historic Guangdong to contemporary Chicago, Enlightenment-era Edinburgh to mid-twentieth century Tokyo, Renaissance Venice to seventh-century Gujarat, it is noted how these kinds of place produce knowledge that is different from traditional ethical, literary, or oral culture. It is a kind of knowledge that stands apart for its skeptical, architectonic, paradoxical, detached, enigmatic, and cosmopolitan qualities, and that seeds great arts-and-science cities and university centers. The intense activity and traffic of these places, and knowledge that they generate as a result, both create the global condition and embody that creation in a myriad of interesting ways.

Chapter 3, 'Portal Power and Thalassic Imagination,' discusses the rise of global cities and intellectual centers in the United States. It charts the interaction between America's portal regions, its philosophies of globalism, the concurrent rise of its great universities and knowledge industries, and the subtle relations between its culture foundations and its world ambitions, its continental system of power and its ability to act-at-a-distance on a world scale. The chapter notes the parallel rise to globalism of another portal region, that of maritime East Asia, and the interweaving of American portal power, knowledge economies, and intellectual traffic with those of maritime East Asia, both before and after World War Two. It also discusses the tensions between parochial and global, national and international strains in the American character, and the relation between the outward-going and inward-looking polarities of the American mind.

Chapter 4, 'The world circumference,' turns to look at the prodigious contribution of the world maritime rim to the formation of knowledge-intensive societies. Societies that are preoccupied with the advancement of the arts and sciences, whether this happens to be today or in the past, are largely concentrated on the world maritime rim; from nineteenth-century London and Baltimore to twentieth-century San Francisco and Tokyo, from New York and Amsterdam to Athens and Rome. The chapter explores the reasons for this, and looks at the particular case of the Australian littoral, the role played by world traffic in goods, peoples and ideas, and the distinctive cultural mentalities and social drivers that have made such intensity of intellectual capital production around the world maritime rim possible.

In Chapters 5–7, Simon Marginson takes us to the present and the formation of the global dimension of the knowledge economy, and the evolution of research universities, the sites of a large part of our creative effort. He examines space-time in the global dimension, global agency, university executive and governmental strategies of space making in the global dimension of higher education; and the global field of higher education and the patterns of power and hegemony of particular universities and nations in the knowledge economy.

Chapter 5, 'Space, Mobility and Synchrony in the Knowledge Economy' works through the changes in space-time in the global era. Communicative globalization and planetary travel have provided new conditions of life. Our reading of new potentials, though, is always an open question. Humans make their own space and time. The fluid flows, horizontal networks and vertical orders of the global knowledge economy are open to any number of permutations. But some elements are common to our experience of the global. First, at this time we engage in acts of 'de-severing' in Heidegger's sense, in which physical and cultural distances are radically reduced. Second, for those who have the means to interact globally (at this stage only a minority can do so), the boundaries of the global seem to be enlarging; and at best we move though the global as a vast realm of freedom. Third, in global space, fertile with opportunities, agents also seek to secure closures in their own interest. This oscillation between openness and closure is at the core of globalization. Fourth, another key to globalization is the enhanced potential for temporal synchrony with each other, across the world, which is manifest in many ways in policy and government, in the financial and industrial economy, in the multitude of 'flat' voluntary networks in civil society, and in the universities and creative work.

In Chapter 6, 'Making Space in Higher Education,' Marginson works with the ideas in Chapter 5 to consider the creation of global spatiality by research universities, and higher education systems. In the wake of communicative globalization and 'thicker' people movement, university executives and research leaders have fashioned a remarkable range of new ways to build capacity and connectivity in the global environment. The geo-spatial strategies reviewed here include the conventional moves such as national investment in innovation, research concentrations, networks and alliances, and commercially marketed international education; and more novel strategies such as global knowledge hubs, region-building as in Europe, e-universities and offshore campuses. The chapter also considers meta-strategies which set out to order the knowledge economy as a whole, such as the WTO/GATS model of higher education as a trading system, and university rankings. These geo-spatial projects rest on different ways of conceiving, arranging and utilizing space. Like all acts of creation, global space making in the knowledge economy rests on openness to the new; like all acts of creation it entails acts of closure often designed for particular interests. Global space making also has unplanned effects. All of this is shaping global potentials.

In Chapter 7 on 'Higher Education as a Global Field' Marginson provides a synthetic mapping of knowledge, research and researchers in higher education. Global flows between countries and between individual universities are shaped by hierarchies and asymmetries, which play a crucial role in constituting the knowledge economy. One global hierarchy is the division of labour between elite universities, whose mission is autonomous and defined by cultural status; and mass institutions, driven heteronomously by governments or market forces. Pierre Bourdieu's notion of a polar field of higher education, developed originally to explain 1960s French universities, has continuing applicability in the global domain. The chapter adapts Bourdieu in framing a tentative worldwide typology of institutional types. The 'Bourdieu-ian' picture is supplemented by the remarkable hegemony exercised by American universities; the rise of higher education and research in China, Korea, Taiwan and Singapore; and a notion of agency in the global setting that is more autonomous and nuanced than that of Bourdieu. A key aspect of the global field is its openness.

In Chapters 8–10 Michael Peters expands on openness, which mediates the conjunction between 'global' and 'knowledge economy,' and the corollary of openness which is the encounter with the Other.

Chapter 8 on 'The Rise of Global Science and the Emerging Political Economy of International Research Collaboration' describes the emerging geography of scientific knowledge and collaboration as an aspect of globalization. It does so by providing a picture of international research collaboration and situating this in historical perspective. The chapter examines three 'moments' in the history of science—classical science, colonial science, and 'big' science—as three illustrative moments in an extended chronology of science that might also recognize other periods such as 'industrial science,' 'Cold War science,' and the rise of multinational corporate science. The chapter begins and ends by raising questions concerning both the role and different models of research collaboration in the age of global science.

Chapter 9, 'The Virtues of Openness in Higher Education,' focuses on the 'open science economy' and science and knowledge as global public goods in the global knowledge economy. The chapter begins by describing and analyzing the significance of open source models of knowledge, science and education and the networked and overlapping spaces that have grown out of the open source movement. The chapter outlines the technopolitical economy of openness, examining three elements—the politics of openness; the economics of openness, and the technologies of openness—before theorizing the development and significance of the open science economy.

Chapter 10, 'Cultural Exchange, Study Abroad and Discourse of the Other' begins by briefly outlining five major models of study abroad including liberal and neoliberal models and the postcolonial model designed to critique the worst features of (neo) imperialism. The chapter also examines the discourse of the Other, beginning with 'first contact' and the myth of the 'noble savage,' demonstrating that ways in which these ideas framed liberal anthropology, ethnography, politics and the multicultural society. The chapter reminds us that assumptions of the discourse of the Other are deeply embedded and the complex ways that they informed cultural exchange and also colonial administration and education. The chapter also investigates the work of the French philosopher Jacques Derrida on the notion and practice of hospitality as a model that provides an ethics for cultural exchange and study abroad, and an ethical basis for understanding modern cosmopolitanism. Finally the chapter reviews the footprint of modern study abroad and raises some questions about its conceptualizations.

Endnotes

1. Lyotard, 1984, 79.
2. Hegel, 2004, 29.
3. *ibid*, 31. Heidegger, 1962, 134
4. Hegel, 2004, 30.
5. *ibid*, 28, 35 & 36.
6. Heidegger, 2002, 121.
7. White, 1960, 216.
8. Hegel, 2004, 39: 'In the positive meaning of time, it can be said that only the Present *is*, that Before and After are not. But the concrete Present is the result of the Past and is pregnant with the Future. The true Present, therefore is eternity.'
9. Hegel, 2004, 36.
10. Smith, 2004 (1759); Smith, 1974 (1776).
11. Drache, 2008.
12. Anderson, 1983.
13. For example, in the otherwise astonishingly perceptive argument about cultural globalization developed by Arjun Appadurai, 1996.
14. Bourdieu, 1993. See Chapter 7.
15. NSB, 2009.
16. Marginson and Mollis, 2001.
17. OECD, 2008; Marginson, et al., forthcoming.
18. e.g. the discussions by Vaughan-Williams, 2008; Basaran, 2008.
19. Hegel, 2008, 51.

References

Anderson, Benedict (1983). *Imagined Communities: Reflections on the Origins and Spread of Nationalism.* London: Verso.

Appadurai, A. (1996). *Modernity at Large: Cultural Dimensions of Globalization.* Minneapolis: University of Minnesota Press.

Basaran, T. (2008). Security, law, borders: Spaces of exclusion. *International Political Sociology, 2,* 339–354.

Bourdieu, P. (1993). *The Field of Cultural Production.* R. Johnson (ed.). New York: Columbia University Press.

Drache, D. (2008). *Defiant Publics: The unprecedented reach of the global citizen*. Cambridge: Polity.

Hegel, G. (2004/1830). *Philosophy of Nature. Part II of the Encyclopaedia of the Philosophical Sciences*. Oxford: Oxford University Press.

Hegel, G. (2008/1920). *Outlines of the Philosophy of Right*. Intoduction by S. Houlgate. Transl. T. Knox. Oxford: Oxford University Press.

Heidegger, M. (1962). *Being and Time*. Transl. by J. Macquarie & E. Robinson. New York: Harper and Row.

Kant, I. (1933). *Immanuel Kant's Critique of Pure Reason*. Transl. N. Smith. London: Macmillan.

Kenway, J., Bulleen, E., Fahey, J., with Robb, S. (2006). *Haunting the Knowledge Economy*. London: Routledge.

Lyotard, J-F. (1984). *The Post-modern Condition: A Report on Knowledge*. Transl. G. Bennington and B. Massumi. Minneapolis: University of Minnesota Press.

Marginson, S. & Mollis, M. (2001). 'The door opens and the tiger leaps': Theories and reflexivities of comparative education for a global millenium. *Comparative Education Review*, 45 (4), 581–615.

Marginson, S., Nyland, C., Sawir, E, & Forbes-Mewett, H. (forthcoming). *International Student Security*.

National Science Board, NSB (2009). *Science and Engineering Indicators*. Accessed on 21 March 2009 at: http://www.nsf.gov/statistics/seind04/

Organisation for Economic Cooperation and Development, OECD (2008). *Tertiary Education for the Knowledge Society: OECD Thematic Review of Tertiary Education*. Paris: OECD.

Smith, A. (2004/1759). *The Theory of Moral Sentiments*. Barnes & Noble.

Smith, A. (1974/1776). *An Inquiry into the Wealth of Nations*. Harmondsworth: Penguin.

Vaughan-Williams, N. (2008). Borders, territory, law. *International Political Sociology*, 2, 322–338.

White, P. (1960). *Voss*. Harmondsworth: Penguin.

CHAPTER 2

The Enigma of Distance

◘ Peter Murphy

Worldviews

The pianist in Wittgenstein (1974, 6.51–7) put it well: 'the most important things in life lie beyond words.' So let us begin by throwing away the ladder of language that we are used to standing on.

Wittgenstein's other life—as an architect, engineer, and musician—conditioned him to do what philosophers often do not bother to do: take seriously what is *not* put into words, or what lies beneath words. Wittgenstein struggled for a way of understanding the silent shape of things. Things that cannot be put into words, he observed, *manifest* themselves. Wittgenstein called this process 'mystical' (6.522). There is a long tradition of thinking mystically about those things that we cannot put into words. There is also another, and equally strong, tradition of thinking about such things. This is to render them in geometric, musical, and architectural forms. There is no obligation on us to choose between these ways of thinking. Indeed, at certain times, these traditions have cut across each other.

Let us call both traditions architectonic. In the pre-modern age, the most important attempts at developing an architectonic view of the world were those of Taoism in China, Jainism in India, Sufism in the Islamic world, the various currents of Buddhism, the succession of Presocratism, Pythagoreanism, Platonism, Stoicism, and Skepticism in the Greco-Roman world and their coalescence with the mystical and paradoxical currents in Christianity and Judaism. The Pythagoreans were the ones who most effortlessly glided between the mystical and the rational—almost as if there was no difference between them.

Architectonics implies a world held together by ties that are neither linguistic nor are they like linguistic ties. These ties are not names or identities. They are not descriptions, words, narratives, imperatives, instructions, utterances, grammars, or syntaxes. This does not mean that such ties are nameless or unidentifiable. Here we should part company with Wittgenstein. We do not have to remain literally silent about such matters. Language can be used perfectly well to name things that are *not* linguistic objects. After all, the world about which we speak is not just made up of the elements of language. All the same, an architectonic worldview is paradoxical. It names and describes something whose nature is not linguistic, and thus is always in some fundamental way indescribable and inexpressible. Some aspect of that nature—the thing-in-itself—will always point beyond words: towards that which is indefinable, unutterable, and unspeakable.

Architectonic worldviews come—in historical sequence—after the appearance of two other kinds of worldview, *viz.* ethical religion and classical literature. Both ethical religion and classical literature distinguished themselves by producing an ethics of distance. They provided the linguistic means that allowed human beings to detach themselves from the territorial confines of tribes and patrimonial kingdoms, enabling them to travel across the face of the earth, and to found the typical political orders of post-archaic civilizations—city-states and bureaucratic empires. The first of these mobile worldviews was revealed religion. This produced religious ethics based on the revelation of divine truth—the utterance of an ethical god. This was truth revealed through the agency of a prophet—the prophets of Israel, Zoroaster, and Muhammad. Revealed religion gave rise to the idea of a free-floating moral law that was independent of a specific geographical locale, and that was 'world transforming.' Other kinds of mobile worldview included virtue literature, such as the Confucian classics, and the epic stories of the Homeric heroes or the Hindu gods. Each gave rise to social bonds independent of a specific locale.

The most interesting of all of the mobile worldviews were a third kind—the architectonic ones, those with an enigmatic core. These generated social meaning through their engagement, often mystical in nature, with un-decidable qualities. The enigmatic worldviews took artistic, religious and philosophical forms. Buddhism and Christianity are the most important examples of the enigmatic religious worldview, although even these often found their highest forms of expression in art, in mystical silence, and paradoxical philosophies. Buddhism's Zen current—and also its syncretism with Taoism—is typical of this. Of all of the three types of mobile worldview, the third or architectonic kind was the greatest solvent on traditional social bonds. The story of the Buddha is archetypal in this respect. It is filled with images of rejection of the household. He gives up his wife; he upsets his father, King Suddhodana, by begging in his own home city; he ordains his son without his father's permission; his principal followers were monks and nuns. His call to carry the truth abroad—and his own traveling through towns, villages, and cities—matches his rejection of the household.[1] The Buddha, 'the Enlightened One' (c. 563–483 BCE), was born Prince Siddhattha in northeastern India, on the border of what today is Nepal. The seers predicted that he would either remain at home and become a universal monarch or would leave and become a Buddha. He did the latter. He gave up the life of princely comfort to become a wandering ascetic on a search for truth.

The search for truth involved the Buddha in renunciation, austerity, self-mortification, emaciation, battles with demons, desertion by his companions, and progress toward enlightenment and the truth (*dhamma*) that everything is relative, interdependent, and impermanent, and that the person who leaves home and goes forth should avoid the two extremes of self-indulgence and self-mortification. Steering the middle path leads to knowledge, calmness, and nirvana. This is paralleled by the idea that the human self is a non-self. The self is constantly becoming different, an ever-changing non-identical identity. This is so because the self is limited, and limits give rise to desire. Desire (what is wanted) causes suffering (what is not wanted). What is desired is transitory, changing, and perishing. The impermanence of the object of desire causes disappointment and sorrow. In other words, desire causes what is not desired. Enlightenment is the overcoming of desire. It is the extinction of passion and cravings—indicated by cool feelings of self-control, cheerfulness and evenhandedness, and symbolized by images of the harbor of refuge and the farther shore.

The search for truth, it turns out, yields little unambiguous truth. But the seeker after truth nonetheless learns some important lessons. Such as that desire is not to be desired—and whoever our self is, is not who we are. Or as Shakespeare put it: 'I am not who I am.' Leaving home, it seems, turns a lot of things into their opposite—home included. Sigmund Freud's word for the uncanny was the un-homely. In the world of the uncanny, everything is its opposite. This begins with the journey away from home, which is also a journey homewards. At home one can be oneself, and yet home, as the homeless mind discovers, is a prison. So the human being who leaves home finds that truth is a fiction or even a lie—in the curious sense that everything interesting in the world is its own opposite. Once this conclusion has been drawn, the searcher can rest. The farther shore of the away home has been reached.

The philosopher Nietzsche, who was not easily pleased by any system of thought, surprisingly had some friendly words for Buddhism. This is possibly because he observed in its corpus something of the same paradoxical thread that he observed and liked in the cases of Pre-Socratic Greek philosophy and early Greek tragic drama. This was the un-decidable union of opposites.[2] Nietzsche supposed that this was the engine house of human creativity. Nietzsche had no friendly words to say about Christianity but, as the French Jewish Catholic mystic philosopher Simone Weil was to point out a little later, Christianity also has its own foundation of paradox (Weil, 1956, 1957). Weil's and Nietzsche's fellow philosopher Søren Kierkegaard had also shrewdly noted that the parables of Christianity—stories of lambs and lions, lost sheep, mustard seeds and fig trees—resonate with paradoxical twists (Kierkegaard, 1978). The sociologist John Carroll (2001, 2007) blended Kierkegaard and Nietzsche in his account of the enigmatic Jesus. This is the Jesus who taught (if that is quite the right word) through paradoxes and parables. These are mysterious, enigmatic expressions that hint at audiences who see but do not perceive, or who hear but do not understand. The paralyzed person who walks, the bed-ridden man who stands up, are metaphors for the spirit (*pnuema*) that animates, uplifts, inspires. Under the impress of *pnuema,* it is grace that rules, not the law. Grace rules through the medium of paradox. Grace is a kind of lawfulness without law, an order without moralism.

Paradoxes baffle—and create other paradoxes in their wake, like the paradox of the twelve followers of Jesus, the intimates who are supposed to have a special knowledge of him, and yet who cannot understand his parables, and who are bewildered by him. These followers are not only bewildered—they are also afraid. His followers fear him. His message to them is that the only thing you have to fear is fear itself. Be courageous! Stand up! Don't be afraid! Trust me! But his followers do not trust him. His followers abandon him. Another paradox—the follower is the one who abandons the one who he follows. With friends like that, who needs enemies? Jesus is the teacher who does not teach, the preacher who does not preach. He speaks in riddles and parables—and stretches language to its breaking point. He enlightens by confusing, and clarifies by spreading bewilderment. The intellectuals in the temple least of all understand him. Those whose vocation is to understand are always the ones who are most mystified. Jesus does not present himself as a savior. He gives every appearance of not caring if his followers perish. What is his response to their timidity? Fear not, trust me. But it is a paradoxical trust. Follow me, and you will be lost—and that is the only way you will find your way. Being saved is very enigmatic in this story to say the least. 'Whoever wishes to save his soul will lose it, but whoever loses his own soul on account of me and my Story will save it.' Jesus is not interested in saving himself either. He does not defend himself against his accusers. To Pilate's questioning, he only has an elliptical reply: you say. Or to his betrayers: what you do, he says to Judas, do quickly. The conclusion of all of this is that only paradox has real power. Ethics has no (true) power. Law has no (true) power. This we learn when we leave home.

Mobile civilization

Prophetic, heroic and paradoxical worldviews each contributed to the sense of 'leaving home'—to a new kind of spiritual independence from one's place of origin. This was expressed not just in the content but also in the media of heroic, prophetic and enigmatic works. Prophecy was expressed through the medium of expectancy, enigma through paradox, and heroism through epic form. Physical media paralleled these formal media. Heroic, prophetic and enigmatic worldviews were transmitted through various types of 'mobile writing.' The principal physical media used for setting down the accounts of the prophet, hero or enigmatic figure were not the clay tablets or the stone of archaic civilization, but the portable media of papyrus, parchment, paper, textiles, or palm leaf (Martin, 1994, 43–52).[3] Correspondingly, 'mobile writing' suited very well the development of both large-scale historic empires and long-distance portal societies. Both of these were types of society whose members developed extensive lateral or peer networks for coordinating administrative, economic, and cultural activity. Councils, assemblies, monasteries, guilds, military corps, scholarly bureaucracies, schools of religious jurists and the like massively supplemented the old social forms of kingship and household. For this to happen, an appropriate ethos and psychology was required. Hero, prophet, and enigmatic figure provided models of mobile characters that moved freely across local or communal boundaries.

In the spectrum that runs from tribe to patrimonial state, face-to-face communications and emotions regulate social conduct. Body language and verbal commands, honor and shame are paramount. Communication between heaven and earth is organized through the rituals of temples and palaces, and is illustrated in pictograms of cosmic events set in clay or in stone relief. The 'books' of ethical prophecy and classical literature, in contrast, are highly transportable. Their effect takes place outside the realm of face-to-face communications. They regulate social conduct in the first case through the emotion of conscience (when the commandments of the prophet are internalized in the human psyche); in the second case, through the heroes' mix of strategy and courage, rational foresight and regulation of feeling; and in the third case, through the sense of wit and irony (that is, when the lessons of the enigmatic figure are internalized in the human soul).[4] Conscience, calculation, and both comedy and tragic irony make it possible for persons to travel widely without bringing their society with them—in contrast to the case of the nomadic or marauding band.

Mobile worldviews provide an alternative to the principal integrative force of face-to-face societies. Before the appearance of this alternative, the commonest social form was a directive hierarchy. Hierarchy is a kind of integrative force that operates through local, personal connections of great strength—through ties of loyalty, service, obedience, honor, and affection. The ethical religions, literary classics, and comic and tragic irony did not so much brush aside conceptions of hierarchy as introduce—side-by-side with them—a new dimension of social action. The wandering Odysseus—for all of his adaptive calculating conscience—is still a king who treats his crew imperiously. Yet his journey means that Odysseus is not tied to a *specific* place or a *specific* community, even if homecoming remains the ultimate goal of the journey away from home. Among the ethical religions, Judaism was an exception in the sense that it remained tied to a specific community, though this community was highly mobile.

The significance of all of this can be understood if we think of social behavior as a kind of geometry. Hierarchy operates in one dimension—up and down. The ethical religions, the literary classics and undecidable enigmas added a second, lateral dimension to human conduct. Lateral relationships were made possible by the emergence of stories of wandering heroes, prophets and enigmatic figures who, in principle, could be adopted as a model by anyone. Their conduct, and the values that they embodied, had the effect of reducing the traditional power of personal hierarchic relations. This had the further effect of enabling social action over longer distances and on larger scales. The stories of heroes, prophets, and enigmas became the basis for forging relations with persons who were neither kin nor hierarchical superiors or subordinates. These stories were the basis for creating new kinds of collegial and contractual relations, for the use of non-kin or non-household agents in transactions, and for developing non-tributary relations between states. The stories encouraged the partial substitution of hierarchical relations with the lateral relations of guild, college, council, senate, corps, assembly, company, agency, and committee. They provided the imaginary basis for 'networks' of relations between persons of equivalent status. Such 'networks' bridged much larger distances than face-to-face hierarchic relations could ever do efficiently. Ethical religions, literary classics, and enigmatic worldviews did not put an end to hierarchic conceptions of the world. Rather they renovated such conceptions. Crucially, various devices of councils, colleges, guilds, and bureaucratic or military corps allowed empires and cities to function over a much larger territorial scale, and for a much longer period of time. We can think of this as the difference between a 'feudal' scale and an 'imperial' scale.

Guilds, councils, corps, and companies provided a basis for interaction that was not modeled on the household and its 'natural' hierarchies. Universalistic religious camaraderie, prophetic preaching, enigmatic images and precepts, and heroic virtue-ethics provided the tacit bonds that linked status groups in networks across distance. These kinds of ethos and enigmas prepared the way for councils to replace tribal chiefs in the Greek polis—and later for Greek cities to form federated leagues and for the theatre of comedic and tragic drama to emerge with its own distinctive enigmas, ironies and inversions. The Buddhist *dhamma* officers of the fourth-century BCE Indian Mauryan Empire, and the Buddhist university monastic centers associated with the later Gupta dynasty (320–600 CE) and the Pāla kings (eighth to twelfth century CE), provided spiritualized corps that both extended and countervailed the power of monarchy. The Roman Senate, the Confucian and Byzantine bureaucracies, and the Ottoman Janissaries are examples of network corps complementing hierarchic power. Where this happened, we have what is conventionally called 'civilizations.'

Spiritualized bureaucracies, though, were not the only social consequence of ethical religions, classical literatures and enigmatic worldviews. What also followed from greater possibilities for action at a distance were greater possibilities for long-distance administrative, cultural, and economic *traffic*. Traffic is not the same as the transactions of spiritualized corps. To visualize the nature of spiritualized bureaucratic transactions, imagine a map-like social space: as the force of ethical religions, classical literatures and enigmatic ideas began to be felt, activity across this space increases. It increases as groups find common bonds rooted in 'mobile writing' and its concomitant psychology. This is a condition of the existence of large-scale or long-distance societies. Side-by-side with this, and deeply influenced by it, emerges the phenomenon of 'traffickers.' These also act on a large-scale but without the controlling structure of council, monastery, or bureaucracy.

To be a merchant from the Persian Gulf living in Canton in the ninth century CE, or a Black Sea Greek artisan or sophist living in Athens in the third century BCE, or a Gujārāt trader in Islamic Sumatra in the fourteenth century of the Common Era required 'literacy'—both in the sense of the correspondence and account-keeping necessary in long-distance business and political transactions, and in the sense of the structures of thought that scriptural religion and literary classics encourage.[5] Even if most people in pre-modern settings still memorized religious sayings or literary episodes, rather than read them, both the textual form and the literary content of these worldviews had powerful effects. Mobile script helped turn secular stories into universal classics, and sacred wisdom into transportable holy 'books.' Reciprocally, images of wandering heroes, sages, and saviors encouraged movement across space into foreign places. The form and content of 'mobile writing' provided the fortification necessary to leave behind the local society of household, tribe, village, court, and patrimonial kingdom. The 'traffickers' though, as we shall see, took an even more adventurous step. In taking this step, enigmatic worldviews and their architectonic power come into full relief.

The clash and concrescence of civilizations

The appearance of ethical religions and literary classics had a staggering effect on human possibilities. Preparedness to venture beyond local social boundaries became much more common place in their wake. Scriptural religions and literary classics became the basis for new political forms—the great post-archaic empires (the Athenian Empire, the Hellenistic, Roman and Byzantine Empires, the Chinese imperial dynasties, and the Abbasid Empire). Venturesome attitudes emerged within the boundaries of these states, encouraged by status groups with strong lateral connections. Persons also began to strike out with ever-increasing frequency to trade with, visit and live in other city-states and bureaucratic empires. They did this for practical reasons, usually related to trade. However, the venturesome encountered political problems specific to their mobility. Ethical religions and literary classics spurred movement across space. But how did these worldviews gel with the folk and patrimonial cultures that they encountered? Were such cultures properly the object of conversion, assimilation, elimination, or coexistence? And even more perplexing: how did ethical and literary worldviews relate to *each other* when they came into contact?

These questions were felt most strongly in portal cities—because these cities are the most palpable points of intersection *between* civilizations. The Islamic Janissary corps or Confucian literati administrators might run an empire, but what happened when they encountered one another? The Buddhist monk and the Catholic scholar-priest might train imperial officials, but when their spiritualized bureaucracies had to deal with each other, how was such traffic possible? Spiritualized bureaucracies have never really effectively answered this. We see this today when the graduate schooled patrician administrators of the United States meet with their Chinese Communist Party schooled counterparts—there is always a moment of incomprehension, no matter how friendly the proceedings. This is why for every Athens there is a Piraeus, for every Rome, an Ostia, or for Constantinople, a Pera; and for every

Washington, there is a New York, and for every Beijing, there is a Shanghai. The denizens of portal cities are masters of trafficking.

One of the great challenges for the portal city has been to answer the question of how can different prophetic and literary civilizations co-exist with each other in the same place—and alongside locals with tribal or patrimonial loyalties? Portals have always been a potential flash point for the clash of civilizations. Scriptural and literary worldviews give rise to civilizations and their component states. The difference between the archaic Chinese feudal state and the Chinese imperial dynasties was Confucianism. The Chinese Empire both produced and was the product of a civilization. This is so in the very straightforward sense that literary bonds and spiritualized bureaucracy were central to its long existence.

In contrast, portals are places where different civilizations come into contact. There is an advantage, sometimes a reluctant advantage, for civilizations and their component states to trade with each other. If they do so, they need portals. Portals provide the entropotic services and ecumenical intelligence to drive inter-civilizational trade and traffic. Even victory in war does not get rid of this question. The spread of Islam by the Arabs did not reduce the imperatives for inter-civilizational contact. The Abbasid triumph did not reduce the necessity of dealing with Franks or Jews or Greeks or Indians or Chinese for commercial reasons. Indeed, such was the power of this necessity, the Ottoman Empire internalized inter-civilizational contact, turning the social basis of what was notionally a Muslim state into a set of elaborate relations between Christian Orthodox, Muslim, Jewish, Armenian, and European law communities (Murphy, 2000). It is also notable that once this inter-civilizational arrangement collapsed—as it finally did in 1922, after long decades of decline—the result was bitter civilizational conflict that continues to this day. The Ottoman Empire devolved into a series of nation-states with different civilizational substrata and a mutual genocidal hatred of each other. Serbs and Croats, Greeks and Turks, Algerians and the French, Israeli Jews and the Palestinians, Shi'ite and Sunni Muslims in ex-Ottoman territories provided examples of some of the worst civilizational clashes of the twentieth century. The attempt to construct nation-states, while still invoking scriptural religions or literary classics, in replacement for empire, was an unmitigated failure—measured simply by the violence it generated. On the surface of things, the Ottoman Empire was pre-modern; the nation-state was modern. But, for all of its modernity, the nation-state did almost nothing to answer the question of how, and whether, inter-civilizational relations could be conducted.

There is clear evidence that the internalization of inter-civilizational relations is only possible in two kinds of cases. The first case is that of empire. We need not think of empire only as a pre-modern political form. Federations provide the model for modern empires. The United States has successfully pioneered this form.[6] There were a number of interesting ideas for federation proposed in the last century of the Ottoman Empire. Had they been adopted, the present dismal politics of the Middle East might well have been avoided. The second model for internalizing inter-civilizational relations is that of the portal city or city-state. Actually, models of portal city and empire are not strictly separable. In the case of empires, portal cities still play the principal role in inter-civilizational relations. Constantinople did this for the Ottoman Empire, and Chicago and New York City have done the same for the United States. Contrawise, the most successful portal cities develop their own empires—as Venice did.

From the history of the twentieth century, it is clear that where inter-civilizational relations fail, portal cities become the targets for extreme communal violence. We see this in the sack of Symrna by the Turkish armies in 1922, or the assault on Dubrovnik by the Serbo-Montenegrin army in 1991, or the civil warring in Beirut in the 1970s and in Bombay in the 2000s. The very function of portal cities—as inter-civilizational hubs—causes them to grapple intimately with questions about the coexistence of ethical religions and literary cultures. We are all familiar with crusading or fundamentalist forms of ethical religions. But national literati, and advocates of literary canons and ideals, have often proved to be just as violent in their prosecution of cultural wars. Portal cities and regions are traditionally major centers of religious and literary publishing. Throughout much of Chinese history, for example, the premier center for printing was in the Canton province. For the very same reasons that portals achieve this kind of print-centric status, they also can end up as a type of prism that concentrates the fierce attitudes of competing literary or religious ethics. In crisscrossing so many worldviews and local views as well, it is clear that the portal city must be based on something else aside from competing varieties of discursive and creedal ethics. Discursive truth claims of virtually any kind are very hard to reconcile with counterclaims. It is here that enigmatic and architectonic worldviews come into their own.[7]

The enigmatic anti-ethics of distance

China is a case in point. As early as the eighth century of the Common Era, Muslim traders were crossing the Indian Ocean to South Asia and China (Chaudhuri, 1985, 44). The impetus provided by religion in the forging of this long-distance relationship is very evident. The drive of Gulf traders (from Basra, Siraf, and Hormuz) to leapfrog across long sea distances to establish direct maritime links with China comes immediately in the wake of Muhammad's life (d. 632) and the Abbasid revolution (749–750). Such was the scale of this that by the ninth century well in excess of 100,000 Muslims, Christians, Jews, and old faith Iranians were living in Canton.[8] Quanzhou just a little further up the coast in Fujian province domiciled up to 10,000 Persians, Syrians, and South East Asians.[9]

Historically, China was less adventurous in its long-distance maritime activity. It was not until the late T'ang period that Chinese vessels sailed to South East Asia, and even more belatedly, it was not till the Sung dynasty that the Chinese reached the Malabar Coast of India.[10] The dominant Chinese literary culture (Confucianism) was anti-commercial and uninterested in explorations overseas. Its major achievement was in the large-scale political unification of China. Beyond that, it was not especially curious. Thus, relations with other states like Viet Nam and Thailand, including official trading relations, were organized on a tributary model.

Tributary relations constitute a form of loose hierarchy between a stronger and a weaker state. Tributary arrangements are an attempt to model relations at a distance on face-to-face hierarchical relations. In the case of the Chinese state, the one very peculiar exception to the tributary model occurred very briefly in the Ming dynasty during the heterodox reign of the third emperor Yung-lo (1402–1424). Yung-lo organized a series of state-sponsored sea-borne expeditions between 1404 and 1433, to ports as far afield as Western India and East Africa, the Red Sea and the Persian Gulf. This was quite evidently an attempt to duplicate the pattern of Muslim traders. (It also had certain parallels with Venetian state sponsorship of trade.) But it was a short-lived policy. Subsequent Ming emperors, responding to Mandarin opposition to this kind of seaward venturing, sharply reversed the policy, and closed China's sea-coasts to foreigners and placed an embargo on Chinese merchants trading overseas (Chaudhuri, 1985, 60–61). This did not kill Chinese overseas trade, though—it just made it unofficial. After 1433, Chinese merchants were never seen again in Indian, African or Arabian ports, but they still ventured (without state sponsorship) to Malacca, the Java Sea and Manila (100). The China Seas, from Japan to Malacca, became the extra-territorial province of heterodox Chinese willing to ignore official prohibition.

What was it that allowed the opening of Canton to foreigners, or later the tenacious pursuit by Fujian Chinese of overseas destinations?[11] There are undoubtedly many causes but one stands out immediately—topography. Fujian province followed the pattern typical of many leading portal city regions throughout the world. They emerge in places where terrain is difficult or confined or unattractive—like for instance Manhattan Island, Amsterdam's marshland rivers, Chicago's swampy portage, or Venice's marshes. 'Fujian had a long history of evil reputation as a fatally inhospitable land: a narrow malarial shore backed by mountains of savages' (Fernández-Armesto, 2000, 104). Often in origin portals are almost extra-territorial, and their subsequent prosperity is tacitly built upon this fact. A place that is not territorial in the conventional sense, and that lacks the conventional resources of territory, can survive only by turning extra-territoriality into an asset. Such places rely heavily on intelligence instead of conventional factors of production.

Extra-territorial places become an asset by virtue of the fact that they provide attractive gateways for trading, exchanges, and contacts. Such intermediation, however, is fraught with difficulty. Canton illustrates such difficulties. To act as a gateway between Muslim Arabia and China, Canton of necessity was an intermediary between the predominately Confucian bureaucracy of territorial China and an Islam that legitimated rule in its own distinctive manner over vast territories. The prophetic ethic of an Islamic empire and the literary ethic of the Confucian empire shared little in common, either in form or content. Because of such incommensurability, the attitude of the portal city had to be premised on something else apart from either prophetic, Salvationist or literary ethics. If not, then the city of strangers—made up of those who come from all over the world and who live in the portal—becomes difficult or impossible to sustain. What is required is another kind of 'ethics'—an *anti-ethics of distance.*

This is often an 'anti-ethics' of non-intervention—or more precisely an 'anti-ethics' of *let it be*. For the maritime mercantile Chinese of Canton and Fujian Provinces, Taoism provided such an 'anti-ethic.'[12] Taoism in effect was the 'religion' of Chinese merchants.[13] Taoism is interesting because it exhibits *in nuce* many of the key characteristics of something that is found repeatedly in portal cities. The basic proposition of Taoism is that there is an inherent but *a-literate* order to the world—the '*Tao*' or the nameless order of the cosmos. This order is *immanent* in the world. There is no transcendent God who has created this order. What is important is not just that the Taoists had no conception of a 'saving' God (in this they agreed with Confucians), or that Taoism drew no distinction between a transcendent heaven and a mundane earth, but rather their 'ethic' was *a-linguistic*. It was nameless (*wu-ming*). *The order of the world was not commanded or scripted.* It was not revealed through prophecy or through the incipient moral law of literary characters or the action of heroes. Rather its core was paradoxical. Its meaning was double-coded and deeply contrapuntal. It did not encourage social activism. It did not attempt to transform the world in the image of 'the word' of a personal ethical God, or through 'the quotation' of academic literary scholarship. In short, Taoism reacted skeptically to discursive knowledge.[14] In the place of discursive knowledge, Taoism emphasized meditation on the *yūan-ch'i*, the primordial 'breath' of the universe.

The skeptical conscience

What is interesting about all of this, from the point of view of the cosmopolitan city, is not the paraphernalia of Taoism—its techniques for contemplation or for the gymnic and respiratory control of the micro-cosmos of body rhythms—or even the spiritual voyage of the Taoist adept to achieve symbiosis with the universe. What is interesting is the underlying assumption that *all* social norms, be they traditional, public or literary, are contingent, not absolute. In the face of the 'nameless,' all linguistic distinctions including those of good and evil, truth and falsity, are relative. In the Taoist view, in the greatest action, nothing is named; in the greatest disputation, nothing is said.

A similar attitude prevailed amongst the Jains of maritime Gujārāt India. The philosophy and religion of the Jains had developed in the sixth century BCE as a protest against orthodox Vedic (early Hindu) beliefs.[15] The attitude of the Jains to every discursive doctrine was that '*it might be*'—*all discursive knowledge was contingent.*[16] The attitude of Jainism to other religions and philosophies was one of non-criticism. It had no proselytizing aspect. While Jainism had its own discursive and canonical literature and body of commentaries, this was a complement to, rather than the determinant of, the Jain imagination. This Jain imagination rested on, and was stimulated by, what might be called 'the power of the non-discursive.' Such power took on meditational and ascetical and mystical forms, but also architectonic forms. Plastic beauty was central in Jain life. Jain architecture and stone carving was of exceptional quality. The non-discursive imagination was also expressed in exquisite paintings on palm leaf and paper manuscripts in Jain monastic libraries.

The relation between the discursive and non-discursive imagination is not one of either/or. A non-discursive imagination does not indicate the absence of discursive faculties—just as (in reverse) discursive themes (literary and prophetic themes) can be rendered in non-discursive media (architecture, painting, and sculpture). Rather, what is of interest to us here is that, under certain circumstances, the non-discursive imagination can take a leading role. This is especially true of portals. Portals present an interesting paradox. They are places where 'mobile writing' is typically very popular, and, for various purposes, highly valued. Yet they are places where non-discursive media are also very prominent. Great portals are distinguished by great architecture (Murphy, 2001, 11–38).

Plastic media provide a powerful counterpoint to the scriptorium and the document. 'Mobile writings' are easily copied and transported, and spread rapidly across the face of the earth. 'Plastic beauty' is relatively immobile, and not easily reproduced. In the mercantile emporium, these two phenomena go hand-in-hand. The paradox of the portal is that long-distance '*entrepôt*' societies, the most freewheeling of all societies, also produce the most spectacular of all plastic civic art. These societies have a profoundly skeptical attitude to norms and rules—no matter whether it is the case of the naked monks of the Jain tradition, the mercurial merchant patricians of Renaissance Florence, or the free-wheeling capitalists of nineteenth-century Chicago. At the same time, their 'building arts' produce monuments of contemplative architectonics that are amongst the most evocative possible intimations of permanence, stillness, and beauty imaginable.

Indeed, in some respects, the architectonics of stone (or modernity's iron) *replaces* norms and rules. Long-distance trading societies place great pressure on norms and rules, whether these are of a traditional or literary kind. Portal societies coagulate many traditions and literatures, and thereby shake up norms and rules of all kinds. Under these circumstances, images of world/*kosmos* tend to replace norms and rules. Such images lay the foundation for a skeptical rational character.[17] Skeptical rational character is little concerned with either concrete rules or abstract norms. It tends to be in varying degrees skeptical of all discursive beliefs. It sets itself apart from ethics understood in either a traditional, prophetic or literary sense. It is impatient with social rules, revealed truths, or literary heroes. It is drawn to anti-heroes and enigmatic characters. Its chief personality type is incognito, capable of assuming multiple roles, masks and personas. Its ethic or rather 'anti-ethic' derives from its sense of the orderliness and continuity (the 'harmony') of the *kosmos*. In the soul this translates into a kind of inner navigational sense. This 'pilot sense' is what makes human beings good at orientating themselves (finding their 'way,' their *tao*) amongst social and natural contingencies.

Fundamental to a skeptical rational character is a detached relation to the world. Detachment is the corollary of a non-discursive orientation to the world. Skeptical reason is 'cool.' Even when over-determined by magical or mystical techniques, it serves the interest of detachment. Take the case of the Jain religious ideal of a perfect nature achieved through an austere, ascetical monastic life. On first glance, the renunciation of the monk seems difficult to reconcile with the fact that the Jain laity were in the main merchants and professionals from coastal Gujārāt and Mahārāshtra. This seeming paradox makes more sense if we think of renunciation as a religious correlate of rational 'coolness.' Renunciation was aimed not at property but at 'attachment.' Attachment, the Jains reasoned (much like the Greek Stoics), was grounded in the passions, and the passions give rise to irrational violence and militancy. Detachment, with its skeptical view of violent passions, made it an attractive worldview for a merchant society for whom the warrior ethos of battling Hindu gods had little to offer. The Taoist 'ethic' of 'non-intervention' is similar in nature. It allowed the Chinese merchant to hold at an arms' length the strong literate social ethic of the Confucians—an ethic that favored the bureaucratic and agrarian life over the traveling and mercantile life.

Of course, for all of the very considerable appetite of ethical religions to intervene in the world, those same religions have engendered their own non-discursive counter-currents. The Cabbalist tradition in Judaism and Stoic currents in Christianity endowed what have been at times militant ethical religions with overtones of pantheistic quietism. In Catholicism, great church architecture and church music have long been a counterpoint to a purely scriptural religion, as have been certain mystical currents as well. The same kind of dual face can also be seen in Islam, the militant religion par excellence. The leading force in the Islamic colonization of Western India, Java and Sumatra—and also of the Ottoman Empire—was the Sufis (Fernández-Armesto, 2000, 395; Bentley, 1993, 174–175, 214–125). Like Taoists or Stoic Christians, or indeed Neo-Platonic-flavored Greek Orthodoxy, the Sufis possessed a heterodox, pantheistic, a-literate sense of world order.

Such an a-literate sense of order tends to flourish in portal cities. It makes possible the cohabitation of scriptive worldviews. We see intimations of this in Manila in the sixteenth century. The city served as a crux of the China Seas' unofficial traffic that linked a putatively closed China with the Malacca Straits passage to the Indo-Islamic world of the Arabian Sea. Manila's ability to function as a cosmopolitan city of strangers—where Spanish Catholics, Filipino converts, Javanese and Arabian Muslims, and Confucian and Taoist Chinese needed to coexist—depended on a strong sense of immanent (non-prescriptive) order. Spanish Manila in the sixteenth century had a huge population of overseas (Fujian) Chinese who perforce had to negotiate trade not only with mainland Confucian China that officially banned overseas trade, but also with local Spanish Catholic officials, indigenous Filipinos, and with Islamic Sumatra and Java.[18] In this portal, nodal world, the Taoist skeptic doubtlessly would have encountered the architectonics of the church builders from Mexico and Spain. Even if the Taoist merchant and the Catholic mason did not recognize themselves in the other, they in fact shared a lot in common—in particular a powerful sense of the world as the product of a-literate design.

Order by aesthetic design

Aesthetic order or order by design is a fundamental alternative to order by commands and order by rules. When skeptics insist on the suspension of judgment, they are not inviting anarchy but rather an order of a musical or architectonic kind. The Taoist skeptic observed that naming, or the name (*ming*), in ancient Chinese thought implied an evaluation that assigned an object a place in a hierarchical universe. If we dispense with names, then how else do we assign objects their places? One answer to this is the Stoic's injunction to 'live according to nature.' But is nature nameless? For the Greek Stoic who thought of the universe as 'breath,' yes it is; for the Stoic in the Roman tradition who represented nature as a kind of 'law,' then no it is not.

If nature in a negative sense is nameless, if its stuff is non-discursive, then what is it in a positive sense? Most often, the Taoists referred to it as rhythmic. What was nameless was the pulse of the universe. It was like the Greek Stoics imagined—a rhythm of eternal return. It was a complex multi-layered rhythm of night and day, life and death, summer and winter, virtue and not-virtue, action and inaction. In short, the universe had a characteristically rhythmic structure of periodicity, transformation and return. In the skeptical view, then, nature was not law. It was an order of rhythm. Such a conception of nature is immensely important to long-distance portal societies. Think of the movement of the denizens of these societies across space. They travel—outward-bound, inward-bound, stopping, re-starting, returning home, going-away. Their mode of life is kinetic. Great energies are expended in this kinetic motion—think of Shanghai or New York, ancient Alexandria or modern Marseilles. But, in order for this kinetic motion not to be chaotic, it must have an order. The natural order of kinesis is rhythm. The most elementary form of rhythm, as the Taoists were aware, is breathing. As we move around the world, breathing is one of the things that set the rhythm for our motion. The in-out, fast-slow, deep-shallow patterns of breath are simple examples of the repetition-difference structure of rhythms. Human beings, of course, create all different kinds of rhythms, including the rhythms that regulate how we breathe. Many of those rhythmic structures are very complex. Complex rhythms become the basis of art.

The formal characteristics of art works define species of rhythm. Balance, proportionality, scale, ratio, color relations, tempo, accent, and so forth allow us to create different rhythmic units. The rhythms of art works structure the movement of eye, hand, foot, and body. On a larger scale—on the scale of the city or the humanized landscape—they structure movement through space in time. Where there is a high premium placed on kinetic activity—as in portal cities and long-distance societies—rhythmic structure replaces some, even many, of the functions of law and command.

A large-scale rhythmic structure, like that of a city, is not a deliberate creation. It happens of its own accord, as the Taoists would say. It is self-organizing, as the social theorist would say. The thought that immediately runs through everyone's mind is that this sounds like nineteenth-century laissez-faire. The Taoist advice to 'let it be,' their paean to inaction, could be taken in that sense. To which the classic reply is Karl Marx's: do we allow things to happen 'behind the backs' of social actors? However, a word of warning: most of what the Taoists said was a kind of paradox. Our Victorians, in contrast, often had little feeling for paradox. What the nineteenth-century mind most certainly had no feel for was the paradoxical nature of creation.

Chuang-tzu's model of creation, like Plato's model of creation, was the artisan. The *tao* was compared with the activity of the potter or the bronze caster. It shaped and transformed the universe out of primordial chaos. But there was something deeply paradoxical about the act of creation. It was more like the in-act of creation. Even more paradoxically than Plato's demiurge who creates according to pre-existing forms, the Taoist ideal was *the carver who does not carve*. This ideal of creative inactivity tells us something quite important about the nature of creation. We know that all creation involves acts of design, in the sense that what is created has form (or intentional departures from form, for the clever amongst us). But great design is not deliberate (in the sense that planning, method and procedure is deliberate). As Kant put it, you do not create great artworks by following rules. Yet mostly what human beings do is to create by following rules. The contrary Taoist advice was to ditch the rites and rules of society, its laws and virtue. The anarchism of the Taoists was deep going.

Even golden-age artisan culture heroes, they thought, were at fault. These heroes had fashioned implements (utilities) and cunning contrivances. In doing so, their carving had blighted the nameless unwrought substance of the universe. True nature lay in uncarved simplicity. At first blush this sounds a lot like Rousseau's romanticism. But only if we forget that this is a philosophical paradox. It is meant to get us to think about what carving or creation would look like if we did not rely on discursive rules—on the rules of guild, bureaucracy, and corporation. To answer this, we need to return in our imagination to the uncarved block (*p'u*) of nature. If the demiurge does not act according to rules, then how does it in-act? It in-acts, seemingly, according to the rhythm or pulse of the universe. Think of this as being a bit like the strains of music. We can suddenly be aware that our foot has been tapping away to the music's beat while we have been concentrating on other things. Something like this happens when we are at our most creative. The highest kinds of creation, as with the best, most virtuous deeds, are like great musical or athletic performances that are pulled out of nowhere. Too much planning, and deliberation, and willfulness destroys them.

Rules and norms like other human creations can contribute to maintaining the order of nature, but should not be confused with it. The skeptic is skeptical of law, indeed of all discursive formations—commands as well as laws, moral fables as well as catechisms. Such skepticism is not irrational. On the contrary, it is highly rational. What is at work here is a particular kind of reason—an enigmatic kind. There are rationalities of societies with thick cultures based on intensive face-to-face relations between client and patron, master and servant, employer and worker, landlord and tenant. Then there are rationalities of larger-scale societies that encourage much more lateral movement across space. These rationalities are based on discursive formations—revealed truths, sagely advice, ethical commandments, literary stories—and on written law or legal principles. Finally, there are the rationalities of a natural or rhythmic order. These rhythms do not command or legislate. They are embodied in the intuitive timing and beautiful phrasing of the writer, not in the writers' advice to the reader. They are to be found in the grace of athletes, not in the rules of the game.

The reason of rhythmic order allows us to organize our movement into 'significant' entities. Human beings delight in beautiful paintings and music. We do so in part because these artifacts structure the movement of our eye, the wanderings of our auditory attention, and the tappings of our toes. They give shape to our motor activity. The skeptic is one who thinks that the power of rhythmic order can in varying measures and degrees replace other kinds of rationality. The detachment of the skeptic is a detachment from social and discursive rationalities.

Anti-ethics

Detachment (a precursor of 'objectivity') is the kernel of an enigmatic 'anti-ethics' of a cosmopolitan kind.[19] The view of the Taoist—that 'one should let men and things go as they can' (Weber, 1951, 188)—is the antithesis of a literate and prophetic ethics of 'care.' Detachment counsels against turning the world into an object of passionate 'concern.' Its maxim is 'don't worry'; its advice is 'do nothing' and 'let the world go its own way.' Such detachment is rife in portal societies. A skeptical atmosphere permeates these societies. The advice to 'let the world go its own way' should not be taken literally. It is a paradox—formulated in the spirit of the carver who does not carve. It does not literally require us to do nothing, but rather to be skeptical of all passionate involvements, be they of an interventionist, fundamentalist, moralist or utopian stripe.

The preference for thinking over passion has a palpable anthropological dimension. As human horizons expand, so does the palette of orientational feelings. These are the cognitive (yes/no) feelings that are crucial to human beings in navigating contingent topographies, social contacts, taste experiences, freely chosen loves and friendships, and vocations.[20] The more cosmopolitan a society, the more human beings rely on orientational feelings of liking, love, interest, intuition, probability, doubt, certainty, caution, and risk-taking to find their bearings. Such cognitive feelings help human beings chart a 'way' in situations where responses are not fixed by tradition, and where there is no clear 'social map.' Passion in contrast replaces the multiplicity of rational orientative feelings with a single (exclusive) focus on one object. Such 'attachments' cause a loss of the ability to navigate contingencies. In place of a mix of interests, loves, tastes, doubts, and certainties, passion elevates *one* love or *one* cer tainty to the exclusion of everything else (Heller, 1979, 107–110, 217–227). For example, either faith (the religious 'yes') or doubt (the scientific 'no') is permitted to rule over all other cognitive feelings.

When faith in literature or religion turns passionate, a discursive ethics can elicit violent and destructive acts. Militant Islam, the Christian crusades, Confucian xenophobia, and revolutionary Romanticism are cases in point. Involvement in an object of 'concern' (an involvement stimulated by the authority of a scribal truth or literary classic) is such that agents lose the capacity to orientate themselves in the world. They lose the internal sense of 'navigation.' The Scottish school of philosophers of the eighteenth century called this internal sense the 'moral sense.' The 'moral sense' was the pilot sense of the skeptical rational character. Adam Smith was a typical product of this school. Anyone possessed by passions, he advised, should take a look at their feelings through the eyes of a stranger. This could be done either through the medium of the imagination or by actually joining an 'assembly of strangers' (Smith, 1969, 213). Strangers have little sympathy for passions. Their company, Smith suggests, restores a mind disturbed by passion to some degree of tranquility and sedateness. The company of strangers encourages in us calmness and composure, and an abating of the violence of passions. Smith and his fellow philosophers knew much about the company of strangers. They saw it every day in the portal cities of Glasgow and Edinburgh. In so many respects, Smith was simply representing the cosmopolitan skepticism of Glasgow, the portal for Irish Sea and Atlantic trade, and Edinburgh, the North Sea *metaxu* with connections across the world.[21] In such places, all of the varieties of social and discursive passions cancel themselves out. Strangers may have their own passions, but they are not interested in other people's passions, or other people in their passions. The coldness of strangers is a perfect foil to the heat of truth and conviction. Ultimately, the important thing for a stranger living in a strange place is to be able to navigate the contingencies of that place, and find a 'way' through their complexities.[22] This is only possible where the full palate of cognitive feelings remains at hand.

Skepticism is not simply 'nay-saying,' or endless 'doubt.' No less than the warrior of faith, the feelings of the perpetual doubter are one-dimensional. The skeptic rather is an epitome of a certain kind of reason. The skeptical character is not prepared to sacrifice any orientative feeling if it can help make a way through contingent terrain. An 'ethic of distance' that promotes the primacy of orientative feelings makes lots of sense in portal cities and emporial states, where so much human activity is devoted to trafficking goods, services, and ideas. Orientation in such a world is difficult. 'Finding a way' requires 'finding a rhythm.' Rhythmic structures provide all sorts of clues for navigating *through space in time* (Murphy, 2001, 11–38). Great portals are filled with complex rhythms. These non-discursive rhythmic structures make for the difference between chaos and complex order. What is very difficult to achieve with either personal relations or rules can be achieved with an abstract rhythmic order and its fascinating structure of repetition-difference or beat-accent. Rhythmic units order the world that we navigate. Where these units are objectivated in stone or iron, or other architectonic media, we create a kinetic-plastic world that we can move through.

The familiar architectonic devices of balance, equilibrium, proportionality, ratio, and scale measure the space of those units—the space that lies between the time-markers of accent and beat. These devices, in subtle but compelling ways, structure the way we move through space in time. From the frame of the door to the edge of the pavement, from the outline of the building to the horizon of the skyline, accents define *a time that is also a space*. It is navigable space. It is plastic, three-dimensional space plus the fourth dimension of time. It is through this movement, and its rhythmical order, that the cognitive ethics of distance makes itself felt.

The aesthetic mode of production

The denizens of portals often have a cynical view of the world. It is cynical in the sense that it does not take any ethical norm as its *sine qua non*. The cynical worldview is one whose ultimate authority is non-discursive and aesthetic. To call something of this kind 'cynical' is simply to remind us of the Greek philosophers, the Cynics, who recommended cannibalism and who did so as an intellectual provocation to make the point that the external authority of their philosophy and the internal authority of their conduct were not normative.

This view is easily misunderstood. Take the case of Adam Smith's cynical and skeptical attitude that we are better to 'leave the market alone' ('laissez-faire'). This attitude, we are often told, licenses social cruelty and the grinding-down of the weak and the poor. But Smith, in fact, was a lot closer in human sympathies to another great cynic of the eighteenth century, Jonathan Swift, than he was to the later Manchester industrialists who were driven by an unremitting theology of Protestant Hebraism. Smith, like Swift, understood the paradoxes of the human condition. He observed that social policy frequently yields the opposite of what is intended. As the skeptic understands only too well, the advocacy of 'peace' is often the cause of 'war,' and vice versa. This is especially so as the world of action grows larger and more distant through trade, communication, and the migration of populations. The more complex the world, the less the outcome of actions correspond with the intentions or desires of actors. Hence, Smith thought, 'it was by far the best policy to leave things to their natural course' (Smith, 1896, 246; see also 180–182 and Smith, 1970, 507–520). He was a proponent of an auto-poietic society.

The cynic is there to remind us that simply insisting on better and more powerful rules against social cannibalism never prevented such cannibalism. Sometimes the very opposite is true. Smith did not suggest that there was no decent order on a cosmopolitan scale—just that whatever this order is, it is not a normative order. It is not an order derived from moral declarations. Rather, it is *an order implicit in history*. Overdetermining all of the intended or wished-for outcomes of human beings is the 'providential' order of history. History is the work of human beings, yet it happens, as Karl

Marx said, behind their backs. It has patterns. Those patterns can help or hinder human beings in the realization of their goals. To be effective, even the moralist had to take cognizance of the patterns of history.

Smith's fellow Scots, the political economists Adam Ferguson, Lord Kames and John Millar, supposed that society moved through stages—hunting, pasturage, farming and commerce. Smith himself refined this schema down to agriculture, manufactures and foreign commerce (Smith, 1970, 483). He was also quick to acknowledge that, although this was the 'natural course of things' (like a river flowing implacably to the sea), in practice this course was often violated or inverted. Thus, contrary to the explanatory schema of the political economists, history was not progressive. 'Foreign commerce'—the activity of portal cities—was a wild card in the pack of history. It did not fit the Scottish Enlightenment idea of progress. In fact, in the portal state, 'foreign commerce' was the cause of the introduction of finer manufactures, or improvements in agriculture, rather than the other way around, in contrast to what the evolutionary model of the political economists supposed. Cities 'situated near either the sea coast or the banks of a navigable river,' Smith noted, were not constrained to derive their subsistence goods or raw materials from the countryside in their immediate hinterland (502). Such cities had 'a much wider range,' and could draw 'from the most remote corners of the world.' They could get their staple goods from far afield 'either in exchange for the manufactured products of their own industry' or else 'by performing the office of carriers between distant countries and exchanging the produce of one for another' (502).

The portal city can disrupt the power of an agrarian society. We see this happening today in China. An agrarian society restricts the mobility of labor because it ties persons to the earth. That is its imaginary horizon. Smith noted that mercantile societies dominated by maritime towns like London, Edinburgh, and Glasgow undermine the relationship to the earth. Marx was later on to note something similar. Smith further observed that manufacturing towns (like the English towns of Leeds, Sheffield, and Birmingham) could achieve a comparable break with agrarian power by inducing the dependence of the countryside on the manufactures of the town (506–520). The crucial point that Smith made was that 'foreign commerce' was a driver of agrarian and industrial development. It was more than an economic form or a mode of production. It was a creator and shaper of economic forms. It was a regulator of progress. It could radically re-order the sequences of progress.

Adam Smith's philosophic history was formulated before the industrial revolution of the early nineteenth century or the post-industrial revolution of the second half of the twentieth century. But its general principle was equally valid for both: moral order and moral solidarity make little sense outside of the non-discursive 'order of things.' The order of things is not composed like a book or a commandment. Rather it is composed of endless numbers of microscopic actions woven into large intelligible structures. The cynic's recommendation not to intervene to stop the 'natural course' of this pattern order did not mean rejecting all social norms—as if anomie was some kind of utopia. All that the cynic proposed was that no ethical, literary, or social norm possessed ultimate authority. Human good, instead, derived from an aesthetic order of things. Please, said the cynic, adapt your social gospel or your literary humanism to that order. Otherwise your gestures—no matter how sincere and no matter how much intended to alleviate human suffering—will be futile. This advice was usually rejected, or simply set on its head. Many nineteenth and twentieth-century messianic personalities thought that History was a vehicle of Moral Truth, or else a deity that they could win to their cause. Adam Smith, himself, talked about Nature having an 'author' as if it were a literary or prophetic creation.[23] But Nature was not a Book of Prophecy to be read or deciphered, no more than History was an enlightened Story of Progress through stages.

Perhaps the best way of understanding the non-discursive 'order of things' is not from the standpoint of enlightenment history, but from the much older, Greek vantage point of *the city*. The Greeks were not without a sense of history. They had their Thucydides. But, unlike Adam Smith's contemporaries, history to their way of thinking was subordinate to the city, not the other way round. The city in the Greek mind was not a set of moral commandments, or a playground of literary heroes. Rather it was *a thing*—a common thing, an impersonal collective artifice. The Greek enlightenment looked at the city as an objective container of human purpose, emotion, and virtue. It was a beautiful reification that conditioned everything human beings could feel and imagine, an anonymous product of endless numbers of human acts and wills, and a human nature that functioned, beyond volition, as the measure of humankind. Nature (human nature) was the growth (*phusis*) of the human being *toward the city*. Knowledge of all kinds was objectified in the city as much as in the individual human mind.

When we think of the development of economies from agrarian to industrial to post-industrial, it is worth noting that the city is common to all stages of economic life. The Scottish political economists had reason to note the eclipse of rural life by emerging industrialism. But it is equally worth noting that at its height the English rural economy produced great wealth. Even more noteworthy, is that the cathedral city and the market towns lay at the heart of the rural economy, and were great exporters. These cities and towns are as much memorable for their great beauty, often unsurpassed by any urban creation that has come along since. The point being that all of the stages or phases or types of economic life have towns and cities at the core, and at the core of these towns and cities is a deep intuitive sense of aesthetic order. It is in this light that we can best understand both industrialism and post-industrialism, and the long history of modern capitalism. It is also in this light that we can best judge the claims made about the role of knowledge in capitalist economies.

One of the first of the great political economists to observe that knowledge was a key factor of production in modern capitalism was Karl Marx. Marx noted in modern capitalist production, the long-term tendency was for the human being to step to the side of the production process, instead of being its chief actor (Marx, *Grundrisse*, 705). He observed this long before robots appeared in factories. He also noted that once labor was sidelined from the productive process, it was no longer the time that persons worked that mattered in wealth creation but knowledge (such as the techno-logical know-how that enabled society's mastery of nature). Indeed, Marx thought that squeezing labor time out of the worker was a miserable foundation for wealth given the knowledge foundation that capital itself had created. For as large industry develops, the creation of wealth depends less on labor time and more on the general state of science and the progress of technology. Indeed, with the passing of time, less and less labor is included in the production process—rather, as Marx observed, 'the human being comes to relate more as a watchman and regulator to the production process…' From a certain angle, Marx thought, this all anticipated the free develop-ment of individuals. It supposed reducing the necessary labor of a society to a mini-mum and expanding the amount of free time devoted to the aesthetic and scientific development of individuals. Marx is among the first to identify the logic of a knowl-edge economy. Wealth in this mode is measured not by command over surplus labor but rather over disposable time—time outside of that needed in the direct process of production. As Marx tartly observed, nature builds no machines, locomotives, rail-ways, or electric telegraphs. Rather these are 'the power of knowledge objectified' (706). In Marx's time, the development of fixed capital was already such that 'general social knowledge has become a direct form of production' and the process of social life had come under the control of the general intellect. Marx regularly complained though that capital behaved in a contradictory fashion in response to this develop-ment. It tried to reduce labor time to a minimum, yet it continued to posit labor time (in contradistinction to disposable creative free time) as the measure and source of wealth.

Marx's complaint was justified—though equally there is a major complaint to be directed at Marx's own theory. It was not until late in the twentieth century, and largely because of post-Marxist social philosophers (Bell, Castells, Marcuse, Lyotard), that there was a widespread recognition of knowledge as a force of production, and even in the 1990s a company like Du Pont did not have a register of its intellectual property (i.e. patents). Notwithstanding this, Nietzsche in the 1870s and 1880s made a telling point that demolishes a fair amount of the salience of Marx's theories of the 1850s and 1860s. Nietzsche vigorously criticized the Socratic view that knowledge was the fulcrum of great societies. Aesthetics, not knowledge, was the driver of human greatness. This was aesthetics of a particular kind. In the opening shot of his first major work, *The Birth of Tragedy* (1872), Nietzsche proposed that the greatness of Greek antiquity could be explained by the uncanny cultural core of Greek society. Greek society was founded on the fusion of aesthetic opposites—the union of the Apollonian and the Dionysian.

Modern economies may grow thanks to the advancement of knowledge, but knowledge does not advance without the stimulus of a deep enigmatic cultural core that is uncanny, ambidextrous and un-decidable, and without the mediation of strong characters and institutions capable of finding ways of holding together the antinomies of creation. In the 1870s, Nietzsche intuited that modern capitalism had already been through its most creative phase and had entered a period of decadence. If true, this would give lie to many of the most pretentious claims today about creative economies and knowledge societies. The empirical evidence suggests that Nietzsche was right. In America, the most creative twentieth-century economy, registration of patents per capita reached its peak in 1900. Registrations of copyrights per capita slightly increased between 1900 and today, though only because the category of copyrightable objects increased markedly in the same period—meaning that copyright registration per capita in real terms actually fell.[24]

The philosopher Cornelius Castoriadis often remarked on the intellectual character of the twentieth century, his own age, and observed something wrong (Castoriadis, 219–242). He carefully noted the symptoms of the problem: the relative dearth or decline in the number of great works in the sciences and the arts produced after the surge from 1890–1920 typified by Cezanne, Picasso, Stravinsky, and Einstein. Castoriadis, like Nietzsche, knew that without the production of great culture, the ordinary working of culture at large is imperiled. So now is the ordinary working of modern economies. The progress of creative decadence in the twentieth century was obscured because of the explosion in the means of distribution of the arts and the sciences. The Internet is the most powerful example of this. But everything from the paperback novel to broadcast radio and television played its part. What we saw develop in the course of the twentieth century was an astonishing array of means of distributing all of the great works of the mind hitherto produced and their endless number of imitators. But living in the ages of mechanical and then later digital reproduction also obscured the relative decline in the creative power of advanced societies. That anyone can within a few seconds find a clip online of Glen Gould performing Bach is marvelous. But that very accessibility does not help explain, let alone facilitate, the forces that will lead to the formation of the next Glen Gould or the next Bach.

It is not self-evident either that the models of the twentieth-century education economies contributed very much either to the act of creative formation at the highest level. Both the empirical evidence and philosophical observation cited above directly confounds the theory of human capital (Paul Romer) and the idea that education is strongly correlated with capital growth—or that massive state and social investment in higher education in particular is a driver of economic growth. Mass higher education has dramatically increased numbers participating (briefly) in the realm of free time. Yet this has also caused a curious colonization of that time. For all of the apparent expansion of disposable time available to social actors in advanced economies during the century-and-a-half after Marx's death, this rarely if at all garnered a commensurate explosion of creative action. The peak period of copyright creation was the first decade of the twentieth century, with short-lived surges in the 1920s and 1980s. Perhaps counter-intuitively for many, these were the ages of Teddy Roosevelt, Calvin Coolidge and Ronald Reagan, not normally considered the avatars of creation. Even in the best-case scenarios, like the close relationship between the San Francisco Bay Area's Silicon Valley and Stanford University, institutionalized disposable time either in the university or in the corporation has rarely produced more than incremental and routine results. The greater per capita investment in research-based companies and universities, the less per capita has been the production of intellectual property.

The paradox of the knowledge economies is that as wealth per capita rises, driven by the application of knowledge, intellectual property per capita declines. Because intellectual property is in part non-exclusive, it disseminates readily. The distribution of knowledge in a knowledge economy is not the problem. In fact, the ability to recycle and resell the back catalogues of creative works has produced huge wealth. The problem rather is the core creation of that knowledge. As distribution of creative work increases, production of it decreases. As the access to creative artifacts grows, and the sale of them expands, the production of those artifacts in a subtle manner shrinks. Note that this shrinkage is hidden by the volume of works being distributed—which means that any shrinkage occurs below the threshold of awareness. It is not visible enough that we pay it any real attention. Why should we? Well, even with the best distribution system for knowledge, eventually as real per capita creative production of knowledge shrinks, we will end up having not enough new artifacts of durable substance and interest value to distribute.

This begs the question then of what is the source of wealth-creating knowledge? There are two closely-related answers to this question: the imaginary of beauty and the portal city. We can see them at play in the most dramatic instance of economic transformation, the Industrial Revolution. The English Industrial Revolution—the most famous and most important example of a revolution in a mode of production—illustrates this perfectly. Factory machinery—the very technology that was to begin to edge labor out of direct participation in the production process—developed out of the artisan clock-making industry that centered on Liverpool and the north bank of the Mersey. This artisan clock-making—the best in England—had developed there in the seventeenth century, underpinned by that century's fascination with the image of a clockwork universe. Such a universe had a strongly geometric aesthetic nature, as indeed all socially prevalent images of nature do. The clockwork universe was a harmonious meshing of gears and wheels, working in elegant cooperation. The clock makers were the creators not just of useful objects but of a precise beauty as well. To achieve this apotheosis of mechanical beauty, the Lancashire clock-makers had to have considerable knowledge of geometry and practical mathematics. The technology for the new industrial factories of the eighteenth century was created by these same clock-makers. Their tools and skills were highly adaptable to the building of industrial machines.

An engineering-clock-making complex developed in the Mersey region centered on Warrington. Warrington was a classic micro-portal. As Peter Hall describes it, Warrington was on the high road from London to Carlisle and Scotland, on the crossroad from Chester to York, at the head of the tidal navigation and the lowest bridge point on the Mersey, and was one of the principal thoroughfares of the north: an entrance from the south to north-west England and to the port of Liverpool (Hall, 1998, 339). Warrington and its clock-makers had other characteristics that are often pointed to when explaining economic success. The area was dominated by Protestant non-conformism. Excluded from the institutions of the Anglican Establishment, the Nonconformists developed their own higher education, literary, and philosophical societies. Warrington Academy was one of the most famous of the dissenting academies. But this re-cycles the human capital argument. Education in the first instance is transmissive, not creative. If education plays a role in stimulating the act of creation, which arguably it did in the Liverpool region in this historical period, then it did so because the worldview of Calvinism that it propagated was a strange one. It was an enigmatic and paradoxical worldview in which grace, freedom and choice were drawn into an uncanny cohabitation with providence, necessity, and destiny. This was the Protestant equivalent of the Greek union of Apollo and Dionysius.

From the standpoint of creation it doesn't matter whether social actors are Taoists or Pre-Socratics, Cynics or Calvinists. What does matter is whether education transmits a type of culture that enables social actors to bear great antinomies. These antinomies are the crucible of creation. Beauty in its myriad of expressions is the sum of the incipient patterns that weld together these antinomies into memorable and durable forms. Beauty is the key to emergent industrial technologies. The clock-makers of Warrington had, in the clock-work mechanism, a model for works of great beauty. This was a model of creation—the image of the clockwork universe. The 'cog in the wheel' would still be an object of fascination in early twentieth-century Futurist and Expressionist art. Such images can be taught, discussed, or argued about in an Academy—although, equally, they might not be. But in order for this to happen, the mute aesthetic dimension must precede education, just as it must precede economic activity. This is what is meant by an aesthetic mode of production—it is one where images of beauty (in the broadest sense), created in free time, provide the basis for the processes of production.

Art and economics

The great Italian Renaissance economies had at their heart an aesthetic mode of production. From Venice to Florence to Milan they constituted a classic portal, thalassic, peninsula economy with riverine features—and a region of astonishing economic and social vitality. By the time that Napoleon conquered Venice, putting an end to the long history of the Venetian Republic, the glory days of Italian art, science, and economics were long gone. The nineteenth-century *Risorgimento* ('Resurgence')—which turned the Italian peninsula into a territorial nation-state—did little immediately to revive those fortunes. In the course of the twentieth century, however, North and Central Italy moved from being one of the poorest to one of the richest regions in Europe. Development, though, remained an insistently regional phenomenon. The South of Italy consistently lagged behind North and Central regions. By the end of the twentieth century, Italy ranked sixteenth out of the top seventeen intellectual property nations, as measured by scientific patents per capita. Without the drag of the South, such a ranking would have been considerably higher.

So impressive was the ascent of North and Central Italy to wealth, that the region was even touted as a model for America when the U.S. economy was making a somewhat rocky transition from industrial to post-industrial economics in the 1980s. The ultimate success of the American transition quieted interest in alternative models. But the strength and distinctiveness of the Arno River and Po River valley economies ensured that they continued to attract attention, and not just as models of economic, but of social and political development as well.

One of the interesting aspects of the Arno and Po River regions is that they went through significant revitalization during the twentieth century, but arguably with little thanks due to either the nation-building set in train by the *Risorgimento* or the imperial masquerade perpetrated by the mid-century Italian Fascists. The ascendancy of these regions, however, had a lot to do with vital cities amidst a chronically weak state and the heritage of civic power in North and Central Italy. The close connection between energetic cities and strong economies on the Italian peninsula extends back to Roman antiquity. Economic activity over many centuries fluctuated in step with the strengthening and weakening of civic power. As ancient Roman cities were eviscerated, so was long-distance trade and economic vitality. Contra-wise, the re-emergence of long-distance trade went hand-in-hand with the development of the medieval commune in North and Central Italy. The city republics that grew out of these communes were the crucible of the Italian Renaissance. These cities—epitomized by Florence and Venice—commanded both great art and great mercantile wealth. When civic power was unable to assert itself, as in the case of the birth of the Italian nation-state, artistic and material wealth did not flourish.

Historically, the South of Italy was a creature of the patrimonial kingdom of Naples. In the South, hierarchic and patron-client relations permeated social and economic life. Correspondingly, the kingdom of Naples had great difficulty projecting its power over distance. In many areas, gaps in the fabric of official hierarchical power were filled by criminal patrimonies (e.g. the Mafia). The most that the national unification of the Italian peninsula in 1870 achieved was the partial, and often fragile, replacement of personalized hierarchies with ineffectual impersonal bureaucracy. Mainly what it achieved, as Antonio Gramsci noted, was the creation of a parasitic administrative class. National unification may have diverted resources from North to South, but it could do little to narrow the gap between the economic proficiency of the North and the sluggishness of the South. As Robert Putnam observed, the difference in economic performance between Northern and Southern Italy could be accounted for by the existence of a civic tradition in North and Central Italy that was absent in the South (Putnam, 1993). Strong forms of civic association characterized medieval and Renaissance cities in those regions. Civic power diminished after the sixteenth century. Putnam's argument was that it began to reappear or reconsolidate after the *Risorgimento*. After Unification, professional and scientific associations, cultural societies, and mutual aid societies blossomed in the Veneto, Emilia-Romanga, and Lombardy. Underpinning these, and stimulated by them, Putnam argued, was the social capital of trust. By encouraging trust, civic associations encouraged cheap and effective kinds of economic cooperation.

Where hierarchy drove economic action through patronage, and the legal-rational nation-state drove economic behavior through enforceable contracts, civic associations drove economic action through the emotional bond of trust. Such associations made possible flexible cooperation and transactions between economic actors. A business owner could find a short-term supplier through social contacts in a choral society. A manager could find reliable technicians through membership of a professional society. Employees could find reliable workmates through their participation in mutual aid societies. In Putnam's eyes, the civic revival in *Risorgimento* Italy was a testing ground for the reliability and rationality of economic actors. The significance of this is not to be denied out of hand. However, it is not a sufficient explanation for the twentieth-century renaissance of North and Central Italy. On empirical grounds alone, it is not fully convincing. As Putnam notes, it is not until around 1900 that North and Central Italy begin to 'take off.' This is *thirty years* after Unification. Even if it took time for a sufficient mass of social capital to accumulate before paying economic dividends, the lag still strongly suggests that there was another factor determining the re-birth of North and Central Italy. This was the factor of aesthetics.

Putnam lays out the basic facts very elegantly (1993, 158). At Unification, Italy had not been touched by the Industrial Revolution. The North was marginally more prosperous than the South. Per capita income was 15–20% higher in the North. However, once industrialization began to drive the North ahead—beginning around 1896—the gap widened sharply. In the period between 1896 and 1911, there is an explosion of development in the North. By 1911, incomes are 50% higher than in the South. By the 1980s, per capita income was 80% higher in the North. It is not the *Risorgimento*, but the period between 1896 and 1911 that is decisive. This is not a period of nation building but of high aesthetic Modernism. This is the same period internationally when Modernist art emerges, and when the Minkowski-Einstein aesthetic-based revolution in geometry and physics takes place.[25] It is also a creative highpoint in the United States, as previously noted. This aesthetic-intellectual explosion is registered in North Italian cities with the rapid spread of artistic currents like Futurism. The national liberalism of the preceding decades may have stimulated the voluntary association of consumers, workers, educators, professionals and artisans, but the real developmental break-through occurred when the North-Central cities became the stage for an intensive imaginative groundswell. The groundswell was characterized by artistic interest in new mathematics and geometries. It produced a number of first-class artists and architects, among them Boccioni, Carrà, Sant'Elia, and Giorgio de Chirico. Of these figures, de Chirico was the one most attuned to the enigmatic foundation of social order. He demonstrated a remarkable intellectual grasp of its strange nature.

Historically, there is a very close relationship between social aesthetics and socioeconomic developments. This was true of the classical Greek city-states, the Venetian-Florentine Renaissance, Shakespeare's London, Amsterdam in its Golden Age, and the American Republic (Murphy, 2001a). Here we see a series of intellectual modernisms characterized by exceptionally high levels of enigmatic socio-aesthetic intuitions accompanied by remarkable socio-economic developments. To understand this, let us return to some basics. Cities have one major advantage over patrimonies and nations. This is their ability to act at a distance. What made Genoa, Milan, Venice and Florence major economic powers during the Renaissance era was their facility for long-distance trade, banking, and manufacture for export—regionally, 'nationally' and globally. It is true that the trustworthiness and reliability of their merchants, bankers, and manufacturers was a significant factor in the success of these cities. Ever since ancient Roman days, *fides* had been an essential ingredient of success in long-distance relations. Merchants, financiers, and manufacturers learnt that even when patrimonial princes or court procedures were unreliable even treacherous, their own sense of fidelity could often make the difference. But this fidelity was cast in a broader context. After all, it was not the reliability of the faithful servant or the rule-following bureaucrat; it was neither a 'social' nor a 'procedural' rationality. It was not even simply a matter of ethical honesty or incorruptibility. Rather it was a type of reliability that had a high aesthetic-cognitive component.

Renaissance Genoa, Florence, Milan and Venice were the initiators of the first great wave of modern capital accumulation. What made this possible was not their citizens' command of social virtues, nor was it methodical procedure or intellectual virtue. All of this was secondary to the uncanny core of an enigmatic culture. This was the driving force of the first regime of true capitalist accumulation. The Genoese-Florentine-Milanese-Venetian model, though, was not a 'one-off.' All of the greatest examples of modern capital accumulation—the Dutch, British, and American—followed this model in crucial aspects. So also did the 'second renaissance' of North and Central Italy in the twentieth century.

What the idea of intellectual capital supposes is that the advancement of knowledge is a driving force of prosperity. But knowledge has many connotations. Anything from the most trivial piece of information to the most abstract philosophical maxim can be called knowledge. However, knowledge comes into its own only if it is surrounded by an architectonic aesthetic. The skeletal frame of such knowledge is made up of uncanny, un-decidable, non-discursive relationships—usually enigmatic or paradoxically, or at the very least radically analogical. These provide the most durable and productive connective force for natural, socio-economic, and personality systems. These relations can be geometrical, mathematical, and aesthetical in kind. Among the more familiar of their type are relations of symmetry, proportionality, harmony, and rhythm. Such relations are the drivers of the beauty, rationality, and efficiency of natural, socio-economic, and 'inner' worlds. They function to create unions out of antinomies, contradictions, and contrasts.

Strong knowledge arises from the understanding, apprehension or intuition of these kinds of relationships and their paradoxical and analogical unions. Knowledge, at its most potent, is an intuition before it is an explication of things. It rests on the mute aesthetics of nature, political economy, and personality that allows individual and collective agents to arrange their actions elegantly, efficiently, and beautifully. Those who do this reap the benefits of prosperity. Take the example of Luca Pacioli (1445–1517). He was one of the mathematicians who made explicit the mathematical basis for Renaissance classical architecture and perspective painting. He collaborated with Leonardo da Vinci, coaching him in the mathematics of proportionality and perspective that underlay da Vinci's great mural *The Last Supper*. The same Pacioli laid the basis for modern accounting. He systematically wrote down the new methods of double-entry bookkeeping that he observed being used by Venetian merchants. So profound was his system that the accounting methods that he laid down remained virtually unchanged till developments in mid nineteenth-century America. Indeed his bookkeeping treatise still accounts for most of the ledger concepts used today (including assets, liabilities, capital, income, expense accounts, and ledger balances). Pacioli's systemization became the basis of all modern business practice.

Pacioli was interested in the aesthetic-mathematical and geometrical relationships between things. His account of bookkeeping (in thirty-six short chapters) was contained in his 1494 treatise *Summa de Arithmetica, Geometria, Proportioni et Proportionalita* published in Venice. Pacioli's aesthetico-geometrical view of the world has had the most massive practical consequences for the modern era. Virtually any modern economic transaction assumes it. But Pacioli's system was not mono-manically 'economic.' He was a mathematician, and, like most mathematicians, he was interested in beauty and elegance, not just in economic utility. This is most fortunate, as economic utility is a by-product of the human interest in elegance and beauty.

Anonymous collective order

The obverse of the aesthetic mode of production is great cities. We cannot separate the two. There is no aesthetic production without great cities, and no great civic power without high levels of aesthetic productivity and creativity. Hierarchies are animated by social obligations; nations by contract and law; and cities by collective aesthetic intuition. Through the medium of such intuition, cities create long-distance and large-scale order. Relations of symmetry, proportion, harmony, rhythm, and the like are the glue of the order that binds unknown persons in and between great cities. Great cities are not the product of associations based on social capital, but of uncanny aesthetic forms.

Take the example of the mutual aid society. This was a very successful late nineteenth and early twentieth century device for insuring workers against the risks and uncertainties of industrial life. Robert Putnam used the example of the proliferation of mutual aid societies in North and Central Italy after the *Risorgimento* to illustrate the hypothesis that economic regions with strong civic traditions of association have a predisposition to foster cooperative relations between social actors. Cooperation is a kind of social capital that sustains economic activity. Through the mutual aid society, workers contributed to a common fund that paid out benefits in the event of illness and unemployment. By reducing personal uncertainty in volatile and dynamic economies, the system of insurance made workers more tolerant of cyclical 'ups and downs' and flexible labor markets, and less liable to look to patrons, sinecures, feather bedding and other forms of neo-feudal, rent-seeking and unproductive economic behavior. The mutual aid society, however, Putnam argued, was only possible because it encouraged and embodied high levels of civic trust. In a mutual aid society, the members could not know each other personally or at least could not know all their fellow members. The society's benefit was unlike a loan that might be extended by a patron or a 'godfather.' For such an arrangement to work, members had to trust each other not to abuse their membership—for example, by joining just before an illness, receiving a benefit, and then bailing out. Such trust was earned—by people doing the right thing. Agents assuming that their fellow members would act reasonably also encouraged trust. Strong civic traditions discouraged suspicious behavior—not to the point of naivety, but sufficient to make trust a self-fulfilling prophecy. But, as Putnam himself observed in passing, it was not just the behavior of peers that convinced society members to pay their dues. It was also the behavior of the societies themselves, with their 'financial rigor and fair distribution of tasks and their political and moral guarantees' (Putnam, 1993, 137–138). What was at stake here was something more than just a social obligation to pay dues, and also something more than procedural probity. What was at stake was the sense of proportional justice, metric beauty, and allocative symmetry that good accounting can inspire.

What this points to is something fundamental about the nature of civic association. Such association, for the most part, is about relations between persons who do not know each other. This is the 'trick' to the development of great cities and towns. They find ways of relating persons who are anonymous and do not know each other. They do this by creating forms of anonymous collective order. At the heart of anonymous collective orders is always to be found a kind of mute aesthetic order. The spotless bookkeeping of the mutual aid society is an example of such at work. The society's members did not need to know Pacioli's aesthetic-mathematical principles to intuitively and instantly recognize the orderly, good and just relations represented by good bookkeeping. Such metrical order, embodied in the collective persona of the mutual aid society, constituted a trusted third party between anonymous or semi-anonymous agents. Members of the society did not have to trust one another personally. Even if the air of the town was filled with general confidence about the deeds of their fellow beings, they were not making or receiving personal loans. The guarantees associated with contributing and receiving money grew out of the fiduciary reliability of the society and the way it managed the commons (the common pool of funds) for its members.

A great city is composed of many such societies. The great city has an anonymous collective order composed of many anonymous collective orders. Each of these collective orders is a commons. Each commons is a form of common space and common wealth located in between strangers. These are agents who are not bound to each other by traditional personal ties of asymmetric reciprocity—vertical ties of patron and client, protector and protected. The collective order is a form of impersonal tie. It emerges between unknown persons in the city of strangers. Unknown persons may come to know some of their fellows well. Even then, the common pool—governed by aesthetic-geometric forms of symmetry, proportionality, harmony, and rhythm—will remain crucial in their relations. Even when strangers become acquaintances, friends or even lovers, this is so. They continue on, as if they were mutual aid societies.

If this is paradoxical, it is not the only paradox that characterizes the kind of order that emerges between unknown persons in and between great cities. The most successful kind of modern capitalism is a product of the impersonal commons—the commons that is constituted not by social norms of reciprocity but by geometric norms of symmetry and proportionality. Such forms, not least of all in the guise of capitalist accounting, have the necessary power required to bind uncanny pairs of large and small, young and old, dark and light, loud and soft. It is this kind of aesthetic order that lies at the core of the most powerful modern economies.

Endnotes

1. As Buddhism develops into an institutionalized religion, the traveling aspect of it declines. Its organization moves from loose groups of mendicant monks to monks living in permanent monasteries with rules and a mix of hierarchic structure and democratic assembly.

2. On the philosophical history of the 'union of opposites,' see Murphy, 2001a.

3. Paper was a Chinese invention. Shreds of paper, made from various fibres (hemp, ramie), have been found in China dating from the first century CE (Martin, 1994, 52). Paper superceded the use of bamboo and textiles as materials to write on. Papyrus, a swamp plant largely cultivated in the Nile Delta, produced a writing material that dates from the first dynasty, ca 3100-ca 2700 BCE (46). Writing on animal skins has been done from time immemorial. The specific technique of producing parchment made from animal skins (skins of sheep, goats, or calves) possibly dates to the founding of the library of Pergamum by King Eumenes II (197–158 BCE), and the efforts to circumvent the quasi-monopoly of the Nile Delta, and thus the Ptolemies, on papyrus production (51). Parchment became a major competitor to papyrus between the first and fourth centuries CE. Papermaking reached the Arab world in the early eighth century. The technique was adopted by the Byzantines in the same century (52).

4. On the role of shame affects in communal, face-to-face societies and the rise of conscience as a regulator of conduct in extra-communal settings, see Heller, 1985, chapter 1.

5. On Islamic traders in India and China, see Chaudhuri, 1985, chapter 2; Fernández-Armesto, 2000, 391–396; Tracy, 1990; Hourani, 1975. On Gujārāt and maritime India, see Fernández-Armesto, 2001, 401–408; Mehta, 1991.

6. The American form of republican empire is discussed at length in Murphy, 2001a, chapters 10–12.

7. For a much earlier attempt to define pre-modern cosmopolitanism, see the discussion of 'traditional cosmopolitanism' in Murphy, 1983, 757–801.

8. We know this because in 878, the rebel bandit leader Huang Ch'ao captured Canton and 'slaughtered 120000 Muslims, Christians, Jews, and Iranians of the ancient faith. This was a period in the history of the T'ang dynasty when southern China witnessed intermittent rebellions, military movements, and banditry.' Chaudhuri, 1985, 51

9. Today we still see the marks of this: a little further up the coast, at Fuzhou, also in Fujian province, the city still harbors a large Christian population.

10. T'ang period (618–906); Sung period (960–1279); Ming period (1386–1644).

11. In Taiwan today, for example, Mandarin may be the official language but Taiwanese, which is a variant of the Fujian dialect, is widely spoken, especially in the southern and rural areas of the island state.

12. Taoism originated in the period of the Warring States [403–221 BCE]. Its classical teachings were those of the *Tao-te ching*, attributed to Lao-tzu, and the *Chuang tzu*, named after its putative author.

13. The majority of the Overseas Chinese in the Dutch East Indes and Malaysia came from southern Fujian. Taoism was significant amongst this group, reflective of the fact that there was a great concentration of Taoists in the Fujian and Canton Provinces. In the twentieth century, the principal concentration of Taoists is to be found on Taiwan. This is a result of the fact that Taiwan was sinized in the seventeenth and eighteenth centuries with a great emigration of persons from nearby Fujian Province. Most Taiwanese speak the dialect of the Fujian Province.

14. Creel called this 'the mystical skepticism of the Taoists.' See Creel, 1953, chapter 6.

15. Founded by Varhamāna, or Mahāvīra ('Great Hero'). Its oral traditions were written down in the fourth century BCE.

16. Other skeptical movements of the time included the Sanjaya Belatthiputta and the antinomian Purana Kassapa.

17. For a discussion of rational character and its relationship to skeptical conscience, see Heller, 1985.

18. On the Chinese—largely from the coastal Fujian province—who defied the resistance of Confucian and other empire ideologies to sea ventures, see Fernández-Armesto, 2000,408–413; Vermeer, 1990.

19. For a criticism of late twentieth-century, pragmatist-inspired attempts to remove objectivity from ethics, see Murphy, 1986.

20. On orientational feelings, see Heller, 1979, chapter 2.

21. Adam Smith (1723–1790) was lecturer at Edinburgh University (1748–51), professor at Glasgow University (1751–1764), the Edinburgh-based Commissioner of Customs and Salt Duties for Scotland (1777–1786), and Lord Rector of Glasgow University (1787–1789).

22. For a brilliant account of the central role played by the stranger in English society, see Scruton, 2000, especially the descriptions at pages 10, 127, 128, 136, and 158.

23. On Christian Stoicism as a constituent (or fellow-traveler) of the modern pagan enlightenment, see Gay, 1966, 295–205.

24. See Chapter 3 of the current volume. This is elaborated in detail in *Imagination*, the companion volume to *Global Creation*.

25. For a further discussion of the parallels between Minkowski-Einstein and aesthetic modernism, see Murphy, 2005, 742–747.

References

Bentley, J.H. (1993). *Old World Encounters: Cross-Cultural Contacts and Exchanges in Pre-Modern Times*. New York: Oxford University Press.

Carroll, J. (2007). *The Existential Jesus*. Melbourne: Scribe.

Chaudhuri, K.N. (1985). *Trade and Civilisation in the Indian Ocean: An Economic History from the Rise of Islam to 1750.* Cambridge: Cambridge University Press.

Creel, H.G. (1953). *Chinese Thought From Confucius to Mao Tse-Tung.* Chicago: University of Chicago Press.

Fernández-Armesto, F. (2000). *Civilizations: Culture, Ambition, and the Transformation of Nature.* London: Macmillan.

Gay, P. (1966). *The Enlightenment, An Interpretation: The Rise of Modern Paganism.* London: Weidenfeld and Nicolson.

Hall, P. (1998). *Cities in Civilization: Culture, Innovation and Urban Order.* London: Phoenix.

Heller, A. (1985). *The Power of Shame: A Rational Perspective.* London: Routledge.

Heller, A. (1979). *A Theory of Feelings.* Assen: Van Gorcum.

Hourani, G. (1975 [1951]). *Arab Seafaring in the Indian Ocean in Ancient and Medieval Times.* New York: Octagon,

Jardine, L. (1996). *Worldly Goods: A New History of the Renaissance.* New York: Nan A. Talese.

Kierkegaard , S. (1978). In Oden, T.C. (Ed.) *Parables of Kierkegaard.* Princeton, NJ: Princeton University Press.

Martin, H.J. (1994 [1988]). *The History and Power of Writing.* Chicago: University of Chicago Press.

Mehta, M. (1991). *Indian Merchants and Entrepreneurs in Historical Perspective.* Delhi: Academic Foundation.

Murphy, P. (2005). 'The N-Dimensional Geometry and Kinaesthetic Space of the Internet.' In Margherita Pagani (Ed.) *Encyclopedia of Multimedia Technology and Networking* Volume 2. Hershey, PA: Idea Group.

Murphy, P. (2001). 'Marine Reason,' *Thesis Eleven* 67, 11–38.

Murphy, P. (2001a). *Civic Justice: From Ancient Greece to the Modern World.* Amherst, NY: Humanity Books.

Murphy, P. (2000). 'The Seven Pillars of Nationalism.' *Diaspora: A Journal of Transnational Studies* 7:3, 369–416.

Murphy, P. (1999). 'Metropolitan Rhythms: A Preface to a Musical Philosophy for the New World.' *Thesis Eleven* 56, 81–105.

Murphy, P. (1986). 'Review of John Rajchman and Cornel West (eds.) Post-Analytical Philosophy.' *Telos* 68.

Murphy, P. (1983). 'Moralities, Rule Choice, and the Universal Legislator.' *Social Research,* 50:4, 757–801.

Putnam, R.D. (1993). *Making Democracy Work: Civic Traditions in Modern Italy.* With Robert Leonardi & Raffaella Y. Nanetti. Princeton, N.: Princeton University Press.

Scruton, R. (2000). *England: An Elegy.* London: Continuum.

Smith, A. (1970 [1776]). *The Wealth of Nations.* Andrew Skinner (Ed.). Harmondsworth: Penguin.

Smith, A. (1969 [1759]). *The Theory of Moral Sentiments.* In D.D. Raphael (Ed.) *British Moralists 1650–1800* Volume II. Oxford: Oxford University Press.

Smith, A. (1896). *Lectures on Justice, Police, Revenue and Arms.* Edwin Cannan (Ed.). Clarendon Press: Oxford.

Vermeer E.B. (Ed.) (1990). *Development and Decline of Fukian Province in the Seventeenth and Eighteenth Centuries.* Leiden, 1990.

Weber, M. (1951). *The Religion of China: Confucianism and Taoism*. New York: Free Press.

Weil, S. (1957). *Intimations of Christianity among the Ancient Greeks*. London: Routledge.

Weil, S. (1956). *The Notebooks of Simone Weil*. London: Routledge & Kegan Paul.

Wittgenstein, L. (1974 [1921]). *Tractatus Logico-Philosophicus*. Translated by D.F. Pears and B.F. McGuinness. London: Routledge.

CHAPTER 3

Portal Power and Thalassic Imagination

◻ Peter Murphy

The collegial society

Hierarchies, networks, and navigations are fundamental social-historical structures. Consider for a moment this typology as it applies to the question of governance. Historically, the most persistent model of governance has been hierarchy. Even today—when hierarchy is rhetorically downplayed in the name of social equality—it remains the most common type of rule. It appears in many guises. Most people find their lives caught up in one or other familial, patrimonial, bureaucratic, clerical, corporate, or party hierarchy.

Hierarchies operate in one, vertical dimension—up and down a line or chain. Such power is a face-to-face, personalized kind of power. Networks add to the one dimension of the hierarchical line, a second or planar dimension. Network power functions across plane surfaces. Technology, law and narrative organize it. Network power operates more impersonally than hierarchy does—which means that its reach across both space and time is greater. The final kind of power, navigational power, is a function of the third, *plastic* dimension of space. It is the most abstract, most impersonal kind of power. Geometries, rhythms, harmonies, ratios, and proportionalities organize it. It has the greatest reach of any kind of power. It is the kind of power most intimately associated with the city or, more particularly, the world city.

Planar orders typically accompany movements to democratize. The most spectacular example of this, in modern life, is the American case. We see the influence of planar or network democracy in America reflected in its model of office holding. America was a leader in the adoption of democratic proceduralism and strong rule-based institutions in political life. But this was slower to occur than is often assumed. We think of America as the antithesis of a hierarchical society. But nineteenth-century America had slavery in the South, political clientelism and the boss system in its ethnic-dominated cities, and a Protestant political gentry elsewhere. Until at the least the 1870s, in what was basically a decentralized rural society, a part self-made, part collegially-formed gentry class of professionals, family business owners, and clergy dominated political life (Hofstader, 1955, 131–173). Governance was organized through relations of eminence and deference. These relations were not feudal, but they were hierarchical. John Adams' phrase, 'a hierarchy of talent,' is a useful way of describing these kinds of relations.

Hierarchy is the typical glue of face-to-face societies. It exhibits its most powerful effects in localized moral geographies. In the American case, outside of the South whose characteristics were *sui generis*, local status groups commanded deference and asserted personal authority. They did so on the basis of 'high-minded' ideals and 'respectability.' The personal nature of American political and social authority was quite long lasting. We should not forget that Jefferson personally answered practically all of the letters sent to him at the White House, or that, until the end of the nineteenth century, a lawyer did not need a degree to tout for business. Andrew Jackson practiced very successfully without qualifications. In ante-bellum America, oratory (delivered in face-to-face forums) was the principal mode of political communication. Through the twentieth century, rhetoric remained a lively pedagogic force in American higher education, where most everywhere else it was eclipsed.

Even after the Civil War, and the spread of distance communications, many key American institutions remained highly localized. Law enforcement in the nineteenth century was limited to counties and townships. There were no state or federal police forces. Many rural areas went effectively un-policed. A criminal who crossed the town or county boundary was immune from the official threat of imprisonment. This is why self-help or vigilante justice was so common in the American nineteenth century, especially in California, Texas, New Mexico, and Montana (Johnson, 2000, 537). It was also why the bounty hunting of absconders developed—as an effective way of extending the reach of local justice. The Federal Bureau of Investigation was a Progressive-era innovation, sponsored by Teddy Roosevelt in 1908 in a political climate pre-occupied with civil service reformism. Prior to that time, the U.S. Department of Justice would hire private detectives or secret service agents to carry out investigations of federal crimes. Pennsylvania created the first State Police force in the United States in 1905—and then there was no stampede. Rhode Island's State Police force for example was not established till 1925.

The voluntary association and the militia, both of them heavily reliant on personal authority, typified early nineteenth-century American organizational forms.

Andrew Jackson conquered Florida using a militia that he personally organized—or rather personally intimidated. Teddy Roosevelt's hand-chosen corps, the Rough Riders, led the American conquest of Cuba at least in a symbolic sense. Personal authority mattered, and not just in war. The Ivy League college was dominated more by social clubbing than by scholarship, and power in America's cities gravitated around political machines like the Society of St. Tammany. In pre-Civil War America, dueling was commonplace. Alexander Hamilton was killed in a duel with Aaron Burr. Honor and even vengeance—bonds of pre-modern face-to-face societies—were remarkably persistent in America. This was particularly true in the Old South and the border-states of Tennessee, Kentucky, and Missouri, and in the pioneering days of the West (Johnson, 2000, 534). The current of violence in American society has at least part of its roots in this. The violent history of American labor relations, or the propensity for assassination in American presidential politics, the use of hand-guns and the high incidence of murders that result from that—all of these are the marks of a society in which dueling is not quite dead and buried. The American attitude was summed up in a 1921 Supreme Court judgment, in a case concerning the judgment of a Texas court that had convicted a man who had stood his ground when an assailant attacked him with a knife. The man had shot the attacker to death. The Supreme Court quashed the conviction. Oliver Wendell Holmes ruled that 'a man is not born to run away' (Johnson, 2000, 534–535).

Despite the persistence of surrogates for pre-modern honor culture in America, the ascendancy of personal authority in American politics and society did change precipitously, and painfully, after the American Civil War. America began on the path of rapid urbanization and large-scale geographical integration. To achieve this integration, Americans had to create ways of relating, and forms of authority, that would permit action across a continent without relying on local hierarchies of notables—or on personal honor, familial preference, and social clubbing. This was never eradicated entirely. The social register and patrician styles continue to be defining characteristics of certain American elites.

The second American revolution

As Karl Marx pointed out, a distinguishing feature of pre-capitalist modes of production is the absence of roads—a characteristic of rural America well into the twentieth century.[1] In such places, Marx also pointed out, where circulatory media do develop, slave or forced labour is relied on.[2] The road and rail and telegraph systems of the ante-bellum American South were extremely limited. The geographical integration of the American continental Union necessarily meant integration through the circulatory media of transportation and communication. The conception of American geography was transformed from one dominated by social place to one dominated by network space. Where personal bonds govern social place, impersonal law and procedure regulates network space. Under the latter conditions, we start to think of geography not as territory dominated by the social colleges ('the bodies') of patricians and gentry, but as something akin to the surface of a sheet of paper criss-crossed with lines. Across the surface of this space are drawn railway lines, telegraph lines, pipelines, and power lines. These lines intersect to create networks (webs and lattices) that induce a historically unprecedented circulation of persons, goods, and messages across vast distances.

Marx identified this as the prime condition for the dissolution of the relationship to the earth which was the defining condition of pre-capitalist and pre-modern societies (Marx, 1973, 497). This was what the American Civil War was fought over. Integration of America through the circulating media of transportation and communication meant augmentation in size, a larger economic market, the consolidation of fully capitalist modes of production and distribution, a mobile population, and the accelerated development of the intellectual forces of production—as spatial networks replaced the relationship to the earth as the defining characteristic of human community. Before the American Union, no continental-scale society—with the partial exception of the Roman Empire—had managed this at all convincingly. Indeed, most historic empires found it very difficult to extend political control firmly over all of their territory. These states were typically poorly integrated the further one moved away from the political centre where social hierarchies were most powerful. Historic empires frequently expended an uneconomic quantum of energy to maintain control at the margins.

The Americans set about with characteristic vigour to realize their 'manifest destiny' of extending control over space. Well before the railways or the telegraph made their appearance, they were already furiously building networks of canals (Johnson, 2000, 376; Miller, 1970, 154–55).[3] Thomas Jefferson envisaged America as a continuous grid of land subdivisions. He also foresaw the power of river networks and highways. Jefferson's 1803 Purchase of Louisiana from the French not only massively expanded American territory but also, as Jefferson very clearly understood, linked the new Western lands to the Gulf port of New Orleans via the Mississippi and Missouri River systems. Many formidable American cities, such as Pittsburgh and Cincinnati, were to develop as up-river portal nodes in this circulatory system (Miller, 1970, 154). Two centuries later these rivers and ports remain major economic arteries. The victory of the Union armies, from the standpoint of military technique, was crucially dependent on the North's use of railroads and telegraph, and the superior ability thereby gained to command, control, and move armies over distances. This represented an unprecedented capacity to move, coordinate, and integrate messages, people, and goods across space. The telegraph allowed the transmission of messages over long distances—without the need for those messages to be carried physically. The railroad revolutionized not only the speed but also the economics of the physical carriage of people and goods across large-scale space. The civilian application of these techniques after the Civil War allowed the consolidation of the Union of States across the North American continent. The telegraph reached the Pacific in 1861, and the transcontinental railroad arrived in 1869. The Sacramento Four—the railroad magnates Huntington, Crocker, Hopkins and Stanford—recast the portal economy of California with a Promethean engineering project that brought the transcontinental railroad over the Sierra mountain region, then extended its networks across the state, down to San Diego, and then back across the continent from San Diego to New Orleans.

The greatest moment in the American conquest of continental distance though arguably was not the transcontinental railroad but the triumph of the automobile. Even those veritable masters of space, the Romans, found land transport prohibitively expensive except for the carriage of luxury goods, and their armies moved no more quickly than they could march. Thomas Jefferson's administration authorized a national highway in 1806 (Miller, 1970, 154, 266). By 1818, it had progressed not much further than a state highway backbone linking Maryland and Ohio, and connected to thousands of miles of private turnpike roads. The turnpikes, notably, priced themselves out of business. Highway and road building on massive scale had to wait until the twentieth century—and it was propelled by automobile technology. While the lack of good roads and highways impeded the early U.S. auto industry, this was reversed between 1915 and 1925 when annual U.S. expenditures on road networks escalated dramatically. It took at least this long, and in some places still longer, for American geographical distances to be truly conquered. Accordingly, the collegial society remained a persistent thread and powerful theme in American life. Even with the automobile, and its mythologizing in the road movie, the ghost of the small-town patrimony was never eviscerated. It just re-invented itself.

America became a large-scale, grid-like territorial state due to its command of law, technology, and narrative. Law defined the scope—the jurisdiction—of its territory; technology provided the means, the media, for administering that space. Technology produced the communicative networks of rail, later road; post, later telegraph and telephone that enabled the communicative integration of a continental territory—no mean achievement. Narratives provided the stories that tied the citizens of a large-scale territorial union symbolically together in lieu of deferential symbols. These stories ranged from the martyrdom of Lincoln to the conquest of the West to the struggle for American independence. The American story was often tinged with religious symbolism—mainly of a Hebraic-Protestant kind. It conjured an image of America as an evangelical nation, a redemptive nation, and Americans as an exceptional, chosen people, capable of doing what the vaguely damned Europeans had proved incapable of: creating a nation based on enlightenment and freedom, and propagating those values to the world. Other, more classical images were woven into this symbolic tapestry as well (Murphy, 2001a, 255–314). Most notable was the idea that America had a Roman-like manifest destiny. In all of this, there was a weaving together of freedom and necessity and a symbiosis of the religious and the classical—something that made it possible for Americans to re-invent ancient civil religion, and to worship their Constitution.

Whatever the symbolism, all of it hinged on the epic story of America as it progressed itself, Virgil-like, from rebellious maritime colonies to con-federal union to constitutional experiment to land acquisitiveness to civil war and bloody nationalism. Throughout the climb to continental epic scale, the American constitution proved a remarkable legal-procedural mechanism for the proliferation and addition of states. The rapid post-Civil War expansion of the Union, though, was equally the function of network communications—rail in particular. The railroad not only allowed for economic and political transport but also provided the model for the development of the modern equity corporation. What all of these institutions—from the constitution to the corporation—shared in common was a preference for proceduralism over local eminence. Law, rules, methods, committees, protocols, and standards were the foundation for constructing institutions that extended well beyond the local scale.

Hierarchies of eminence and deference forged out of talent nonetheless remained central to the workings of American managerial institutions. Modern American bureaucracy was a hybrid of patrician hierarchy and administrative proceduralism. Moreover, surprising numbers of non-bureaucratic patrimonial structures (e.g., the municipal 'boss system') survived and flourished in America, a long time after the ethos of managerialism appeared—as did patrician styles amongst the established wealthy and powerful. American legalism cohabitated with the county sheriff and 'good old boy,' who knew everyone and disliked strangers on principle.

Thus by the turn of the twentieth century America was an uncanny place, and was to remain so. It had its patrician notables who claimed and acquired democratic precedence based on moral conviction and precocious (or at the very least self-promoting) talent. It had its emergent corporate and communication networks that spread in planar fashion across the continent following along behind the railroads and the indubitable American sense of manifest destiny. This space of lateral expansion— what Andrew Jackson dubbed the 'area of freedom' (Stephanson, 1995, 31)—was defined not by a geographical boundary but by the scriptive (and in a tacit sense scriptural) boundary of the American nomos, the law of the constitution. Finally, in the ecumene that stretched along the Hudson River and across to the Great Lakes, between New York City and Chicago, an urban revolution unprecedented since the Roman Empire started to explode, confounding the Protestant gentry of rural America. This urban revolution began, inchoately, to define a civic order of rhythm in contrast both to the impersonal space-defining nomos of legal order and the personal heroics of an Andrew Jackson or the less heroic personalized bonds of local voluntary associations and rural township authorities. It was also this urban revolution—one of the greatest urban creations in history, involving one of the largest and swiftest shifts from rural to urban society of any time in history—that provided a nodal interface, a portal and pipeline, between continental America and the rest of the world.

The third American revolution

The political expression of the urban-portal eruption was the rise of American globalism in the 1890s. This decade was to bring a third revolution in American life. The first revolution laid the basis for the rule of the self-made gentry of Jeffersonian and Jacksonian America. The second revolution, which began with the Civil War, was a nationalist revolution. It resulted in a strong territorial state, an integrated national economy based on the railway, and the distinctive American managerialism of chain, branched, and franchised network organization. The third revolution was played out in the period from the 1890s to the 1920s. Its beginning moment was the Spanish-American War (1898). The third revolution created an American empire.

Let me stress—this was, from the beginning and was to remain, a very strange kind of empire. It was an empire with limited territorial ambitions. Brooks Adams (1848–1927) imagined it in the following way: Adams was a friend of Theodore Roosevelt, the first President of America's global age, and the last of the self-made heroes. In *The Law of Civilization and Decay* (1896), Adams conceived of an American empire based largely on the control of maritime trade routes. This was an empire that had much more in common with the maritime empires of Venice and Amsterdam than it did with the Russian or Austro-Hungarian Empires, or even with the British Empire, which in its latter phases rushed to command vast swathes of the earth. The emergent American global power was an emporial kind of empire. It was based to a very large extent on maritime power and world trade, and *not* on the possession of land, or for that matter on international law or legalitarian proceduralism.

Correspondingly, land war proved to be the least distinguished aspect of American warfare overseas. The classic example is the Vietnam War. While the Americans never lost control of the maritime delta region in Vietnam, the interior land and mountainous war defeated them. Less obvious, but in a way even more illustrative, was the European theatre of war in the Second World War. America defeated Nazi Germany, and successfully occupied Germany for a short period for the purpose of democratic reconstruction. But in the larger theatre of European geopolitical territory, America made a significant mistake. In the closing stages of World War II, Roosevelt resisted Churchill's pressure to invade Europe via the Mediterranean and Eastern Europe. Had that been done, Soviet domination of Eastern Europe would have been checked, and the Cold War would have been minimized. Roosevelt preferred the quick advance to Berlin via France to the slower slog through Eastern Europe. Another way of understanding this is that the American genius is for aerial and naval and cavalry wars of movement, and not for infantry wars of position.

This attitude to war is an expression of the larger American sense of geopolitics. American geopolitics in large measure has downplayed territorial possession and mercantilist regulation of trade, relying instead on a mix of command of the seas (via fleets and bases) and economic intelligence (market information). The United States rarely sought to acquire more than 'points of safety' for the projection of its power. It has exhibited little appetite for territorial acquisition beyond its continental homeland. At the end of the nineteenth century, the United States began to imagine itself as an enigmatic imperial power—one with great power but very few colonies or protectorates. The colonies and protectorates that it did acquire were the exception that proved the rule. In the American-Spanish War of 1898, which was engineered by the United

States, America acquired the maritime colonial territories of Cuba, the Philippines, Puerto Rico, and Guam from Spain. These were the sclerotic remains of the once formidable Spanish Empire. America ceded Cuba its independence (albeit with various back-handed qualifications) but held onto the other territories—eventually granting them various and complex forms of ambiguous status as 'insular areas' of the United States.[4] (America would keep a toe-hold on Cuba through its perpetual lease of the naval base at Guantánamo Bay, with an eye on the geopolitics of its Houston-New Orleans-Florida portal zone.) 'Insular' became the principal epistemological category of American empire. This was a watery empire, and one that was shy of territorial incorporation. Insular defined an uncanny, ambivalent status. It was not an incorporated territory that could apply for statehood and American citizenship. Insular status ranged from Commonwealth status to Unincorporated Territory status to Associated State status—none of these entailed U.S. citizenship or a pathway to statehood and incorporation in the American Union. In some cases American law may apply to an insular state, in other cases the state may be legally independent in all but foreign and military affairs.

In 1903 the United States laid a transpacific cable that linked San Francisco with Manila via Honolulu and Guam. This represented a chain of power that was visibly different from a continental model of power. The role of these insular stepping stones was to amplify the projection of American power into East Asia, sufficient to ensure that the doors of East Asian states (China, Japan, and Korea) remained open to trade. Underlying this was a further geopolitical consideration. By the end of the nineteenth century it was clear that there were three long-term loci of world wealth and power. One was maritime Europe—Northwestern Europe stretching from the North Sea to the Baltic Sea, the zone that had created early modern capitalism. The second was the portal regions of the United States, which had already outstripped Europe by the beginning of the twentieth century. The third was the China Seas region of East Asia.

Alfred Thayer Mahan set out the particulars of the American doctrine of 'navalism' in a set of lectures he gave at the US Naval College and published in 1890 as *The Influence of Sea Power on History 1660–1783* (Mahan, 1987).[5] Mahan provided an analysis of historical naval warfare, and offered a set of observations about the relation of sea power to national prosperity that went a long way to defining the distinctively American imperial attitude that was emerging in the 1890s. In Mahan's view, naval power was a key to a commercial state projecting its global interests. 'Control of the seas…is chief among the merely material elements in the power and prosperity of nations,' he was later to write in 1893 (Mahan, 2002, 52). '…From this necessity follows the principle that, as subsidiary to such control, it is imperative to take possession, when it can be done righteously, of such maritime positions as contribute to secure command.' Unlike the British disposition to turn 'maritime points' into 'colonial planes,' the Americans thought of 'maritime positions'—and the slivers of territory they occupied—as being much more like bases than colonies. Mahan maintained that the US must occupy positions that would give it control over the Panamanian isthmus—anticipating that a canal would be soon built there for commercial and strategic reasons—and he proposed bases in the Pacific to protect American interests in the Far East from British, French, Russian, German and Japanese competition. The creation of Panama was engineered in 1903. This convoluted territorial sleight-of-hand was done with the ulterior purpose of building a trans-isthmian canal and having Panama concede a Canal Zone colony, the artifice that enabled the US to administer the canal and secure trans-oceanic traffic.[6]

Much about America is enigmatic, not least of all the building of an empire without territory. This is a society that is habitually misunderstood by both its friends and its enemies. Its character is inherently ambidextrous, even contradictory. It certainly is uncanny. We have on the one hand the world of Jacksonian American that Alexis de Tocqueville described—a world that managed to be both egalitarian and patrician in the same breath. Then we have the world of the network revolution that arrived with a vengeance in America after the Civil War. Railroad, later road—and telegraphic, later telephonic, broadcast, cable, and packet-switched—networks became the technology backbone of commercial and administrative networks that were to reach into the most isolated rural areas creating, with great ingenuity and a significant amount of violence, a national polity. From this emerged branded, chain store America in contrast to the small-town Main Street America of the Jeffersonian and Jacksonian eras. The 1890s added yet another 'American character.' In this protean moment, world cities—the great portal cities of Chicago and New York—emerged as nodes that not only tied America's continental networks into a global system of commerce and politics, but also became centers that attracted massive concentrations of intellectual capital. Like their analogous predecessors—Venice, Amsterdam and London—New York and Chicago emerged to world standing not just as centers of commercial wealth but also as centers of epistemic and plastic power.

These were places in which the power of design, the ability to think and act architectonically, was as important as dynastic-patrician power—symbolized by power-families and power-couples in the White House—and as important as network power, the managerial power of the franchise and the chain command organizations that the inventive managerial genius of the Americans spawned. In 1896, right at the opening of America's thalassic age, the Spanish-American philosopher, George Santayana, immediately grasped the nature of the power underlying America's third revolution. In Santayana's view (1896/1936), this was the power of form based on the sense of beauty. America's embrace of the 'city beautiful' idea mirrored its most creative age—the Progressive Era and the Presidency of Theodore Roosevelt—when more measurable creative artifacts were produced in the United States per capita than any time before or after.[7]

The aesthetic power of the urbs, though, did not go uncontested. For America at the beginning of the twentieth century was a head-spinning mix of high-minded Protestant moralism, small-town sanctimoniousness, big-city corruption, developmental blight, aspirations to national procedural fairness, and emergent plastic power. American Progressives demanded the removal of ethnic patrimonialism from municipalities and urged the passage of social laws to regulate working hours and conditions.[8] At the same time they protested large-scale corporate power, and dreamt of a return to a pastoral world dominated by independent lawyers, local business, and moral conscience. Such was the paradox of America that, at the very moment Progressive opinion decried the evils of the city, the very nature of the city was being reinvented. The vertical-skyscraper city of Chicago and New York was the first new city form since the medieval gothic type. The countervailing hope of Progressives lay in the developing suburbs that mixed neat orthogonal street grids with the green space of the Pilgrims' New England countryside—a reconciliation of a rural topos with the legalitarian space of Thomas Jefferson's infinitely extensible Cartesian network.

Nothing has changed today. American democracy is still distinguished by the same mix of patrician morals, fascination with law as the panacea of all ills, and a mute aspiration for an architectonic spirit that rises above the other strains in the American character. It combines legislative proceduralism with congressional patrimony (aka earmarks). It hankers after personal moral authority, its voting power lies in the suburbs, and its wealth and global influence extends outwards from its vertical portal cities, with their world trade centers and their maritime sea regions.

Traffic

The sea-based or thalassic aspect is the least well-understood feature of American democracy. In republican America before the Civil War, the maritime economy, centered on New York and Boston, had been very large (Miller, 1970, 80–85). It extended across the Pacific as well as the Atlantic. In fact it was so large that states like Massachusetts and Connecticut refused to send militia to fight in the 1812 War against England—to try and avoid the damage this war caused to their Atlantic trade with Britain. Yet, after that, nation-building and territorial politics in the nineteenth century focused American attention away from the seas. From the 1780s onwards, Eastern seaboard towns and cities of New England, New York, Pennsylvania and Maryland had a major interest in the Pacific. This included whaling fleets and trade in sea otters, fur and hides. 'These interests were so strong as to develop a sense of ownership over the Pacific coast long in advance of the event' (Van Alsytne, 1974, 106; see also 95). In 1816 and 1820, John Melish, the official cartographer for the U.S. government, published maps showing the Pacific coast from the 52nd parallel and then the 49th parallel as part of the United States. America belatedly returned to larger thalassic preoccupations in the 1890s. Models of territorial imperium are useless to explain what happened thereafter. So also is the supposition that thalassic power is a kind of unprincipled globalization in which American vices are projected indiscriminately across the surface of the globe. In fact, thalassic politics has a *sui generis* logic and well-developed, if not especially well-understood, principles.

It was the Delft-born Dutch theorist Hugo Grotius (1583–1645) who defined the core principle of thalassic politics: the freedom of the seas (*Mare Liberum*). Grotius developed this notion in opposition to attempts by Spain and Portugal to treat the oceans as just another form of territory. He argued that the liberty of the seas was an essential correlate of *the right of nations to communicate with each other*. Significantly, the first foreign policy act of America was to engineer the removal of pirates from the Mediterranean Barbary Coast. It was the commitment to protect maritime commerce and passenger cargo in the Atlantic that brought the United States into World War One. Support for Britain in the Second World War, prior to the Japanese attack on Pearl Harbor, hinged on much the same considerations. But it is notable that America interpreted Grotius' right of nations to communicate with each other also as *the duty of nations to communicate with each other*. The long-term premise of America's East Asia policy, beginning early in the nineteenth century, was the maintaining of an open door to maritime trade. This was vigorously enforced. A loathing of hermit states might be thought of as basic American principle.

Trade with China and Japan attracted American attention from the early nineteenth century. The Boston merchant William Sturgis sailed to Canton as a vessel captain in 1800. He made four round-the-world voyages in the following eight years, 'Canton being the principal destination of each voyage,' and later established a major business trading between China and the Pacific coast (Van Alsytne, 1974, 170). In 1813, the American naval captain David Porter, who had been on assignment searching for British merchant shipping in the Pacific, wrote to President Madison:

> We border on islands which bear the same relation to the N.W. Coast as those of the West Indies bear to the Atlantic States… The important trade of Japan has been shut to every nation except the Dutch… Great changes have since taken place in the world—changes which may have effected [*sic*] even Japan. The time may be favorable, and it would be a glory beyond that acquired by any other nation for us, a nation of only 40 years standing, to beat down their rooted prejudices, secure to ourselves valuable trade, and make that people known to the world. (Van Alsytne, 1974, 125–126)

In 1835, the United States established an East India squadron with an eye to the China trade. In the 1840s, under pressure from the West, China acceded to demands to open its doors, and allowed the establishment of treaty ports where Western nations could freely trade on equal terms. In 1844, U.S. Ambassador Caleb Cushing negotiated a commercial treaty with China opening five China ports to U.S. merchants. In 1847, President Polk declared that Californian harbors 'would afford shelter for our navy, for our numerous whale ships, and other merchant vessels employed in the Pacific ocean, [and] would in a short period become marts of an extensive and profitable commerce with China, and other countries of the East' (Van Alsytne, 1974, 145). Foremost among those other countries was Japan.

Once the China door had been opened, the Americans immediately turned their attention to Japan. Naval commander Perry was sent to Japan with instructions to use force if necessary to open Japan to the world. 'The world has assigned this duty to us,' Perry declared: 'we have assumed the responsibility and undertaken the task, and can now not hold back' (Van Alsytne, 1974, 173). The Commodore's hope was to turn the island of Okinawa into an American *entrepôt*, and to negotiate the establishment of treaty ports with Japanese authorities. By 1858, six treaty ports had been opened, and Americans had been granted rights of trade, residence and consular representation. The U.S. was also able to establish naval depots at Nagasaki, Kanagawa (near Yokohama) and Hakodate (Van Alsytne, 1974, 175).

Open door policies, which suppose that there is a universal duty to communicate, are often thought of as simply a matter of economics—as if history hinged on an economic interpretation. But, when Grotius declared the freedom of seas, he had something more than commerce in mind. Let us call this 'something else' the system of circulation. Circulation represents the distinctive space that exists within and between portal cities. The signifier of the port city is its traffic. This traffic is created by the rapid circulation of persons, goods, services, and ideas *in and around*, and *between*, cities. This traffic takes place in the portal space of 'backwards and forwards,' 'in and out' (Murphy, 2001, 11–38). Practical politics, including 'real politic,' concentrates on keeping this circulation going. When such circulation stops, we end up with what happened in the Mediterranean in the seventh century CE. When the Mediterranean was divided between Christian and Islamic powers, trade ceased and the European dark ages began. The fall into a dark age is not simply a commercial matter or a matter of material wealth. It is fundamentally also a metaphysical and spiritual matter.

It is metaphysical in the sense that it is the kinetics of traffic, or navigation, that brings alive the third or plastic dimension of space. The third dimension of space is rather peculiar. *Movement through space in time* creates it. This is not the epic circulatory movement *across* space; nor is it the static place *assigned* by patrician hierarchies. As the great modern painter of the plastic, and a master of enigmatic form, Georgio de Chirico, understood well, *the third dimension of space requires the fourth dimension of time*. De Chirico's art helps us answer the question: is there a *sui generis* architecture of the portal? The commercial architecture of Amsterdam's stock exchange or Chicago's skyscrapers might come close, as might the design of Sydney's harbor quays or London's docklands, Venice's canals, and so on. But Chicago produced architecture for plutocratic patricians and university mandarins alike, while court cities have produced portals—St Petersburg—and Venice had its Doge's Palace. De Chirico was more precise. The key to understanding the portal is its uncanny plastic order in which time and space merge to become one. Great plastic order gives form to our navigations. It incites in us a sense of profound rhythmic structure. Instinctively the makers of the great plastic cities—*viz.*, those who created Periklean and Demosthenes' Athens, Hadrian's Rome, Florence, Venice, New York and Chicago—have always tacitly understood this.

So far as the city is concerned, the fourth, kinetic dimension of space—that is to say, movement through space in time—is musical. I mean this in the sense that movement through space in time is governed by the order of rhythm. What makes kinetic-plastic creations great are their marvelous rhythmic qualities—qualities created by all sorts of architectonic devices. These devices help us to mark out, in gorgeous time, our passage through space. These are the devices of proportionality, ratio, harmony, accent, beat, and so on. Our most beautiful, our most just political orders are mirrored in this implied music. This is a beauty and a justice that is something more, and less, than words. There are moments when the declarations of presidents and the rhetoric of those in legislatures surprise us with their intimations of something beyond words. This does not happen often, but it does happen. It happens when their voice suddenly becomes musical and architectonic. This is what set the great British statesman Winston Churchill apart from his peers. His oratory did not always serve the greatest of causes or even the best calculated ones. But when it did, it entered another dimension that is immediately recognizable. In those moments, we are confronted with unbelievably beautiful contrapuntal words, with a rhythmic force that exceeds all verbal meaning but has a meaning all of its own. When we hear those words, the hair on the back of our neck stands up. It is the same feeling we have when we enter a plastic masterpiece like the Pantheon or St. Peter's or Rockefeller Plaza. It is the metaphysical sense we have when we enter and exit great plastic space. It is the sense that we have when we move round a sculpture in the public square, or through the halls of a university, a parliament, a monastery, a palace, or a house that has been designed with a musical sense.

Like its form, the sound of the portal city is uncanny. It achieves this through polyphonies and poly-rhythms in which low and high, the near and the far, slow and fast become almost enigmatically identical (Murphy, 1999, 81–105). This musical-style movement through space in time occurs on multiple levels and through multiple channels. The great Renaissance and early modern music-making of the Flemish and the Venetians was polyphonic, as was the Catholic musical tradition of New Orleans. The latter was to leave its mark on the demotic musical genres that originated along the Mississippi—ragtime, jazz and blues. These were to reach mature form in New York City and Chicago in the first half of the twentieth century and were to provide an acute aesthetic counterpoint to the polyrhythmic ethos of the American metropolis.

In the first two decades of the twentieth century, the great New York composer Charles Ives captured exactly this sense of polyrhythmic order. In Ives' case, it was a polyphony that bordered on near cacophony. It was a type of musical cubism. Ives's life is a perfect miniature of America in transition through the era of its third revolution. His personal metaphysic looked back to the philosophic Transcendentalism of gentrified Boston. His politics were a type of radical democratic Progressivism. He advocated a procedural utopianism of direct voting on laws and ballots to recall errant legislators. His music, though, was something altogether different. His *Fourth Symphony* (1910–1916) sounded as though it had come directly out of New York's rush hour—a vertiginous, riotous yet coherent sound collage of staggering rhythmic complexity and enigmatic beauty. Ives created a musical form whose planes of movement and time generated a surface of chaos that betrayed an extraordinary underlying sense of order.

Portal knowledge

The kind of order that Charles Ives portrayed is an outgrowth of the peculiar crosscurrents of portal cities. These crosscurrents are produced by the very nature of a portal that is inherently 'open to world'—indeed to the cosmos—but which, in order to succeed, must structure and orchestrate and schematize the flows that pass through it. The signature of this 'opening to the world' and the first schemata that a portal adopts is its relationship to other portals. The cosmos, from the standpoint of the portal, might be thought of as the sum of all relations between portals.

This is not just a philosophical observation. Contemplating what was destined to make the United States 'the world's historical center,' an anonymous American Whig editorialist writing in 1849 observed that technological advances would shrink distances. 'The barriers of time and space will be annihilated.' The result would be the opening up of commercial opportunities. 'The trade of China and of a large portion of Asia must find its way across the Western ocean to our Pacific shores, building up great towns and cities there, and thence across to the Atlantic coast, there to meet the trade of Europe coming over the Atlantic on its western route' (Stephanson, 1995, 58). In this modern cosmos, what was essential was not just trade in a generic sense, but trade intertwined with 'building up great towns and cities' on both sides of the Pacific that, in turn, linked with nodal cities on both sides of the Atlantic.

Great portal cities only exist in tandem with other cities. There is no New York without Chicago, London or Shanghai. There is no Venice without Constantinople. Likewise, great cities are composed of cities within cities, typified by the boroughs of New York City or the multiple urban ecologies of Los Angeles. Circulation within and between cities generates a flow of news, letters, reports, and speculations. This establishes relations of correspondence. Already even centuries ago the scale of this could be staggering. For example, Datini, a Renaissance-era Venetian merchant, exchanged over 125,000 letters with his factors and agents between 1364 and 1410 (Jardine, 1996). Relations of correspondence are different from the communicative structures of the procedurally-defined or law-defined citizen city. Notices of assemblies and proposed new laws, news of the violation of laws and of impending threats, reports on the state of the city's planar networks of power and utility, and investigations of the relation between country and town, earth and artifice, define the 'progressive' city. Circulation supposes a different or additional kind of knowledge to that of the citizen city.[9] Circulating knowledge is based on having been to other cities, or other parts of the city, and on the assumption that audiences have also been to, or may one day go to, those places. Knowledge of this kind arises out of the milieu of contacts, friendships, embassies, transactions, traffic, trade, and voyages in and between cities.

Circular knowledge and its works arise for a number of reasons. Traders want to know whether crops have failed or rivers are silting up or war has broken out in some distant place. Envoys want to know the mood and disposition of the officials they are going to meet. Travelers to religious and sporting festivals want to know about travel conditions, lodging, and the reputation of the place or the event they are going to.

This is elementary knowledge—*information*. But, in the course of time, this stimulates *speculation* concerning much more fundamental questions about large-scale structures of geography, climate, warfare, dynastic change, security, hospitality, and sacred life.

Consider the example of price information. Like political news—indeed like any type of information—it is ephemeral. This is the nature of information. It is disposable. It is only important for the moment. It is generated by our responses to contingencies and uncertainties. On the other hand, the good use of information requires frames of interpretation. Is a slump in prices likely to be short-term or long-term? Does the agent sell now or hold onto their commodity? Is the spy providing good information or misleading disinformation? To answer such questions assumes that we can make inferences about large-scale systems—the impersonal order of things. The behavior of markets, war, and government are not random. They have patterns, as difficult as these are to figure out. This is the work of intelligence. Charles Ives is a good example of this. As well as a composer, he was a highly successful businessman in New York's insurance industry. His genius for understanding the patterns of the insurance market not only made him a millionaire but also had direct parallels with the kind of mastery of complexity that his composition required. Intelligence is the discernment of long-range and long-term patterns, which may range from knowledge of the seasonality of monsoons to the political cycles of states.

The intelligence of the portal requires both heavyweight and lightweight media. Portals typically excel in both. The 'built environments' of historic Venice, golden age Amsterdam, London, and New York are collective works of art. At the same time, each of these portals have been great centers for publishing and for the dissemination of information—Venice in the sixteenth and seventeenth centuries, Amsterdam since the seventeenth century, London since the eighteenth century, and New York since the nineteenth century.[10] They are places for the bartering, sale and storage of information. London produces the Reuters news service because 'the world passes through' the portal, and because the portal city exists as a 'carrier' to the world. But information is a kind of raw material, only of the meanest value, until it is given form and structure. This is what writers and anthologists, editors and publishers, librarians and curators do. They organize information into navigable forms—whether this is a gallery display, a newspaper layout, a web page or a searchable database. While most of this architectonic work is prefabricated, it rests on an important principle: intellectual capital is accumulated where cultural and scientific labor extracts something like orderly, architectonic structure from the random, stochastic, or contingent nature of information.

Thalassic power and the right of nations to communicate

Portals are foci for the accumulation of intellectual capital. They are locales where intelligence is highly concentrated. Plastic spaces play an essential role in this concentration. Plastic forms serve as *a model of and stimulus for pattern creation and recognition*. In light of this, it is unsurprising that the portal city should have become, in the middle and late twentieth century, the major center for the development of information technologies. This technological revolution had as great an impact on the world as the industrial revolution of the late eighteenth century. Just as the Mersyside portal-region was the birthplace of industrialism, it was American portal city-regions that pioneered technologies for the electronic manipulation, storage and distribution of information. The most spectacular example was 'the Californian coast,' encompassing the San Francisco-Oakland Bay Area (with its Palo Alto/Santa Clara/Silicon Valley off-shoot) and the mirror city-region of the Southern Californian strip-polis that stretches from Santa Barbara to San Diego-Tijuana (and may, in all probability, one day eventually extend far down into Mexican Baja California).[11] In the same border-hoping sense, America's Puget Sound-Seattle region, another post-industrial pioneer, extended its influence into Canadian British Columbia. These city-regions geographically front the Pacific Ocean, and each constitutes a kind of simulated sea region underpinned by military-industrial economies of great sophistication.

What made all of this possible? In the mid-nineteenth century, and largely because of the building of railroads and the coincidental spread of the telegraph, America hit upon a new kind of planar power. Its communicative technology was to prove more far-reaching than anything since the age of Roman road building. Just as the Roman roads were a network medium that linked and integrated Roman society—and its administrators and armies—across vast distances, America's rail and electric networks made possible a new class of American rulers who replaced the collegial patricians and the self-made gentry of the Jeffersonian and Jacksonian ages. Of course, it is not technology but culture that makes a class, which is why the Germans or the French, who had the same technology, did much less—or certainly very different things— with it. The Americans in the age of continental empire building—with the land deals they transacted with the French and the British, and their wars against the Indians and the Mexicans—were the modern Romans par excellence. Their mastery of planar network power, if anything, eclipsed the Romans.

But, here, now: a word of warning. Despite the popularity of the analogy, American global power—the power that grew out of America's third political revolution—*is not Roman in character*. A society that had ambitions in the mid-nineteenth century of incorporating Canada and Mexico could reasonably be described as Roman. Insofar as NAFTA (the North American Free Trade Agreement) may eventually produce such a territorial empire by peaceful union, the tag Roman remains valid. However, it is not valid to describe the thalassic, global, post-1890s reach of America. Something very different from the Roman model gradually started to take shape in America during the twentieth century. Theodore Roosevelt, former Assistant Secretary of the Navy, a key architect of United States naval power and doctrine of globalism, and the defining President of the American Progressive Era understood very well the subtleties of this power, its distinctive scope and limits.[12] In 1904, Roosevelt stated, with classic American brevity, both the scope and limits of American power.

> All that this country desires is to see the neighboring countries stable, orderly, and prosperous. Any country whose people conduct themselves well can count upon our hearty friendship. If a nation shows that it knows how to act with reasonable efficiency and decency in social and political matters, if it keeps order and pays its obligations, it need fear no interference from the United States. Chronic wrongdoing, or an impotence which results in a general loosening of the ties of civilized society, may in America, as elsewhere, ultimately require intervention by some civilized nation, and in the Western Hemisphere the adherence of the United States to the Monroe Doctrine may force the United States, however reluctantly, in flagrant cases of such wrongdoing or impotence, to the exercise of an international police power.[13]

Although Roosevelt's comments were directed at Latin America in the first instance, they neatly summarize the defining principle of American global power as it emerged from the 1890s. Since that time, there has been no shortage of American isolationists—or alternatively advocates of multilateralism—who have disagreed with Roosevelt's principle and the resulting practice of American globalism. Indeed they have disagreed with the principle and the practice at great length and with great energy such that the debate about globalism has become a recurring staple of American politics.[14] Yet what is often overlooked, in the midst of the heat of that debate, are the explicit limits on American power that Roosevelt summarized. Yes to intervention, but only occasionally, only reluctantly, and only in cases of chronic wrongdoing and impotence that results in a general loosening of the ties of civilized society. All things considered, in the case of a great power that is a sound and measured and sensitive principle.

In the 1920s the U.S. Congress made an historic decision to strategically concentrate its overseas military forces around harbor locations in San Diego, Los Angeles, San Francisco Bay, and Puget Sound. In 1928–1931, a Bay Area lobby organized a tough political campaign that was successful in getting the U.S. Navy to site a major facility at Sunnyvale, at the southern end of San Francisco Bay. The lobby offered the U.S. Navy free land for its base, and beat the initially favoured candidate, San Diego, to the prize. Through the 1930s, San Francisco continued to attract naval and air bases to the Bay Area. By 1941, when America entered World War Two, the Bay Area was crowded with military establishments. Suppliers of naval equipment like Westinghouse and of aerospace equipment like Lockheed came to Sunnyvale in the 1950s. The presence of the military bases and their suppliers was the stimulus for massive indirect and direct support for research and development. Federal funds flowed to Berkeley and Stanford universities for science and technology research that had any vaguely conceived military applications. By the 1960s, California received the lion's share of U.S. federal research and development monies (Hall, 1998, 433). The most striking thing about the American naval and naval-air power was that it was never 'just a military force'—in the same way that Venetian or Dutch military force in the golden age of those states was never 'just a military force.' Thus it did not produce a garrison-city, or a presidio-like culture. In fact, if anything the very opposite in the case of California, for the very interweaving of research and defense meant that the military and its fiercest critics, the universities, lived in a symbiotic relationship.

American globalism was a product of the doctrine of 'navalism,' a doctrine that was subordinated implicitly and explicitly to the thalassic principle—to Grotius' principle—of *the right and, in the American interpretation, the duty of nations to communicate with each other.* Thou shalt communicate, or else. This was a complex, and historically unprecedented, world-view. The U.S. naval captain, David Porter, neatly summed this up in 1813. After a spell chasing British merchantmen in the Pacific, Porter wrote to President Madison. In the letter, he observed of Japan: 'The time may be favorable, and it would be a glory beyond that acquired by any other nation for us, a nation of only 40 years standing, to beat down their rooted prejudices, secure to ourselves a valuable trade, and make that people known to the world' (Van Alsytne, 1974, 125–126). This is a perfect synopsis of the American doctrine of globalism. There is the frank, even disarming, admission of trading self-interest. Yet this is combined with a political and moral metaphysic. This metaphysic supposes both the right and duty of nations to communicate with one other. States that retreat into the incommunicado of prejudice—behind impervious walls of tradition—violate the principle of free communication. It is correspondingly the duty of America to break down such barriers to communication, and to make those who have closed themselves off from the world known to the world.

Without question this is not just a doctrine of trade, though doubtlessly it squares neatly with trade interest. It is not even just a doctrine of enlightenment, even if beating down a state's rooted prejudices represents a rather assertive form of enlightenment. What really makes the American doctrine stand apart is the self-incurred duty to make closed societies known to the world. On the world stage, the American conception of enlightenment was not formulated in terms of rights or liberties, but as duty and destiny. It carried with it the burden and the gravity of responsibility for the world at large. This was no mean consideration.

To assume responsibility for the freedom of the seas and open communication between nations supposed a military power that was of a very distinctive kind. Grotius' basic point was that the oceans were not territory. They could not be commanded like territory. Neither traditional tribute and resource-extracting hierarchies, nor Roman techniques of legal and planar network power worked effectively over seas. It was the Dutch and the Venetians who first found effective ways of projecting power over distance without behaving territorially. The key was their accumulation of intellectual capital. The Venetians at their peak built the best boats and invented financial accounting. The Dutch at their height built the best boats and invented the stock exchange. Both learned to command distance rather than territory. Both learned to command distance through information as well as technology. Both learned to do this because each had an architectonic sense. Both eschewed social and even legal power for the power of abstract relations—relations of aesthetic design, form, number and structure. You see it in their art, their science, their architecture, and their town planning.

It is this condition that American thalassic power groped towards. Through the twentieth century, United States military spending, spearheaded by its naval and naval-air establishments, helped create the phenomenon of 'the knowledge economy.' A classic example of this is the Oracle software company, whose first contract in the late 1970s was struck with the Advanced Technology Division of Wright-Patterson Air Force Base. As Oracle founder Larry Ellison (1944-) was later to observe: 'Who but the Federal Government would buy database technology from four guys in California?'[15] Another early Oracle customer was the U.S. intelligence agency, the CIA. U.S. military spending funded a regime of perpetual innovation by technology and science companies spun off from research universities, primarily located in its thalassic cities, and shielded to some extent from short-term market perspectives by the system of defense contracting. Other nations look at this and try and replicate bits and pieces of this model. They fund technology research but miss the military and political and architectonic dimension. Venice did not become either prosperous or immortal just because its denizens were great ship technologists. Rather what the Venetians learnt with painful experience was how to command distance rather than territory. Ultimately, what made the Venetians brilliant at this, for several centuries, was their exquisite plastic, architectonic, and aesthetic sense. In a more contradictory way, the same is true of the Americans. Typical of the American story is Ellison, the South Side Chicago-raised boy, whose first vocational passion was architecture and one of whose abiding intellectual loves was Japanese landscape architecture. Commercializing the idea of relational databases made Oracle's fortune. But conceptually the relational database was just that—relationships: the transference of the architectonic schema of relationships into the field of information.

Thalassic power and plastic creation

Pattern media are the primary media of the creative imagination.[16] Wherever pattern media are socially prevalent, creative action will take place. Thus, it makes perfect sense that the Californian railroad magnate-turned-Governor and U.S. Senator, Leland Stanford, when he built a university at Palo Alto should also have built an architectural masterpiece.[17] Stanford University—founded in 1885, opened in 1891 and named in memory of Stanford's deceased son—was not just a rich man's folly and Stanford was no fool. Of course, an isolated architectonic work does not constitute a creative ecology. But where such works are repeated on an urban and regional scale then one of the key conditions of creative production is in place. San Francisco's Bay Area managed this, though not to extent of ancient Athens or modern New York, and not in the prolonged fashion of Florence or Rome.

Plastic form is a paradigm of pattern creation. This is creation achieved by the ordering forces of harmony, proportion, rhythm, scale, symmetry, and the like. The most effective way of acting at a distance is through pattern media. The great sea powers, in addition to hierarchy and command, law and technology, were masters of pattern creation. When we look at the Americans, we see a thalassic power with a divided allegiance. For territory also commands part of the American heart. The phrase 'the heart land' sums it up. 'Country' still has an enormous pull on the American psyche. Yet, in the history of the city, New York and Chicago are as remarkable plastic creations as any. These cities grew to maturity due to their ability to command distance rather territory. They accumulated vast artistic, scientific, and commercial wealth on the basis of the principle of the right and duty of nations to communicate with each other. In targeting the Twin Towers in New York City, the terrorist attackers in September 11, 2001 understood more than most the intimate connection of plastic and thalassic power, and the centrality to the American empire of the portal principle of the right and duty of nations to communicate with each other.

Plastic-thalassic power has different expressions. American West Coast cities lack the iconic plastic form of New York and Chicago. Los Angeles in particular is a planar city par excellence. It was created in the image of the railways. It grew around their networks. Its freeways follow their demolished tracks. Even its principal harbor (Long Beach) is an artificial creation. Nonetheless, a kind of plastic genius was central to Los Angeles' rise to maturity. For its endless suburbs and its aero-space economy would never have taken off without two great engineering projects—its aqueducts and the Hoover Dam in Nevada that supplied the hydroelectricity, the cheap power, that drove the most dynamic economy in the world since the days of the industrial revolution. By the end of the twentieth century, California was the sixth largest economy in the world. The availability of cheap power rested on a crucial judgment made in the 1920s. The American President Herbert Hoover made the decision.[18]

Hoover's interest in hydraulic power reflected another aspect of American thalassic power—the command of rivers. Had the political conditions of America been otherwise, Hoover-style engineering politics might have even seen the emergence of a kind of hydraulic despotism in America.[19] If you think that is a frivolous notion, then consider the Mississippi slave economy. It set a powerful precedent in American history for such a thing. However, as it was, Hoover, the engineering graduate from the Bay Area's Stanford University, was a spirited defender of liberties and much more interested in the control of nature than persons. Just as Teddy Roosevelt backed William Mulholland's aqueduct (1913) for water-hungry Los Angeles, Hoover backed the scheme of Ezra Scattergood to dam the Colorado River system at Boulder Canyon to provide hydroelectricity for California. The latter, renamed the Hoover Dam and completed in 1935, was to supply phenomenally cheap electricity to Los Angeles and San Francisco. The Grand Coulee Dam (1942) provided the same for Seattle.[20] But as well as the crucial power, these kinds of projects also provided a plastic imaginary for America.

A strong sense of artifice or 'second nature' has been central to all intellectual capital-intensive societies in history. Great acts of artifice on a public and symbolic scale provide a spur to general pattern creation. California found the locus of its designing mind in some remarkable feats of engineering. When the Hoover Dam was completed, it was the largest man-made structure on earth (Nye, 2003, 244). This was without a doubt a prodigious Promethean act, but creating intake towers as tall as skyscrapers was also an incitement to artifice in general and a stimulus for the kind of designing intelligence that city building in New York and Chicago at the turn of the twentieth century had unleashed. Both power and plasticity were decisive for the creation of the first truly post-industrial economy. As a result, the California coast and Seattle—supplemented by the technological science of maritime Boston and (at least till the 1950s) New York—produced for a time the most dynamic economy in the world since the industrial revolution. As with England's industrial revolution, its incubator was a naval economy and its technology demands.[21] California's most iconic structure was not a traditional architectural edifice but a brilliant hybrid engineering-architectural masterpiece—the Golden Gate Bridge (1938). The structure spans the Golden Gate Strait, the entrance to the San Francisco Bay from the Pacific Ocean. It was a collaborative work by engineers (Joseph B. Strauss and Leon S. Moisseiff) and architects (Irving F. Morrow and Gertrude C. Morrow). It is an astonishingly beautiful structure—a work of enormous span, sweeping cables, elegant lines, soaring towers, delicate accents, and subtle art deco styling.

The kind of economy that America's naval and military economy helped generate is well illustrated by San Francisco's Bay Area. The allying of science-based production and the United States defence force goes back, in the case of the Bay Area, to the turning-point era of the late 1890s. The relationship between the two is complex and interesting. America's 1899 war with Spain stimulated Bay Area interest in wireless communications—much as previously the 1844 war with Mexico had stimulated popular enthusiasm on the East Coast for Samuel Morse's telegraph. A pattern was established in San Francisco of amateur clubs, and of graduate students and faculty, experimenting with communication technologies. Stanford University's electrical engineering department was a locus of this experimental culture. A further pattern was established of turning this hobbyist and experimental activity into commercial ventures. Stanford faculty, for instance, backed the commercialization of Stanford graduate Cy Elwell's 1909 wireless telephone. Elwell's company became a major U.S. wireless firm, benefiting from the 1913 radio law that came on the heels of the sinking of the *Titanic*, making ship radio mandatory.

Americans borrowed the idea of the research university from Berlin—and they took to it with alacrity. In 1870 there was one American PhD graduated. By 1880 that had risen to 53, and by 1900, 382 (Murray, 2003, 433). Yet there is nothing in German academic culture that is a precedent for the American triangulation of faculty science with amateur experimentalism via the energies of graduate research students. In the 1970s the development of the personal computer and networked computing in significant part was driven by the experimentalism of hobbyists, popular science enthusiasts, and graduate students in the Bay Area, Boston, and Chicago.[22] Elements of this pattern extend backwards—to Thomas Jefferson and Benjamin Franklin, both of whom were inveterate technology experimenters. The attitude of experimentalism was also woven deeply into the fabric of the philosophy of Pragmatism, which was one of a number of the central threads of American thought that emerged in the Progressive era, another being the Chicago School of Sociology, with its emphasis on the collective creative force of the city (Murphy, 2006, 64–92). What all of this indicates are the kinds of non-institutional forces that drive discovery and innovation. The alternative story of American creation that is told supposes that individual experimentalism does not scale and cannot explain how discovery and innovation work when for example hundreds of individuals have to collaborate on the design of an airplane or the making of a film. It does not explain defence-funded big science or the Hollywood studio system.

The question, though, to be asked is which of them has worked better? There is no question that, in the nineteenth and twentieth centuries, America has been the most creative nation on the face of the earth. But looking at America alone, in its own terms, what worked better? Was America more creative at the end of the nineteenth century or at the end of the twentieth century? At the end of the twentieth century, like many of the most powerful countries across the globe, America took to calling itself a 'creative economy' and a 'knowledge society.' This was not nonsensical. Since the beginning of the nineteenth century, a handful of economies developed vast and historically-unprecedented levels of wealth based on knowledge. These societies adapted acts of creation from the arts and sciences, and translated these into durable innovation in economy and society—which in turn generated enormous increases in productivity and finally in wealth. The question, though, is whether or not this creative leviathan was more vital at the start of the twenty-first century than at the start of the twentieth century? The answer to this question is no—it was not.

Both the rate of discovery and the rate of innovation in the United States broadly trended downwards over the last century.[23] Why did this happen? The short answer to the question is summed up in one word: enigma. At the core of the widely-regarded greatest work of visual art, Leonardo da Vinci's *Mona Lisa*, is a mystery—an enigmatic smile. What the smile communicates is undecidable. There in lies the heart of creation. That is how Charles Ives composed. The heart of his work was enigmatic. It took decades for music experts to unravel it or even to play his works properly.[24] Ives suddenly stopped composing in 1920. This is a metaphor for what would dog the American century. It is not that no great works were produced in that century, or that there were no major creative events in the period. Rather their rate of incidence declined. There were fewer of them per capita. John Cage continued the American tradition of experimentalism in his composition. John Adams wrote first-class operas, orchestral works, and chamber music. Miles Davis and Bob Dylan were exceptionally gifted performers and composers. But the larger collective force of creation declined. The mystery at the core of culture, its undecidable enigmas, seemed to abate. It did not disappear. America has remained a foremost creative power. Yet, in real per capita terms, its power has subtlely, almost imperceptably, waned.

The American golden age of creativity occured during the Teddy Roosevelt Presidency. It coincided both with rise of America as a world power and its fascination with the 'city beautiful'. Since then there has been a falling away in its creative force. This falling away has not been uniform. Creative upsurges occured in the 1920s and 1980s. The latter produced, among other things, the communication and information technology revolution. These upsurges, though, were not sustained at their peak levels. This hints at a long-term slackening of the architectonic imagination in America. The architectonic imagination is what links and binds uncanny pairs. It is what makes the disimilar, similar. It expresses itself through individual works that have an intimate bond with the collective power of the city. The work of Charles Ives is sui generis, and yet unimaginable without New York City. In the act of creation, the individual and the collective merge. Relations of this kind are enigmatic—like creation itself. To sustain the engima of creation is an enigma in itself. For a very long time that most enigmatic of nations, America, has drawn on an uncanny cultural core—one that is ambidextrous in its own terms and ambigious in the eyes of others. America has enormous powers of reinvention, and it has often deployed those powers in suprising ways. Whether it can do so again and again, and revisit the heights of its own creation, is simply an open question whose answer lies in the unknowable future.

Notes

1. 'The sea route, as the route which moves and is transformed under its own impetus, is that of trading peoples… On the other side, highways originally fall to the community, later for a long period to the governments, as pure deductions from production, deducted from the common surplus product of the country, but do not constitute a source of its wealth, i.e. do not cover their production costs. In the self-sustaining communes of Asia, on one side no need for roads; on the other side the lack of them locks them into their closed-off isolation and thus forms an essential moment of their survival without isolation (as in India).' Marx, 1973, 525.

2. Marx (1973, 528) notes 'the violent rounding-up of the people in Egypt, Etruria, India etc. for forced construction and public works.' Exactly the same applies even post-bellum in the American South: technically slavery may have been abolished but chain gangs and other forced labor was used to maintain the levee banks of the chief circulatory medium of the South—the Mississippi River.

3. State canal building was prodigious. By 1840, 3,326 miles of canals had been constructed in the U.S. Typical of pre-Civil War developments, these networks were mainly in the North and the West. The economic effects of this canal building were dramatic. New York State's Erie Canal—which linked the port of New York to the ports of the Great Lakes—cut freight rates per ton between Buffalo and Albany from $100 to $15. In contrast to canal building, most railroad building was privately financed and organized—though it was only government land grants, and government preparedness to allow railroad companies to use this land as collateral for their bond issues, that made railroad corporation securities a marketable proposition. (Miller, 1970, 243)

4. At various points since 1898, the following have been insular areas (unincorporated territories, commonwealths, or free associating states) of the United States, some inhabited and some

uninhabited: American Samoa, Guam, Northern Mariana Islands, Puerto Rico, United States Virgin Islands, Wake Island (disputed with Marshall Islands), Palmyra Atoll, Baker Island, Howland Island, Jarvis Island, Johnston Atoll, Kingman Reef, Midway Atoll, Navassa Island, Republic of the Marshall Islands, Federated States of Micronesia, Republic of Palau, Navassa Island (disputed with Haiti), Wake Island (disputed with Marshall Islands), Serranilla Bank (disputed with Colombia), Bajo Nuevo Bank (disputed with Jamaica), the Philippines and Cuba.

5. Mahan in 1902 also coined the term 'the Middle East.'

6. Under the terms of the Hay-Bunau-Varilla treaty, November 18, 1903.

7. On the effect of the city beautiful idea in America, see Murphy, 2001a, 281–314.

8. Which meant in actual practice the regulation of factory hygiene. The Upton Sinclair novels were written to scandalize the conscience of the Protestant middle class about factory working conditions. What really upset Sinclair's readers, however, were the depictions of hygiene (or lack of it) in the factories. This triggered the modern movement for consumer laws.

9. For a discussion of these types in the ancient Greek setting, see Lewis, 1996.

10. On the origins of Dutch book publishing in Antwerp, Leiden, and Amsterdam, see Steinberg, 1955, 127–132.

11. The expatriated English art critic, Reyner Banham, in his insightful book on *Los Angeles: The Architecture of Four Ecologies* (1971) called this strip-polis, '*surfburbia*,' which goes someway to capturing its *sui generis* qualities.

12. Among his many books, Roosevelt was the author of a major history of *The Naval War of 1812* (1882). He was appointed Assistant Secretary of the Navy in 1897 by President William McKinley, Roosevelt was President of the United States from 1901 to 1909.

13. President Theodore Roosevelt, 'The Roosevelt Corollary to the Monroe Doctrine' (1905) in Richard B. Munro, *Basic Documents in American History* (New York: Van Nostrand Reinhold, 1965), pp. 145–147.

14. Charles Beard in the 1920s developed the mature form of the national liberal view, which painted America overseas as an inveterate imperialist. William Appleman Williams recapitulated this view in a vaguely Marxist version. More recently it was re-done in an institutionalist guise by Chalmers Johnson. Mark Twain was a prominent early anti-imperialist.

15. Smithonian Institution Oral and Video Histories, Interview with Larry Ellison, http://americanhistory.si.edu/csr/comphist/le1.html. Accessed September 2003.

16. Janet Burroway put it very well: 'The fusion of elements into a unified pattern is the nature of creativity, a word devalued in latter years to the extent that it has come to mean a random gush of self-expression. God, perhaps, created out of the void; but in the world as we know it, all creativity, from the sprouting of an onion to the painting of Guernica, is a matter of selection and arrangement…At the conception of a fetus or a short story, there occurs the conjunction of two unlike things, whether cells or ideas, that have never been joined before. Around this conjunction other cells, other ideas accumulate in a deliberate pattern. That pattern is the unique personality of the creature, and if the pattern does not cohere, it miscarries or is stillborn.' *Writing Fiction* (2002)

17. Stanford endowed the university in 1891 with a gift of $20 million 'at the time one of the largest philanthropic gifts ever made…' (Hall, 1998, 426).

18. Hoover's presidency is one that has been much misunderstood. The cliché about Hoover was that he was an unreflective free-market President who failed to deal with the on-set of the Great Depression. But, in fact, he was a pioneer of great public work projects and created prototypes of some of the better New Deal institutions Franklin Roosevelt later became famous for. In

reality, neither of the two Presidents understood the causes of the American depression and both contributed to it in similar ways. The Roosevelt administration's lack of understanding of the role of money supply in the economic equation prolonged the 1930's recession in the United States far longer than necessary.

19. It is not difficult to imagine the New Deal's Tennessee Valley Authority as the prototype of a rationalized hydraulic state.

20. On the dam schemes, see Johnson, 2000, 704–706, 757; Nye, 2003, chapter ten.

21. The knowledge needed for English machine building derived from the Liverpool-region clock-making industry that serviced British naval ships.

22. Examples include the Harvard drop-outs Bill Gates and Paul Allen (the Microsoft operating system), Ed Roberts (the first personal computer, designed for the science hobbyist market), Steve Jobs and Steve Wozniak (Bay Area hobbyists and founders of Apple Computers), Ward Christensen and Randy Suess (graduate students in Chicago who wrote the first modem program in 1977). A classic example of the methodology of this boot-strap science is provided by the case of Roy Tomlinson, an MIT graduate working for BBN (Bolt, Beranek and Newman) in Cambridge, MA in 1972. Computer users could already send mail from one user to another on the same (time-shared) machine. Tomlinson looked at two such machines sitting in the lab, and asked himself could you send mail between them? He experimented secretly with idea; like most inventions on company time, he was not supposed to working on the project. The first piece of electronic mail between two computers was sent and received in 1972. An early version of file transfer protocol (ftp) was modified so that it could send a text message from one machine and drop it into another. Immediately the resource sharing function of computer networking was eclipsed by its capacity as a messaging system. As early as 1973, an ARPANET study found that 75% of all traffic was email and this despite the fact that emailing was an unofficial use of network resources. ARPANET officials identified the success of network mail as the largest single surprise of their program. Tomlinson invented the @ symbol for separating the name of the sender of an email from the network ID of the machine on which the user had a mailbox.

23. The evidence for this is explored in detail in *Imagination* the companion volume to *Global Creation*.

24. The first complete performance of the *Fourth Symphony* was in 1965.

References

Adams, B. (1896). *The Law of Civilization and Decay: An Essay on History*. New York: Macmillan.

Banham, R. (1971). *Los Angeles: The Architecture of Four Ecologies*. Harmondsworth: Penguin.

Boldrin, M & D.K. Levine. (2008). *Against Intellectual Monopoly*. Cambridge: Cambridge University Press.

Burroway, J. (2002). *Writing Fiction*. London: Longman.

Hall, P. (1998). *Cities in Civilization: Culture, Innovation and Urban Order*. London: Phoenix.

Hofstader, R. (1955). *The Age of Reform*. New York, Vintage.

Jardine, L. (1996). *Worldly Goods: A New History of the Renaissance*. New York: Nan A. Talese.

Johnson, P. (2000). *A History of the American People*. London: Phoenix.

Jones, M.A. (1983). *The Limits of Liberty: American History 1607–1980* (Oxford: Oxford University Press.

Kasson, J.F. (1977). *Civilizing The Machine: Technology and Republican Values in America, 1776–1900*. Harmondsworth: Penguin.

Lewis, S. (1996). *News and Society in the Greek Polis.* Chapel Hill: University of North Carolina Press, 1996.

Mahan, A.T. (1987) *The Influence of Sea Power upon History, 1660–1783.* New York: Dover.

Mahan, A.T. (2002). *The Interest of America in Sea Power, Present and Future.* Boston: Adamant.

Martin, H.J. (1994 [1988]). *The History and Power of Writing.* Chicago: University of Chicago Press.

Marx, K. (1973). *Grundisse.* Harmondsworth: Penguin.

Marx, L. (1964). *The Machine in the Garden: Technology and the Pastoral Idea in America.* Oxford: Oxford University Press.

Miller, W. (1970). *A New History of the United States.* London: Granada.

Murphy, P. (2006). 'American Civilization.' *Thesis Eleven: Critical Theory and Historical Sociology* 81, 64–92.

Murphy, P. (1999). 'Metropolitan Rhythms: A Preface to a Musical Philosophy for the New World.' *Thesis Eleven* 56, 81–105.

Murphy, P. (2001). *Civic Justice: From Ancient Greece to the Modern World.* Amherst, NY: Humanity Books.

Nye, D.E. (2003). *America as Second Creation.* Cambridge, MA: MIT Press.

Roosevelt, T. (1965). 'The Roosevelt Corollary to the Monroe Doctrine (1905).' In Richard B. Munro (Ed.) *Basic Documents in American History.* New York: Van Nostrand Reinhold, 145–147.

Santayana, G. (1936 [1896]). *The Sense of Beauty.* New York: Charles Scribner's Sons.

Smart, J. (2005). 'Measuring Innovation in an Accelerating World: Review of 'A Possible Declining Trend for Worldwide Innovation.' Acceleration Studies Foundation. http://www.accelerating. org/articles/huebnerinnovation.html Accessed 25 March 2009.

Stephanson, A. (1995) *Manifest Destiny: American Expansionism and the Empire of Right.* New York: Hill and Wang.

Van Alsytne, R.W. (1974 [1960]).*The Rising American Empire.* New York: Norton,

CHAPTER 4

The World Circumference

◻ Peter Murphy

World history and patrimonial states

Most states in human history have been patrimonies or have possessed significant patrimonial features. Today patrimony, or more precisely neo-patrimony, is still the most common state form to be found across the world. Under the surface of modernity lurks a deep and abiding archaism. Patrimonial states took shape sometime in the fourth millennium BCE, and attained a mature form with the Sumerians, Hittites, and Egyptians. These states replaced technological adaptation to nature—prized by the first human societies, the nomad societies—with the social organization of labor. Whereas peripatetic nomad societies advanced through technological metabolism with nature, patrimonial states advanced by escalating the range and types of face-to-face social relationships. This was far from a happy condition. They deployed techniques of slavery, status hierarchy, serfdom, patron-client relations, and command-and-obedience relations to enforce or compel sedentary life. The state in effect asserted ownership over human beings. Even while patrimonial states produced the first urban communities, their command of face-to-face social structures proved more often than not to be sadistic, punitive, and terrifying. Cruelty was the norm of these thick social relationships.

Patrimonial state building is not a matter of historical or anthropological curiosity. Indeed, for all of human history since their emergence, thick patrimonial social structures have dominated human thinking and doing. Patrimonial techniques may have changed with time, but patrimonial-type relations still remain the commonest of human bonds. Whether it is Russia, China, Iraq, Iran, Colombia, or Indonesia—the list is huge—the claustrophobic nature of patrimonial-type relations dominates contemporary social transactions. Deified emperors and human-sacrificing priestly castes may have been relegated to history, but many different kinds of neo-patrimonial regimes have mutated in their place. Contemporary neo-patrimonialism presents a rich array of military regimes and clientalistic democracies, genocidal dictatorships and corrupt bureaucracies, single party states and murderous theocracies, relationship-driven electoral parties and criminal-run oligarchies. "Neo," notably, does not always mean new. Some of the contemporary neo-patrimonies still attempt human deification and sacrifice. The worship of the Communist leaders of North Korea and the killing machines of Pol Pot and Saddam Hussein are cases in point. In the latter cases, the endless procession of sacrificial victims appears to be necessary in order to exorcise the archaic fears of their rulers.

The old thin peripatetic societies that dated from the dawn of the human species had a built-in release value. As social pressures accumulated, defiant bands and contrary individuals simply 'went their own way.' Patrimonies closed down this kind of exit strategy. Vicious forms of social bondage were created to confine the transients. Locality and village became the norm of human spatial experience in place of distance. Distance was transformed into territory. Rule over territory was organized by bolting local social units into feudal, imperial, theocratic, and bureaucratic hierarchies. This type of power first emerged on the alluvial plains of the Nile, Sumer, and Indus Basins, and eventually was replicated across virtually the whole of the Eurasian landmass, and in various pre-Columbian imperial states in the Americas. Patrimonial social power showed little capacity for the kind of technological innovation that humanizes nature, but enormous capacity for the organization of social labor.[1] It is understandable then that amongst its few great innovations were the techniques of writing and numerical notation. Writing and adding up are the basic technologies of hierarchic social organization. Such organization proved expedient for large labor-intensive schemes, like draining marshes, irrigating land, clearing forests, or building ziggurats and pyramids.

This model of social organization has been astonishingly persistent in history. The Russian Empire exhibited many of its features. The Soviet Empire that replaced the Russian Empire promoted the organization of labor as its chief ideology. Admittedly, though, the slaves who built the Egyptian pyramids were probably better looked after than the prison labor in the Gulag Archipelago. The necrophilic genius of the twentieth century was to kill the state's slaves because the slaves were educated—they were from the classes that wrote and were numerate. The epitome of the self-devouring state was Pol Pot's Cambodia and Hitler's Germany. While these states were extreme cases, their extremity was the product of a norm. The historical norm was patrimony. The extremities were caused by failed transitions from this norm. Germany and Russia and China in the early decades of the twentieth century attempted the shift from patrimonial empire to modern republic. But these transitions were disastrous, and new totalitarian empires quickly arose in their place. The transitions failed not least because patrimonial social power has been the norm of the Eurasian landmass for most of its recorded history. If you doubt the role of persistence in history, then consider the scene today. In Democratic Russia, the successor of Communist Russia, oil-rich oligarchs and ex-secret police bureaucrats vie for power. Markets and elections not seen since the late Tsarist days have been restored, and the ideology of labor glorification sidelined. Yet, despite this, a potent neo-patrimonial capitalist economy has emerged in place of the retrograde Communist command economy. Take away electoral competition for party supremacy, and China looks much the same. In the post-totalitarian era, consumer markets and stock markets have been unleashed, but China's party state still controls the allocation of key social goods—offices, employment, residence, travel, contracts, and information.

To step outside the state's realm of bureaucratic law, except in officially endorsed and carefully demarcated arenas like stock markets and retail shopping, means going into the zone of illegality. For example, large numbers of contemporary Chinese defy internal residence laws to go to dynamic cities. But, because they have an illegal status, these migrants can't turn whatever micro-resources they might accumulate into legal capital. They represent an exaggerated case of what everyone in a neo-patrimonial society suffers: viz., exclusion from the abstract system of legal title in property and qualifications. This means that they cannot get insurance, register what they own, form business partnerships, bargain on the basis of certified skills, and enter large-scale markets driven by abstract skill-sets and title-based transactions. The Greeks, Romans, Dutch and British evolved this system of abstract law to enable long-distance transactions between strangers. The announcement at the end of 2003 that the ruling Chinese Communist Party would alter China's constitution to protect private property is a sign of an internal recognition of limits of bureaucratic law. Words on paper do not necessarily bring real changes, though. China's constitution, after all, is just another species of bureaucratic law.

Maritime power and the administration of things

What's the alternative? The single, only, truly effective alternative to patrimonies and neo-patrimonies has come from the maritime circumference of Eurasia. A hint of this occurs around the thirteenth century BCE. We possess sketchy evidence of sea peoples who overwhelmed the Hittite Empire and who threatened the Egyptian Empire.[2] This is the first suggestion we have of the kind of maritime power that would eventually provide the key historical counter to the territorial power of patrimonial states. The decisive appearance of sea power in world history occurred at the battle of Salamis in 480 BCE. This was the event in which Greek warships routed the invading Persians, and thwarted the attempt by the Persian Empire to conquer the Eastern Mediterranean. The city-state of Athens and her allies defeated a much larger Persian fleet. This was the first great set piece confrontation between a territorial state and a maritime society.

Persia was a classic patrimony. It was the acme of some 2,500 years of evolution of such states in the Middle East. The Greek cities on the other hand were a product of the Eurasian maritime circumference, and acquired traits from earlier circumferential maritime societies—the Minoans and the Phoenicians especially.[3] These circumferential societies—variously island, peninsula, and archipelago city-states—had certain shared characteristics. They had limited land and natural resources. Large-scale mobilization of labor—using slavery and other coercive techniques to orchestrate tens of thousands of bodies for the purposes of extracting or controlling natural resources—was pointless in circumferential societies.[4] Even the sea, on which they spent a considerable part of their time, was not a resource in the sense that a fishing society treats the sea as a resource for exploitation. The sea was a place of carriage.

In the ancient world, sea carriage was much more economic than land transport. Maritime societies became adepts at foreign commerce. These elementary facts determined their character. This character was solidified in the hundreds of Greek city-states. The power of these states was neither proprietary nor was it territorial. They did not have state patrimony in land, office or persons. They did not pursue large landed empires. Their farms were not extravagant landed estates. They used neither slave nor mercenary armies. Their military forte was not on land but on the sea. Their edge was naval rather than territorial. These states were self organized rather than hierarchically organized. Yes, they had status divisions, even slavery. But the essence of the state was not an elaborate hierarchy of land, office and persons. Land was predominately in the hands of citizens. Citizens did whatever fighting was required. Government was in the hands of citizen councils and assemblies, not bureaucracies supported by a patrimonial surplus.

Citizenship in maritime societies began as the collective rule of aristocratic or oligarchic peers who knew one another. Citizenship initially allowed forms of acting together that did not rely on the directions or threats, intimidations or depravations of hierarchical superiors. But, significantly, citizenship also evolved beyond the rule of peers. It gradually acquired the characteristics of persons meeting anonymously and acting according to impersonal abstractions. Abstraction became a general medium in circumferential societies. From local exchanges developed markets, from councils developed assemblies, from aristocratic symposiums and contests developed artistic and scientific publics. The rule of artificial persons gradually replaced the rule of natural persons.

It was Thomas Hobbes who drew the distinction between the artificial and the natural state (Hobbes, 1972, 82–85; 1962, 168–172).[5] The natural state is modeled on the relationships between father and son, or patron and servant. It is either paternal or despotic (Hobbes, 1972, 85). The artificial state sets aside the interactions of natural persons in favor of artificial persons. Interestingly, Hobbes pointed out that, in the civil state, an inanimate thing can be a person. As he put it: a temple or a bridge, indeed any thing requiring money for its upkeep, can act in law. Artificial persons act for and speak for these things (Hobbes, 1972, 171).[6] In this sense, a thing can be a ruler. This is intrinsic to the nature of civic power. Remember that Henri Saint-Simon spoke of the political ideal of socialism as the administration of things. I know this notion is disparaged today. But that is just because it is not understood—or perhaps it is understood all too well by those who regard socialism simply as a superior form of patrimonial reciprocity, rather than its radical opposite.

In contrast, in state-mediated societies, if a manufacturer wants a contract, or an administrator wants a promotion, or a student wants a scholarship, they present as natural persons petitioning other natural persons. In one manner or another, directly or indirectly, they have to get the backing of the agents of the imperial-state or party-state. This may be done within the framework of bureaucratic law, but the pseudo-legality of bureaucratic permissions is quite different from the abstract 'rule of law.' Abstract law is economical and impersonal. It involves relatively few permissions or procedures, and these are governed by abstract criteria. Bureaucratic permission seeking in contrast is personalized, multi-stepped, delay-ridden, and tortuous. It typically has ten times as many steps per transaction as abstract law. Each steps costs money. To cut 'red tape' involves illegal payments. In purely legal-rational terms this system is corrupt. In its own terms, it is unexceptional. The agents of the state provide benefits in return for support, money, legitimacy, votes, or even sexual favors. Access to virtually any social good—from export licenses, loans, and contracts to offices, stipends, and tax waivers—can depend on meeting the private terms of the state and its agents.[7]

The idea of government as the administration of things is a way of drawing a clear-cut distinction between the natural state and the civic state. The civic state is an order of things. It is an artifice. If we think of the great maritime powers, what we find is that they are all artificial states. We see this first of all in the fact that they are not states at all in the ordinary sense of the word. Rather they are constitutional combinations, federations, and unions of states. In one form or other, they are all 'united states.' Such unions of states are quasi-geometric or device-like artifices—what the eighteenth century liked to call 'clock-work mechanisms.' Such mechanisms are meant to reduce the personal element in politics.[8] Indeed these commonwealths, republics, and unions are densely populated with artificial persons. This means not just Alexis de Tocqueville's voluntary associations, but bridges, churches, laboratories and libraries acting in law. Artificial persons such as universities and business corporations have real effects in the world. Without question, artificial bodies subsume and contain natural persons and social hierarchies. But these are over-determined by the human capacity for artifice and design. Successful institutions have a marvelous capacity to over-ride social imperatives for much higher, more abstract civic designs. Artificial persons, and the collective actors who constitute those persons, adopt the mask of impersonality to do so. Likewise, even when natural persons are involved, the transactions of markets, publics, and law courts have powerful impersonal, often anonymous, dimensions. They are subject to forceful abstractions like economy, democracy, science, truth, and justice. This is so even in spite of the ritual complaints about 'the lonely crowd' and 'lack of community' that allegedly characterizes 'automatic' or 'artificial' societies based on abstract forms. While participation, connections, communities and neighbors are popular cultural tropes, their assertion has little actual impact on behavior in societies based on high levels of artifice. While the lonely crowd is supposed to be incurably anomic, in practice it is palpably happy. Its individualism—and skepticism about too close connections—works well. In fact, the individualist sense of impersonal order is a very effective foil for egoistic and narcissistic anomie.

The ability to abstract is a remarkable thing. It is one of humanity's species-essential capacities. It certainly does not just belong to the humanity of modern times. During its long gestation in pre-state societies, the human species distinguished itself as a consummate artificer of tools. Tool making, and making things with tools, requires great designing intelligence. It is important not to romanticize this. Early tool making concerned primarily the relationship between humanity and nature. Pre-state societies show little evidence of making civic artifices. However, the Greeks, who knew a lot about creating civic artifices, repeatedly used the artisan as an image of how civilization, indeed the cosmos, was made. Whenever this is mentioned, anxious hands are raised to tell us that Greek citizens loathed labor and that they used slaves to avoid having to labor. Indeed they did. Greek citizens even loathed the manual aspects of artisanship. So much so that even the skilled use of hand tools presented them with moral problems. While handicraft was not labor, repetitive production without imagination was considered illiberal and beneath the citizen. It lacked the full creative weight of humanity's designing intelligence.

The Greek attitudes were not contradictory though. They were absolutely consistent. They were the radical antithesis of the cult of labor of state societies, i.e. of patrimonial societies. Low levels of labor-replacing technological innovation and application have characterized all state societies. This was true, not least of all, of twentieth-century state socialist societies. State societies invariably preferred to rely on the social organization of labor for their enrichment. Karl Marx, in Notebook V of the *Grundrisse*, observed the peculiar economic power of concentrated labor that was to be found in pre-capitalist societies. With the help of violence, the state orchestrated the concentration of labor on big projects. The productive consequence of bringing laborers together was represented not only by the sum of their labor, but also by what could only be achieved through the massive combination of laboring effort. 'Hence the violent rounding-up of the people in Egypt, Etruria, India etc. for forced construction and compulsory public works' (Marx, 1973, 528).

Circumferential societies, in contrast, invariably have had a low opinion of labor. This is a fundamental reason why they used slaves—for the very opposite reason that the Egyptians or Persians used slaves, or the Russians and Germans turned their prison camps into slave labor black holes. Maritime societies used slaves to do the labor they could not replace with tools or with the cunning of reason. Aristotle, twenty-two centuries before Adam Smith and Karl Marx, even speculated about tools that operated independently of the human hand—i.e. machines. The Greek cities invented the idea of economy—literally the 'law of the household.' The first and fundamental economy always was the economical use of labor. Economy, or efficiency, was the principle of *doing the most with the least*. The Greeks observed that nature was economical. It was so arranged or ordered as to avoid waste or (as the Greeks put it) excess. This order was achieved through various geometrical principles—such as symmetry, branching, gnomic addition, golden ratio spiraling, and rhythmical structuring. The abstract principles that the Greeks observed in nature were applied to social organization. These abstract principles made possible the auto-poietics, the self-making, of the human artifice in place of hierarchic social organization. Markets, assemblies, military drills, and publics were built on abstract patterns rather than on face-to-face social interactions. From the deep geometries of the Greek imagination grew market pricing, the rule of law, science, and distance warfare.

There is no clearer example of auto-poietics at work than in the case of warfare. Distance warfare was the antithesis of ritualized face-to-face combat. Drill and discipline first used by the Greek phalanxes allowed for impersonal engagement with an enemy, and for an increasing distance between combatants. Over the centuries, the science of ballistics gradually extended this distance. Drill and discipline created the cohesion of troops, and thus the ability to effectively control them on a battlefield. This enabled tactical adaptation to fresh intelligence and changing circumstances. Distance warfare was amplified by sea power. Sea power permitted the transport of troops over long distances, the supply of troops who were far from home, and the provision of amphibious capacity to withdraw troops who were facing strategic defeat.

A similar auto-poietics was at least dreamed of by Greek political economy. In the first volume of *Capital*, Marx noted Aristotle's anticipation of the machine in *The Politics* (1253b35–1254a1).

> 'If,' dreamed Aristotle, the greatest thinker of antiquity, 'if every tool, when summoned, or even of its own accord, could do the work that befits it, just as the creations of Daedalus moved of themselves, or the tripods of Hephaestos went of their own accord to their sacred work, if the weavers' shuttles were to weave of themselves, then there would be no need either of apprentices for the master workers, or of slaves for the lords.' (Marx, 1967, 408)

Aristotle's term for the slave was striking and utterly Greek. The slave was the self-moving tool or possession—the animate or ensouled (*empsukhon*) tool (*organon*) or possession (*ktēma*). Self-movement, the soul-like principle of self-regulated movement from within, was the Greek utopia, and one that foreshadowed the end of labor. From water-powered tools to industrial machines to the artificial intelligence of computers, the dream of applying self-movement to the things that make things implied the emancipation of humanity from labor.

Ironically, in Greek hands, slavery (the worst kind of human labor) was also an anticipation of the termination of labor. Equally ironic, what is often considered the epitome of human culture—script—emerged as an accounting tool for patrimonial states. In order to build their pyramids of sacrifice and water their fields, these states employed computation and writing. With writing they recorded the state's appropriation of the surpluses that were produced on irrigated fields. Rituals (some of them very cruel and very bloody) carried on in the houses built for their gods legitimated this tribute economy. With numbers, they calculated the boundaries of fields that were periodically washed away by river floods. To Greek eyes, though, this was mathematics in the service of forced labor. The real—the divine—function of mathematics was *to eliminate labor*. The Greeks imagined things not as a patrimony but as a system. A system had inputs, operations, and outputs. A well-ordered system was well designed. The human imagination was the ally of this designing intelligence. It asked how things could be better designed. Better design meant making systems more beautiful, elegant, efficient, and economical.

Just how powerful such a designing intelligence could be was demonstrated in the victory of the Greek allies over the Persians in the battle at Salamis. Just how pivotal this battle was can be gauged by its size. By some estimates it is still the largest single naval engagement in history.[9] To this day, modern naval engineers still do not properly understand the subtleties of the design of the Greek war ships or triremes—'their extraordinary ratio between weight, speed and propulsion' (Hanson, 2002, 49). The same geometrical spirit underlay the discipline of the Greek naval formations—their ability to think of battle not as the heroic action of the individual warrior in face-to-face combat but as the collective force of impersonal disciplined formations capable of acting at a distance. Such force is governed by the geometric principles of line and column, and by the abstractions of tactics and strategy.[10] Circumferential maritime societies would only ever constitute a relative handful of human societies. But their power and influence has far exceeded their size or their numbers. The reason for this is the same reason that the vastly out-numbered Greeks won the day at Salamis. This is because they owed allegiance not to other persons but to beautiful, and sometimes fierce, abstractions. They owed allegiance to the artifices of city, constitution, science, and cosmos—or if you prefer to beauty, freedom, democracy, and any of the other multitude of abstract conceptions that the Greeks bequeathed to humanity.

Circumferential power in world history

Like all societies, particular circumferential societies come and go. Yet, as a species, circumferential societies have always managed to reproduce themselves. Their spirit seems to be immortal, even when the expressions of this spirit rise and fall like any other society. In this respect, Greek history is salutary. Alexander's armies swallowed the Greek ecumene. It was subsumed by an aspirational Greek patrimonial state, led by a ruthless charismatic general with a brilliant nose for landed warfare. But the Successors of Alexander were as much Hellenized by the Greeks as Greek civilization was subject to patrimonial ways of doing things. This hybrid was a precursor for an even more influential template for merging sea and land power that was to follow. This was the model of the Romans.

Originally a society of yeoman farmers, Rome recast itself first as a citizen soldier city eager to rule the Italian peninsula and then as a sailing republic in order to defeat maritime Carthage and assert itself over the Mediterranean. In its final mutation, Rome became a land power that ruled from London to Antioch. The Romans' merger of sea and land power propelled them into the invention of a third kind of power—network power. Rome scaled itself into a massive force using networks of roads, law courts, alliances, and colonial cities. This enabled it to rule over vast lands without relying exclusively, or even primarily, on patrimonial techniques. Certainly Roman consuls and emperors borrowed from the satchel of the Asiatic despots. But more importantly Rome figured out that it could apply the rule of abstract law and citizenship grants, template-type colonial city building and treaty alliances to the management of expansive territories. These devices allowed Rome to rule large terrestrial geographies without turning the state into one giant slave estate.

The principal difference between the Roman and the Greek models was the matter of citizenship. Rome granted its allies, and its conquered enemies, citizenship. The Greek cities jealously kept citizenship to themselves, even though they welcomed strangers as resident aliens. What Rome and Greece shared in common was a faith in an impersonal order of things—an inhuman order. The impersonal force of natural law, city, and cosmos surrounded the Greeks and the Romans wherever they went. On the battlefield, in the market place, in the arena, the theatre, the literary and scientific publics and academies, a-social or extra-social norms applied.[11]

In history, there have only been a handful of societies that have gravitated to this kind of order. Overwhelmingly, they have been littoral or circumferential societies. All have attracted the criticism of being heartless or cold societies—steely in their mentality. High levels of creativity in arts, sciences, or politics have characterized each one of them. This is not surprising when we read the overwhelming conclusion of empirical studies of the psychology of creative persons, *viz.* that creative people are highly likely to have personality traits characterized by social hostility, aloofness, unfriendliness, and lack of warmth. This is the flip-side of the psychological autonomy, independence, introversion, and self-confidence of the creative personality; just as it is also the flip-side of the openness, nonconformity, and norm doubting necessary for creative action.[12]

Circumferential societies have had a disproportionate influence on world history. This pattern, which began with the Greeks and Romans, was followed by Genoa, Venice, and Pisa-Florence, and later by the Anglo-Scottish-Dutch North Sea maritime triangle. From the early seventeenth century to the mid nineteenth century, the British created a maritime circumferential power that ringed the African-Eurasian landmasses. Anglo-Irish, Anglo-Scottish, Anglo-Chinese settlements dotted the world—from the tip of South Africa to Australasia, the Atlantic seaboard of North America, the Pacific North-West, and the China Seas. Littoral colonies and cities were created at Virginia in 1607, on the Indian littoral in 1640 at Madras and Calcutta in 1690, on the Australian littoral in 1788, on the South African Cape in 1795/1806, on the island of Singapore in 1819 and the islands of New Zealand in 1839, and at Shanghai and Hong Kong in 1842. Following this, the late nineteenth century saw the rise of the United States as the world's leading maritime power.

One of the basic reasons for the disproportionate influence of circumferential societies on world history is their command of human creativity. Charles Murray, in his study *Human Accomplishment* (2003), provides data that demonstrates this clearly. In the study, Murray sets out statistically-based lists of the greatest achievers in art, science, literature, philosophy, and music in the period 800 BCE to 1950. The lists are based on empirical measures of citations in dictionaries of biography, encyclopedias, and other standard reference works. One of the most interesting things that Murray does with his data on Europe and America is to ask the question: where in Europe and the United States has eminent achievement in the arts and the sciences been concentrated? His answer is an overwhelming confirmation of the importance of the maritime circumference (295–308). In the United States, 90% of eminent figures were resident in the maritime regions of the Eastern seaboard, California, and the Great Lakes-Hudson ecumene. In the case of Europe, from 1400 to 1950, the highest concentrations of major figures in art, science, literature, and music came from London and Southern England (excepting for art in the period 1400–1800), Tuscany and Venice (in decline after 1800), Holland-Belgium, and Paris. Science figures came in significant numbers from the Glasgow-Edinburgh region (in the period 1600–1950). The Göttingen-Berlin region, again one of the few non-circumferential creative concentrations, was also important in science (in the era 1800–1950). The only non-circumferential locale that consistently figures 'across the board' in achievement in art, science, literature, and music in Europe from 1400 to 1950 is Paris. Whether this was because of Parisian court power or because of transcriptional riverine power, or because of both, is an interesting question.

One important fragment of German-speaking Europe that appears repeatedly in the geo-history of the creative mind after 1600 is the triangular region bounded by the Elbe and Salle Rivers, and that includes the cities of Freiburg, Jena, Halle, Bayreuth, and Weimar. In the period 1800–1950, two other riverine regions—a triangular region bounded by the Maas (Meuse) and Rhine Rivers and the triangular area of Baden-Württemberg bounded by the Rhine and Danube Rivers (converging at its southern tip on Zurich)—show a distinct spike as sources of outstanding literary and science talent. Science in the period 1800–1950 is the only creative activity (of any period since 1400) that shows evidence of being broadly sourced through Northern Europe. Even in this case, the series of riverine and littoral centers cited above remain dominant.

What we can infer from this is that liquid regions are key sources of creative activity. What distinguishes creative potential from realization of that potential, however, is politics. London-Southern England, Tuscany-Venice, Holland-Belgium, and the United States all created political structures that galvanized and focused creative action. In contrast, notably, the Elbe-Salle, Maas-Rhine, Rhine-Danube triangulations failed to generate commensurate political structures. The failure of the 1848 Revolutions in these areas may have been a decisive cause of this. These regions failed to turn pre-existing imperial free cities and patrician-burgher cities, or university cities, into powerful polities—thereby allowing Bavarian and Prussian state structures to absorb them. Politically weak, these triangulations tended to be characterized by a pattern of cities—often times small cities—that by per capita standards were the birth place of large numbers of eminent creative persons. Murray's figures (356) are again revealing: Whereas London was the origin of 6 eminent figures per million in the period 1800–1950, Stuttgart (in the Rhine-Danube triangulation) produced 91 per million. Cologne in the Maas-Rhine triangulation produced 10 per million, while Zurich produced 17 per million. There is a comparable example of this same paradox from the thalassic edge of Europe: tiny Königsburg on the Baltic produced the equivalent of 33 eminent persons per million from 1800–1950. In general, the sea-edge of Europe was without question the crucible of invention. While most European cities produced few or no eminent achievers in the arts and sciences in the period 1800–1950, Hamburg produced 17 per million, Bristol 20 per million, Dublin 17 per million, and Edinburgh 22 per million. Of course, very often these 'birth places' were not the final places of 'destination' for creative minds. They would leave for politically stronger centers (e.g., London). Paris would appear to be the only European city that has been both a producer and retainer of exceptional talent. It was the birth place of an impressive 24 per million significant figures during the period 1800–1950, far in excess of the 8 per million of St. Petersburg and Moscow, Madrid's 7 per million, Rome's 4 per million, and Berlin's 5 per million.

Demiurgic power

Athens, Rome, Venice, Britain, and America all became the greatest powers of their time. The littoral states of Holland and Portugal also managed to create far-reaching though ultimately less dynamic examples of circumferential power. Beginning with a sea base, each of these littoral powers developed a circumferential curtain, sometimes defensively, sometime expansively, that hemmed in both nomadic societies and patrimonial states. They despised centralized landed power and eliminated nomadic no-fixed-address insurgency. Despite the many illustrious examples, circumferential power has not been uniformly successful. Historically it has waxed and waned. The great Baltic venture that was the Hanseatic League of merchant cities failed to evolve into an effective commonwealth. In the seventeenth century the Swedish monarchy encircled the Baltic from the north—at its height absorbing Finland, Baltic Russia and Estonia. It fought for control of the Baltic ecumene with Denmark, a littoral rival, and with the territorial powers of Poland, Russia, and Germany. Despite its seaboard location, Swedish power failed to develop a marine character. In many ways it was a classic landed agricultural and natural resource state. It lacked the knowledge-based markets and publics of North Sea capitalism. Unsurprisingly, it left Baltic trade to the British and the Dutch.[13]

While maritime porosity, intellectual capitalism, and inter-state mobility increasingly came to characterize Scandinavian states in the twentieth century, the effect of Tsarist policies, Bolshevism, Nazism, and the Cold War was to split the Baltic Sea down the middle. With the collapse of the Soviet Union came signs of a resurgent

Baltic political economy. Those Baltic states that had been the Cold War captives of the Soviet Union gained their independence. At the same time, old romantic Scandinavian nationalisms inherited from the nineteenth century were in visible decline. The Baltic emerged from the era of the Soviet Empire a bit like the Rhineland in Karl Marx's time or the Baden-Württemberg intersection of the Rhine and the Danube in twentieth-century post-war Europe. Each of these economically dynamic regions had the 'in principle' capacity to forge a kind of liquid power. Yet each was subject to the massive pull of the Franco-Germanic heartland of Europe. The long-term outcome of this invisible tug-of-war cannot be predicted. But it is clear that the geopolitics of Europe continues to be shaped at deep levels by swings between landed and liquid power. For this reason, the same sorts of questions addressed to the Baltic periphery of Europe can be asked of all of the states in successful transition from Soviet-type state socialism: Is Budapest aligned to the riverine economy of the Danube or to Franco-Germanic Europe? Does Prague follow the logic of the Elbe-Hamburg axis or the logic of territorial-autobahn Europe?

Littoral power in the modern age was based on the command of the oceans. Oceanic power was in part a technological achievement, typified by Portuguese development of the 'great ship' for the voyage to India and the accompanying innovations in naval gunnery such as building gun ports into the walls of ships (Modelski, 1987, 72–73). The Portuguese also exploited the idea of network power. The idea was not original, the model for it had previously existed in the Mediterranean. The Attic Empire and the Venetian Empire were prime examples of it. The idea was to control strategic harbors and islands, nodes in a network of power that protected trade routes. The Portuguese adapted this nodal model of power to global conditions. From the 1420s, the Portuguese explored the Atlantic ocean and coastal Africa, developing the Atlantic islands of the Azores and Madeira, and establishing trading posts along the African coast.[14] In 1487, Bartholomeu Diaz sailed around the Cape of Good Hope, establishing a new (oceanic) route to India. Strategic settlements (nodes) around the circumference of the 'world-island' of Eurasia followed. After 1500 Portugal sent annual fleets to the East and by 1515 a world-wide network was in place that stretched from the cod fisheries off Newfoundland, and Brazil, to East Africa, the Persian Gulf, the Malabar Coast, Malacca, and the Spice Islands. Soon China and Japan would join a world system that had a circular network structure, each region now being accessible from every other region via the oceans (Modelski, 1987, 73).

However, Portugal was a world power only for a very short time. Almost from its start, Portugal's global influence began to unwind. The reasons for this are instructive. They tell us much about the conditions of this new kind of nodal, stepping-stone global power. To become a world power, Portugal had to develop an oceanic orientation. Yet, for all of its exploration of the world circumference, Portugal's economy was still built around the Venetian-North Sea network. Portugal had strong relations with Bruges and Antwerp and other watery cities of Flanders, Zeeland, and Friesland. Correspondingly, when Portugal's integration into the North Sea ecumene was upset, its nascent world power shriveled. At the time the Portuguese began their world venturing, the cities of the Low Countries were under the influence of the Burgundian court. Through the Portuguese Crown's close relationship with Burgundy, Lisbon had strong connections to the portals of Flanders and guild-dominated cities like the island city of Ghent.[15] This changed decisively in the mid-sixteenth century.[16] During this era, the Hapsburgs subsumed the Burgundy Court, while the Netherlands revolted (1565–1579) gaining its independence from Hapsburg Spain, and the Portuguese and Spanish Crowns were united in 1580. In place of strong ties with the maritime Low Countries, Portugal's primary focus became Spain, a state with a strong continental, territorial and national orientation. While Spain had large overseas possessions, these were of a continental type. Spain had no interest in the circumferential nodal power of the kind that the Portuguese briefly pioneered.

The Netherlands, on the other hand, had a great 'feel' for such power. At the local level, the new Dutch Republic was structured around a network of city-provinces.[17] The Dutch republic was not a traditional 'strong' state. Its system of power was divided between the States-General, a federation of seven provinces, and the Stadholder (the commander in chief of army and navy). This gave its system of state power a porous quality that, among other things, was attractive for intellectuals wanting to escape the pressures of more traditional European court cultures. A notable example was Descartes, who moved to the Netherlands in 1628, beginning in that year his first major work, *Essais philosophiques* (1637). Descartes spent most of the rest of his life there, variously in Amsterdam, Deventer, Utrecht, and Leiden. The porous quality of the Netherlands in this period (its Golden Age) is reflected in its system of higher education. Of the 38,000 students who attended Leiden University between 1575 and 1700, nearly 17,000 of them were foreigners from places as far afield as Norway, Ireland, Spain, Poland, the Ottoman Empire, and Persia (Steinberg, 1955, 129).[18]

From the time of their first resistance to the Spanish in the sixteenth century, the Dutch provinces began to assume the characteristics of a knowledge society. The United Provinces had a high level of literacy and education. They quickly became a major center for printing and publishing. Widespread collecting of art (paintings) and reading of books distinguished the seventeenth-century Dutch Golden Age. This was accompanied by popular interest in voyages of exploration and in the science of cartography. What explains this? The majority Protestantism of Dutch society, and its rejection of priestly authority, was one cause, as was the disappearance of courtly and princely authority in the Dutch Republic—and also the general weakness of the central authority of the Republic. All of these factors combined discouraged censorship and encouraged the type of freedom of thought required for the advancement of art and science. Yet there are many examples of societies without censorship that are not knowledge societies. The success of the Dutch in the seventeenth century was based on something more than liberty of thought.

The Dutch foundation can be explained in the following terms: The United Provinces saw the dismantling of traditional social and pastoral hierarchies. Additionally, these old hierarchies were not simply replaced by legal-rational hierarchies typical of modern administered institutions. Rather, the seventeenth-century

Dutch relied as much on anonymous collective power as on explicit institutional power. The latter was weak and porous while the former, benefiting from the porosity, proved to be remarkably robust. This picture is typical of all successful portal states and regions. They are characterized by the removal of traditional hierarchies and their replacement not by administrative and bureaucratic power alone but in significant degree by forms of aesthetic and architectonic power.

The relationship between architectonic power and a knowledge society can be explained in these terms: The seventeenth-century Dutch Republic had a massive upsurge in literary, artistic, technological and scientific activity. It produced works both in quantity (such as the moralizing verse of Jacob Cats) and in quality (the philosophy of Spinoza). If we ask ourselves what made this possible, the answer is an underlying architectonic sense. As in all comparable cases of knowledge explosions, such a sense is not explicit in all or even most works produced. Nonetheless it is a tacit presupposition of knowledge production, and is explicit in the characteristic works of the period. Nothing better sums up the Dutch Golden Age than the paintings of Jan Vermeer (1632–1675). Obscure in his own time, Vermeer nonetheless captures the spirit of his age consummately. The 'heroes' of his paintings are letter-readers and letter-writers, music-makers and map-readers. His emotional tableaus are cognitive. The order of his paintings is calm, cool, and full of quiet concentration.

Vermeer's is a world of enlightenment, literally. For him, light defines the shape of things. It pours through windows into rooms, creating the illusion of volumetric space. In that three-dimensional pictorial space, Vermeer carefully locates human figures and their worldly objects. There is no murkiness or chaos in this world. Each figure and object is clearly defined thanks to Vermeer's mastery of light. His arrangements of figures and objects in space create a perfect balance without any sense of this being contrived. The pervading effect is of calm. Vermeer's palette of silvery blues and cool yellow underscores this. What he achieves is an intimation of creation. His colors capture the enigmatic double nature of creation. This is reflected in the characters he portrays. He captures them in moments of deep concentration. The maidservant pouring milk, the lady weighing gold—each is hard at work, yet calmly, quietly, deliberately. They embody thoughtfulness and its paradoxical expression in motionless movement. Outwardly the girl with the pearl earring is still, but inwardly she betrays a lively intelligence, her eyes piercing into the soul of the viewer. The blue and lemon, and the pearl grey, of the painting impart the entrancing emotional cool and warmth of Vermeer's gorgeous subject.

Aristotle once observed that knowledge begins with the unmoved mover. So it is with Vermeer. This is the antipodal order of the letter-writer and the music-maker, and the geographer who mulls over latitudes. The blue and yellow, the subdued dark tones and the sparkling light, are the mystical pattern of thought before it emerges into language. In this primordial state, thought is mutely architectonic. Even when (in the case of the letter-writer) creation's overt medium is language, its real power derives from its capacity for design, arrangement, and placement. Blue against yellow, light against dark—everything in Vermeer's paintings is carefully arranged. It is this arrangement that generates the beauty that persists indelibly in the mind of the viewer. It does this because it touches the pattern order of the mind directly.

Vermeer's thoughtful world is calm and contemplative. It is demotic and knowing at the same time. There is nothing in it that is fantastic or ethereal. Its very ordinariness heightens the sense that it is special. Vermeer's characters weigh gold and measure distances and pour milk. It is this that helps us understand how the worlds of power and painting, trade and art that ordinarily stand apart are also intimately linked. Everything that is ordinary has its own mysticism simply because the mind and the world are analogously patterned. Thus the merchant who imagines the world as a nodal-network is like the painter who sees with the mind's eye the invisible architecture of color that gives the painting its endlessly fascinating form and its uncanny power. The anonymous collective power of a golden age, whether it is in art or trade, is the power to give form, to find the pattern-arrangement that enables prodigious human activity and that by forging subtle unions of contrast and contradiction unleashes great energies. Not every age is great, but seventeenth-century Holland, like Elizabethan England, was. Both were grand masters of intersecting forces and paradoxical unities. Vermeer's palette of silvery blue and cool yellow is the aesthetic equivalent of the odd coupling of the Anglo-Dutch, Scottish-Dutch and Anglo-Scots who for a time transformed the world. In international affairs the Dutch, English and Scots cohabited and fought in the same breath. They formed an agonistic unity—and a notably successful one. The closeness of the North Sea states in the seventeenth century did not exclude antipathies, competition, cultural loathing, or trade warfare between them. Indeed the antagonisms, up to a point, were essential to their union.

Such sympathetic antagonism was similar in kind to the historic 'mirror' relationship between Venice and Constantinople—and is central to precocious art and trade in general. The mastery of intersecting forces is a key to both. The ancient Greeks were cultural masters because they commanded both Apollo and Dionysius. The Low Countries were trade masters because they were the nodal point at which the Maas and Rhine Rivers met the North Sea, and traders from the Mediterranean and the Atlantic met those coming from the Baltic Sea. The Netherlands had the typical precarious topography of a portal—limited land that it had to drain and reclaim from the sea. It flourished not because it was a territory, but because it was an intersection. At the same time, the explanation for the spectacular rise of the Flemish or the Dutch portal zones was not only that the Low Countries was a crossways. The power of this zone was based also on the existence of mirror cities (Amsterdam and London, Amsterdam and Edinburgh, Amsterdam and Rotterdam, and so on) that provided the structural pivots for a network spread across an ecumenical sea region—a large-scale regional order distinguished by the multiplication of centers and virtual connectivity between them, enabling action at a distance. The cross-linkages of the ecumene were subtle but powerful. Finally, it must be emphasized, the mastery of intersections was also at its core a cultural phenomenon. The Vermeers and the Shakespeares set the tone for a culture of doubling (Murphy, 2009). It was the resulting cultural command of contradictory forces and forms that drove the advancement of knowledge.

Thus the North Sea ecumene was not simply a network of trade, or even of diplomacy, but, most crucial of all, an extraordinary cultural crucible. The outward expression of this was a striking capacity for knowledge productivity that has extended across centuries. The Dutch, English, and Scots collectively created in the seventeenth century a remarkable set of intellectual and scientific innovations. This in turn fed back into the creation of all sorts of instruments that allowed their respective nodal-networks to expand. These innovations ranged from Grotius' international law and Hobbes' and Spinoza's social contract philosophy, to the commitment by the English monarchy to repay its debts, the expansion of contract and property rights and civil courts, the development of insurance, limited-liability corporations,[19] and stock exchanges,[20] through to the federalist, commonwealth and republican models for mediating complex relations between cities and states, and major advances in mathematics, astronomy, and geography. It is estimated that, in the seventeenth century, more books were printed in the Netherlands than in all the rest of Europe put together (Haley, 1972). Many of these were surreptitious printings of editions of books banned or difficult to publish elsewhere, like Thomas Hobbes' *Leviathan*.[21]

To make it clear: the core of all of this is the phenomenon of cultural doubling—the enigmatic union of antithetical cultural deities. The Romans earlier had summed up this idea in the cultural image of Janus—the god of January who looked both ways, backwards and forwards (Murphy, 2001a, 94). Janusian thinking is the core of creative action.[22] We could, if we wished, think of the act of creation simply in terms of art or science, but, in the end, the working of the imagination is also mirrored in social power. The Janus-like power of the imagination is replicated in the distinctive dual power structures of creative societies. Rome is a case in point. Partly because of their early experience of being ruled by an Etruscan monarchy, Republican Romans were wary of power, and created structures of countervailing power. Power in the Roman Republic was divided between consuls, Senators and the Roman people. After Rome became a formal Empire, with the rise of Augustus, there still remained a desire to strike a balance between city and empire, and to somehow 'divide' power. This is represented in imperial Rome's retention of institutions like the Senate. Even when republican institutions lost explicit power, they remained symbolic of an order of divided power, and, most crucially, of the 'gap' between those explicit powers, the interstice through which the demiurgic power (the implicit, shaping power of the city and of creation) manifests itself.

Such 'divided' power is a condition of the existence of cosmopolitan cities and knowledge societies. It creates the 'breathing space' within a political order with vast reach—a 'breathing space' for the city and its creative spirit to flourish. Put in more abstract terms, divided power is the condition under which the ineffable collective creative power of the city emerges. The Greeks and the Romans liked to represent the power of the city in the form of myths—like the myths of Poseidon and Athena, and Romulus and Remus.[23] Myths are a way of talking about a power that is not the explicit power of the one, the few or the many, but rather the power of no one, of nobody.[24] Myths transform explicit power into tacit creative power in the same way that a rare handful of great architects transformed social power into the anonymous power of numbers (geometry) or the plastic power of sculptural form. In analogous fashion, Greco-Roman constitutional models of the union of the one, the few and the many can be thought of as experiments that provide a mathematical representation of the paradoxical power of no one.

Looked at in this way, Rome was the expression of the power of collective creation. The greatest works of Rome—which even the Renaissance popes wanted to re-create—flowed from this. Like Athens before it and Venice after it, ancient Rome was the objectivation of the anonymous power of collective creation. In order for there to be space for such a power (the power to give form) to be exercised, there needs be a constraint on the power of the one, the few and the many. It does not matter whether a state is ruled by the one (emperor), the few (aristocrats, oligarchs, courtiers) or the many (guilds, democratic councils, the people), the cosmopolitan city and the knowledge society and all of the rest of the expressions of the demiurgic act of creation flourish only if the arrangements of explicit power make room also for the mythic power of nobody, that is, the poietic power of creation, the Janus power of doubling.

Historically, models of countervailing power have varied. For example, Constantine instituted the symbolic counterweight of the Senate in his eastern war capital, and encouraged the power of the church; the Byzantine Empire was premised on the invisible power of Christendom as a check on the visible power of secular rulers; the Ottomans allowed substantial autonomy to the *millets* as the institutions of communal law and to the *vakifs* as the builders and guardians of the city's great mosques and charities; Venice hemmed in its rulers with the most elaborate controls of their conduct; Greater London kept separate the city of Westminster (the seat of royal power) from the city of London (the locus of commercial power) and (much like Constantinople before it) allowed a panoply of trusts and charities to endow the city alongside private and government benefactions and speculations. In each of these cases, power was 'divided,' not in a liberal constitutional sense, but nevertheless in a real and effective sense. In the interstices between explicit institutions, in the uncovered gaps, the power of nobody exerted itself. It is this power that is the most decisive force in shaping the preternaturally beautiful city. It is an interstitial power—arising from what is 'in between' court city and merchant city, emperor and bishop, coast and plain, oligarchy and guild, ghetto and patria.

Thus the world city is always a tale of two cities—Piraeus and Athens, Latin and Sabine Rome, Senatorial and popular Rome, Byzantium's two demes, Golden Horn and Galata, Westminster and London, the boroughs of New York, the four ecologies of Los Angeles, the rivals Sydney and Melbourne, Tokyo's cities-within-a-city—and the demiurgic space between them.[25] Venice, the Serene Republic, seems outwardly to be an exception to the rule that 'out of division arises the city beautiful.' Venice is the mirror image of the other great portals. Justinian I crushed the riots of the Blues and the Greens—and proceeded, over the bodies of 30,000 dead, to set Anthemius of

Tralles and Isidore of Miletus to work to create Hagia Sophia (Church of the Holy Wisdom). In contrast, Venice had a morbid fear of such factionalism. Venice's desideratum was stability. Yet, to avoid division, it devoted itself to perpetual architectonics—fashioning the same breath-taking beauty that elsewhere seeped out through the cracks of divided power. Venice was the exception that proved the rule.

Dual power

In London's case, the outline of a dual power emerged in the depths of British history, well before even the Norman Conquest. Self-confident behind its city walls, medieval London was a prosperous trading and processing center, while the royal city of Westminster evolved separately but in tandem further upstream on the Thames River. A long-term, mutual relationship developed between the monarchy (always in need of money for wars, expanding administration, and court expenses) and 'the city' of London whose wealth—generated by international sea-borne trade and skilled artisanship—was a source of money that the Crown could covet. Strikingly, London never became a royal city subject to the 'king's men.' Through the medieval period, it maintained a large and well-resourced volunteer army, and, by custom, the king had to ask permission of the lord mayor to enter 'the city.' When William the Conqueror built the Tower of London for the 'protection' of 'the city,' the Crown's intent was obvious. Yet, despite such gestures, 'the city' continued to function virtually as an autonomous republic within the king's realm.[26]

London's medieval walls—enclosing some 677 acres—set apart a tiny space filled with intense commercial activity. Even after the walls were demolished, these boundaries continued to define a nodal concentration of cooperative antagonism and amiable congestion. By the nineteenth century, this space contained a remarkable array of banks, inns of law, stock and commodity exchanges, newspapers, insurance and shipping companies concentrated in its precincts. Upstream at Westminster there was an equally remarkable concentration of palaces, royal parks, parliament buildings, and government offices. Considered separately, neither Westminster nor London was naturally brilliant. As Greater London built towards its nineteenth-century climax, we see a Westminster that was dominated at times either by extravagant royal taste or else by stilted government taste. The former is exemplified by the various awkward attempts of John Nash, the London architect with princely social connections, to work on a baroque scale, and the latter by Sir William Chambers' Somerset House with its overworked design that suffocates architectonic rhythms and energy. The City of London, on the other hand, was a bricklayers and carpenters' municipality subject to rather lurid mercantile appetite for 'fat cornices and enormous iron-work shop-signs' (Summerson, 1978, 59). It was only at the intersection of these antithetical forces that a truly interesting city emerged.

As Britain coaxed itself into building an oceanic empire—resting on a complex balance of official and commercial interests—it eventually created something that was neither one nor the other of these but rather a distinctive portal space. Portal London can be thought of as the third term between commercial and official London. This is an architectonic space that emerged out of the explosion of Britain's overseas interests. The results are visible in the immaculate works of Christopher Wren, but also in a vast series of splendid demotic works like George Gwilt's warehouse at West India Dock (1800) on the Isle of Dogs, Daniel Asher Alexander's Piranesi-influenced warehouse at Wapping's London Dock (1802) and John Rennie's bridges (Waterloo Bridge, 1811–17; Southwark Bridge, 1815–19).[27] By the 1820s, London had become the greatest city of an empire with an enormous maritime reach. This empire had been first conceived in the early eighteenth century as a projection of naval power (based on a series of naval bases beginning with Gibraltar and Minorca, Jamaica and Antigua, Boston and Nova Scotia),[28] which was then developed into a world system of maritime nodes, global territorial possessions, and regulated (mercantilist) trade that spread from the Atlantic to the Indo-Pacific.

Rear Admiral Philip Colomb elegantly summed up the subtleties of the British view of Empire in his magisterial work *Naval Warfare* (1891). Colomb outlined the conjunction of sea power, commerce and colonies that characterized the British Empire. 'In these three things,' he wrote, 'production, with the necessity of exchanging products, shipping, whereby the exchange is carried on, and colonies, which facilitate and enlarge the operations of shipping and tend to protect it by multiplying points of safety—is to be found a key to much of the history, as well as of the policy, of nations bordering on the sea.'[29] In this view of empire, commerce and navies were natural partners. Sea-power, Colomb observed, 'includes not only the military strength afloat, that rules the sea or any part of it by force of arms, but also the peaceful commerce and shipping from which alone a military fleet naturally and healthfully springs, and on which its security rests…' The natural affinity between commerce and navy was aided and abetted by 'points of safety' en-route. In the British mind, initially, such points were naval bases that could re-provision ships with ammunition and food supplies, and provide barracks, dockyard facilities, hospitals and so forth, and later (in the age of steam) provide fuel along sea routes. With the passage of time, the imaginary of bases ('points') became a chain of circumferential cities as well as a colonial imaginary that devised 'planes' of administration, 'borders' on maps, and the 'lines' of territories that were populated by settlers and governors, armies and factories, farms and plantations.

Between 1850 and 1900 Britain laid the first global communications (cable) network.[30] Such was its monopoly of this technology that other governments (the Germans and the French) had to use the British network for their own political communications, even when confronting the British. The British organized a world system of undersea cable. This was done in a private-public partnership between the British state (the Admiralty and its cartographers) and the private companies that financed the cable laying, produced the cable and sourced the copper and rubber from which the cables were made. The first cable (Calais to Dover) linked London with Paris. In 1865, a transatlantic cable was laid, an intimation of the later North Atlantic system of oceanic power. A link between Malta and Alexandria enabled London to communicate with India. This was followed in the 1870s by a network that spread outwards to include the West Indies and South America, Southeast Asia, China and Australia. Africa was incorporated in the late 1880s and early 1890s, and the British concluded their world-encircling efforts with a transpacific cable in 1902. Indicative of the fact that Britain was the only true world power in the nineteenth century, and that its nearest rival (France) looked at the world much more from a continental than a maritime perspective, is that Britain's fleet of cabling ships was ten times that of France. Britain laid two-thirds of the total undersea cable in the nineteenth century. Britain's naval supremacy and the power of its commercial shipping became intertwined with its dominance of this geopolitical (distance) technology.

The rise of oceanic power—and the corresponding shift of the locus of amphibious commerce from coast and sea to ocean—caused a fundamental change to the power of the portal. Oceanic power, like sea power, relied on naval power to keep trade channels open and enforce trade agreements, customs and migration rules, protect overseas property, and eliminate piracy. The Mediterranean city (Venice) had been able to supply its own naval power, and do so convincingly in its heyday before the 1490s. It was able to amass large fleets (that doubled as merchant and military craft, according to exigency), and it had control of strategically-placed bases in a semi-circle from the Adriatic to the Aegean. However, with the rise of the Ottomans, Venice had to confront the fact that, all of a sudden, it could not match the naval power of (what was primarily) a territorial state that had (to everyone's surprise) adapted very quickly to amphibious power. The weakness of the city in its own watery domain—made embarrassingly clear by the Ottomans—was compounded, in the era of oceanic power, when the British pioneered a new 'maritime military—maritime civic' relationship.

Britannia ruled the waves in large part because the English Crown had been frustrated at home by the limits placed on its landed forces by the British parliament. Out of this check-mate between the Crown and Parliament grew the projection by the English Crown (a power firmly rooted in English soil) of naval strength, and a global division of labor between the City (London) which concentrated on trade and commercial colonization (typified by the East India Company) and the Crown which managed a mix of maritime force and mercantilist law. As a consequence the City no longer had to provide its own navy, which was timely, as maritime republics in the age of oceanic power—if Venice is any guide—were no longer a match for the shipbuilding capacities of larger, territorial states. By the eighteenth century, Venice's Arsenal lagged badly in shipbuilding technology. To fall behind in naval power not only meant being unable to keep pace with the British, Portuguese, Dutch, and others in their domination of oceanic (Atlantic, Indo-Pacific) trade and mercantile-colonization, but it also meant having to surrender the seas to the control of the oceanic powers. For Venice that development meant not counting anymore even as an Adriatic power, let alone an Aegean power, or a sea power that once had even contemplated controlling the waters of Black Sea.

Ironically it was one of Britain's earliest, and longest lasting, emporial ambitions to become a Mediterranean power. To achieve this it began by creating a naval base at Gibraltar (taken from Spain in 1704), and then at Malta (taken from Napoleon in 1798).[31] It arbitrated in those places where there had been a centuries-long tug-of-war between the Venetians and the Ottomans. Britain established protectorate rule over the Ionian Islands (1815–1864), Crete (1898–1913), and an even more convoluted patrimony over Cyprus that began in 1878.[32] Beyond these historically contested waters, Britain moved to create a form of protectorate rule over Egypt (1882–1922) and forestall the coming-to-power of a nationalist regime. One can speculate indefinitely about the motives of a great power. Certainly the unexceptional desires for wealth and power figured in Britain's ambitions. Horatio Nelson's report to the British Admiralty on the prospect of taking Malta—'as a most important outwork to India, that it will give us great influence in the Levant and indeed all the southern parts of Italy'—illustrates the pragmatic material relationship between geopolitical microcosm and macrocosm (Bradford, 1971, 483). But the imaginary dimension of this ambition should not be ignored either. In Britain's Mediterranean aspirations there is an aspect of *erōs* for the Mediterranean city and a desire for communion with the power of beauty that the city had so convincingly exhibited over the course of centuries. There is also (in the Victorian and Edwardian ages) a streak of evangelicalism in British imperial attitudes. There is a sense that the decline of the Mediterranean city is due to moral weakness, and that beauty is culpable in this, for beauty (the evangelical sometimes supposed) is no substitute for morality. The conviction of some of the British was that biblical morality was the cause of imperial strength, while the card-playing, music, dancing, and the rest of the enjoyments of the Venetians was a symptom of decline of a society in the thrall of beauty.

Britain never quite proved the argument one way or the other by achieving hegemony over Venice—that dubious honor fell to Napoleon in 1797.[33] But in truth and in practice, aesthetic power was crucial to the British dominance of the world circumference. The British ruled their empire through hierarchies, through laws, and through aesthetic abstraction. As a general rule, hierarchies were loathed, laws were of mixed value, and aesthetic power was the most effective and least dispute-causing means of exerting power at a distance. The masters of the British Empire wisely limited the amount of direct Foreign Office rule from London. They often used local hierarchies instead. In some cases, they invented new local hierarchies, some of a regular kind, some based on race. But, overall, hierarchy was incompatible with distance. It assumed an intimacy of interactions between agents that distance confounded. Law was a somewhat better medium for coordinating action over distance. Notably the British planted sound formal legal and law-creating institutions in countries like India and Australia. But a single law, like a single hierarchy, for multiple nations was impossible to achieve, or rather quickly fell out of favor. Integration on a world scale requires cosmopolitical or demiurgic power. Its most potent vehicle is the creation and replication of civic forms. The British creation of the 'Victorian city' from Liverpool to Bombay to Melbourne is a manifest case of this (Briggs, 1982).

As ocean trade replaced the old Silk Route from China to Constantinople, a number of strategic mercantile city nodes (Shanghai, Singapore, and Hong Kong) were created under the watchful eyes of British and Western powers in order to guarantee access to China and the trade passage through the Malacca Straits. Parallel developments occurred in the settler societies of Australia and New Zealand. The enigmatic power of doubling, mirroring and twinning permeates the history of these nodes. The special status of Hong Kong in relation to mainland China, the failed union of Singapore and Malaya (and their subsequent tense coexistence as city state and nation state), Shanghai's history as an extraterritorial treaty port on Chinese soil, the equal power of Sydney and Melbourne that precluded both of them becoming the national capital and relegated Australia's capital territory to a rural back block, and the parsing of commerce to Auckland and government to Wellington—each of these is a variation, though some of them more compelling than others, on the theme of dual power.[34] Each proved, in varying degrees, to be successful portals—and some acquired the characteristics of great portals. Each managed to mix global trade with international hospitality, host émigré communities, discourage confessional, ethnic and ideological hatreds, value the intelligent trafficking of goods, persons and information, move along at an energetic pace, and make good use of limited space. It was notable that Shanghai in the early 2000s should produce the most authoritative international ranking index for global universities. The issue remained, though, whether any of these cities, Shanghai included, managed to tap into the kind of enigmatic cultural power capable of infusing cosmopolitan cities and knowledge societies with a creative driving force—one that would make them a compelling model rather than simply an interesting replica of creation.

Circumferential power: The Australian case

Throughout history, sea powers, and later on oceanic powers, have been the most successful creators of forms of liquid, non-territorial power.[35] The Mediterranean, the North Sea, and America's multiple seaboards stand out for their inventiveness. From their crucible was created a bevy of highly adventurous city-based republics, constitutional unions, commonwealths, and settler-colonial empires that provided an enduringly tough, no-holds-barred counter-weight to both nomadic and patrimonial power. The first true cases of countervailing maritime peripheral power—the city republics and republican empires of the classical Mediterranean—also proved remarkably enduring and exceptionally flexible models of how to construct such a power.

The British, for example, drew extensively on the Roman model. Yet they did so without dogma, and always with their own decisive innovations. The British baulked at the idea of extending English citizenship to their colonies. They repeatedly knocked back the idea of representing the colonies in the British parliament.[36] This forced the Americans into rebellion. For the pivotal half century after that bruising experience, the British were content to retreat to a somewhat more Hellenic model of colonization, creating a string of soon-to-be self-governing colonies tied by common values to Britain but otherwise free to run their internal affairs. The key to the creation of self-governing colonies was city building. We see this spectacularly represented in the case of Australia. Virtually from their inception, the Australian colonies were among the most highly urbanized societies in the world.[37] Their dominant coastal cities were also among the greatest urban colonial creations in history—not least because a model of self-governing order was implicit in their design.

Originally the Australian colonies were intended to be highly compact settlements, with a tight agrarian perimeter around an urban core. To this Hellenic model, however, was soon appended the Roman model of rule over an extensive continental geography by means of law and roads. The assiduous development of communicative, civil administrative, law court, road and rail networks allowed for the extension of a civil power across an insular continental hinterland that lay behind Australian coastal cities.[38] The center of gravity of Australian political economy, though, never shifted from these circumferential cities and towns. Just as Australia stood as a circumferential society to the 'world island' of the Eurasian landmass, so its cities were built as a circumferential chain around the inland of its own island continent.

Contrast this with the case of British imperial India. In his 1853 articles for *The New York Daily Tribune* Karl Marx brilliantly prophesizes what the British were to do for India: *viz.*, give it the telegraph, military drill, a free press, private property, the railways, and an educated class able to govern and armed with European science. The result, as Marx predicted, would be real unity across the sub-continent and integration into the world market.

> The political unity of India, more consolidated, and extending farther than it ever did under the Great Moguls, was the first condition of its regeneration. That unity, imposed by the British sword, will now be strengthened and perpetuated by the electric telegraph. The native army, organized and trained by the British drill-sergeant, was the *sine qua non* of Indian self-emancipation, and of India ceasing to be the prey of the first foreign intruder. The free press, introduced for the first time into Asiatic society, and managed principally by the common offspring of Hindoo and Europeans, is a new and powerful agent of reconstruction. The *Zemindars* and *Ryotwar* themselves, abominable as they are, involve two distinct forms of private property in land—the great *desideratum* of Asiatic society. From the Indian natives, reluctantly and sparingly educated at Calcutta, under British superintendence, a fresh class is springing up, endowed with the requirements of government and imbued with European science...The ruling classes of Great Britain...intend now drawing a net of railways over India. And they will do it. The results must be inappreciable. (Marx, 1962, 353–354)

Yet, as canny as Marx's anticipations are, they miss the key, indispensable role of the city. What Marx describes for India is Rome transplanted to Asia, but without Rome's nodal city building capacity. Australian modernity, by contrast with Indian modernity, was distinguished practically from its origins by the largest concentration of urban dwellers in the world. The urban node was supplemented by continental spanning networks.

In a short order of time, the Australian landmass was subjected to the rational abstractions of transport networks, scientific farming, map grids, and the like. One consequence of this was to replace the relationship to the earth with a relationship to networks. A second consequence was to decisively strip the land of nomadic significations. Aboriginal hunter-gatherer societies were marginalized by paternal administration, police actions, and intermittent settler violence. Many aboriginals became subsistence pastoral laborers. Under the impetus of 1960s romanticism, there was an attempt to re-assert earth over network with official policies of aboriginal land rights and communal self-determination. The practical effect of the policies was to replace aboriginal pastoral labour with welfare dependence. The extraordinarily effective Roman model granting citizenship or free status to the defeated was not repeated in Australia—or rather only very belatedly.[39] The Romans seamlessly integrated Gallic, Celtic, and German tribes in this manner.

Settlement in Australia was a relative term. What arose in place of the pre-existing nomad societies was nothing like the locality-bound structures of patrimonial states with their static mentalities and internal passports. Like North America, Australia was a mobile society. The pattern of its travel was in, through, and between its coastal cities. These urban nodes in turn were part of a world-chain of circumferential cities ranging from Bombay and Alexandria to Liverpool and Boston (Murphy, 2004). Bush legends about itinerant Anglo-Celtic trans-national pastoral workers, and (later on) accounts of the pre-European nomads, found audiences in these cities. But the stories of such inland peripatetic thin-textured societies had little impact on the actual structure of the emphatically urbanized Australian form of life. After all, this was a place where by the 1990s, four out of five people lived in cities, one in four of the population lived within fifteen minutes drive of the coast, and population growth was almost entirely confined to urban coastal corridors.[40]

This commonwealth of urban coastal dwellers had effectively de-territorialized its territory, and by forging a commonwealth the coastal dwellers had also created a non-proprietary state. Non-proprietary states arise when natural persons no longer have a direct ownership stake in the state. The state becomes an artificial entity. It acquires a strong civil or public character. Offices are clearly distinguished from persons, as law is from command and permission. Government as an artificial person interacts with other artificial persons: citizens, corporations, cooperatives, universities, trade unions, benefit-holders, municipalities, legal titleholders, qualified experts, share owners, automobile associations, returned soldiers leagues, environment lobbies, and so on. The range of possible civil classes and artificial bodies is exceptionally large.

Construction of Australia's artificial state was the work of the nineteenth century. From this patient work emerged a structure of power whose logic was geometric in spirit. This crystallized in the commonwealth idea—a subtle design for a constitutional arrangement that was architectonic in nature. This arrangement orchestrated states into a federal union, organized around a separation of powers that created a dynamic equilibrium of great ingenuity. The mechanism of forming such artificial bodies proliferated through all dimensions of Australian life—from cooperatives, schools and museums to science organizations, public broadcasters, and political parties. At the heart of this process was a genius for replacing natural persons with civil artifices that could act on behalf of social classes and natural environments, old buildings and new bridges, boundary-crossing river systems and national industrial sectors.

The Australian political economy

The mix of circumferential life, a state-subsuming commonwealth, and de-territorialized territory in Australia had far-reaching ramifications. One of things that it created was a very particular type of political economy. This was an economy in which agriculture, industry, and service sectors alike were transformed by a deeper logic of circumferential urbanism and intellectual capitalism. The Australian agricultural heartland illustrates this perfectly. In the world of coastal dwellers, farmers produce for world markets. In this, Australia has always been much more aggressive than the United States. Australia never developed an enduring political apparatus of farm protection or family-farm style agrarian populism. Correspondingly, it never developed the rash of inland cities that the United States did in its period of continental empire building during the nineteenth century. Though a substantial source of wealth, extractive mining, pastoralism, and cropping (even at their height in the nineteenth century) were never the principal source of livelihood for Australians—most of whom were never to be found in the countryside, except on day trips for recreation. Nor was Australia ever a full-fledged industrial nation. Its manufacturing industry took off late (in the 1920s) and declined early (in the 1980s). The label post-industrial doesn't adequately characterize the Australian economy either, in any of its phases. Generally there was great wariness about developing the kind of back-office tertiary service economy that, for instance, millennial India began to experiment with on the back of the information technology revolution. The propensity of intellectual capitalist economies like Australia is to develop such jobs and then to export them. A lot of phony political battles in intellectual capitalist societies have been defences of (variously) agrarian, industrial, and post-industrial jobs, when the very nature of such economies is that they avoid and evade such typecasting. What really matters in these economies is the capacity to invent new forms of work.

In short, neither agrarianism, nor industrialism, nor post-industrialism really describe an economy like Australia's. These terms obscure the nature of circumferential power. A much more instructive way of understanding such a political economy is to think about it first and foremost as a civic economy. The gravitational center of its mode of production and distribution is the city. Its primary driver is a mix of urbanism and knowledge. Littoral societies typically invest heavily in urban development. Their signature is brilliant demotic cities. These cities are notably different from the other premier urban creations in history: the court, palace, and capital cities of patrimonial and neo patrimonial states. The point of the demotic city is not the creation of bureaucratic court power through splendor and ritual. Rather these cities are the crucible and model of a designing intelligence. As exporting states, circumferential powers rely heavily on such intelligence to drive the long-distance traffic, transfer, and circulation of commodities. Equally, they rely heavily on such intelligence to design what they produce and how they produce it. A significant and (over time) escalating portion of the value of these products lies in their design—whether this might be the design of a crop, an animal, a machine, a manufactured item, a landscape, a written page, an oral address, a painting, or a song.

The faculty of intelligent design propels the political economy of circumferential powers in very practical ways—as the Australian case demonstrates. In 1870, the Australian colonies had a product per head that was more than a third greater than the next wealthiest countries: Britain, Belgium, the Netherlands and the United States (Williams, 1988, 281–291). Notably all of these were littoral societies, or societies with powerful seaboard-portal economies. Australia achieved what precedence it had not because it was a 'lucky country' enjoying the patrimony of nature but because its notional agrarian economy was based on science, technology and management innovation.[41] Its sheep industries depended on intelligent breeding programs that focused on fleece rather than carcasses, fencing of sheep runs, and the invention of shearing machines. Its wheat industry depended on the development of mechanized strippers and harvesters, the design of wheat strains resistant to drought and rust, and the use of super-phosphates to replenish phosphorus-deficient soils (282–283). Science-based production meant that by 1870 only thirty percent of the workforce in Australia was employed in agriculture in comparison with fifty percent in the United States, Germany, and France. Mirroring this, the Australian propensity to patent technologies was higher than in Britain, the United States or Germany (Inkster & Todd, 1988, 119).

The Australian political economy did not emerge in a vacuum. It is part of a much larger history of civics and science—and their circumferential geographies. Science-based production and what corresponds to it (viz. intellectual property in technology) are labor shedding. They are quite different from other technology traditions in which technology supports the social organization of labor. The history of imperial Chinese technology illustrates the latter. Its innovations in paper and printing were efficacious social technologies for a literate bureaucratic society. The wheelbarrow was a perfect complement for backbreaking labor. Gunpowder found uses in rituals and in signaling. It had to wait however for transplantation to Europe before it found an application in military science and (later on) engineering.[42] Please note: the argument here is not a rehash of the thesis of 'the West and the rest.' Archipelago Japan took the sciences of artificial intelligence and robotics, and applied them with great success to factory production in the 1970s. This reflected its own version of a condition that repeats itself time and again in littoral and peripheral maritime societies. They share a fascination for mathematical sciences and applied art. Even a state like Japan, where social connections and social power remain very important, at times to the point of claustrophobia, a counter-tradition of aesthetic economy and of mathematical science produced a powerful industrialism and a typically oddball but highly productive circumferential capitalism. This long preceded the pressure to integrate Japan into the world trade system in the nineteenth century. From the mid seventeenth century, the Japanese began to show interest in Western science, including mathematics, surveying, ballistics, astronomy, geography, and medicine. This was systemized in the eighteenth-century 'Dutch' studies or *rangaku* (Goodman, 2000). Japanese modernity was built on this potent knowledge acquisition combined with strong aesthetic traditions.

Littoral states and riverine intersections have long been a critical seedbed of the mathematical sciences. One of the most interesting of the riverine intersections is the Baden-Württemberg triangle bounded by the Rhine and Danube Rivers, that converges at its southern tip on Zurich. Not at all incidentally, this region produced both Karl Marx and Albert Einstein. Marx was born at Trier on the Mosel River in the eastern Rhineland on the doorstep of Luxemburg and Belgium. Einstein was born at Ulm on the Danube in historic Württemberg. If you think that the geography of thought does not matter, then consider this: Einstein was schooled in Munich and absolutely loathed the rote learning, coercive authoritarianism and landed militarism of German Barvaria. In defiance of its mindlessness, Einstein taught himself mathematics and physics, most especially from a little textbook on Euclid, his 'holy geometry book.' Einstein eventually rejected German for Swiss citizenship, and enrolled himself in Zurich's Eidgenössische Technische Hochschule. There one of his teachers was the Lithuanian ex-Königsburger Hermann Minkowski, whose 1907 work on four-dimensional space-time was to provide the crucial geometrical interpretation of Einstein's Special Theory of Relativity. Minkowski and Einstein created a revolution in thought as dramatic as the two Baltic coast geniuses, Copernicus and Kant.

Copernicus in Frombork [Frauenberg] on the Polish Baltic coast and the great Königsburg philosopher, Kant, are part of a spell-binding cohort in the geography of thought. Königsburg, the city of Minkowski's higher education and Kant's working life, was also where Hannah Arendt was schooled. Arendt, alongside John Rawls, was the great political philosopher of the twentieth century.[43] Astonishingly, the University of Königsburg also produced Theodr Kaluza. Kaluza's 1919 paper postulating a five-dimensional geometry—based on the assumption that each point in a one-dimensional universe is really a circle, and thus every line is actually a cylinder—is tipped to provide the mathematic foundations for theories that will eventually unify Einstein's universe with quantum physics (Kaku, 1995). The liquid, littoral, insular cohort includes Eudoxus in Athens, Archimedes in Syracuse, Ptolemy in Alexandria, Newton in Woolsthorpe and Cambridge, and Descartes in Amsterdam. Its impact extends from science to society. Eudoxus' friend Plato exemplifies the impetus of this cohort to wed aesthetic beauty and abstract form with economy and politics. As do Hobbes and Shaftesbury, each of whom (like Newton) hailed from coastal English provinces.[44] Geometrical-mathematical sciences or formalistic abstraction provide a worldview for littoral states. It is city building that translates this formalism into demotic terms. Thus, it is Christopher Wren who is the great populariser of Newton, Shaftesbury, and Hobbes. This is not because he set out to depict the Newtonian universe in stone—even less so would he have approved of Shaftesbury's Whig politics or Hobbes's secular politics. Yet these distinctions mean very little when compared with the belief in civil artifice and elegant design that all of these figures tacitly shared. Their common ground was a kind of civil religion, in which God is a synonym for the rational design of auto-poietic or self-organizing systems—from macro-cosmos to micro-cosmos.[45] The city is the visible representation of this designing intelligence. Thus an intuitive civic deism bridges between Tory and Whig, royalist and republican. Its consensus product is the idea that an auto-poietic commonwealth will replace the social state. The city becomes the laboratory for learning how the impersonal equilibrium of a complex self-regulating system is achieved.

Wren was the master city builder. The mathematician turned architect oversaw the rebuilding of London after the Great Fire. Newton called Wren one of the three great geometers of his age. Wren consistently understood visual problems as geometrical problems. For Wren there were two kinds of beauty—natural and customary. The cause of natural beauty was geometry (Downes, 1971, 46–49). Wren's London was a template. It was translated around the world during the era of English maritime colonization. This circumferential colonization is not to be confused with the land-grabbing imperialism that took off in the middle of the nineteenth century, with the extension of British rule over vast territories, especially in the tropics. Four factors caused Britain's shift from maritime to territorial empire. The first was the vacuum of power caused by the declining Mughal Empire in India. This caused the East India Company after 1757 to turn itself into a quasi-state, assuming control of Bengal. This was not yet a norm. Indeed the Pitt Act of 1784 outlawed the East India Company from further wars of aggression or annexations. The real turning point in British attitudes was the defensive reaction by the British state to Napoleon. This was reinforced by a third decisive factor: the spread of romantic ideologies in the nineteenth century. Romanticism drew an equation between power and earth. The fourth factor that explains British territorial acquisition was the British success in World War I. After the war, German colonies instantly became protectorates of Britain.

The vision of Wren was worldly not earthly, geometric not terrestrial. Its aesthetic-geometric-mathematical spirit—altered through many Augustan and Victorian iterations—allowed it to be reproduced across the world, like the Greek and Roman colonial city before it. This model of colonization through city building was astonishingly efficient. Colonial cities were an approximate re-creation of the metropolitan city. This template allowed Australia to emerge in quick time as 'a new, large, self-governing country, automatically recreating British institutions and re-forming familiar clubs and societies'—as one historian put it (Serle, 1963, 381). The spectacular capacity for civic mimesis meant that institutions of science developed in Britain through the era of scientific enlightenment were quickly and faithfully reproduced in Australia. In this sense, the dominance of science-based production in Australian political economy was a function of the pattern of colonial settlement inspired by the

Greco-Roman model of colonization. The type of city that Wren inspired was a brilliant, subtle, everyday reminder of and education in the geometrical-mathematical spirit. Wherever one walked, this spirit was present.

The effect of this spirit on nineteenth-century Australia is fascinating. It was a place where state-funded science flourished. Government departments employed large numbers of surveyors, engineers, geologists and other science officers and experts. Yet this science was an open book. It held no secrets of state. Its theoretical and practical fruits were disseminated widely to a discriminating public and to interested parties. The state supported scientific reconnaissance and expeditions and, later in the nineteenth century, university research science. It did so without turning the processes or the products of this science into the patrimony of the state.[46] Scientific offices were integrated into a public sphere of science learning, debate, exhibition, and publication. The city was the crucible of these publics. Australian cities saw assiduous investment and participation in self-regulating civil artifices like mechanics institutes. These offered broad-ranging forums for science and technology discussion and dissemination.[47] There were some eight hundred mechanics institutes in the colonial state of Victoria alone. Learned societies, royal societies, exhibition buildings, libraries, universities, and botanical gardens proliferated widely throughout colonial Australia. Each was an artificial person that contributed to the larger civil artifice of an emerging commonwealth.

Frank speech and mystic silence

Crucial to the development of such a commonwealth was frankness of speech. Australians did not invent this. The Greeks did. They called it *parrēsia*. Australians, however, have practiced it wherever they could. Samuel Huntington, in his book *The Clash of Civilizations and the Remaking of World Order*, described Australians as 'the most direct, blunt, outspoken, some would say insensitive, people in the English-speaking world' (1996, 153). I have never seen a better description of the antipodeans.[48] Let us dwell for a moment, though, on why this is a true description. Australians are not congenitally rude. In fact, with their origins in late eighteenth-century English Augustan society, they have the typical Augustan virtues. Much more so than the United States or Canada, Australia was the great Augustan fragment of the British cosmos. Its foundation period—1877 to 1820—was the late Augustan era. Much of the mentality of the era was replicated in the founding nature of Australia, not least the Augustan love of wit and humour. Australians are cheerful, optimistic, and friendly—a nation of happy skeptics. But they are also brutally frank, and sometimes ice-cold in their judgments and actions.

Their frankness of attitude stems from the fact that Australia in crucial respects is a post-social society. It was built on a refusal of social power. The same rejection of social power marked the Greeks, the Hellenized Romans, Spinoza's Dutch, Deist America ('In God We Trust'), and generations of British Whig and Tory, socialist and liberal radicals. All of the societies that I have just referred to, of course, had countervailing movements that urged social power on them. Sometimes this social power was of the most awful kind, as in the case of American slavery. Sometimes it was of the dim-witted kind, though even bumbling power caused its share of catastrophes as when the Edwardian estate gentry led their troops into battle in the First War World.

The Australians were to prove themselves among the most successful in replacing social power with the power of artifice. Already at the Australian foundation, a deep and abiding architectonic spirit conditioned the Augustan cheeriness of the antipodeans. This spirit was displayed in an extraordinary talent for city building. This spirit acquired a mature form as early as Governor Lachlan Macquarie's Sydney in the 1810s. This was remarkable considering that Sydney was still then essentially a penal colony. The speed with which a durable civic fabric arose—visible even today amidst Sydney's skyscrapers—is the first sign of a society that had begun to construct itself as an artificial person. In such a post-social, or civil, society, geometric-style relations of equilibrium, grace, balance, proportion, and rhythm replace social-style relations of deference, nepotism, corruption, service, and social sensitivity that characterize hierarchical and gentrified societies. The post-social society is the automatic society.

The post-social or automatic society is one that devalues social connections and relationships. Its existential slogan is 'leave me alone.' Its workers work best when they are—exactly—left alone. In the Australian case, this mentality is a product of distance—its denizens originally came from somewhere else, they invariably came a long way to get to the antipodes, and most had the capacity to move on had they been too disappointed with what they found. In that limited respect at least Australians proved to be a little like the nomads they displaced. The unofficial Australian national anthem is about a sheep-stealing itinerant shearer who dances his backpack across a mostly empty country. Even Australia's labor movements, which had (and have) a strong attraction to the social power of 'mateship' and other peer-type social solidarities, in their founding years were made up of large numbers of transcontinental and transnational itinerant workers. Notably when these itinerants finally settled, they turned with a passion, and in a mimesis of macro-sociological evolution, to horticulture—in the shape of the Australian domestic garden, the epitome of designed nature.[49]

Itinerancy is an interesting phenomenon. Non-state societies in pre-history dealt with social conflict by itinerant dispersion. People who clashed moved away from each other. The social state prohibited flight. Not uncommonly, it bound natural persons to the soil. Those who were forced to stick together in this way had to 'get on.' They had to develop social manners and social virtues. 'Harmony' in social interaction was often the highest virtue. Smoothing over and organizing relationships became the pre-occupation of these societies. Frank speech was discouraged. Ritual speech took its place. Tool-making also was downplayed, in favor of the social technologies of recording and writing, and organizing labor for big projects.

Pre-historical peoples in contrast were more interested in object-creation than in relationship-formation. Their symbolic societies were small-scale; their functional social units even smaller. They survived not by deference to superiors or through the back slapping closed-shop social solidarity of peers, but by fashioning better tools. The Greek innovation was to figure out how to create larger-scale societies without sacrificing human independence. They did this by posing the question: how is it possible to have cooperation between those who have the liberty to go away? The answer was to organize interaction through abstraction: cooperation through the artifices of market, public, assembly, law court, science, federation, and above all, the city.

These artifices constituted spaces where people could gather and communicate. In these publics individuals spoke frankly, even brutally. They could do so because their cooperation did not depend on social manners or social virtues. The Greeks had no sense that anything important depended on 'getting on' and 'fitting in' with their fellows. They celebrated contest and competition. What they discovered, though, is that price-driven markets could coordinate even the behavior of total strangers thousands of miles apart. Likewise they discovered that persons with no social ties could be solicited to do things in common—such as provide charity or build a navy or accommodate overseas visitors. Assemblies were based on mathematical systems, carefully constructed to avoid tribal and family blocs, and made general laws and provisions for the common wealth. It was also discovered that beautiful and functional cities could be built by having strangers, who were chosen by lot, sit on public committees.

We would be shocked if we were to listen in on some of the discussions of these assemblies and committees. The Greeks for instance regularly declared their victorious generals in war to be naves or criminals.[50] Generals who personalized combat in the savage-heroic mode, or who ignored the rule of the city, or who courted gratuitous violence and senseless risks were held to account, and words were not minced. Frank speech was a practical assertion of a citizenry that understood that their armies won victories not because they were social bodies based on slavish deference or sycophantic peer solidarity but because they were impersonal 'machines.'[51] Sometimes people spoke frankly because they feared these 'machines.' Also sometimes they thought the human element to be irrelevant. Both were wrong. But still it is true that the Greeks, who were often out-numbered, won wars because their citizen soldiers and generals understood the military geometries of leverage, force and resistance, and least effort. This did not make generals dispensable. But it did make them part of an artificial person that was deadly in war but not the proper subject of normal social sensitivities.

Frank speech is the sign of liberty in a society where persons can 'walk away'—and yet who also have powerful ways of cooperating through artifice. This is a society that is good at creating objects, artificial persons, and self-regulating systems composed of combinations of objects and persons. This is a society that is structured not by social virtues or social manners but by the Platonic forms of proportion, equilibrium, and rhythm. The larger nature in which this society and its civic fabric is embedded is also a nature of forms. It is not a nature that mimics social relationships. Its cosmos has a mathematical-geometric character. From Eudoxus and Plato to Copernicus, Newton and Kant, and finally to Minkowski and Einstein, the geometric interpretation of nature has been the over-riding consensus of scientific cosmologies. The great demotic cities of the maritime commonwealths habitually interpolate this nature. I think this is so because these accomplished city makers, who have no especial sense of modesty, nonetheless have a powerful sense of the impersonal character of their enterprise. So while they create, they do so with an abiding sense of objectivity. Correspondingly, the best of their work, and there is a lot of it, avoids the social language of moralism and sentimentality. It is (in a manner of speaking) hard-hearted. It eschews ethical religion and social virtue, whether it be a modern or a traditional, evangelical or Confucian kind. Yet the a-social is not irreligious nor is it unjust—quite the contrary.

Justice, objectivity, and impersonality share a family resemblance. On their back arises the sense of the sacred typical of post-social societies. The Australian sense of the sacred can be thought of as an answer to Max Weber's anguished question (Murphy, 1983, 757–801): how do modern societies live with their warring gods? Somewhere in the nineteenth century modern societies lost faith in a single God. In this vacuum appeared a swarm of competing cultural deities that immediately began to war against each other. Socialism, communism, nationalism, rationalism, liberalism, environmentalism, and a host of others have claimed omniscient status. The response to the resulting cultural wars has either been dogmatism or relativism. There is though a third response: a flinty, often witty, objectivity that lives ironically in the presence of all of the competing gods (Murphy, 1994, 193–238). For want of a better term, we might call this a kind of civil religion. It is civil in virtue of its skeptical tolerance, and religious in light of the enigmatic, mythic forces that it summons up in order to reconcile the obdurate deities of contentious modernity.

The Australian civil religion has its sacred artifices. The greatest is the Sydney Opera House.[52] It is the Australian Parthenon. It sits like a white trireme on Sydney Harbor, eternally ready to sail into the distance. In conceiving the idea for the design of the Opera House, its architect, Jørn Utzon, took an orange and divided it into segments. That was the indispensable act of creation. Those segments, transformed into the shells of the building, and arranged artfully with regard to its site on Bennelong Point, are the essence of the Opera House. In some sense, this act of creation was child's play, but child's play of an impossibly high order. An act of creation that will last millennia, and that is not just vogue or fashion, is elemental. That which is the most difficult is the simplest of all. The segmented hemisphere on which Utzon based his design echoes the form of the orb or sphere that is found throughout nature—from the glories of planetary systems to, yes, the humble orange. What great architecture does is to mimic the forms of nature. In the architectural act of creation we see the re-creation of the proportions, symmetries, ratios, and shapes of nature. Architecture is pure artifice. But, at its most powerful, it is an artifice that is a second nature. Such architecture is different from nature but also very much like nature. From that paradox, it draws its power.

The mystic characters of Patrick White's novels represent a similar uncanny quality—in White's case, it is the rising up of silence out of sound.[53] It is ironic, to say the least, that the frankest and most insensitive nation of talkers on the face of the earth should produce a mystic writer as its major literary figure. White's Australian characters personify the sway of mute intuition over noisy reason. White writes about what cannot be written about, and makes explicit that which can only ever be tacit. This means that his words become something else altogether. At the heart of such experiments in thought lies the double nature of creation.

The characters that White created spoke of speechless intuitions and possessed hermaphrodite-like identities forged out of enigmatic unions of oppositions: male and female, colonial and metropolitan, bourgeois and bohemian.[54] Such dazzling two-in-ones animate creation. Creation is double. Global creation emerges from the to-and-fro, the eternal return, of the portal. In creation, one thing is always two, and two makes one. All creation is an analogy. One thing is the same as and different from something else—its twin, its mirror, its other. Creation is the representation of one thing by another thing. It is the making of one thing in the medium of something else, and it is the making of a new thing in the image of something old. Utzon did all of these things when he recreated the sea-side shells of his childhood in tiles. To the viewer at a distance, the huge tiled sound shells he created look like the sails of a ship billowing in the wind. This is the double nature of creation, the paradox of Pygmalion: the sculpture that comes alive. It is the immortal icon of the portal city—the sacred enigma that elicits eternal fascination.

Endnotes

1. 'Before the [agrarian] revolution comparatively poor and illiterate communities had made an impressive series of contributions to man's progress. The two millennia immediately preceding 3,000 B.C. had witnessed discoveries in applied science that directly or indirectly affected the prosperity of millions of men and demonstrably furthered the biological welfare of our species by facilitating its multiplication. We have mentioned the following applications of science: artificial irrigation using canals and ditches; the plow; the harnessing of animal motive-power; the sail-boat; wheeled vehicles; orchard husbandry; fermentation; the production and use of copper; bricks, the arch, glazing, the seal; and—in the earliest stages of the revolution—a solar calendar, writing, numerical notation, and bronze. The two thousand years after the revolution—say from 2,600 to 600 B.C.—produced few contributions of anything like comparable importance to human progress. Perhaps only four achievements deserve to be put in the same category as the fifteen just enumerated. They are: the 'decimal notation' of Babylonia (about 2,000 B.C.); an economical method for smelting iron on an industrial scale (1,400 B.C.); a truly alphabetic script (1,300 B.C.); and aqueducts for supplying water to cities (700 B.C.).' Childe, 1951, 180.

2. These may possibly have included the Anatolian coast dwelling ancestors of the Etruscans, Sardinian and Sicilian tribes, and the Cretan Philistines.

3. For a depiction of the rise of a Phoenician mercantile upper class, the near elimination of the power of kings, and the emergence of civil law and oligarchic governing councils, see Edey, 1974, 88–92 and Harden, 1971, 69–73. All of this occurred in the Phoenician cities despite a religion that held to notions of the slavish and sacrificial relation of humans to the gods.

4. The Lavrian silver mines of classical Greece and the large slave estates of southern Italy in Roman times were the exception rather than the rule.

5. 'On Artificial Man' from *De Homine* and 'Of Persons, Authors and Things Personated' from *Leviathan*.

6. 'On Dominion' from *De Cive*.

7. The workings of modern neo patrimonial reciprocity are nicely depicted in Harold Crouch's description of the Malaysian ruling party UMNO—United Malays National Organization. UMNO's dominance of Malaysian politics in the second half of the twentieth century is attributable to its ability to get and keep the support of the Malay community: 'This has been partly due to its control over patronage distribution at all levels. Business people wanting contracts, bureaucrats wanting promotion, peasants wanting land and parents wanting scholarships for their children have all found it helpful to be recognized as UMNO supporters' (Crouch, 1993).

8. On nineteenth-century advocates and critics of the machine society or mechanistic society, see Leo Marx, 1964, 145–226.

9. '…there must have been somewhere between 300 and 370 Greek vessels arrayed against a Persian armada of well over 600 ships. Both Aeschylus and Herodotus, however, were certain that the Persian armada was even larger, numbering more than 1,000 ships and 200,000 seamen. If they are correct, Salamis involved the greatest number of combatants in any one engagement in the entire history of naval warfare' (Hanson, 2002, 44).

10. On this kind of warfare, see Hanson (2002), especially 46, 230–231, 316.

11. On the emergence of this kind of order, see Murphy (2001a).

12. For a summation of 100 years of empirical psychology's study of creativity, and the persistent conclusion that creativity and a-social norms are very closely related, see Feist, 1999, 273–296.

13. This is why Kant's dinner-table companions and friends in Königsburg were British merchants.

14. One expedition in 1482—the construction of the fort of El Mina on the Gold Coast, instrumental for capturing the gold trade of Guinea—included Christopher Columbus among its number.

15. Today, the port of Belgium.

16. The roots of the shift lie in the event in 1519 when Charles V of Spain was elected Holy Roman Emperor, combining the crowns of Spain, Burgundy (with the Netherlands), Austria and Germany.

17. In 1579, the Union of Utrecht brought together seven northern, Protestant provinces of the Netherlands against Catholic Spain.

18. Leiden's university was established in 1575 in reward for the courageous actions of its citizens during the Spanish occupation.

19. The first example of the limited liability (joint stock) trading company was the Muscovy or Russia Company created by English merchants in 1553 looking to fund exploration for a northeast passage to Asia.

20. Stock exchanges were a creation of the sixteenth century. The first one appeared in Antwerp (today part of Belgium), an historic portal city. There, in 1531, traders started the practice of gathering together to speculate in shares and commodities. Another historic sea portal and mercantile center, Hamburg, followed suit in 1558. Amsterdam furnished the next stock exchange, in 1619. London and Paris created exchanges toward the end of the seventeenth century. The New York Stock Exchange was created in 1792.

21. After the 1651 English edition of *Leviathan*, there were attempts to suppress the work in England. A subsequent Latin translation of *Leviathan* was issued at Amsterdam in 1668. The first edition of Hobbes' collected works was published in Amsterdam in 1688.

22. Albert Rothenberg in *The Emerging Goddess: The Creative Process in Art, Science, and Other Fields* (Chicago: University of Chicago Press, 1979) called creative thinking Janusian. Arthur Koestler in *The Act of Creation* (New York: Dell, 1964) termed it bi-sociation

23. Nietzsche put the spotlight on this with his theory that the duality of Apollo and Dionysius were the crucial twin source of Greek culture. The idea of the origin of strong culture in myth is re-worked in dramatic ways by John Carroll (2001, 2004).

24. Cornelius Castoriadis introduced the idea of the power of nobody. See for example Castoriadis, 1991, 150.

25. Byzantium's 'two demes' refers to the Blues (landowners and Greco-Roman aristocracy) and the Greens (the party of trade, industry, and civil service).

26. In Shakespeare's Henriad, the mayor of London is an important figure.

27. If this was non-academic, engineers,' architecture, it was no less powerful for that, and, in any case, found an academic translation in the work of the Berlin architect Karl Friedrich Schinkel (1781–1841). Schinkel undertook a historically well-timed study tour of Britain in 1826. As part of this trip, he visited several of London's premier architects, including the influential John Nash. But he was not particularly interested in the princely cachet of Nash's work. (Schinkel, the Prussian architect-bureaucrat, was to pointedly note in his diary that Nash lived like a duke.) What he was really interested in were the workshops, factories, warehouses, bridges and docks and markets that Britain's maritime empire was inciting. Contra-wise, on Wren's architecture as a signifier of portal urbanism, see Murphy, 2001, 11–38

28. Gibraltar passed from Spanish to British hands in 1704 during the Spanish War of Succession.

29. Quoted in Howard, 1962, 235.

30. On this and what follows on sea cables, see Mattelart, 2000.

31. Napoleon had himself just wrestled it from its historic governing military order, the Knights of Malta, on his famous expedition to Egypt.

32. After the fourth Crusade, in 1204, Venice purchased Crete from crusaders. Crete stayed in Venetian hands until 1669, when it passed to the Ottomans. Greek forces ousted the Ottomans in 1898, and the British managed the island as a protectorate until its union with Greece in 1913. The British assumed control over Cyprus in 1878, in an agreement with the Ottomans. Under this arrangement, the Ottoman Emperor remained the nominal sovereign. During World War I, the British annexed Cyprus. The island was offered to Greece in 1915, but the offer was allowed to lapse. Cyprus became a Crown Colony of Britain in 1924.

33. That same year the city was handed over to Austria. Following Austria's defeat by Prussia in 1866, Venice was ceded to the kingdom of Italy.

34. In 1627, Japan was closed to the outside world except for a Dutch trading post. In 1853–1854, the American Commodore Matthew Perry forcibly opened up Yokohama as a 'treaty port' for overseas trade, ending Japan's isolation. Yokohama subsequently became the focus for foreign settlement and for overseas trading houses, and later on the hub of the country's electronic industries. Even though the Japanese were reluctantly pressured into trading relations with the West, the treaty ports that the Europeans gained access to had a long subtle influence. The rapid urbanization of Japan in the late nineteenth century occurred in and around the international port cities of Yokohama, Kōbe, Niijata, Hakodate, and Nagasaki, and the naval bases of Yokosuka, Kure, and Sasebo. The reciprocal causality of ports, industrialization, and

city growth was set in train. Japan rose to become one of the principal seagoing nations with one of the world's largest merchant marines. Also noteworthy is the case of the Chinese Communists. They decried the Treaty Ports as a colonial evil and the source of unspeakable national humiliation. This is in part true. But when Mao's nationalist and isolationist strategies of economic development ('socialism in one country') finally collapsed in the 1980s, it was the old treaty port cities that became the vehicle for a new economic mode of production. This reorientation was based on special economic zones (SEZs) located on China's south eastern coastal belt near Hong Kong and Taiwan. These zones in effect reopened the old treaty ports including Shantou (Swatow) and Xiamen (Amoy)—and, later on, coastal cities such as Wenzhou, Ningbo, and Guangzhou (Canton). The zones removed administrative control from local authorities and offered preferential treatment for foreign investment. Investment came from Hong Kong, Japan and Taiwan. Development was characteristically robust, lawless, Dickensian, and successful—though largely in sunset industries that the Taiwanese and others were exporting aboard rather than in high-technology industries that Chinese political leaders at the time dreamed of. While this development was driven by the second coming of the pre-war treaty ports, with all that implies as being European and Japanese trade colonies, just as significant in retrospect was the fact that the majority of Thai overseas Chinese originally came from Swatow and the majority of overseas Chinese in Malaysia, Singapore and Indonesia came from Hokkien-dominated Amoy. The ironies of history should not be ignored.

35. The distinction between the 'world island' of the Eurasian landmass and the circumference of societies that ring that landmass comes from the founder of modern geopolitics, Halford Mackinder (1981).

36. Without concomitant representation, the notion of an Anglophone imperial federation thus was still born. This idea, which had some currency between 1900 and 1939, was side tracked into schemes for an imperial trade bloc based on trade preference and protection. The free-trading British and Australians scuttled these schemes in practice, whatever their official rhetoric. The one-time friend of Marx, and founder of the British Social Democratic Federation, H.M. Hyndman, was one of the advocates of a democratic imperial federation.

37. 'The growth of towns was a distinctive feature of these prodigious settler colonies. Even during the gold rush and the wave of agricultural settlement that followed, two out of every five colonists lived in towns of 2500 or more inhabitants. By the 1880s towns encompassed half of the population, a higher proportion than in Britain, higher also than in the United States or Canada... In every colony the capital city consolidated its dominance. It was the rail ferries and the principal port, the place where the newcomer disembarked and, after the gold rush, usually stayed. It was the commercial, financial and administrative hub, and used its political leverage to augment control over the hinterland. Brisbane, Sydney, Melbourne, Hobart, Adelaide and Perth, each one of them a coastal city established before the settlement of its inland districts, were separated from each other by at least eight hundred kilometers and movement between them was by sea' (MacIntyre, 1999, 109–110).

38. Railway networks expanded from 243 miles in 1861 to 1042 in 1871, 4192 in 1881 and 10,123 in 1891. The means of freighting exports and imports rose correspondingly, from one million tons of shipping in 1851 to five million in 1861 to sixteen million in 1891. See Fitzpatrick, 1946, 68.

39. Citizenship was granted in 1966 by referendum.

40. A good snapshot of the statistical evidence for this in the 1990s is contained in Drew, 1994.

41. The term 'lucky country' was the ironic title of a 1960s book by the Australian author Donald Horne. This book warned Australian governments against relying on extractive industries—i.e. the lucky deposits of nature—for an economic future. The Scottish-Australian philosopher John Anderson provided the philosophical foundation of Horne's polemic. Anderson took seri-

ously the Stoic warnings against relying on fortune. Goods, in Anderson's view, were the product of the kind of enterprise typified by science. See Anderson, 1962.

42. Gunpowder appears to have been invented in China in the tenth century CE. It arrived in Europe in the fourteenth century. Some attribute the invention of firearms to a fourteenth-century German monk by the name of Berthold Schwarz.

43. Strikingly, the general region of the Baltic States produced the American painter Mark Rothko, possibly America's greatest painter, and the families of Bob Dylan, Leonard Cohen, and Saul Bellow. The latter three grew up on the rim of the Great Lakes ecumene, the former settled in New York City.

44. Newton hailed from Woolsthorpe, Lincolnshire, a county in the east of England that extends along the North Sea coast. Cambridge is located in an adjacent county. Hobbes grew up in Wiltshire, a county in Southern England located between the Bristol and English Channels. Shaftesbury's home and power base was coastal Devon.

45. This theology emphasized the rationality of the universe. While God's workings might have been mysterious, behind all experience was a great design.

46. A countervailing example is the secret science cities that emerged under Soviet state socialism.

47. This paid dividends. The United States began to add figures to the roster of 'most accomplished' figures in the arts and science about 150 years after European settlement. Australia's record is comparable. Three figures with Australian origins—W. Lawrence Bragg (physics, active in the 1930s); Frank Burnet (medicine, active in the 1930s); Howard Florey (medicine, active in the 1930s)—appear in Charles Murray's index of world figures before the study's cut-off date of 1950. See Murray, 2003, Appendix 5.

48. Perhaps the only true competitors in the blunt talk stakes are New Yorkers. New York and Chicago, at tail-ends of the Hudson-Great Lakes ecumene, are typical of the way that liquid portal regions produce frank speech. This bluntness stands in sharp contrast to the politesse of agrarian-tutored Middle America.

49. On the Australian garden culture and economy, see Hogan, 2003, 54–75. On the placing of the ubiquitous demotic Australian garden in the English tradition of humanized nature and the landscape garden, see Crozier, 2003, 76–88.

50. '...there was not one great Greek general in the entire history of the city-state—Themistocles, Miltiades, Pericles, Alcibiades, Brasidas, Lysander, Pelopidas, Epaminondas—who was not at some time either fined, exiled, demoted, or killed alongside his troops. Some of the most successful and gifted commanders after their greatest victories—the Athenian admirals who won at Arginusae (406 B.C.), or Epaminondas on his return from liberating the Messenian helots (369 B.C.)—stood trial for their lives, not so much on charges of cowardice or incompetence as for inattention to the welfare of their men or the lack of communication with their civilian overseers.' Victor Davis Hanson, *Why The West Has Won: Nine Landmark Battles in the Brutal History of Western Victory* (London: Faber, 2002), pp. 35–36. These episodes did not always have merit. One of the cruelest cases was the treatment by Athenians of their great general and statesman, Phocion (402–318 B.C.E.) who was tried on trumped-up charges and condemned to death. On this episode, and its profound resonance in the art of Poussin, see Carroll, 1997.

51. The machine metaphor here sounds like a soulless Babylonian compulsory labor detail, but the contrary is true. The idea of the machine derives from the idea of the ensouled human being with its principle of self-movement. All machines from water-wheel technologies to computers are in debt to this idea. If frank speech represents the individualism of the citizen or the free person with liberty to leave the city and speak their mind, then the 'machine' of the battle formation is an example of the collective soul of the many kinds of self-regulating systems that

the Greeks and their civilizational heirs were to invent. It would be entirely mistaken to think that individualistic societies with liberty of movement and speech are not also strongly collectivist in nature. Their collectivism is not that of the serf or the slave hierarchy but the collective reason of self-regulating systems binding strangers in common action through abstract media of law, drill, theatre, assembly, and the like. The Romantic critique of the machine, which underlies much contemporary anxiety over the machine metaphor, implicitly and explicitly dreamt of a return to organic hierarchy. Yet the creation of nineteenth-century 'machines,' like the modern political party, was decisive in edging out patrimony, patronage, and personal obligation from politics. On a defense of artifice against Romantic organics, see Murphy and Roberts, 2004.

52. For a more sustained analysis of the philosophical significance of this work, see Murphy, 2001, 11–38. See also Murphy, 2009.

53. Mary Hare, Alf Dubbo, Mordecai Himmelfarb, and Ruth Godbold in *Riders in the Chariot* (1961); Arthur Brown in *The Solid Mandala* (1966).

54. Most memorably, the characters of Mordecai Himmelfarb in *Riders in the Chariot* (1961) and Eudoxia/Eddie/Eadith in *The Twyborn Affair* (1979).

References

Anderson, J. (1962). *Studies in Empirical Philosophy*. Sydney: Angus and Robertson.

Aristotle. (1955) *The Politics*. Trans. Saunders, T.J. . Penguin: Harmondsworth.

Bradford, E. (1971). *Mediterranean Portrait of a Sea*. Harcourt: New York.

Briggs, A. (1982 [1963]). *Victorian Cities*. Harmondsworth: Penguin.

Carroll, J. (2007). *The Existential Jesus*. Melbourne: Scribe.

Carroll, J. (1997). 'What Poussin Knew,' *Quadrant* 41:7, July 1997.

Carroll, J. (2001). *The Western Dreaming*. Pymble, NSW: HarperCollins.

Carroll, J. (2004). *The Wreck of Western Culture*. Melbourne: Scribe.

Castoriadis, C. (1991). *Philosophy, Politics, Autonomy*. Oxford: Oxford University Press.

Childe, V.G. (1951). *Man Makes Himself*. New York: Mentor.

Crouch, H. (1993). 'Malaysia: Neither authoritarian nor democratic' In (Eds) K. Hewison, R. Robison & G. Rodan (eds) *Southeast Asia in the 1960s: Authoritarianism, Democracy and Capitalism*. Sydney: Allen and Unwin.

Crozier, M. (2003). 'Simultanagnosia, Sense of Place and the Garden Idea,' *Thesis Eleven* 74, pp. 76–88.

Downes, K. (1971). *Christopher Wren*. Penguin: London.

Drew, P. (1994). *The Coast Dwellers: A Radical Reappraisal of Australian Identity*. Ringwood, Victoria.

Edey, M.E. (1974). *The Sea Traders*. TimeLife: New York.

Feist, G.J. (1999). 'The Influence of Personality on Artistic and Scientific Creativity.' In R. J. Sternberg (ed.), *Handbook of Creativity*. Cambridge: Cambridge University Press, 273–296.

Fitzpatrick, B. (1946). *The Australian People 1788–1945*. Carlton: Melbourne University Press.

Goodman, G.K. (2000). *Japan and the Dutch 1600–1853*. Richmond: Curzon.

Haley, K.H.D. (1972). *The Dutch in the Seventeenth Century*. London: Thames and Hudson.

Hall, P. (1998). *Cities in Civilization: Culture, Innovation and Urban Order*. London: Phoenix.

Hanson, V.D. (2002). *Why The West Has Won: Nine Landmark Battles in the Brutal History of Western Victory*. London: Faber.

Harden, D. (1971). *The Phoenicians*. Harmondsworth: Penguin.

Hobbes, T. (1962). *Leviathan*. Ed. John Plamenatz. Collins: Fontana.

Hobbes, T. (1972). *Man and Citizen* (De Homine *and* De Cive). Ed. Bernard Gert. New York: Humanities Press.

Hogan, T. (2003). "Nature Strip': Australian Suburbia and the Enculturation of Nature,' *Thesis Eleven* 74, 54–75.

Howard, M. E. (1962). 'The Armed Forces.' In *The New Cambridge Modern History* XI [Material Progress and World-Wide Problems 1870–98]. Cambridge: Cambridge University Press.

Huntington, S. (1996). *The Clash of Civilizations and the Remaking of World Order*. New York: Simon and Schuster.

Inkster, I. & and Todd, J. (1988). 'Support for scientific enterprise, 1850–1900.' In R.W. Home (Ed.) *Australian Science in the Making*. Cambridge: Cambridge University Press.

Kaku, M. (1995). *Hyperspace*. New York: Doubleday.

Koestler, A. (1964). *The Act of Creation*. New York: Dell.

MacIntyre, S. (1999). *A Concise History of Australia*. Oxford: Oxford University Press.

Mackinder, H. (1981). *Democratic ideals and reality: a study in the politics of reconstruction*. New York: Greenwood.

Martin, H.J. (1994 [1988]). *The History and Power of Writing*. Chicago: University of Chicago Press.

Marx, K. (1967). *Capital* Volume 1. New York: International Publishers.

Marx, K. (1973). *Grundrisse*. Harmondsworth: Penguin.

Marx, K. (1962). *Selected Works* Volume 1. Moscow: Progress Publishers.

Marx, L. (1964). *The Machine in the Garden: Technology and the Pastoral Idea in America*. Oxford: Oxford University Press.

Mattelart, A. (2000 [1996]). *Networking the World 1794–2000*. Minneapolis: University of Minnesota Press.

Modelski, G. (1987). *Long Cycles in World Politics*. London: Macmillan.

Murphy, P. & D. Roberts. (2004). *Dialectic of Romanticism: A Critique of Modernism*. London: Continuum.

Murphy, P. (1983). 'Moralities, Rule Choice, and the Universal Legislator.' *Social Research*, 50:4, 757–801.

Murphy, P. (1994). 'Pluralism and Politics.' In John Burnheim (Ed.) *The Social Philosophy of Agnes Heller*. Amsterdam: Editions Rodopi, 193–238.

Murphy, P. (2001a). *Civic Justice: From Ancient Greece to the Modern World*. Amherst, NY: Humanity Books.

Murphy, P. (2001b). 'Marine Reason,' *Thesis Eleven* 67, 11–38.

Murphy, P. (2004). 'The City of Ideas: Cavafy as a Philosopher of History.' *Modern Greek Studies* 11/12, 75–102.

Murphy, P. 2009. 'Sacred Icon: Jørn Utzon's Sydney Opera House' in Makarand Paranjape (Ed) *Sacred Australia*. Melbourne: Clouds of Magellan.

Murphy, P. (2009 forthcoming). 'The power and the imagination: the enigmatic state in Shakespeare's English history plays.' *Revue Internationale de Philosophie*. Brussells: Presses Universitaires de France.

Murray, C. (2003). *Human Accomplishment*. New York: HarperCollins.

Rothenberg, A. (1979). *The Emerging Goddess: The Creative Process in Art, Science, and Other Fields*. Chicago: University of Chicago Press.

Scruton, R. (2000). *England: An Elegy*. London: Continuum.

Serle, A.G. (1963). *The Golden Age: A History of the Colony of Victoria 1851–1861*. Carlton: Melbourne University Press.

Steinberg, S.H. (1955) *Five Hundred Years of Printing*. Harmondsworth: Penguin.

Summerson, J. (1978 [1945]). *Georgian London*. Harmondsworth: Penguin.

White, P. (1961) *Riders in the Chariot*. London: Eyre & Spottiswoode.

White, P. (1966) *The Solid Mandala*. New York: Viking Press.

White, P. (1979) *The Twyborn Affair*. London: Cape.

Williams, B. (1988). 'Wealth, Innovation, and Education.' In *Australia: The Daedalus Symposium*. Ed. Graubard, S.R. Sydney: Angus and Robertson, 281–291.

CHAPTER 5

Space, Mobility and Synchrony in the Knowledge Economy

◻ Simon Marginson

A break in space-time

On Saturday 7 February 2009 it was 46.4 C (115.5 F) in Melbourne, a city of almost four million people, capital of the state of Victoria on the southern coast of Australia. Though a temperature of 46 (115) would not seem strange to citizens of Tucson or Riyadh or Khartoum, in Melbourne it was the highest reading since the British settlement was founded in 1834.

The continent of Australia is located north of the Southern Ocean. This great body of water stretches right around the earth. It has extraordinary momentum and gigantic swell, the most fearsome stretch of water for shipping on the planet. The circumpolar Antarctic current flows through the Southern Ocean, moving from west to east. It regulates the oceans and the weather of the world and has done so since the Australian plate broke away from the Antarctic 60 million years ago and moved north, enabling the present current to form. One effect of the polar current is that most of Australia is arid. Summer in the southern parts is hot and dry.

The number one problem is fire. The dominant flora in the countryside are eucalypts. These are beautiful trees in their natural setting, but their oil burns readily when there has been little rain for months and the hot north winds are blowing from the centre of the continent. With bushfires an annual event, protocols for protecting life and property have developed. Victorians have become accustomed to fires that fall within the observed range of speeds and with a known intensity based on an identifiable set of global ecological conditions. They know how these fires behave and how to manage them. Residential and commercial zones in rural areas and on the city fringe are surrounded by fire breaks created at public expense, and each individual home is enclosed by another no-burn space around it. Householders are warned of approaching fires as early as possible by the public authorities. At that point residents have the legal choice of either fleeing the fire and leaving their property, or staying to protect the houses, outbuildings, and in the case of farmers the animal stock. These are vulnerable to the smaller fires generated by flying embers propelled from the main fire-front, which should have been held at bay by the fire breaks. In other words, the protocols for regulating human conduct in the face of bushfires have been carefully crafted on the basis of a defined spatiality, a particular space-time configuration, reinforced regularly by experience of the natural world.

But in Melbourne climate and weather are changing, as they are changing in many other places. Through the interface of climate with natural and social systems, this is creating new potentialities in the spatiality of those systems. In the last two decades rainfall in the city has fallen to a level which is just over half the historic annual average. The winds that bring rain to southern Australia are synchronized with the Antarctic current. They blow across the continent from the Indian Ocean west of Perth till they eventually reach Melbourne on the southeastern side. Climatologists have identified a heating pattern in the Indian Ocean that is weakening the intensity of these rain bearing winds. Inexorably the whole of southern Australia is becoming hotter and drier. Inland towns are running out of water. The desert spreads, turning cattle country into late Permian landscapes bare of vegetation. In vegetated areas closer to the coasts and the Eastern ranges, where there is still some rainfall, the annual fire danger is growing.

The vectors of space and time that comprise our world and structure our subjectivity lie at the core of the way we live. At any given time they seem eternal to us. They scarcely need to be articulated. They are taken for granted. But space-time is not eternal, it is a human construct. It is also continually conditioned by the experiential world, in which spatial materialities alter as the result of human actions and natural events, and this in turn changes our subjective potentials. The natural conditions underlying human experience vary more slowly than the cultural forms that we use to interpret those natural conditions. But even those natural conditions are not fixed in stone. All things must pass; and this is as true of the global vectors of space and time (natural, social, natural/social/cultural) as anything else.

When the natural, social and/or cultural conditions change sufficiently, our experience of movement through space is transformed. Our spatiality changes. Perceptions of time change with it. We feel the changes in spatiality as novelties of location, distance or tempo. Our old version of space-time 'breaks,' and new kinds of space-time become possible. Sometimes we are conscious that humans have chosen a space-time break, as in the intensified global cultural changes in the late 1960s. Other space-time breaks seem to have been generated from outside us, as in the case of changes in the ecology of the planet. Likewise, many people around the world experience global communicative convergence and knowledge flows across borders as an external force. For many people also, the 2008/9 global financial crisis and world recession, synchronized to a degree unprecedented in economic history and flowing to all parts of the world at speed, hit them as an external force beyond human control. However, even in the case of global ecology, the global economy and globalizing communications, past human actions contributed to the space-time changes. And the new spatialities, the space-time configurations that we create from the range of options before us, are within our control.

Perhaps the global vectors of space and time are more open to change than they were. Perhaps also this is one of the signature features of the age of the global knowledge economy. Certainly, the global dimension is more important to us than before. We feel global ecology, global economy and global cultural systems directly. Changes in each affect the others.

On the morning of 7 February a hot north wind was blowing, and as the temperature rose, fires began to break out across the state of Victoria, some apparently spontaneous and others deliberately lit. In the wooded zone 50–75 kilometres north of the city of Melbourne lines of fire raced forward, pointing from north to south in the direction of the wind with a narrow front facing the city. Then in the afternoon, as the heat climbed towards 46C the wind changed direction, swinging round to west south west and becoming stronger. It pushed across the long thin lines of fire stretching north-south and turned them into wide fronts advancing east.

Smaller fires became joined into larger and gathered unprecedented speed and intensity, roaring through the tinder-dry bush. Balls of flame shot forward ahead of the firefront, and the fires attained a mighty height, walls of flame that stretched up to 70 metres in the air. There was little time. Some communities were warned of the approaching firefront less than ten minutes before it hit. Many decided to stay on defend the homes, as they had in previous years, until they realized what they were up against. Others decided to leave immediately. For both groups, though they did not know it, global conditions had so changed that the old space-time perceptions and established protocols were now obsolete. The previous calculations of fire movement across space and time were about to be overturned. Those who wanted to survive the fire no longer had an option to stay and defend their property or to shelter inside their homes; and for some who decided to leave it was already too late.[1]

The fires powered into the vicinity of the townships of Kinglake and Kinglake West, Strathewen, and Marysville with almost lightning speed, moving from treetop to treetop and jumping the long fire breaks that had been designed to stop them. When people realized the fire was close to the town it was already on them. Even before the fire reached many of the houses they exploded into flame. The radiant heat ignited domestic gas cylinders, killing those who were still inside their homes, aside from a few people with access to basements. This had never happened in bushfires before. These fires were much hotter than their predecessors. Temperatures close to the front reached 800 C. As people ran for their cars some were incinerated by the radiant heat. Nor could those who reached their cars a little ahead of the fire escape that way, because the firefront was travelling at 120–130 kph and it caught them on the road. Others perished as they ran across open fields: all hope and all life lost as they were enveloped by the great roaring wall of flame.

Some bodies were consumed so completely that the remains could scarcely be discerned or separated one from another.[2] The deaths cannot finally be known. The best estimate is 178. 'Black Saturday' in Victoria was as bad as it gets and after the fires there was a protracted debate about fire management, which dug deep into the old assumptions about the possible. One suspects that this debate was just the beginning of a transformation in spatially-vectored practice. The latest scientific consensus suggests prospects of a rise of average global temperature by up to 6 C by the year 2100, making the earth hotter than at any time since the Oligocene 30 millions years ago; associated with further Antarctic ice melt, a possible rise in worldwide sea levels of 6 metres and the substantial advance of desert in regions like southern Australia.[3] This suggests that in future we will see a sharper space-time 'break' than in 2009, in the conditions of fire management.

We find that just as the first global communicative community is emerging, with its vast opportunities for humans to fashion space-time for themselves, together, the one-world ecology has burst upon us with an unstoppable material as well as subjective force. To compound this coincidence of global events, it is happening at a time when the financial and industrial economies, which are more globally synchronized than ever before, are caught in a common disaster. Even so there are a broad range of strategic options for the way we order the new ecologically-sensitive spatiality and thereby order ourselves. And if that is true even of our handling of climate change, with its brute facts that demand a speedy response, it is doubly true of the global knowledge economy, which is where the solutions to global financial crisis and global ecological transformation will be discovered, brokered and disseminated.

This chapter is about how we understand global movement (mobility) and convergence, and global space-time, and how these are playing out in our imaginings and actions. The objective of the chapter is to grasp more closely the new spatiality of the knowledge economy, which shapes our handling of climate change and fire management and so much else. The knowledge economy is fertile ground for novel forms of space making. As with the handling of climate change, innovations in the k-economy are associated with changing space-time coordinates. As with climate change, both outer-direction and inner-direction are at play. Some of the global initiatives in knowledge production and in education can be understood as responses to new space-time vectors, to changed conditions: changes driven by global technologies that alter space, and also by the moves of other human agents. Other global initiatives are more clearly original, and themselves constitute new conditions and sensibilities in the global knowledge economy. All of this contributes to the creation of the global.

Mobility

To say that globalization is associated with the growing mobility of people, communications, ideas, knowledge, technologies and capitals is to repeat a truism. But how potent is global mobility in face of the channels and barriers which also constitute our world? How might we give definition to global mobility in order to better grasp its potentials? The terms we use to explore global movement are 'global networks,' 'global flows' and 'global technologies.' There is a long literature that turns 'networks' inside out. But there has been little interrogation of the term 'flows', while the use of 'technologies' is problematic. We will begin with flows.

Flows

Why has the liquid metaphor of 'flows' become so central to the discussion of cross-border relations and effects? The first need is to explain communicative globalization: the emergence of one-world systems operating in real time in communication, information and finance. This momentous change in human affairs is still reverberating through our lives, our imaginations and our vocabularies, and it is still only half understood. Between them, 'flows' and 'networks,' which invoke water and electricity respectively—ways of talking about connectedness that have been drawn from different parts of our history—carry some of the sensibilities of moving and joining, of soaking and flooding, of linkages, circuits and systems bearing power, that talk to our sense of living in the global. 'Flows' and 'networks,' which are everywhere, allow us to escape Cartesian notions of linear cause and effect set by a pre-global age. This is not a small achievement. More than effects of globalization, 'flows' are carriers of global effects and creators of global effects that keep on circulating in continuous feedback loops, so that in a sense the global flows *are* globalization and we begin to free ourselves from the notion of globalization as an invisible essence. In this ubiquity, that is also a refusal of closure (a refusal that is threatening for some and liberating for others) we feel ourselves moving closer to what is distinctive about our present, which is the thing that we seek.

But there is more to it than this. Old habits die hard. We evade the notion of globalization as an invisible essence only to universalize, all too easily, the global flows themselves. And the term 'global flows' encourages us to do this. 'Flows' carries a pervasive seductive sense of being carried along with gentle motion; so that the other-determined becomes inevitable, irresistible; an imperative to read the trends and go with the times; in other words, to surrender to our fate. This ought to set our alarm bells ringing. After all technologies are inscribed in social and economic life, they enable cultural practices, they are deployed by identifiable interests. Do we want the language that we use to advance this? 'Global flows' offer the familiar promises of modernity: the prestige and wealth offered to those whose method is to manage time, those who adroitly position themselves just under the top of the wave as it breaks. But in letting ourselves be carried along in this manner our sense of agency disappears. Swept forward by 'globalization' or 'competition' or some other unstoppable structural force, we forget about older questions like 'is this the kind of world that we really want?'

The conventional utilities of the term 'global flows' do not destroy its potential as an analytical and explanatory tool. If we condemn a concept by the company it keeps, rather than understanding it as a zone for exploration and conversation, then the terms 'democracy,' 'equality,' 'globalization' itself, and many others would be lost to scholarly use; and much good work of the last two decades would have to be rewritten. But what can 'flows' tell us about what is distinctive about the global in the knowledge economy? If we want to know agency and make choices, 'flows' will not get us there. Something more is needed.

Technologies

In the first mainstream discussion of communicative globalization in the 1990s, political economists and social theorists wrestled in an ungainly fashion with the effects of technologies. Was global convergence a function of communications and transport? Or were world markets the decisive cause, as the neo-liberal imaginary suggested, driving white hot technical innovation and the NASDAQ industries and the rivers of gold they were going to bring? Discussion oscillated between technological determinism and economic determinism, both of them externalized, abstracted from the realm of human subjects. But there was an afterthought. Was there something 'cultural' at work? Where did that fit in to technology?

Since then the theoretical ground has shifted. Most commentators now agree that communications are foundational to what is new about globalization in this era; that globalization and the knowledge economy embrace economic and cultural changes together; that they are manifest in many spheres of life; and they are associated with new behaviours. It is hard to ignore the impact of networked technologies, virtual worlds and knowledge abundance on, say, work, or friendship. These insights have triggered a weakening of economic determinism, even though it retains its hold on mainstream political discourses. For it is clear that in the global setting (and other settings) people do *not* do things for money alone. They also create science and art and global forms for other reasons. How else can we explain social networking and open source knowledge which have grown much faster than world markets? Far from globalization being an artefact of neo-liberal government and world markets, as the advocates and critics of economic globalization have often claimed, in many respects global creation is an *alternative* to the neo-liberal project. University executives often flourish the symbols and talk the talk of corporate capitalism. Yet often they pursue non-capitalist ends. Consider: offshore research ventures rarely make money. They are mostly subsidized and at a high price. But every university president and research professor wants to maximize them. Which is not to say that economics is out of the picture. Creativity has many traffic conditions and cars and drivers. Much of the dynamism of creativity in the age of the global knowledge economy (and any age) has economic roots. Creativity also has economic manifestations and outcomes. Basic research is the ultimate source of most of the innovations in business and industry. University research trains those industry personnel who innovate.

It has also become more widely recognized that the Internet and air-transport (virtual and corporeal flight) are *necessary but not sufficient conditions* of the global knowledge economy. Material changes in technologies open up new human practices, with endogenous effects that accumulate over time. The resulting evolution, often spontaneous and unpredicted, races ahead of profit-making and all deliberative intentions. It is true that the vectors of space and time have been dramatically altered by communicative ecology and travel. Yet those same global technologies and systems are created and exploited by human subjects.

Technologies are fecund tools for exploration. They expand the range of our experiences. At the same time, in determining how we move across space and in shaping the horizons of what we can see, technologies also set boundaries and blockages of the imagination (though these limits are also constantly changing). Each single technology, just like every act of thought, illuminates some things only by placing other things in shadow. We always see the part and we imagine that we see the whole only by blinding ourselves to our own ignorance. Nevertheless it does seem that in the age of the global knowledge economy our total mental capabilities are expanding. We multiply our means of reflexivity. There is an ever growing set of models, templates, grids, rules and questions with which to interrogate our mentality, its ideas and its artifacts. There are ever better search engines, ever more works at our disposal, ever more permutations of imagining, ever more means of synthesis.

Whether our stellar creations are increasing—as distinct from the growth that we can see in mental capabilities—is a different and more problematic question for us.

Space and space making

Space and time are the vectors of our world. And as Kant, Hegel[4] and Heidegger were all at pains to point out 'space' and 'time,' which frame our understanding of the world, embody an essential subjective element. They are shaped by us. Hegel argued against the notion of space as 'one thing,' as a kind of universal out-there. It can have more than one character, he said.[5] This insight is crucial to understanding the global dimension and the space-forming strategies that have emerged in the wake of communicative globalization and are constructing that global dimension. The world in which we live our lives is not 'present-at-hand in space,' to use Heidegger's term.[6] The materiality of the physical universe can be interpreted in a very wide range of ways. The civilization of the Maya in pre-Columbian America produced a brilliant astronomical calendar based on a circular rather than linear notion of time. The 'aroundness' of space (Heidegger) and our spatialities, our understandings of space within that aroundness, are human constructs.[7] In many respects the spatial forms we inhabit have been brought into being by human activities: by our imaginings, by our productive activities, by the kinds of policy and regulation we employ.

In *Being and Time* Heidegger engaged in an extended discussion of subjective modes of space making.[8] He talked of 'insideness,' the process whereby we create an enclosed space for ourselves. He also talked about the process of 'de-severing,' the mental process whereby we bring remote locations close to us and vanish physical distance. 'De-severing' is a crucial notion for understanding global space-time. Space and closeness are not simple functions of physical distance or the speed of messaging. '"De-severing",' said Heidegger, 'amounts to making the farness vanish—that is, making the remoteness of something disappear, bringing it close.'[9] He noted that de-severing is essential to modernity. In *Being and Time* (1962/1926) Heidegger remarked that 'all the ways in which we speed things up, as we are more or less compelled to do today, push us on towards the conquest of remoteness.' De-severing is accomplished 'in a purely cognitive manner' and it can also be powerfully conditioned by technology. Heidegger's example was the radio. Through the radio our everyday environment is so expanded that we have accomplished 'a de-severance of the world.'[10]

In the age of the knowledge economy air travel and geo-navigation and facility in the realms of the virtual have rendered de-severing more central to the way we live. It seems that no place on earth is now beyond our imagined proximity. There are no more 'secret islands,' no more 'lands that time forgot,' those essential motifs of nineteenth century fiction, Moreover, and in contrast with Heidegger's account of de-severing, in bringing the remote places close to us, we do not forgo communication with our immediate environment which he called the 'ready-at-hand.'[11] For example, there is no necessary tradeoff between the virtual environment and the environment of our bodies. We have become masters of the multiple location for whom each and every distance is relativized; and each act of relativization, each de-severing, is beginning to intersect with all the others. We experience the 'ready-at-hand' and the far distant place simultaneously. This is an astounding change. It is might seem easy to jump from de-severing into hyper-space, into hubris, into the notion we can imagine anything and make anything. But like all techniques, de-severing has its limits. However much that we shrink space and time in our minds towards a single point, we have yet to abolish them.

For physical space is always there. It was there before we inhabited the earth and it will still be there after we have gone. Heidegger distinguished the spatial universe of the human subject, 'being-in-the world,' from the 'reality' of the world. Space is plastic. We shrink and elongate space at will. We use our technologies (Heidegger's example was the radio) and our minds to change our spatiality. We rework the coordinates of the beings, the institutions and the other objects we encounter. In placing all the different entities, while locating ourselves in one moment above them *and* among them, we constitute a strategic landscape for ourselves:

> When we let entities within-the-world be encountered in the way which is constitutive for Being-in-the-world, we 'give them space.' This 'giving space,' which we also call 'making room' for them, consists in freeing the ready-to-hand for its spatiality. As a way of discovering and presenting a possible totality of spaces determined by involvements, this making room is what makes possible one's factical orientation at the time. In concerning

itself circumspectively with the world, [we] can move things around or out of the way or 'make room' for them.[12]

In the path dependent institutional settings of government, traditional universities and innovation systems, few people can be said to determine spatiality. Most people work with spatial constructs inherited from the past, or spatial strategies of another's devising. 'Those who define the material practices, forms, and meanings of money, time or space fix certain basic rules of the social game,' noted Harvey.[13] In the global setting, which is largely unmade and unmapped, social relations are 'flatter' and there is more scope for venture and adventure than in other dimensions of life. There is a larger freedom to 'make room' for ourselves.

Place

Given this plasticity, the malleability of space, how important then is place or location within the strategic landscape of the knowledge economy? In one sense place is everything, or at least the starting point for everything else. Place is the platform on which human agency is erected. Place is identity. Place is the concentration of space and time taken together. 'The Here is at the same time a Now, or it is the point of duration. This unity of Here and Now is Place' (Hegel).[14] Yet in the global setting we find that place is less constant than it once was. Some locations are sites in which mobility is uppermost, such as some research centres in Singapore. Many people, and institutions, now live in more than one place. Some agents claim for themselves a strategic advantage in having no place at all and a license to roam free across the globe. Or their place lies in passage, in global movement itself, as if they are inhabitants of the void (and sometimes airport lounges and the absences that they create bring us close to imagining the void). As we shall see, this mobility and multiplicity of the 'here and now' is one of the primary features of the global spatial strategies of universities. By changing location within the global field institutions and individuals create differing potentials. For example, by centring some of their activities offshore, and by referencing their own performance against the global disciplines rather than comparators within the nation, research universities are able to secure a partial independence from regulation by national government. At the same time they experience places other than their own, positioned in observable ways, as a field of opportunity. 'As spatial barriers diminish we become more sensitive to what the world's spaces contain.'[15] In short the importance of place in the knowledge economy lies not just in its fixity but in its alterity. The paradox is that each quality is necessary to the other.

Boundaries and boundary making have also changed in the global setting. Boundary making has always been significant in human affairs: it is as a primary means of defining identity, interest, coverage, ambition and reach. Boundary making allows us the place an 'other' beyond the boundary and shape the self in opposition to it. At the same time the creation of a spatial horizon makes it possible to imagine a move beyond the horizon. Thus Hadrian's Wall in Roman Britain, and the Great Wall in China, were simultaneously means of identifying, understanding, excluding and managing the 'barbarian world' beyond.[16] But the spatial dynamic of globalization is radically different. In the process of global convergence, the other begins to disappear. Everything becomes placed inside the margin of the world. All is part of 'us.' We can still create boundaries within the world, but only in the form of cultural creations, which are arbitrary and always vulnerable to re-negotiation. Wall building, the old strategy of naturalizing social-cultural borders in geo-spatial terms, is no longer accessible.

If there is a founding historical moment in the formation of the global mentality, as noted in Chapter 1, it lies in the conjunction of two sixteenth century events. The first event was the circumnavigation of the world by Magellan's expedition in 1522. The second was the assertion by Copernicus that the earth was round, that it circled the sun and it was not the centre of the universe; a conclusion he reached around 1510 but did not publish until 1543. At that point it became possible to model the earth as a sphere, to mount it on a table and locate oneself outside it in the sun position. It was a powerful image. It captured attention in its day: 'The Globe' was the title of Shakespeare's theatre. Visualization is essential to imagining. But neither Magellan's expedition nor Copernicus could actually see the earth spinning in space, and thereby complete the process of boundary definition, externalisation of the self in relation to the natural and human world, and inclusion of the other within the purview of the self, in a spatial setting in which the other was subordinated. The second stage in the visualization of global space was when the image of the planet in space beamed back from the 1960s astronauts and cosmonauts. From that moment we could see the edge of the world and mark it as the boundary of our condition. Only then could we fully grasp the interdependence, the boundedness, the singularity of the global dimension. Only then was it possible to surmount the world as a whole, strategically, from an imagined position outside it and above it.

Space-time

Nevertheless, space is not solely something in our minds. There is an irreducible materiality about space. Heidegger remarked that it is when we focus on objective distances that we uncover 'the "reality" of the world at its most real.'[17] This distinguishes space from time. Time is pre-eminent in our social practices, and also pre-eminent in the interpretations of those practices by social theory as David Harvey noted.[18] 'Economy of time, to this all economy ultimately reduces itself' (Marx).[19] But what is the materiality in time, in duration itself, that matches the 'thereness' that we find in the physical universe, the thereness that is altered by transport and communications? When we first reached all parts of the solar system via radio communication, the solar system was experienced as a single space for the first time. We could cross it end to end almost instantaneously. But though a new space was opened up by radio communication, in which distance as measured by time had become radically shortened for us, the passage of time as such was not altered. We can experience time differently, we can manage time differently, but duration itself is not plastic in the material sense.

Our fiction is filled with ideas of moving forward in time, backward in time, the suspension of time, differential rates of ageing, wistful longings for eternal youth, and so forth. But time is impervious to our imagining and our technologies. It is not plastic in the same manner as space. Despite the metaphor of time as the fourth dimension of space, space-time constitutes a heterogeneous couple.[20] In space making there is a reciprocal relation between the subjective and the objective not evident in the case of time. Globalization as a process of convergence does not 're-make time.' Nor does it enable humans to re-make time. Rather, space making and the conquest of distance create a changing experience of time.

As has often been pointed out by theorists of the space-time potentials of the global knowledge economy, notably the early contribution by Harvey on *The Conditions of Post-Modernity*[21] and the trilogy by Manuel Castells on *The Information Society,*[22] we perceive the global changes in spatiality as space-time compression. We experience shorter durations, heightened instantaneousness, and a greater potential and desire for temporal synchrony. It is important to emphasize that in the global knowledge economy, space is altered by *both* objective and subjective changes. On the objective side space is changed for us and this affects the possible choices. On the subjective side, we engage in space making strategies that we select from this range of possible choices. Spatial changes in climate and weather, in wind velocity, the distribution of rainfall and of fire-risk, created new space-time potentials in the ecology of southern Australia. Likewise, a succession of changes in spatial potentials have made it possible to imagine the space-times accessible to us in the global knowledge economy: the synchronous linking of locations by telegraph and telephone in the nineteenth century; the spread and cheapening of air travel in the second half of the twentieth century; and above all the abolition of distance in complex communications though the virtual sociability created by the Internet, in the context of our growing propensity for global synchrony. In synchronous world-wide communications and complex data transfer, in the shortening of travel distance-as-time, in our ease of virtual travel and instantaneous communications from the other side of the world, global community has an immediacy and depth that the Romans, the Tang, the Mongol horsemen, the Portuguese and Spanish, and the British—all of whom in their time were masters in managing physical distances over land or sea—never knew.

Space making

In sum, space making, which is the creation of global spatiality, is the construction of the global dimension as a set of spatial relations. Material space is a given, but there is always more to space and spatiality than this, including the scope for deliberate space making and the effects of new spatialities in our experience of time. The global spatial strategies of universities and their agents, and of governments and national higher education systems, which are the topic of chapter 6, can be variously observed as acts of the imagination, acts of production and acts of regulation. Space making involves distinct and observable acts of economic and cultural production.

Space making also derives from policy and regulation: governments have always governed in and through space. Further, and especially in global spatiality, where the potentials are relatively novel and the terrain more open than at national level,[23] space making strategies in higher education can involve acts of radical imagining.

It is important not to lose sight of the subjective factor, the scope for imagination and choice. We cannot derive changes in the perceptions of space-time in linear fashion, from quantitative changes in the speed and cost of travel or in the extent of the Internet. To repeat the point, the changes in material spatial conditions, especially in the capacity to communicate and synchronize across borders, have provided new potentials for imagining and creating spatial forays. The precise contents of the global imaginings and strategies in the university sector cannot be predicted on the basis of the material shifts in space any more than the fathomless depths of the piano solos in Mozart's 22nd concerto can be derived from the urban economy of eighteenth century Vienna or the vicissitudes of Hapsburg policy on the Ottoman border. Global space making does *not* mean the 'discovery' of a new set of 'natural' relations, borders or territories put in place by globalization, or inherent to or necessary to it. Even if globalization was so predictable, and it is not, spatiality is always constructed by human agents. Globalization re-makes space, and enables and compels us to re-make space. Space making occurs within identifiable limits. Within those limits are many possibilities.

Openness and freedoms

Like all social settings, the global dimension of human activity does not *exhaustively* determine our mentalities, groups, practices or personal trajectories. We are never entirely determined by class, culture, language, country, history or planet. We are thinking, practicing beings with the capacity to dream dreams and make choices. We can alter our fate, within limits, providing we have the resources with which to do so. But all else being equal, our conditions and histories affect our desires, perceptions and choices. The circumstances in which we find ourselves suggest certain things to us. They tend to highlight some possibilities rather than others. Life is a continuing dialectic between the settings in which we live and ourselves as self-determining agents. This is as true of the global dimension as the local dimension. What is distinctive about the global dimension is that in going global we find that new freedoms are opening up. There is more scope for human agency in the more global setting than there was prior to communicative globalization and the knowledge economy.

One reason is that when compared to the local and national dimensions we find that the global realm is unusually open in the scope for initiative and action. The scope for action rests on the capacity to act. The capacity to act globally is partly a matter of raw economics, the cost of plane travel and of communications infrastructure. It is partly a matter of political economy and the stability of nation-states, for example the ability to sustain long-term research programs. But in the weightless world of information, knowledge and virtual networking the capacity to act is more cultural than economic. It takes in language of use and the space for innovations. Here global freedoms are within reach of every child with access to the Internet. It is easier for children at ease with English and mathematics, again reminding us that the distribution of global capacities is highly uneven and unfair. Even so this is an epochal expansion of free creative potentials. Consider also the coordination of the science of global climate change. The global setting allows us to configure complex information on the basis of consensus. We begin to approach the world mind. In the global setting individual and institutional agents reach further and have an enhanced capacity for alliances. The field of initiative is vaster. It seems that we make up the rules as we go. We seize and create global opportunities at the same time. In doing so we continually create the global dimension itself.

Kant talked about one form of freedom, 'freedom in its cosmological meaning,' as the power of spontaneously originating an event or a state of being.[24] In that sense the creation of the global dimension is an act of freedom. This new global openness and freedom have little in common with the romanticism of marketing prospectuses, which seems undiminished by the global recession; or the hyper-claims of Internet educational enterprises; or tourism in which freedom is always an escape into leisure and hedonism. The new global freedoms are more than illusions, and they are incessant and demanding and not always comfortable. In the global dimension, both negative and positive freedoms are enhanced. In the absence of a global state, with little regulation, we range beyond nation-states and their tools of constraint and control. Hence the neo-liberal enthusiasm for market globalization in the 1990s. For neo-liberalism negative freedom sui generis, freedom as freedom from constraint by the state, is sufficient. The contradiction is that in the global dimension as in all social settings, freedom requires also the capacity to act. It requires positive freedom, and it requires this in the global context. We must become global selves and part of the global dimension. Otherwise the global dimension confronts us solely as an external constraint on our local and national selves. Here global cultural capacity, which confers on us global personality and the means of communicative initiative, is all important. We cannot put a price on the value of an email address and a website in this era. In turn the enhanced negative and positive freedoms provide more favourable conditions for what Amartya Sen[25] calls 'agency freedom,' the liberty of the will which fashions itself even as it fashions its settings.[26] Agency freedom entails self-determination within the shifting limits of the global. It is the liberty of the human agent *for itself* and its own project, not just of itself and still subject to external causation.[27]

Self-will alone does not ensure creativity. Openness to the world and its possibilities is the sea in which the creator swims. But where to swim? Possibility is not actuality. The will that becomes locked into internal brooding on the infinite range of possibilities has lost itself. The totality that is harboured within asserts itself in the manner of an external determination. The self-determining agent sets aside both other-determination, and the personal striving for absolute openness as totality. Personal acts of creativity embody not just attention to the prospect of the world and to the range of possibilities within it but closures as well, the refusal of the paths not taken. Acts of creativity embody both openness and closure. It is a necessary antinomy. 'Only by resolving can a human being step into actuality' (Hegel). Hegel quoted Goethe: 'Whosoever wills something great must be able to restrict himself.'[28]

For the self-determining human agent, life is a succession of creations and self-creations. Causality implies identity and dependence. Escaping from causality makes independence, difference and Mozartian originality possible. If freedom lies in the escape from causality, including the refusal of totality, while at the same time enhancing our potentials for both voluntary action and contingency, then the realm of the global is quintessentially free.

And yet these global freedoms and creative potentials are both within and beyond our control. The global dimension is the visible consequence of our actions. It is also unknown to us. In the continuing formation of the global knowledge economy, the acts of creation by all of the different agents interact with each other with outcomes that are not foreseen or devised. The endogenous evolution of the global is irreducibly complex and subject to unpredictable events and developments. It changes the conditions of human agency and changes that agency itself, so that we ourselves are being continually created and recreated. This imposes limits on us. The global dimension is like all aspects of the social in that we experience it as one of the conditions of freedom. We are both subjects of the global and are subject to it. We experience the global setting both as a field of our own creation and as an objective force confronting us. Freedom is enlarged, the global is enlarged, and the stakes in global freedom are also larger. If freedom lies in escaping determination by nature and history, then global creation offers an enhanced potential for moves that take us beyond the constraints of nature and naturalized history. If so it is just in time. Nature is beginning to rebound on us with gigantic force.[29]

If openness is a defining feature of both the global dimension itself and of creativity and creative association in this era, this suggests that openness might be one of the clues to global creativity. Michael Peters expands on this theme in Chapters 8 and 9. A striking feature of policy and popular/media discussions of the global is that openness and mobility are nearly always presented in positive terms. One example is the free movement of skilled labour across borders, which is discussed in positive terms even in many nations that are in deficit in the global process of brain circulation. Yet global openness is not always easy to live with. As well as room to move, we crave a stable and predictable home to which we can return at will, the durable shelter against continuous modernization that Hannah Arendt talked about in *The Human Condition* (1998),[30] the solid location that we still imagine for ourselves within what Zygmunt Bauman called 'liquid' modernity.[31] When pressed, we crave certainty about the self. Global convergence, mobility and prolific cultural exchange have rendered agency more fraught, or at least human agency in the static categorical form commonly called 'identity' (to which many people cling like a life-raft even while it is transforming underneath them!), but there has been a shift within even these cravings for a stable home. There may be more than one such home. Multiple locations might be one kind of insurance against the disappearance of our origins. George Orwell talked about that sense of loss of self in *Coming up for Air* (2001/1939). The book's central character, George 'Fatty' Bowling, returns to the pristine place of his childhood in Lower Binfield, expecting to find the stillness and green water he remembers that he loved. He is devastated by its transformation into a housing development in which everything he knew and valued had vanished.[32]

Here, much depends not just on where but on how we position ourselves. If we believe that we belong to one soil and no other, then when our sense of place becomes destabilized we ourselves are destabilized with it. Yet in opening ourselves up to multiplicity we can also become hostages to it. When our locations are multiple, one inescapable consequence of this greater freedom of movement is that we are made more changeable, a process we never wholly control. While there is a thread of continuity in the self we transport from place to place, it is affected by successive encounters. It evolves. If this is freedom it is liberation by insecurity. Nevertheless, the variety and alterity that we derive from greater geo-spatial and linguistic-cultural mobility expand not just uncertainty but our creative range.

Even so, despite the broadening of choices that this entails, the creative possibilities before us are never infinite. The lesson of history is that creativity follows patterns and pathways as Peter Murphy discusses. Creativity is anchored in history as well as technology. Creators are also profoundly influenced by their needs and experiences. It is in the continuous interaction between our material practices and our imaginative resources that global creation is shaped. Our mentalities, our conditions and our lives seem to spiral upwards together.

Projects of closure

There is another constraint. It points to the indeterminate, sometimes over-managed and potentially politicized character of the global dimension. Not every action of global agents is designed to enlarge our common freedoms. The global dimension is cluttered with projects that set out to exploit, and often in that process to augment, its openness: a flurry of strategies designed to make and manage and manipulate its new potentials. Peter Murphy's chapters suggest that it always has. Global strategy making can be a little unnerving. It is a terrain always partly unknown that invokes a recurring tension between local pragmatism and bold cross-border initiatives. 'Can we afford to invest in this? Is this really core business' are the questions asked. But often the excitement is more compelling: 'Can we afford to miss out?' The opportunity costs of not going global bulk larger than the opportunity costs of not doing more for local stakeholders (sometimes, of course, local and global initiative go together). Here not every strategy is path-breaking. In the global setting individuals and organizations exhibit a mix of mimetic behaviour and innovation. They hunt down a trilogy of goals. All want to build global capacity. All seek global connectivity. These means are readily turned into ends in the minds of executive leaders. In turn capacity and connectivity are used to construct global relations, which is the third objective.

In these essays in strategy global spatiality and temporal rhythms are defined. Chapter 6 reflects on how the creation of global relations plays out in the range of space-making and space-using strategies in higher education and research.

The irony is that many strategies designed to open the global and work it as a virgin field are also intended to secure its closure. In the nineteenth century European settler states in the global south, in Argentina, South Africa and Australia, the first act of farmers in new terrain was to fence their claim. Soon after that they built a familiar garden of plants from the home country around the settler house, so forming an enclosure within the enclosure; the first enclosure territorial, the second cultural. In going global today, companies and universities try to seize a first mover advantage via status systems (for example the methods of ranking universities), market values (intellectual property) or nation-state decisions (favoured foreign provider status within a national education system) that create an enclosure and then busily work to turn that first mover advantage into something more permanent. Global enclosures serve several functions: for example as a means of defence and the protection of identity; and as a method of concentrating privilege while shutting the competition out, like the gated cities of the privileged in urban precincts around the world. University rankings and intellectual property rights use the classical instruments of status hierarchy and property ownership to turn global reach and openness into closure. Elite research universities advocate global systems for valuing knowledge that guarantee their interests first. Companies research the rainforest to monopolize its pharmaceutical potentials. Partnerships and consortia create new opportunities for some while shutting the others out. Global communications and knowledge spread English everywhere, creating a one-world cultural space by occluding all other languages. Americanization of the knowledge sector constitutes an enclosure that advances US interests abroad while protecting the hegemon at home from the challenges of global difference.

We have seen that the antinomy between openness and closure is endemic to acts of personal creativity. An antinomy between openness and closure might be endemic also to globalization. In this respect it resembles the oscillation between diversity and homogeneity, which is not identical with the antinomy between openness and closure, but partly overlaps with it. But not every closure is essential and desirable. Openness and closure both have implications for the play of interests and the imposition of hierarchy. We can evaluate global projects in terms of who gains from the moves to widen openness, who gains from the tactics of closure, and how deeply those closures become entrenched.

The oscillation between global opening and global closing, between the space for freedom and the certainty of causation, can take many different forms. In 2001 the 9/11 attack on civilians and military in the USA prompted a partial closure of the communicative trading globalization that had marked American foreign strategy in the Clinton era. The desire for trade did not stop. But the ethical basis for communicative globalization between the USA and the Muslim world was exploded; cross-border people movement between these zones was weakened and later the war in Iraq undermined trade as well. We can note here in passing that the hegemonic character of the Clinton brand of communicative globalization, which imposed on the world not only the universal use of the English language but Americanizing cultures of consumption, sexualization, sport and celebrity, was one of the conditions of 9/11, which savagely ruptured the common space to escape its contents, using the act of aggression to create a pre-global cultural zone protected by global military polarity.

As the symptoms of global warming accelerate these will prompt similar desires for particularist closures designed to protect established interests and familiar ways of life, cutting off the potential for new and combined solutions to new problems—in other words, closures that block the larger scope for global creation. All strategies embodying global closure are designed to protect the strategist against global contingency through an act of will, a small contingency pushed up against the larger.[33] But strategies of particularist closure have a two-fold price. First, once the closure is set, those executing such strategies have forgone the larger part of their own agency freedom in the global setting. Second, they deny agency freedoms to others, for whom such strategies are experienced as external determinations. But particularist strategies of closure always prove futile in the end. No one can evade global contingency for long, especially in the form of ecological transformation. This suggests a first principle for the politics of the global: *always keep the global dimension open for collaborative action.*

In other words, the larger irony is that sooner or later each successive closure is exploded. No global strategy is wholly or finally plausible. This is one of the paradoxes of the global. Every project designed to open the global and exploit that openness is also a closure, and a closure always doomed to fail. The spatial possibilities are almost infinite. And yet the passage of time ensures that finitude is never so apparent as in the global dimension, where the slow geological evolution of the planet is belied by the whirlings of culture. Each shift in the global setting confronts the pre-existing forms and enclosures with arbitrary force. The other side of the enhanced scope for agency freedom is the greater scope for contingency in the global era.

'Newness' in creativity

The successive obsolescence of all projects again underlines Arjun Appadurai's point that globalization is modernization writ large.[34] We have more freedom in self-making than ever. Correspondingly our capacity to install ourselves as permanent and transfix our descendants, embodying in cultural forms the evolutionary instinct to pass on our characteristics to our offspring, the driving force behind the pyramids of Giza and the Ming tombs in China and the skyline in New York, is reduced. The shortening of duration tends to flatten out differences in value between the various kinds of creation.[35] Is the knowledge economy doomed to the ephemeral? It would be easy to conclude that it is: that the difference between on one hand an award-winning 30 second commercial for soap, on the other Bach's 'innovation' in counterpoint or Haydn's development of the sonata form, has narrowed, meaning 'why bother', and thus we are less likely to dig deep inside ourselves. Yet great creations retain a power to move and inspire, a power that is continually renewed. And we know a good idea when we see one, even if its novelty is often more dazzling than its depth. Perhaps that was always the case.

The crucial point for the inquiry in *Global Creation* is that all these developments—the novel configurations of space and time and of the strategic spaces that we make for ourselves; the larger set of cultural forms now at our fingertips; the openness, the greater mobility, the new freedoms, the enhanced potentials for self-made agency with a more fecund set of reflexivities at our disposal—suggests there might be greater scope for non-path dependence (or at least lateral shifting) in creative work. *For more 'newness' in creativity.* On the other hand the compression of duration and the evident superficiality of most of what is disseminated globally suggest that profundity is all too readily emptied out. We suspect the jury is still out on the question of the scope for 'newness.' It bears watching. Whether the greater scope for newness, if any, is actually being realized in practice is another question.

Synchrony

Whether in the global dimension there is more scope for path-breaking creative work or not, the way we relate to each other has changed in important ways. This affects highly creative individuals along with the rest. Indeed, they are among the main contributors to the change.

Traditionally, creative work was divided between lone individuals, the model for scholars and some artists, and tightly knit groups who shared premises in one location. Group work in the artists' workshop, the musical academy or the sciences followed an apprenticeship system in which one or two creators were supreme and the younger members of the group were copyists, laboratory technicians or third violins. We now find that increasingly, creative work is organized between loosely tied individuals for whom electronically mediated networks and data transfer provide highly flexible systems for monitoring, producing and disseminating knowledge. The beauty of loose ties is that they sustain voluntary behaviour, encourage autonomy and are open to initiatives from all members of the group. They permit a larger diversity of perspectives than a command system, and can even (within limits) cut across the preexisting hierarchies. Potentially, loose networks magnify the role of intellectual merit as a regulative value, rather than status, and provide more space for innovations; which is not to say that networks automatically generate these benign effects.

How is it that loosely tied voluntary networks, ranging across borders, so often deliver the goods in creative work? The benefits of diverse talents, variety of perspectives and global standards are only part of the explanation. In a global environment both local diversity and common benchmarks can be accessed from any location. On the face of it the pull of local obligations should be stronger. Conventional organizational logic suggests that surely local command systems, career jobs and grounded loyalties are more motivating than loose voluntary networks. The answer is that electronically mediated networking positively *encourages* creative people to join with kindred spirits, and to synchronize with them in real time or close to real time on the basis of relatively 'flat' organizational relations. Electronically mediated synchrony provides for their needs. Why? Loosely tied networks happen because the technologies permit and encourage networks, and because people want them to happen. The first factor is much discussed. The second deserves more attention.

The term 'synchrony' (or synchronism) refers to concurrence at the same point in time. Kant referred to three modes of the temporality of the subject: duration, sequence and simultaneity-as-culmination.[36] To this we can add a fourth mode of temporal experience, synchrony. Synchrony is the sharing of time. Our time sense is always individualized; 'time is never promordially universal' as Heidegger put it.[37] To live in the same rhythm we must synchronize our time with the times of other people. Synchrony is essential to our sociability. It is especially important in the operations of people-heavy institutions such as schools and health care facilities, and foundational to co-production in intellectual and artistic life. One of the keys to globalization and to global creativity in the age of the global knowledge economy is that there has been a major change in the conditions of synchrony.

'Concurrence at the same point in time' is deeper than accidental coincidence. Synchrony is driven by our desire to relate to each other. Once synchrony is achieved, in familiarizing ourselves with each other it tends to reproduce that desire to relate. Global synchrony is more than simply establishing a communicative link across borders. It consists in living in a common time, for at least part of our lives. Global synchrony, which is the achievement of a common time space and rhythm with people located across national borders who could be anywhere in the world, is the temporal partner of the spatial practice of global de-severing, which is the process of imagining ourselves close to those in distant locations. Faster global mobility and the 'thicker' global traffic in people and ideas have better enabled both global de-severing and global synchrony while rendering them more attractive to us. The desire for global synchrony drives global de-severing. Global synchrony is its culmination and measure.

In the *Theory of Moral Sentiments* Adam Smith explored our need for human association. His findings about human sociability were brighter than Jonathan Swift's had been in *Gulliver's Travels*,[38] but then Adam Smith was always interested in how we behave at our best. He noted that people were adept in achieving an emotionally satisfactory harmony with strangers; and that much of the time, mutual understanding seemed to function as an end in itself.

> Generosity, humanity, kindness, compassion, mutual friendship and esteem, all the social and benevolent affections, when expressed in the countenance or behaviour, even towards those who are not peculiarly connected with ourselves, please the indifferent spectator upon almost every occasion.[39]

In sympathizing with others, he said we put ourselves in their shoes. We do so to a limited extent. Our own interests are mostly foremost. But we respect 'wisdom and virtue' in others and this motivates us to associate with them; and we appreciate concurrence, with its sense of 'fellow feeling.' We admire concurrence in others and it reinforces our sense of self.

> Nothing pleases us more than to observe in other men a fellow feeling with all the emotions of our own breast; nor are we ever so much shocked as by the appearance of the contrary....To approve of another man's opinions is to adopt those opinions, and to adopt them is to approve of them.[40]

In face-to-face conversation with a person, synchrony is achieved in what we talk about and the non verbal gestures and expressions that establish communication, as when eyes meet. We talk of 'reaching understanding' after a pleasing encounter. There is 'chemistry.' But there is also the social and emotional noise that accompanies a face-to-face encounter, information that contributes nothing to synergy; and visual symbols and day to day settings can inhibit agreement. When meeting someone who is a stranger, it can be difficult to disentangle the core business at hand from the institutional, social and emotional flotsam that accompanies it.

Globalization does not change time in the same manner as it alters the forms of space. But the alteration of space brings with it a transformed set of space-time potentials. If temporality has the four forms of duration, succession, simultaneity-as-culmination and synchrony; then in the global dimension succession is accelerated; duration is compressed; every simultaneity-as-culmination quickly gives way to another; and synchrony, the metric of social rhythm, must be continually remade. Here the news is good. Global system convergence, faster communication and the diversification of means of communication—together they add up to a remarkable advance in the conditions for synchrony in creative work. In an electronically mediated world the rhythms of global synchrony pull us into alignment with each other. We can hardly bear to remain unconnected for long. The desire for global synchrony is as universal as the desire for global mobility. The forms of both global mobility, and global synchrony, allow us to expand connectivity while sustaining the self. We can be open and bounded at the same time.

Synchronous electronic networking allows us to test and negotiate agreement on the task at hand, with all the practical and emotional benefits that brings, to do so in relation to novel and complex texts, ideas, data and images; and to do so in a manner of our own choosing and with rights of exit uninhibited by the politeness regimes that govern a face-to-face encounter. The threshold for achieving 'chemistry' is not as high. Self-recognition of the other is easier to achieve, depending less on visual cues and more on the homogenized written languages shared by educated people. In electronically mediated synchrony we empty out much of the 'noise' of human association, dispense with non essential institutional baggage, and focus squarely on the task at hand. In electronic communication, the pleasures of synchrony require no special act of virtue. 'Loose ties' in this form are as compatible with Jonathan Swift as with Adam Smith. And in technical terms, global synchrony enables us to move with speed and precision to accomplish common and several objectives. It is free of unit cost. Once the network is running it is cheaper to connect electronically across the world than to travel in one city. Like all forms of virtual travel it is faintly glamorous and exotic, more so when it extends to sites and cultural sets very different from our own. Global synchrony also has an extraordinary speed in disseminating results and building reputations world-wide. Each day the expansion of the reach of the Internet renders it more effective. 'Our goodwill is circumscribed by no boundary,' said Adam Smith, 'but may embrace the immensity of the universe.'[41]

For creators, global synchrony offers the security of voluntary relations on grounds of autonomy. It works against, around and in between global closures. Every move to lock up creative work as intellectual property is sooner or later subverted by free conversation between 'competitive' creators. Creative people need connectivity and mirror recognition. They also need solitude,[42] an unlimited space in which to be different, and rights of exit largely free of protocols. They need ease in adding members to the group and in changing the labels on informal teams. They need sharp minds, complexity, immediacy and communicative intimacy. Global synchrony provides for these needs. At the same time, the need for synchrony also helps to explain mimetic (imitative) behaviours, *non-creative* behaviours, in fields as wide-ranging as consumption, politics and research. Imitation is a means of entering systems and signaling empathy with their requirements. The process of repetition maintains synchronic rhythms. Mimetic behaviours provide a ready means of gaining a footing in global time/space. This does not mean that synchrony in creative fields always brings mimetic behaviour with it (though it is a tendency to guard against). The point is that global synchrony in itself does not deliver or enhance creativity. It changes the conditions and potentials of creativity.

Global synchrony is flexible. It can be re-arranged in many ways. In the global setting, in which we see more and a more diverse set of particulars and our cultural potentials are much more varied, something stops it all from fragmenting and flying apart. Something pulls us into the same places as each other within this elastic set of possibilities. That something is synchrony. It is a means of global relations and creation. Like all means we come to desire it as an end in itself, for our ends are always in process. Global synchrony is the 'glue' that binds together the flowing circuits of knowledge and makes cosmopolitan cities possible.

The desire for global synchrony, which is the desire for connection, for agreement and for co-production on the ground of freedom, has become a powerful human motivation in creative work and in everything else. In growing our products together in the common field and time of our choosing we reach deep into our Neolithic selves. It is not surprising that synchronous social relationships via communicative technologies have become highly attractive, even addictive to us. Here weak ties trump all others. Here the future world society is being born.

Policy synchrony

Global synchrony and desires for global synchrony touch most of our endeavours. Consider global policy borrowing in higher education. The process of voluntary convergence between national higher education systems sustains the Bologna and Tuning projects in Europe, where universities are converging in degree structures and in the description of curricula. The Bologna process extends to more countries and has more momentum than Europeanization in other spheres.[43] As was discussed in our previous volume,[44] voluntary convergence is apparent in the reform of higher education institutions in many nations to bring them closer to the dominant template, that of the comprehensive science-based university on Anglo-American lines. This form of institution, which could be called the Global Research University,[45] is powerfully valorized by university ranking systems.[46] Voluntary convergence is especially evident in the systems for organizing and managing science which was always the most globally-referenced facet of higher education. At bottom national systems want to synchronize effectively with each other; the individual institutions want to synchronize with each other; and both want to be seen to do so. Nations maintain their strategic independence. They diverge from common templates where it suits them. But they do so more surreptitiously than before. The prima facie assumption of convergence is strong. Roger King remarks:

> It is quite rare in these days of policy internationalism within sectors to find outright rejection by national governments of global governance templates and agreements, even if some countries would prefer that they could reject them. Rather, in such circumstances overt or formal acceptance of worldwide 'best practices' is often accompanied by behavioural foot-shifting, or other forms of passive and unenthusiastic implementation. The objective is to avoid the full impact of globally-inspired reforms while seeking to avoid the international and other criticism that would follow outright non-adoption. Strategies of 'mock compliance' and 'regulatory ritualism' are two examples of formal policy adherence being undermined by actual behaviour.

> 'Mock compliance' is especially likely when the costs of global compliance by a country tend to fall disproportionately on influential domestic interests. These ensure that implementation is often inconsistent with the new standards. The result tends to be regulatory forbearance ('turning a blind eye'), administrative failure as a result of a lack of governmental impetus and monitoring, and private compliance failure, simply behaving as before.... The European Bologna Process, for example, aims at converging national systems' architectures by 2010, but quite significant harmonization on the surface masks continuing national differences and varied local interpretations.[47] 'Regulatory ritualism'[48] is another form of behavioural divergence from intended outcomes. It tends to develop over time rather than at inception (unlike mock compliance). In higher education systems it can be found in the strategizing by institutions and academics in the face of increased external accountability, such as associated with quality assurance. After a period, regulatory processes such as those based on audit, become a 'ritual of comfort' or an 'institution of pacification' rather than evidence of successful and effective compliance.[49] There is an acceptance of institutionalized means for securing regulatory goals combined

with losing focus on achieving the goals or outcomes themselves. Both processes of mock compliance and regulatory ritualism may help to mask persisting national variety in higher education systems that lies below formal policy internationalism on the surface.[50]

A case of exceptions that prove the rule. With global referencing now commonplace, national identity is sustained within a game-frame in which synchrony is uppermost. Hannah Arendt noted in relation to the public realm that despite differences in position and variety of perspective, 'everybody is always concerned with the same object.'[51] This enables the public realm to function. So it is with global synchrony and the common policy space. In the global knowledge economy all nations, and all institutions, share desires for global capacity, connectedness and success as measured by recognized templates. At bottom they do so because they have been drawn together into the single interdependent system of the global knowledge economy in which isolation is punished and there is no choice but to engage.

Policy borrowing and policy convergence have been drivers of globalization since the eighteenth century.[52] They have reached a high level in policy on higher education, research and innovation. Here the spontaneous synchronies of individual scholars with each other, researchers with each other, and institutions with each other are matched by mimetic approaches in government. In the knowledge sectors (though less so in policy in some other areas such as immigration, defence, and manufacturing) we have moved decisively beyond the Hobbesian world of sui generis national states perpetually on the brink of zero-sum conflict. Conformity to common global norms has been intensified by the global ranking of universities that began in 2003 and the move of research performance measures to the centre of policy attention.[53] National exceptionalism in approaches to higher education and science remains an option but is obvious only in the USA and a handful of countries. Even in those cases, proud claims of divergence mask conformity with or parallel evolution to global norms, so that even the national differences have become expressed in common ways. In the case of American exceptionalism the practices of American universities themselves constitute global norms.

The near universal adoption of the techniques of the new public management (NPM)[54] is a striking example of policy synchrony in higher education, research and the creative and expressive arts. The NPM is the dominant set of forms and strategies for modernization in public administration. In its origins in the UK Thatcher government in the 1980s it slightly predated the communicative globalization touched off by the Internet, but 1990s globalization became a powerful medium for the spread of NPM practices on the world scale, and as such a vehicle for the partial fashioning of the knowledge economy along Anglo-American lines.

The NPM imagines formal education, research and the arts in term of business models, particularly US business models. It identifies specific goals, and policies and strategies for achieving them. It finds 'bottom lines' difficult to define in curiosity-driven research and the arts, where by definition the outcomes are unknown, but has invented proxies for desired outcomes, including product formats such as the research 'project,' and money targets such as revenues accruing to research or the arts. The

NPM uses competition between producers to drive allocative efficiency and (it is assumed) continuous quality improvement. The NPM also emphasizes surveillance, transparency of outcomes and performance management. It employs reporting and accountability processes so as to enable a managed devolution of responsibility from government to individual institutions, and within institutions from managers to units under their control. Often the NPM entails expectations about income raising by institutions/organizations and their units, especially in universities and the arts, which masks a partial transfer of financial responsibility away from government. The NPM fosters professionalized executive managers and entrepreneurial staff, and where possible client-style relations between producers and users of the knowledge-intensive products: students, parents, employers, industry that accesses research, patrons and consumers of the arts. At the national level the NPM imagines education and research/innovation in terms of single systems that can be managed from a central pivot via competition, funding-based incentives, negotiated or formula-based agreements, targets, performance measures and accountability/audit.[55] There is a prima facie tendency towards system architecture in which all sectors and all institutions within sectors can be controlled simultaneously. In many nations the NPM is also associated with the introduction or augmentation of private sector institutions, partly regulated by government, which is seen to bring production closer to the ideal of a field of competing firms.

Once installed the NPM drives a continued critical reflexivity, sustained by ongoing techniques of performance monitoring, evaluation and accountability. These techniques are often grouped under the heading of 'quality assurance.' Production is punctuated by frequent reviews and the structural overhaul of work organization, which simulates the continuous product development, shifts of focus and internal reorganizations typical of private industry. Periodically targets are lifted so as to simulate the drive for market expansion and profitability typical of the business firm. In essence these are simulations of continuous modernization.

The tendency to policy borrowing is universal but the timing and transformative potentials of reform are not. The roll-out of the NPM is a worldwide process with national-cultural and local variations. In some policy settings, such as the 'Westminster' polities of the UK, Australia and New Zealand, all 'NPM-ed' by the mid 1990s, and also parts of Eastern Europe and East and Southeast Asia, thoroughgoing NPM reform has been implemented. Signs of this are the comprehensive cultures of corporate management with a caste of trained managers steeped in the new values, the actual (rather than just nominal) conformity of disciplinary groups to comprehensive performance requirements, and the installation of an internally coherent system of financial incentives at all levels of operation. In other settings such as the USA and parts of Western Europe the full-blown adoption of performance controls; and, in Western Europe, the adoption of devolution-based systems; have been slower. In some nations, especially where communicative globalization is slowed by language factors and/or lesser communications capacity, for example parts of Southeast Asia and Africa; or there are strong non-NPM traditions in higher education, as in parts of Latin America;

first stage NPM reforms such as university 'corporatization' are only now being introduced, and managers of academic departments or research centres are not as yet completely soaked in the NPM culture. Nevertheless, once introduced into policy systems NPM reform can be more rapid in follower nations than those where partial modernizations were introduced earlier.

Limits of knowledge markets

While all forms of NPM are simulacra for business activity, NPM systems also vary in the extent to which they install functioning economic markets. In its original Thatcher government form the NPM was conceived in terms of a neo-liberal 'social imaginary,' to use the term developed by Charles Taylor.[56] In this social imaginary all goods produced in education, research and the arts were understood as private goods, with rare exceptions. It was believed that all such production could be organized in terms of profit-driven economic markets: Milton Friedman, along with F.A. Hayek one of the two high priests of neo-liberalism, argued that in education market-based production could be used to produce even the public goods. The notions of human sociability and agency were attenuated. Neo-liberals adopted Adam Smith's argument in *The Wealth of Nations* about the benefits of market rather than state coordination of the economy, but not his argument in *The Theory of Moral Sentiments* about the motives for human association. Neo-liberalism became the ideology of the financial economy, of the City of London and Wall Street. Neo-liberals imagine sociability only in terms of competition and market exchange. They emphasize negative freedom, which is understood in terms of freedom from constraint or coercion, usually by the state. At the same time they resist notions of positive freedom, which is the capacity for self-determining action, and resist strategies of public action to secure social improvements that would enlarge positive freedoms.[57] Neo-liberalism promotes a choice-making individualism as such but not the capacity to exercise choice. It sources its political energy not in visions of a better society but in anti-statism. In his critique of negative freedom, freedom limited to choice-making, Hegel called it 'the freedom of the void which rises to a passion and takes shape in the world.'[58]

Neo-liberalism has proven ideologically powerful, and as such has contributed to the more general momentum for NPM business modeling. However the full neo-liberal vision for education, research and the creative arts was never implemented in Thatcher's UK, and though Australia and New Zealand took it further than the UK, it was not adopted in full in those nations either. It has never been adopted in full anywhere else, nor will it be in the future. While specific neo-liberal ideas and ways of seeing/imagining have left their mark on the knowledge economy, particularly in the ubiquitous presence of competition games in system organization, the neo-liberal drive towards the universal commodification of knowledge has failed.

While competition between producers is widely used in national system management and in the allocation of resources between units within universities, no nation has introduced a full-cost commercial tuition market into schooling or first degree university education. In all nations tuition is either free, or subject to nominal standard charges well below actual cost, or in the case of the American Ivy League set nominally at high cost levels but heavily subsidized by government and or philanthropy. There are commercial tuition systems in international education in many countries, and also in some mass vocational education and in the equity-financed for-profit sector chains such as the University of Phoenix, but not in the mainstream of citizen education. Likewise, basic research is government financed all over the world. The neo-liberal idea is manifest in the common desire of policy makers to shift part of university research activity from basic research into the development of commercial intellectual property, but after two decades of such policies, all over the world, the industry share of the financing of university research in all nations remains modest. It is typically 6 per cent or less even in the USA where the pharmaceutical industry has made significant inroads into the universities.

We can identify at least five reasons for the failure to implement in the knowledge sectors the policies of commercial market formation that are imagined in the neo-liberal variant of the NPM. First, as was discussed at greater length in *Creativity in the Global Knowledge Economy*,[59] the neo-liberal premise about the economic nature of knowledge is flawed. An increasing number of commentators argue that knowledge is predominantly a public good not a private good, because once the moment of first creation has passed and knowledge has passed into the common domain it is non-rivalrous and non-excludable.[60] Thus both the new knowledge produced in research, once disseminated, and the contents of what students learn which are based on existing knowledge, are largely public goods. Public goods are typically under-provided in commercial markets. It is true that degree certificates, and the networking benefits of attendance at elite institutions, can be produced as private goods. But because the knowledge contents of learning are public goods, and learning is essential to the institutions in which the private credentials and networking benefits are acquired—except perhaps in the most cynical of the diploma mills, in which learning contents are emptied out and the 'piece of paper' is the only thing—then even the acquisition of the private goods depends on the simultaneous production of the public knowledge goods inherent in student learning.

Second, to the extent that degree certificates and networking benefits are private goods, these are status ('positional') goods, not conventional market commodities.[61] The production of high value degrees in elite universities cannot be expanded infinitely without exploding the economic value of those goods; while degrees in low status diploma mills have negligible market value as status goods. This sets limits on the economic character of production.

Third, related to the point about public goods, neo-liberalism has never been able to explain or even acknowledge the extraordinary growth of communicative sociability and open source knowledge goods mediated not by economic markets but by the Internet. Synchronous open source association is more cooperative than competitive and is unmotivated by direct profit-making. This is not to say considerations of personal interests and advantage are absent, only that they do not take the forms that populate the neo-liberal imaginary.

Fourth, in the neo-liberal imaginary, education and research (even the arts) are understood in terms of national systems. NPM reform is driven by the goal of national competitiveness in the global setting. But global reflexivity in the form of global comparison and relativization quickly takes us beyond a solely national view; and global knowledge flows constantly undermine the idea of a closed national market-system. It makes even less sense in relation to the knowledge sectors than it does in relation to the 1940s idea of 'Gross Domestic Product.'

Finally, the principal economic contributions of education and research in the global knowledge economy lie not in the production of goods directly turned into financial values. Some such production does take place, for example in the international education sector. But the more important economic contribution of education and research is that they provide for long-term conditions of production in all other sectors, via the level of social literacy, the training of particular skills and professions, and the provision of knowledge and research training through research systems. Given the public good character of learning contents and research, if educational participation and knowledge creation were largely market determined, their fecund contributions to productivity and innovation would be weakened.

In short, far from the neo-liberal reflexivity driving globalization, as some critics of neo-liberalism claim, neo-liberal notions in policy and administration constitute an increasing barrier to global creation. Turning all relations into economic market relations and all knowledge-inflected goods into commodities, thereby magnifying a lesser part of the global knowledge economy into the blueprint for the whole, would stymie its potentials. It would negate the larger part of communicative globalization and the knowledge goods that are produced and disseminated. It would bear down more heavily on cultural diversity than does the present global standardization of knowledge forms. It would eliminate all particularism in value, imposing a single standard of exchange value in place of a diversity of use values. It would elevate the financial economy from the role of significant presence and driver within the knowledge economy to its supreme architect and arbiter. It is now obvious that the universal commodification of knowledge will not happen. This is not, as some neo-liberal commentators have argued, because of political factors, such as the failure of government will or the capture of policy by special interests. It is because the neo-liberal policy blueprint in education and the creative sectors is out of synchrony with the actual knowledge economy.

The collapse of the neo-liberal vision points to the limits of all mono-cultural conceptions of the global knowledge economy. Orthodox political economic ideas have much to offer in explaining the k-economy. We can point to acts of investment and entrepreneurship by individuals, institutions and states; forms of production; patterns of exchange; rates of return; and the generation of surplus. We can analyze the effects of regulation and of regulated deregulation in conditioning creative activity. Quantitative economic data illuminate trends and point to futures, though all measures have specific purposes and limits, and data-based predictions are habitually disrupted by complexity and contingency. However, it is less helpful to treat economics as the final horizon of explanation, for example by imagining agency and sociability in terms of the exclusive and universalizing notion of 'economic man,' as if all motives boil down to the maximization of financial or psychic returns to single individuals, and all resources are scarce rather than (as in the case of information) hyper-abundant.[62] It is also unhelpful to impose a single system of financial valuation across the whole corpus of scholarship, research and the arts with their heterogeneous rhythms, outputs and purposes.

Where then does that leave the NPM mechanisms for managing the global knowledge economy, which are shaped in terms of economic incentives and a single system of financial valuation and are now implemented very widely via global policy synchrony and flows? A key issue is whether and to what extent NPM systems support or inhibit free creative work. The area is under-researched. For example, what are the effects of modelling creative work in terms of financial activities and outputs, in shaping the patterns of activity? What consequences flow from the imposition of heteronomous control systems that override creator independence? What about the widespread use of short-term product formats and reporting cycles? How much does the requirement for income raising inhibit the flow of public knowledge goods, especially those with downstream and long term benefits? These issues go not just to the critique of neo-liberalism but to all NPM systems. The NPM is superior to the collegial and bureaucratic practices it replaced in terms of the goals of efficiency, transparency and the installation of performance cultures. This is not to say that the means by which these goals have been advanced have been optimal for creativity. Here the OECD is concerned:

> The shift to project-based research funding in TEIs [tertiary education institutions] raises a number of issues that need to be considered in relation to the long-term development of the research and innovation system. Competitive funding may promote more ad hoc and short-term research in cases where evaluation mechanisms and incentive structures focus on quantifiable and immediate outputs. As a result, researchers may be reluctant to engage in research that will not produce results that can be demonstrated over short time-spans. In addition, precisely because project-based funding is competitive, sustained funding is not guaranteed, which may impede the autonomy of researchers working in controversial fields. If project-based funding has a short duration, it may also mean that researchers need to spend time preparing applications to secure funding on a more frequent basis. Atkinson remarks that young faculty in particular spend an excessive amount of time preparing project proposals. Liefner found that competitive or performance-based funding could have an impact on the type and field of research because some academics avoided research with riskier outcomes. Likewise, Geuna notes that 'short-term research and less risky research may reduce the likelihood of scientific novelty.' Furthermore, Geuna and Martin argue that 'research may become homogenized' because safer research is rewarded. Morris and Rip point out that the stage of a researcher's career needs to be considered in relation to the type of research undertaken. Some of the questions raised are: does the researcher need quick results to bolster his or her next job application? Is he or she senior

enough to get a five-year rather than a three-year grant? and these questions are pertinent in the context of project-based funding.[63]

There is a particular problem in emerging research systems, in which indigenous research cultures are embryonic or older scholarly traditions have been displaced by English-language modernization, and the dominant influence is a government-led investment based on NPM blueprints. Investment in public communications and knowledge production is crucial to capacity building, but over-management can truncate the potentials for local creative work.

This suggests the need for developing a new set of techniques of reflexive modernization for organizing knowledge-related institutions; techniques more in tune with communicative globalization, with the diversity of knowledge goods and with the predominantly public good nature of knowledge, including the gift-based character of much knowledge exchange.[64] Refashioning the organizational instruments would provide an opportunity also to factor in a more diverse set of models of knowledge production, moving beyond the fixation with the highpoints of Anglo-American university culture to take account of multi-polar traditions and capacities including East Asia, South Asia, the Arabic world, Latin America and Europe.

Regardless—and despite the NPM and all other top-down systems for organizing creative work, which underplay creator independence and hinder as much as they help—there are solid reasons to be optimistic. The global flows of knowledge are touched by university rankings and the NPM but also elude them. Every effort to channel and limit knowledge and its communication leaks copiously. Perhaps most knowledge is produced outside the formal scientific institutions and major disciplinary journals, in the open source ecology. In emerging national university systems, much depends on the capacity of local scholar-researchers to use communicative linkages, especially with those in like circumstances in other countries. But the preconditions are there. Providing that the Internet remains a commons, and both the knowledge produced and disseminated in the formal codified parts of the k-economy, and the knowledge produced in the open source sector, are broadly accessible, then direct cooperation between creators has the potential to trump all control systems as it did in Mozart's Vienna.

This chapter has established that the knowledge economy is fertile ground for space making. The next chapter focuses on one bounded set of actions in the knowledge economy, the geo-spatial strategies of university executives and governments, the new sensibilities of space-time these actions indicate, and the global creation thereby taking place.

Endnotes

1. In California authorities have the power to direct people to leave their homes in the face of fire, an option which the Australian police and fire brigades do not have. Recent Californian fires have destroyed more homes and killed fewer people, relative to the Australian experience.

2. Creative fiction anticipates the event: 'Many charred bones had there their roofless grave; for many of the Noldor perished in that burning, who were caught by the running flame and could

not fly to the hills.' J.R.R. Tolkien's account of the Dagor Bragollach, Battle of Sudden Flame, in the *Silmarillion* (1977), 151.

3. University of Copenhagen, 2009.

4. e.g. 'time, like space, is a *pure form* of *sense* or *intuition*, the non sensuous sensuous…' (Hegel, 2004, 34).

5. Hegel, 2004, 30.

6. Heidegger, 2002, 135.

7. See also the discussion of space-time in Harvey, 1990, 201–323.

8. Heidegger, 2002, 134–146.

9. Heidegger, 1962, 139.

10. *ibid*, 140.

11. *ibid*, 142.

12. *ibid*, 146.

13. Harvey, 1990, 226.

14. Hegel, 2004, 40.

15. Harvey, 1990, 294.

16. Some scholarly literature on Hadrian's Wall is caught in a debate between on one hand the Wall as exclusive/defensive of the barbarians, and the Wall and the outlying forts such as Newstead located north of it as the foundation of a forward presence and a means of managing the population beyond. As if the boundary could not have both functions at once. In academic debate scholars habitually create binary arguments and 'other' their opponents, creating partial truths represented as whole truths, in order to stake a claim; and perhaps also because larger meanings are too dependant on complex judgment rather than simplified and selected empirical 'facts.' Other scholars make their move via the arguments for re-unification and synthesis. These are oscillating rituals.

17. Heidegger, 2002, 141.

18. Harvey, 1990, 205.

19. Marx, 1973, 173.

20. This is one point where the present argument deviates from Harvey, who works with an orthodox notion of space-time equivalence.

21. Harvey, 1990.

22. Castells, 2000a; Castells; 1997, Castells, 2000b.

23. Appadurai, 1996; Marginson, 2008a.

24. Heidegger, 2002, 16.

25. Sen, 1985; Sen, 1992.

26. 'Pure will—pure practical reason—the lawfulness of the fundamental law of factical action—self-responsibility—personality—freedom. All these necessarily belong together'—Heidegger, 2002, 201.

27. 'It is not until it has itself as its object that the will is for itself what is in itself'—Hegel, 2008, 34.

28. Hegel, 2008, 37.

29. Stern, 2007; University of Copenhagen, 2009.

30. Arendt, 1998.

31. Bauman, 2000.

32. Orwell, 2001 (1939).

33. 'Arbitrariness is contingency manifesting itself as will'—Hegel, 2008, 37.

34. Appadurai, 1996.

35. Here the status values imposed by university rankings, a conserving function that slows the process of obsolescence, function as a partial corrective (see Marginson, 2009).

36. Heidegger, 2002, 107. Simultaneity 'expresses the relationship of that which is present to time as a summation of everything present' (p. 112).

37. Heidegger, 2002, 90

38. Swift, 2001.

39. Smith, 2004, 45.

40. *ibid*, 9 & 14.

41. *ibid*, 281.

42. Murphy and Pauleen, 2009.

43. Van der Wende, 2008.

44. Marginson, 2009.

45. Ma, 2008; Marginson, 2008b.

46. Marginson, 2009.

47. Witte, 2006.

48. Braithwaite, 2008.

49. Power, 1997.

50. King, 2009.

51. Arendt, 1998, 57–58.

52. Bayly, 2004.

53. Marginson, 2009.

54. Marginson, 2008a.

55. Rose, 1999.

56. Taylor, 2002.

57. e.g. the classical statement of this position by Hayek, 1960.

58. Hegel, 2008, 28. 'Choice, therefore, is grounded in the indeterminacy of the I and the determinacy of a content. Thus the will, on account of this content, is not free'—*ibid*, 38.

59. For example, in Chapters 1 and 8.

60. Samuelson, 1954; Stiglitz, 1999.

61. Hirsch, 1976; Frank, 1985.

62. Peters, 2009.

63. OECD, 2008, 176.

64. Kenway et al., 2006.

References

Appadurai, A. (1996). *Modernity at Large: Cultural Dimensions of Globalization*. Minneapolis: University of Minnesota Press.

Arendt, H. (1998). *The Human Condition*. Chicago: University of Chicago Press.

Bauman, Z. (2000). *Liquid Modernity*. Cambridge: Polity.

Bayly, C. (2004). *The Birth of the Modern World: 1780–1914*. Oxford: Blackwell.

Braithwaite, J. (2008). *Regulatory Capitalism*. Cheltenham, UK: Edward Elgar.

Castells, M. (1997). *The Power of Identity*. Volume 2 of *The Information Age: Economy, Society and Culture*. Oxford: Blackwell.

Castells, M. (2000a). *The Rise of the Network Society*, 2nd Edition. Volume 1 of *The Information Age: Economy, Society and Culture*. Oxford: Blackwell.

Castells, M. (2000b). *End of Millennium*, 2nd Edition. Volume 3 of *The Information Age: Economy, Society and Culture*. Oxford: Blackwell.

Frank, R. (1985). *Choosing the Right Pond: Human Behaviour and the Quest for Status*. New York: Oxford University Press.

Harvey, D. (1990). *The Condition of Post-modernity*. Cambridge: Blackwell.

Hayek, F. (1960). *The Constitution of Liberty*. London: Routledge and Kegan Paul.

Hegel, G. (2004/1830). *Philosophy of Nature. Part II of the Encyclopaedia of the Philosophical Sciences*. Oxford: Oxford University Press.

Hegel, G. (2008/1920). *Outlines of the Philosophy of Right*. Intoduction by S. Houlgate. Transl. T. Knox. Oxford: Oxford University Press.

Heidegger, M. (1962). *Being and Time*. Transl. by J. Macquarie & E. Robinson. New York: Harper and Row.

Heidegger, M. (2002). *The Essence of Human Freedom: An Introduction to Philosophy*. Transl. by T. Sadler. London: Continuum.

Hirsch, F. (1976). *Social Limits to Growth*. Cambridge: Harvard University Press.

Kenway, J., Bulleen, E., Fahey, J., with Robb, S. (2006). *Haunting the Knowledge Economy*. London: Routledge.

King, R. (2009). *Governing Knowledge Globally: Policy Internationalism, Global Science, and the Open Society*. Paper to a seminar at the Centre for the Study of Higher Education, University of Melbourne, 6 April. Accessed on 22 April 2009 at: http://www.cshe.unimelb.edu.au/research/res_seminars.html

Ma, W. (2008). The University of California at Berkeley: An emerging global research university. *Higher Education Policy*, 21, 65–81.

Marginson, S. (2008a). Academic creativity under New Public Management: Foundations for an investigation. *Educational Theory*, 58 (3), 269–287.

Marginson, S. (2008b). 'Ideas of a University' for the global era. Paper for seminar on 'Positioning University in the Globalized World: Changing Governance and Coping Strategies in Asia. Centre of Asian Studies, The University of Hong Kong; Central Policy Unit, HKSAR Government; and The Hong Kong Institute of Education: The University of Hong Kong, 10–11 December. Accessed on 20 April 2009 at: http://www.cshe.unimelb.edu.au/people/staff_pages/Marginson/Marginson.html

Marginson, S. (2009). University rankings and the knowledge economy. In M. Peters, P. Murphy & S. Marginson (eds.) *Creativity and the Global Knowledge Economy*, 185–216. New York: Peter Lang.

Marx, K. (1973). *The Grundrisse*. Transl. by M. Nicolaus. Harmondsworth: Penguin.

Murphy, P. and Pauleen, D. (2009). Managing paradox in a world of knowledge. In M. Peters, P. Murphy & S. Marginson (eds.) *Creativity and the Global Knowledge Economy*, 257–276. New York: Peter Lang.

National Science Board, NSB (2009). *Science and Engineering Indicators*. Accessed on 21 March 2009 at: http://www.nsf.gov/statistics/seind04/

Organisation for Economic Cooperation and Development, OECD (2008). *Tertiary Education for the Knowledge Society: OECD Thematic Review of Tertiary Education*. Paris: OECD.

Orwell, G. (2001/1939). *Coming up for Air*. Harmondsworth: Penguin Modern Classics.

Peters, M. (2009). Introduction: Knowledge goods, the primacy of ideas and the economics of abundance. In M. Peters, P. Murphy & S. Marginson (eds.) *Creativity and the Global Knowledge Economy*, 1–22. New York: Peter Lang.

Power, M. (1997). *The Audit Society: Rituals of verification*. Oxford: Oxford University Press.

Rose, N. (1999). *Powers of Freedom*. Cambridge: Cambridge University Press.

Samuelson, P. (1954). The pure theory of public expenditure. *Review of Economics and Statistics*. 36, 4, 387–389.

Sen, A. (1985). Well-being, agency and freedom: The Dewey lectures 1984. *The Journal of Philosophy*, 82 (4), 169–221.

Sen, A. (1992). *Inequality Reexamined*. Cambridge, MA.: Harvard University Press.

Smith, A. (2004/1759). *The Theory of Moral Sentiments*. Barnes and Noble.

Stern, N. (2007). *Stern Review on The Economics of Climate Change*. London: HM Treasury, UK Government. Accessed 20 April 2009 at: http://www.hm-treasury.gov.uk/sternreview_index. htm

Stiglitz, J. (1999). Knowledge as a global public good. In *Global public goods: International cooperation in the 21st Century*. In I. Kaul, I. Grunberg & M. Stern (Eds.), 308–325). New York: Oxford University Press.

Swift, J. (2001). *Gulliver's Travels*. London: Penguin.

Taylor, C. (2002). Modern social imaginaries. *Public Culture*, 14 (1), 91–124.

Tolkien, J. (1977). *The Silmarillion*. London: George Allen and Unwin.

University of Copenhagen (2009). *Key Messages from the Congress*. Outcome of international scientific conference on 'Climate Change: Global risks, challenges and decisions,' 10–12 March. Copenhagen: University of Copenhagen. Accessed 20 April at: http://climatecongress.ku.dk/ newsroom/congress_key_messages/

van der Wende, M. (2008). Rankings and classifications in higher education: A European perspective. In J. Smart (Ed.) *Higher Education: Handbook of theory and research*. Dordrecht: Springer.

Witte, J. (2006) Changes of Degrees and Degrees of change: comparing adaptations of European higher education systems to the Bologna Process, Doctoral Thesis, CHEPS, University of Twente, Netherlands

CHAPTER 6

Making Space in Higher Education

◻ Simon Marginson

Universities at large

How is it global space making in higher education has come to take strategic form? Who are the strategic actors? Some of the space making moves that are remaking the global dimension in higher education and research are carried out directly by governments or semi-autonomous state agencies. But the larger part of strategic global activity is triggered by higher education institutions themselves, especially the research universities with which this chapter is mostly concerned. In most countries the presence of universities with a highly active international portfolio under their own control is still a fairly new departure. Until the mid-1980s at least international activities were conducted mostly on the margins and the cross-border movements of university personnel were more influenced by national higher education system authorities. But the Internet, global flows of knowledge and the freer mobility of people in higher education have changed all of that. Providing that they have access to global communications, all university personnel have the potential to be global players without leaving the office. Some governments find it difficult to let go. The degree to which research universities are 'disembedded' from national control[1] when outside the country varies from case to case. But it is a common fact that the formation of the global knowledge economy has become associated with more autonomous research universities. It is significant also that research universities have more freedom in global affairs than in their national and local work. In sum, globalization rests on, and has advanced, the 'entrepreneurial' or 'enterprise' university.[2]

The roots of the enterprise turn lie in early twentieth century United States,[3] but it became general to national higher education systems in the wake of the new public management (NPM). From its beginning the NPM imagined the university as a quasi-corporation, and its field of operation as a national and later global market. These conceptions have never become fully hegemonic in higher education in the USA or elsewhere, but they are congruent with the main line of policy and regulation and have helped to shape research universities. This shows in the growing materiality of the institution qua institution, as distinct from a container for a miscellany of academic disciplines. Associated with the rise of the institution qua institution is the accumulating weight of the administration, and the professionalization of management; the rise of university branding, in which the old coat-of-arms is dusted off and placed in neon lights; and the growing role and effectiveness of executive leaders, mostly risen from the professorial ranks, with financial and directive power and a strategy-making brief.

Here again the American university is the model. The US created an executive university presidency in the nineteenth century, which over time gathered special responsibilities for external relations, fund-raising and the trajectory of the institution. National traditions are not always congruent with the corporate university forms; some academic cultures resist strongly; countries are at different points along this road. The single CEO has not been universally adopted. For example Dutch research universities are led by a small oligarchy in which sometimes one person is dominant and sometimes power is more distributed. Among the majority of institutions that have invested in the CEO model, some of their leaders have more discretion than others. Some have more raw power to move people and resources than do others. In some universities leaders are enmeshed within a complex system of checks and balances; in other cases leaders have a marked capacity to create contingencies, functioning almost as a force external to the institution. The capabilities of leaders vary. Yet all research universities seem to be moving over time towards a centralization of institutional strategy.

On the whole the rise of the strategic executive has facilitated global formation in the knowledge economy, by strengthening the agency freedom and formative capacities of universities. Associated with this the enlargement and diversification of global spaces have facilitated global creativity. There are exceptions to these generalizations. The relationship between executive power and global formation is not simple or linear, while relations between the executive and creativity are often problematic. The leading American research universities have largely managed to avoid the wholesale fall into business modelling that can limit the reach of NPM reforms, or alternatively, where such reforms are imposed successfully on hapless institutions on a thoroughgoing basis, can stunt university work. Strong academic cultures are not always optimal for path-breaking creativity but they serve to check the capacity of executive power to stymie research by second guessing the fields of knowledge. However, many institutions inside and outside the USA are affected by the trend to closer surveillance and managed augmentation of internal performance and activities. In some universities below the top level, especially in the English-speaking world where NPM reforms have been more comprehensively applied than elsewhere, as in Australia and New Zealand, executive authority can bear heavily on the disciplines.[4] Likewise government systems that define and fund research activity and manage it as a financial economy, and set out to shift the balance of research from basic inquiry into applied and commercializable activities, can also restrict creative potentials. In short, if government and/or executive management blocks or unduly limits the global dealings of scholar-researchers in the disciplines, rather than facilitating open creativity and knowledge dissemination, much can be lost. But this critique of the NPM is widely made and now well understood.[5] The point less widely acknowledged, especially in the critical literatures on the university and on globalization, is that in global strategy making, university executive leaders can be as creative as scientists and scholars.

Status and display

The novelty of this strategic globalization should not overstated. In dancing the global dance universities do some things that are new. The purpose of their creativity is older. Global research universities are playing an age old part: the public display of virtue. Consider Republican Rome. In Rome the realm of the household was largely held in contempt and the public realm was seen as the realm of excellence (*virtus*). It was only in striving for public achievement that one could distinguish oneself from all others.[6] The compelling desire for public excellence drove Julius Caesar, Cicero and their contemporaries. They had established forms in which public excellence could be achieved and celebrated. A century later Nero scandalized the city when he attempted to transfer the model of publicly displayed virtue from military glory, public oratory and the erection of civic buildings, to performance in the sports and arts. The attempt to substitute entertainment for gravitas, and personal values for communal ones, only contributed to the collapse of his popularity. Today's universities also work within conventions that govern the display of excellence. Compared to the Romans we are more positive about the private realm. Ends such as personal enrichment that for them were not fit for polite society, so that Senators were expected to hide their business interests, are now seen as signs of virtue. But the notion of the public realm as the realm of display and recognized virtue retains some of its old force. Perhaps the role of status has been strengthened in the knowledge economy. Not only is it modern and post-modern. It is also pre-modern.

Universities need public recognition. Increasingly, as we have seen, they need this recognition as institutions and brands. The essence of higher education lies in the formation of student subjects, the transmission of knowledge, and the production of new knowledge and ideas and forms of knowing. But all of this eludes ready quantitative measurement and other forms of consensual recognition. This has created a vacuum, a need to demonstrate their worth, which the universities fill with continuous acts of public display. In particular, the virtual world is pre-eminently a theatre for display. And again, as in ancient Rome, the marks of virtue are well-defined and prominently displayed in websites and other communications. The most important sign of virtue is research performance, measured in rankings and publication/citation volumes, and tabulated in breakthrough discoveries and applications of public benefit, particularly in medical fields. Research, with its ready indices of winners/losers and competitive firepower, is the contemporary equivalent of military achievement in the ancient world. The Nobel Prize is the k-economy equivalent of the grass crown for valour in Roman wars. Another form of public virtue is care for students, which is manifest in a rhetoric that is part pastoral and partly about respect for the consumer. The tangible signs of this caring for students are displayed in buildings, facilities and services. That is much as it was in late Republican Rome, whose citizens were endowed with bread, circuses, basilica and aqueducts; and were fostered with a mix of parental care—Augustus, who drew all the elements of the Republican tradition into himself, was 'father of the country'—and the nominal respect paid to electors. (In universities today pedagogy and the fostering of intellectual growth are virtues less attractive and more elusive than pastoral care and services, less open to public display: words like 'intellectual challenge' and 'rigorous curriculum' have entered the marketing lexicon, but their role is restricted.) Then there are the superficial statements that recur in many university websites, about cultural diversity, respect for 'difference,' and education as a process of educational and cultural 'exchange' between locals and foreign students. These too had their equivalent in the inclusive politics of the late Republic. In Rome the plebeians occupied an honoured second place in the system of government, the Italian tribes had recently been admitted to the franchise, and all knew where the real power still lay.

As in Rome, whose foreign wars were crowned by the triumphal procession of the victorious general through the streets of the city to popular acclaim, the international ventures of universities are among the most important items for competitive display. Globalization is a high status form of modernization writ large. Global activity and scientific discovery are the two leading signifiers of modernity in universities. Often they go together. International research collaborations and cross-border teams focused on global problems such as climate change, water, cities and epidemic diseases, are especially obvious in university marketing. The functions of Deputy President International and Deputy President Research are combined in one person often enough to suggest a pattern. Julius Caesar reconnoitred in the fabled island of Britain, and planned the conquest of Parthia via the invasion of Dacia and an expedition round the far side of the Black Sea, outdoing Darius and Alexander; Caligula feinted at the conquests of Britain and Germany; his successor Claudius did invade Britain successfully in 43 CE: all to impress, please and appease the rapacious public opinion at home. So it is for universities. Leading and not so leading Anglo-American and increasingly, European research universities establish beach-heads in other countries in the form of campuses and joint programs, send off staff and students like colonists, and sign much photographed treaties with kingdoms of knowledge in fabled India and Cathay. Because international ventures are a high prestige and prestige-building activity, in the stronger research universities the global activities of executives are often well resourced. The international work of the institution entails business class travel, ceremony and diplomacy. It is not just a driver of national and global prestige; it is a source of status within the institution and one of the rewards that flow to internal authority. As with the international ventures of consuls and emperors in Rome, some of which beggared the Treasury, the financial returns from the global strategies of universities are mostly uncertain, except in the commercial tuition market. International ventures are sold as loss-leaders, to be followed by 'downstream benefits' at some future time. Yet the displays of global might and public glory function as ends in themselves. Mutterings are muted.

Acts of freedom

All the same, there is more at stake here than the internal organizational cultures and the budgets of the universities themselves. The more novel global strategies emerged only in the last 15 years, and the advent of global university rankings in 2003 seems to have accelerated creativity. The range of projects is remarkable. As we shall see, some open up the global dimension for activity; others build enclosures within it. Some involve nimble moves across or between multiple sites; some call for multiple partners or create networks; others are grounded, working outwards from a single location. Some work with a small slice of the global dimension. A few global moves by universities or governments seek to reconstitute the global as one space. In the open higher education setting, spatial variation (space making) has become a primary strategic device in the hands of university leaders and national systems.

Given this it would be easy to exaggerate the extent of planning and forethought. Not all outcomes are intended. Global creation is not always pre-meditated, and the relation between imagining and practices is not always happy. Some of the imagination-heavy global strategies in higher education gain purchase. Other prefigured strategies fail spectacularly. The global dimension does not always conform to the abstractions made of it, whether those abstractions are grounded in observation or imagining. Bold efforts to impose an imagined global spatiality are combined with outcomes that emerge unexpectedly in the course of the formative act, or become justified as part of the plan, after the event. Many university leaders and research entrepreneurs follow their noses, grabbing at opportunities as they appear. Still more seem to follow trails laid out by other universities without much reflection. It hardly needs to be said that most of the global strategic behaviour of universities does not involve path-breaking creativity. Mimetic behaviours provide the easiest means of gaining a footing in global space-time. Path-breaking researchers are often disdainful of the plodding of 'management' and they might be right. Even so many researchers benefit from globally-projected university status and the options that institutional moves have opened up.

Not all executive strategies are mimetic. A handful of space making moves creates new forms in the global knowledge economy.

University leaders consider themselves to be realists, who happen also to be patrons of the arts and the sciences. Parallels with Machiavellian nobility in Renaissance Italy spring to mind. As executives, they are governed by medium term contracts rather than the lifetime academic tenure habitual to professors. This serves to emphasize the element of practicality. Like all leaders entrusted with decision power, university executives produce their number of harebrained schemes. Some presidents make wasteful errors. And no doubt there are many more who have erred by failing to take the opportunities that thrust themselves into the foreground under the presidential nose. All the same many university presidents engage in forays that are as hard-headed as the ideal business executives they would like to be; there is real boldness in many quarters, and a few leaders are genuine originators. Aristotle said that the actual is prior to the possible.[7] What we imagine is based on what already is and what we know. Heidegger remarked that freedom is an occurrence wherein subjects appropriate their proper being.[8] For Hegel freedom brought the subjective and the objective into alignment. We are always creatures of our history. But there is also something more, a space to make the new. And (and this is the point) amid the dazzling enlightenment of the knowledge economy there is no clear way forward in the dark. There is more 'newness' than there was. Yesterday's audacious move provides today's conditions of existence. We know those conditions will evaporate again tomorrow. The actual often *has to be* anticipated. With our 'being' in perpetual transition, altering ourselves and our forms of imagining are always on the agenda.

At best the global strategies of universities are acts of freedom that build at the same time global imaginings, global agency, global capacity and the global field of action. Both the large successes and the large failures of strategy are interesting. If the global spatial moves made by universities fail as often as they succeed, in this they are no different to other acts of creation.

Types of global strategy

In the global strategies of universities and national systems there are two early objectives. Some strategies emphasize one objective, others both. The first objective is to build *spatial capacity* in the global setting. Strategies such as research concentrations are designed to accumulate powers of action and attraction in knowledge-oriented institutions in particular localities. These strategies do not necessarily break new ground in the use of space but can shape the global knowledge economy, including the distribution of activity between sites. The second interim objective of global strategy is to build global engagement and *spatial connectivity*. Being designed to build relationships, strategies focused on connectivity such as the creation of consortia and other networks are more formative of the global dimension itself.

When a university builds spatial capacity and connectivity this has its own performative and self-satisfying ends, but there remains the question of what to do with an augmented global presence. Geo-spatial strategies such as the creation of commercial export, global hubs and knowledge cities use the knowledge economy as a site of *global production* and in doing further form the global dimension itself, often in unplanned ways. These strategies advance the interests of particular territorially-bound nations or institutions and are mostly grounded in existing activity and identity (though certain knowledge hubs constitute 'greenfields' localities alongside existing ones). But over time these strategies change the role of institutions, the forms of higher education provision, and the patterns of global flows and relations.

Beyond these moves we find more radical geo-spatial strategies that break out beyond national boundaries to explicitly create a *distinctive global space*. Europeanization in higher education has foundations at the national level but also creates a new kind of domain in the meta-national setting which encloses part of the globe and has a global strategic agenda. Likewise, universities that are active in transnational education establish new campuses in foreign sites, with one foot in their traditional location and another beyond it. This again is a new way of doing things, based on plural identity, that qualifies nation-state regulation. These institutions are regulated by more than one jurisdiction and teach more than one curriculum. E-universities are organized solely in the global realm, altogether beyond national control.

A final group of strategies is focused explicitly on the *constitution of the larger global dimension* itself with greater or lesser effect. These include global publishing, university rankings, and the WTO/GATS attempt to remake education as a world trading system.

The chapter will now review the various strategies, moving from those that in their space making potentials are the least radical to those that might be the most radical.

Spatial capacity

The first strategic move in the global knowledge economy is an old move, dating from Sumer, Egypt, China and Teotihuacán Mexico: build the competitive capacity of the nation at the behest of its state. This imperative has its equivalent at the level of the institution: build the 'world class university.'[9] Here globalization as global convergence, and the enclosure of the world-from-space as a bounded whole, have deepened the sense of national and local interest. That is, the role of place within the global relational space is heightened. As Harvey noted:

> …the more unified the space, the more important the qualities of the fragmentations become for social identity and action. The free flow of capital across the surface of the globe, for example, places strong emphasis upon the particular qualities of the spaces to which that capital might be attracted. The shrinkage of space that brings diverse communities across the globe into competition with each other implies localized competitive strategies and a heightened sense of awareness of what makes a place special and gives it competitive advantage. This kind of reaction looks much more strongly to the identifica-

tion of place, the building and signalling of its unique qualities in an increasingly homogeneous but fragmented world.[10]

(For 'capital,' substitute 'capital and knowledge.' They are not the same. One difference is that in the global setting knowledge flows more freely than economic capital. The former is less susceptible to the blockages created by national regulation and economies of scale).

Since 1960 policies of nation building through education and research have been framed in the language of human capital theory.[11] Governments believe they can enhance competitive advantage through higher participation in tertiary education, better educational standards, imported high skilled labour, more high quality research outputs and the enhanced take-up of research in industry innovation. Here globalization has sharpened the nation-by-nation comparisons, raised the stakes and quickened the nation- and region-building strategies. A global 'arms race' in spending on innovation has emerged. In Europe the Lisbon protocols have positioned Europe as the would-be leading knowledge economy.[12] The k-economy, for example the high level of school student achievement as measured in the OECD's PISA comparisons,[13] is seen as central to Finland's economic and social success in the 2000s. A similar narrative has emerged around Korea. In Asia China, Taiwan China, Singapore and Korea have all invested massively in higher education (see Chapter 7). India and Malaysia also position themselves as future k-economies. A subset of the nation building investment policies is the growing emphasis on concentration of research capacity. Research rankings and the mobility of talent have catalyzed this trend.[14] Raising the investment in R&D unleashes a virtuous circle. Augmented research capacity attracts more research talent, especially cross-border talent, further building capacity and ranking, provided that other nations are not doing the same.

In Europe the Lisbon goal is for each nation to devote 3 per cent of GDP to R&D. This provides a favourable policy climate for policies of concentration in particular universities and centres of excellence, as the distributional politics within nations are easier to manage during a period of overall growth. The German *Exzellenzinitiative* of 1.9 billion euros may lead the regeneration of German higher education. France is pursuing a 3 billion euro merger plan designed to push French institutions up the global rankings. China is building a cohort of strong research universities with additional funding.[15] In the USA the winner-take-all higher education market, in conjunction with federal research funding, constitutes a de facto concentration of resources, research power and status power. The USA houses nearly all of the top research universities. The British research assessment exercise has concentrated research support in a group of leading institutions. Other countries such as Canada, Switzerland, Sweden, Denmark and Finland foster a small number of outstanding research institutions. These developments suggest that Westminster neo-liberalism no longer sets the global pattern of investment in education and research. The heyday of 'doing more with less' has gone. It is probable that coming out of the global recession there will be a widespread lift in the level of investment in knowledge capacity building. If so such a trend would be transformative. The dynamics of competition ensure that leapfrogging investments flow from country to country on a global scale. Each nation drives all the others. In the longer term, the general growth of nation building investments will remake the world political economy as a set of contending knowledge economies. This will not necessarily expand global community but it will enhance global referencing and grow the global synchrony and commonality in policy. By augmenting the capacity of each national innovation system to read all of the others, the common process of capacity building will advance space-time compression and de-severing on the global scale. Inescapably, it will also grow the size of the pool of mobile experts with no fixed loyalties.

Policies designed to concentrate national and local advantage through the building of capacity in education, research, and industry innovation have no inherent tendency to enhance global openness or create new arenas of global action. Given its self-referential intention, capacity building does not exclude a closed and defensive stance on the world. That stance is never wholly absent in state thinking. However, nations and institutions engaged in capacity building welcome the opportunity to range freely in the global setting. Openness is a virtue universally encouraged in others! More positively, most nations and all institutions come to recognize that engagement is essential to global as distinct from local capacity. Projects for building spatial capacity lead logically to projects for building spatial connectivity.

Spatial connectivity

The second spatial move in the global setting quickened in the early to mid 1990s, amid the rise of communicative globalization. This strategy is the formal building of connectivity through alliances, pursued by individual institutions, not nations (the important exception is Europeanization, discussed below). These alliances take two forms: bilateral partnerships, and multi-agent networks. Formal institutional alliances have their equivalents in the decentralized dealings of research centres and individual scholar-researchers with each other. Sometimes these informal alignments are congruent to and aided by institutional ones, sometimes not.

Partnerships

Relations in the knowledge economy are both cooperative and competitive. In a networked communicative system based on loose ties, the same parties might be connected by each, in different domains. Formal partnerships embody specified cooperative activity. They do not assume or create identity, though if successful over a period of time they might generate convergence. Partnership agreements offer shelter from the world—and from each other—and the potential for sharing of intelligence and resources, and more instrumental connections.

Partnership building is also an end in itself. Global partnerships, like global mobility, enjoy the status of an unambiguous good. Throughout the university world there is explosive growth in the number of signed Memoranda of Understanding (MOUs). No comprehensive figures are available, but the rate of increase might match that of the expansion of the Internet. Though each international vice-president makes noises about sweeping away the clutter of inactive MOUs, the truth is that agreements with possible partners in every country of interest, potentially enabling of activity, are a functional approach: easy to secure and dormant with potential. A university never knows which of the deals might be useful, even essential, in future. The conspicuous signing ceremonies also have a performative element. They are visible demonstrations of the university's commitment to internationalization and global modernization; tangible proof of the status of its brand and its research in the eyes of the world. In the moment of signing, the parties are symmetrical, or can be represented so. Thus Harvard, Stanford, MIT, Oxford, Cambridge and other top 'brands' are much sought after as partners. And surely having MOUs in all major countries signifies that the university offers more than mere breadth of coverage and an energetic international office? This can only signify a deeply global mission, and a profound capacity for engagement? Sometimes it is so.

Other cross-border partnerships between universities are driven by activity. The MOU follows the global strategy rather than leading it. The evidence of websites suggests that these more substantial partnerships are also becoming 'thicker' in number and weight. Active partnerships between institutions can involve resource sharing, particularly information resources and the software of administrative systems; benchmarking and quality assurance of each other's programs; or administrative staff training. They often incorporate subsidized research collaborations. In educational programs, there are various forms of sharing and semi-integration, including student and staff exchange, jointly badged degrees, 'twinning' programs whereby students complete one part of the degree at home and the other part abroad, and the 'franchising' of foreign university degrees by local providers. In a study of international networks Beerkens[16] finds that partnerships between institutions broadly similar in functions and status are more common than partnerships between institutions that form a division of labour on the basis of differing status, resources or missions. However, the second kind of partnership is widely used in the cross-border commercial markets in tuition. Franchising and twinning arrangements couple universities from mostly Anglo-American developed nations with local providers, particularly in Asian nations and in Mexico (see below).

A small number of universities exhibit an outstanding level of networked cooperation, such as Tsinghua University in China and Leiden University in the Netherlands. In most research universities outside the USA, global engagement is becoming a central role but in these exceptional institutions global engagement has been at the core of the mission for some time. The National University of Singapore (NUS) is a byword for global engagement (see below).[17]

Consortia

Multi-agent networks or consortia constitute the partnership building strategy on a grander scale. Though consortia may involve preference for members, they are rarely designed to create tight enclosures. Most research universities are members of more than one such network. Nearly all involve at least personnel exchange. Only some trigger joint educational activities. Much depends on the level of drive from the institution where the secretariat is housed. If international networking is a continuum between MOU tokenism and the 'thick' practical connections of universities like NUS, then most consortium activity falls closer to the MOU end of the spectrum. Nevertheless, consortia provide a space in which institutions develop bi-lateral and plural linkages of a practical kind; and strategic and organizational perspectives are shared between leaders at regular meetings, encouraging convergence.

The effects of consortia and smaller partnerships at the local level are modest unless the institution is one of the small number of universities that has moved beyond the level of weak ties and voluntary consent to a deeper agreement, dependency and identity in some areas. This only occurs if the partnership adds something additional to the activities of each member, without substantial opportunity costs. These are difficult conditions to fulfill. But the agreements at lesser levels still contribute to the global knowledge economy. The spreading lattice of small agreements and prosaic cross-border passages and activities, those regulated formally and those unregulated and under-recognized, all accumulates over time. In many respects the global dimension *is* this web of relations and activities. Within it institutions are brought closer in sympathy, de-severing geographical and cultural distances. They become more accustomed to each other's policy jurisdictions, more adept at moving activities to where they are optimized, more ready to consider multiplying their own locations. The mobility of personnel grows. New collaborations emerge. Synchronies become habitual. Mimetics spread.

The symbolic dimension of university partnerships and consortia might seem hollow, but it is not. Amid the thickening and normalizing of global linkages of all kinds, based on voluntary association and a growing personal sympathy between leaders in different national domains, the invisible ties of symbolic partnership can be surprisingly effective in generating action at a distance, much in the manner that without a word being spoken the values shared between colonist and colonizer still hold an ongoing synchrony across the sea. Formal global consortia are also regularly displayed and highly visible. In moving beyond the limited spatiality of inter-national links they give form to the global dimension. If the network also fosters mandated activity in each member's local domain it makes the global still more visible.

Global production

It is remarkable just how often in universities the development of global capacity and connectivity are seen as ends in themselves. This points to the symbolic and performative character of much 'internationalization policy.' Nevertheless, many systems and institutions also have more practical ends in view, utilizing their developing global attributes to produce education and research in the global dimension. Several strategies of production have developed, each with distinctive implications for the formation of global space.

Education export

The most conventional of these strategies of global production, building on the longstanding phenomenon of cross-border student mobility, is commercial education export. Between 1975 and 2006 the number of students crossing borders to receive tertiary education grew from 0.6 to 2.9 million.[18] Cross-border students grew by more than 6 per cent a year, twice the rate of growth of local tertiary students in the OECD countries. Part of the growth in international students is driven by desires for migration to the country of education, especially if it is English speaking. Growth is also driven by the visa, marketing and recruitment policies of the national systems and institutions engaged in education export. In those countries, which have learned to transform the desires for foreign education and for migration into economic capital, the education of international students is a trading business. More than a third of the world's international students pay full cost tuition fees and are regulated by the nation of education not simply as tertiary students but as non-citizen consumers purchasing a service, akin to tourists. More than one million students are now positioned as consumers of the commercial service. Their numbers are growing faster than those of international students in subsidized places.

In little over two decades in Australia, the UK and New Zealand, education export has grown from nothing into a service industry providing a significant chunk of tertiary education costs: about 15 per cent in Australia and 10 per cent in the UK. In Australia the education of international students is the third largest of all export sectors, behind coal and iron ore but ahead of tourism, gold and the agricultural products that sustained the settler state for most of its history: wool, wheat and beef.[19] In certain Australian institutions, including universities with a global role in research that are prestige providers to local students, a large minority of all students are fee-paying internationals. Australia has 14 designated research universities each with over 7000 full fee-paying students.[20] In many smaller private colleges specializing in business studies or English language teaching, foreign education is the core business.

The business model of international education was pioneered by the Thatcher government in the UK in the early 1980s. Australia enrolled its first full fee-paying students in 1987. New Zealand, the Malaysian private sector, Singapore and China followed. With the exception of the Malaysian private sector, most of the provider institutions are ostensibly non-profit institutions, classified 'public' except in the UK, that manage commercial international institution as a business legally separated from domestic education (though subsidized local students and full fee foreign students share the same classroom). Commercial cross-border education is also provided by

Masters programs in some European universities, English training colleges in many countries, and vocationally oriented for-profit institutions such as the University of Phoenix with branches in Mexico, India and Western Europe. The US doctoral universities subsidize international education, which is treated primarily as a branch of foreign policy and research provision rather than a revenue-generating venture. However, full fee commercial places are provided by some non profit institutions. In Europe foreign education of other European nationals is encouraged by the Europeanization process and provided on the same basis as domestic education. The education of non-Europeans is often subsidized and in some cases, such as parts of Germany, is free of tuition charges. Outside Europe and Japan the commercial mode is more dominant. In total 12 per cent of all international students are educated in the UK, 10 per cent in Australia, 2 per cent in New Zealand, 3 per cent in Singapore and 2 per cent in Malaysia. China educates 6 per cent of all international students, many on a commercial basis.[21] The worldwide value of the industry is now estimated at $40 billion dollars USD. Most of this money flows as transfers from the emerging economies to the Anglophone zone. In 2005 exports by the USA were valued at $14.1 billion, the UK $6.1 billion and Australia $5.6 billion.[22]

Education export is transformative. It draws global capital flows and flows of talent into exporting nations and strengthens the global presence of their institutions. It does more than build local resources and global capacity and connectivity in those nations. It improves the number and perhaps quality of graduates in importing nations. Here the business of international education is sustained by and augments the common process of global convergence. In that respect it parallels the capacity building strategies of nations that invest in basic research as a public good within the global circuits of knowledge. Like global research flows the export industry strengthens the role of English as a global language. In other respects two kinds of flows have differing implications for the global space. First, knowledge flows are open in form. The export industry produces exclusive and rivalrous private goods that enclose some but exclude others, partly reworking the knowledge economy as a commercial space in which people mobility is the commodity for trade. This fragments international education between student places that are market commodities and those governed by subsidies or foreign aid.[23] Second, research flows are primarily generated by open source synchrony in civil society and in higher education and other research institutions. Commercial education exports, framed and regulated by nation-states, are the product of national positioning strategies and the governmental drive for export revenues.[24] In the UK, Australia and New Zealand education export has been partly fostered by the under-funding of local educational institutions, at some cost to long term research capacity, which drives them to expand international student places; and the partial phasing out of aid-based student places.[25]

An older political economy is at work in this industry, grounded in an imperial imagining of the global. The old imperialism saw English-language education and/or Western culture as intrinsically superior and one of the means and the justifications for global domination. In spatial terms it saw emerging nations as places to control politically and exploit economically. In this framework there was little obligation for imperial nations to adjust to the cultural other. It is no longer feasible to exercise direct political control of global giants like China and India, the two nations supplying the largest numbers of international students. Instead Anglophone exporters pursue the imperial mission by other means, and the cultural assumptions have not much changed. Commercial advantage is secured through what is seen as the superior status of universities in the developed world, particularly the English-speaking nations. But there is more than one possible explanation for the status of English. No doubt for many 'consumers' of education exports, the dominance of English is not a mark of virtue but a reflection of the world dominance of English-speaking powers since the eighteenth century. But in the export nation itself the superior status and market value accorded to English is both common sense and readily slotted into the old imperial imagining. As Harvey stated: ' …the problem with Enlightenment thought was not that it had *no* conception of "the other" but that it perceived "the other" as necessarily having (and sometimes "keeping to") a specific place in a spatial order that was ethnocentrically conceived to have homogeneous and absolute qualities.[26]

Like all people movement in higher education, the commercial market sustains the de-severing of cultures within a cosmopolitan space. International students maintain contact with families and friends at home while engaging with the country of education. As they grow as self-determining agents they become media of pluralization. In their struggles to survive and change they draw the world closer together. Boundaries fray and people begin to understand each other. This is global integration on a scale of millions. In this manner commercial international education produces incalculable global public goods. Its Marxian dynamic of capitalist expansion inadvertently powers the growth of these public goods. Yet commercial international education falls short of full sharing. It is asymmetrical in form (students from emerging nations travel to developed countries but not vice versa) and imperial in contents. Far from the 'cultural exchange' promoted on university websites, studies of international education in the English-speaking nations persistently find there has been little change in the contents and pedagogical methods of institutions in the export nations. The presence of large number of students schooled in other educational and cultural traditions seems to have little impact on educational programs. There is little obligation to engage with international students' own learning histories and traditions in the classroom; not as a gesture of politeness to the students (many of whom are pleased to be doing something new) but to create more room for transition and perhaps hybridity, to increase the purchase of pedagogies and to bring the locals something new. But international students are typically modelled as in language and learning 'deficit.' Few bi-lingual and multi-lingual approaches have emerged. In short, the sources of students are multiple but formal learning is not. Given that local students are under no obligation to respect the cultural identity of international students, it is unsurprising that the level of mixing between international and local students is disappointingly low. This is another persistent finding in the literature.[27] For their part, international students struggle to synchronise with the host country. Often they feel pressured to choose between original and host country identities. In mono cultural settings a supple pluralism is difficult to reach.[28] The commercial industry is open to ever more consumers but not the cultural baggage they bring. The NPM rhetoric about responding to the consumer/customer/stakeholder is negated. This is unsurprising. Belief in cultural superiority is intrinsic to the market commodity itself.

Global hubs

Global hubs take the evolution of global production one stage further. In the knowledge economy global education hubs are designed to position a particular national system or city as a pole of attraction and capital accumulation, centred on its education and research activities. The aim is to divert part of the global flows of talent, knowledge, ideas, technologies, fee paying students and capital investments in knowledge through the hub; and to wrap around the hub a larger set of industries such as tourism, knowledge-intensive manufacturing and perhaps financial and regulatory services. Typically, government invests in infrastructure and offers favourable terms to foreign providers who may wish to locate onsite. The classic hub is seen as a medium of modernization that will position the nation or city as a centre of global and regional development. The first and only real knowledge hub is Singapore in Southeast Asia.

Singapore

For Singapore the global dimension is not just a field of opportunity it is necessity and destiny. Singapore is an island city-state of 710 square kilometres with a population of 4.8 million in 2008. The city-state has much geography but little history. It is strategically located at the end of the Malay Peninsula on the Straits of Malacca along a major seaway and roughly equidistant between China and India. The site was an 1819 British foundation. It broke away from post-colonial Malaysia in 1965. In the last half century Singapore has created its own national identity centred on economic development. Multi-cultural in character, three quarters of its people use a Chinese language, mostly Putonghua (Mandarin) which is known as Huayu in Singapore. Smaller groups speak Malay and Tamil. However, the dominant language of civic intercourse, business and education is English. Singapore is a bi-cultural Anglo-Chinese zone which, like Hong Kong, has advanced capacity in both the English-speaking world and China, reinforcing the role of global medium and portal city that its geography suggests.

The city-state has built a Western European level of per capita income as a transport and trading economy with advanced manufacturing and financial services. It is one of the world's busiest ports and sustains a high volume of currency dealings and other financial transactions. Manufacturing industries include electronics, petroleum refining, chemicals, mechanical engineering and biomedical sciences. The only wealthy economy in Southeast Asia, Singapore has positioned itself as regional centre and broker and often hosts pan-Asian organizations and meetings. Its ambition is to broker international dealings on a global scale, and it emphasizes links into Europe and the Americas as well as different parts of Asia. It is a regional city on par with Seoul and a little behind Tokyo and Shanghai that wants to become a world city. Its exemplars are Paris and San Francisco and beyond that London and New York. The capacity to leverage global mobility, and the capacity to manufacture and renovate social and cultural relations, are at the heart of the Singapore project. It is friendly to foreign businesses and to tourists. Regulation is enabling, subsidies for industry and universities are designed to attract and hold, the civic services are well organized and urban precincts are transparent, safe and clean. Every effort is made to provide the right local and imported cultural activities. Having eliminated the original rainforest, Singapore has constructed a small wilderness zone for the eco-tourist. In keeping with the sanitized urban precinct and the manicured lawns there is a whiff of artificial display—even tweeness—about some of the state-sponsored art and design. Singapore is Disneyland for grownups. Here is 'a small, small world' in more than one sense.

Nevertheless, Singapore's formidable powers of invention make it the quintessential knowledge economy. The city-state is led by a data-rich and far-sighted apparatus expert in global positioning and reflexive self-creation. It knows its own national project, which is also a global project, and the understanding is widely shared in the city. The long-term stability and objectivity of the state apparatus are protected by one party rule. As with all governments in some domains, but more so one party regimes, transparency is lacking. The state observes the world accurately and interacts with it effectively but it does so from within a cone of silence with one-way glass. Open and bounded. Singapore has no resources except people and location and must continually define itself, make its own fate and live on its wits, its agency freedom applied strategically in the global setting. Both global engagement and national 'insideness' are essential and each has developed almost to caricature. As Sidhu notes:

> At different historical moments, the Singaporean government has mobilized different themes to promote its vision. For the past decade the discursive language within its developmental blueprints, ministerial speeches and newspaper reports has used the global imperative—globalization. Global benchmarks and imaginaries are a vital part of the educational, political, social and semiotic landscape. Billboards on buses, train stations, and motorways, along with government commercials proclaim the island as 'a global city'; its national university as a 'Global Knowledge Enterprise.'[29]

Singapore's economic planners believe survival and prosperity depend on 'establishing high value industries and services such as design and engineering, education, communication, marketing and management.'[30] They are global hub strategies in several areas in addition to education and research, including financial services; medical services; creative industries in the arts, media and communications; conventions; and tourism. Singapore sees the knowledge industries in parallel to other, familiar, global-forming and globally-formed industries such as transport and finance. The lodestone is the short-term and long-term contributions to capital accumulation. Within the knowledge sectors, basic research and cultural creativity are encouraged, as a part of the conditions of accumulation. In what Singapore calls its 'Global Schoolhouse' strategy the nation invests in both its own knowledge infrastructure; and in the enticement of foreign universities and business schools on the basis of medium term partnerships. It is hoped that the creation of a zone of institutions with world reputations will draw a strong flow of fee-paying international students of good quality, particularly from China, and also firms interested in the potential for commercializable intellectual property, especially in electronics and biomedicine; and the presence of foreign universities of quality will drive improvements in Singapore's own institutions. Amongst the foreign institutions that have set up shop are Wharton, the leading business school in the USA, the Chicago Business School, the MIT research laboratories, the leading European business school INSEAD, the Technical University of Eindhoven in the Netherlands, and Munich University of Technology from Germany. The Schoolhouse strategy is state-dependant but it is also flexible, in that the city-state has the option of scaling down foreign involvement at a later time, thereby shifting the balance more towards locally-controlled activity. In Singapore there is also now 'greater recognition that for Singapore to meet its knowledge economy aspirations, the development of indigenous capacity in entrepreneurship and technological innovation is vital.'[31]

> In the Global Schoolhouse, we have a state-sponsored project devised to establish a 'knowledge and education hub' which attempts to brings together *networks* of ideas, knowledge, technology, and world-class universities, aligning them with the professional aspirations of people who are anticipated to contribute to Singapore's knowledge economy ambitions. The Global Schoolhouse, then, can be said to have multiple policy functions: it is anticipated to act as a magnet for other 'value' added knowledge-intensive services and industries; it is expected to attract high quality human capital-dubbed 'top talent' from all over the world' …it is also expected to set world-class standards for local universities and local staff. The policy approach to leverage off the branding potential of a group of renowned foreign institutions ('World-class Universities'), extended to the provision of government support to establish centres of excellence in research. It was anticipated that these centres would link up with domestic industry and MNCs with a regional and Singaporean presence, as well as local research institutes to establish a self-sustaining 'research ecosystem.' Only 'high quality' institutions were invited and supported....[32]

Sidhu notes that 'global knowledge spaces such as the US$300 million Biopolis (biomedicine) and the Fusionpolis (IT and creative media) draw inspiration from the cluster technopoles of Silicon Valley and Route 135.'[33] There is talk of Singapore becoming a 'Harvard of the East.' Negotiations with each of the Universities of Warwick in the UK and New South Wales in Australia, to create a large-scale campus focused on fee-paying international students, came to nothing, but research partnerships are simpler to organize because the funding of research activity is unequivocally dependant on government, in this case Singapore. Foreign research partners are required to make only modest financial commitments in exchange for up front subsidies and can bid for Singapore research funds. In the case of Johns Hopkins, where the partnership collapsed, the American university committed just $60,000 to the establishment of the Johns Hopkins Medical School in Singapore. Singapore spent about $53 million USD.[34] A key sticking point in partnerships and a potential weak spot in the hub strategy is the character of the foreign contribution, whether it is a peripheral international venture or the real thing. The foreign branch campus must be as hard to enter as the home institution, the people it sends to Southeast Asia must be cutting edge, and it must be a magnet for talent in the manner of its parent. Singapore's local birthrate is below replacement and a primary aim of the Global Schoolhouse strategy is to attract talented expatriates, especially those from the 'creative class' in Richard Florida's sense.[35] Much thought in Singapore has gone into what constitutes a 'creative economy' and 'creative culture,' terms which have been translated in a straightforward manner from their European origins. Planning focuses on forms of entertainment, stimulation and sociability that creative people are expected to enjoy. Singapore knows innovations are rooted in ideas and that synchrony across diverse fields can spark them.[36] Nevertheless rather than migrating permanently, outsiders often stay for only limited periods. Some expatriates become frustrated by the inner enclosure of decision-making. Perhaps this, too, is what Singapore wants.

Singapore's own education and research institutions are already strong. The schools exhibit relatively high levels of student achievement in standardized tests. In terms of the total volume of scientific papers produced in 2003–2007, moderated by citations per publication and normalized by academic field, the National University of Singapore (NUS) ranked 63rd in the world, just in front of the University of Edinburgh in Scotland and Georgia Tech and the University of California Santa Barbara in the USA, further ahead of the Universities of Melbourne and Sydney in Australia, and not far below each campus of the University of Texas at Houston and Austin.[37] This is a fine performance for an institution with modest research three decades ago and will improve in future counts. The extent to which foreign presence in Singapore is essential to local performance is debatable; but Singapore's three universities are outstanding in the extensity, intensity and acumen of their global networking. NUS has located partnerships and centres of student exchange across all of the advanced industrial regions and in all main cultural zones. It has alliances with most major institutions in Asia, Western Europe and the English-speaking countries, in both teaching and research; plays a leading role in consortia such as the Asia Pacific Rim Universities (APRU) and the ASEAN country networks; and hosts regional Southeast Asian and global meetings. NUS's space-making on the global scale is an essential complement to its capacity building in the island state itself. In some other respects the Global Schoolhouse might have become too Singapore-enclosed

Singapore's hub strategy is a notable creation of human imagination. It is global modernization writ large: in the internal scale of transformation Singapore is exceeded only by the remaking of China. Starting from a clear understanding of its geography and capacity, consumed by the problem of size, an embattled interest at the feet of the giants, the city-state set out to secure a leading vantage in the more compressed and synchronous world to be. The bold vision has been followed through with honesty of purpose. Self-marketing is at the behest of strategy in Singapore, not strategy at the behest of marketing. Free of the burden of tradition, Singapore is culturally open and flexible and can mix and match. The fit between global observation, global vision, national regulation and local incentives has been beautifully crafted and is continually tuned. The hub strategy has captured the attention of emerging states around the world, though none match Singapore's clarity of purpose and execution. No doubt if the Global Schoolhouse strategy had worked exactly as planned the global dimension would now be thick with hubs jostling each other, cities would be transmogrifying into a clutch of hubs in different sectors; though only a few nodes in each global network could achieved the sought-after dominance. But the Global Schoolhouse has not altogether worked as planned.

For the foreign partners Singapore offers a favourable location for operations in Asia that is supplementary to core operations. For Singapore the Global Schoolhouse *is* core business. Thus Singapore has assumed most of the costs and risks, but in asymmetrical partnerships it can be difficult to align expectations. A persistent complaint in Singapore is that the foreign partners have not located their best work in Asia. In the case of Johns Hopkins', a key point of contention' was the failure by the American institution to hire '12 senior investigators with international reputations to reside in Singapore' as had been agreed.[38] The Hopkins Dean of Medicine noted that persuading Americans and their families to relocate to Singapore was 'a challenge.' Singapore lacked the stimulation derived from proximate US health science and health services, and the research performance indicators set by Singapore were too inflexible. 'Hopkins [considers] serendipity vital to the scientific process.'[39] Similar difficulties have attended other partnerships. The bargains driven by Singapore in exchange for generous up front funding have proven hard to deliver, while Singapore has been overly focused on direct national economic returns for its investment in global education and knowledge. Singapore makes its partners offers that are too good to refuse, but on the creative side of the knowledge economy, commercial deal-making is no substitute for partnerships regulated by voluntary synchrony. A case of 'money can't buy me love.' Without love, it can't buy new ideas either.

There might be two difficulties here. One is ideological. Reflecting the neo-liberalism that is the price of a British heritage, Singapore models the knowledge economy as akin to finance or transport in that it is seen as a site of direct economic returns; but in a capitalist economy the more important economic roles of education and research lie in the creation of conditions for innovation and productivity advance in other sectors. While Singapore acknowledges the need for basic research, it may have under-estimated the leakage from national innovation systems in the open source setting and have been optimistic about the potential patent income and local payoff in product innovations to follow from that same basic research.[40] Likewise the plan for a University of NSW campus faltered because a poor business model over-estimated the likely income from international students and made the mistaken assumption that a mass teaching campus operating essentially as a commercial service-provider would sustain a front rank research effort at the same time. However, if the neo-liberal model was set aside (and after all, policy on NUS has been handled differently), and the time scale for economic returns was elongated, it would be possible to pursue a version of the hub strategy.

The second difficulty is more fundamental. It goes to the spatial form of the hub strategy. A study by Kong and colleagues of creative economy policies in Asia finds the Singapore strategy is 'non-spatial, or at best aspatial.'[41] There is little discussion of spatial configurations inside the city. The benefits of fine-tuning local proximity are missed. Sidhu notes the failure 'to translate the global imaginary into globalizing practices and outcomes' and suggests that factors of location and 'adjacency' have been underestimated. 'Pronouncements about the "end of geography" and the deterritorialized university…should be approached with caution.'[42] Both comments only capture part of the problem—after all, Singapore's hub strategy is premised on a hyper-awareness of geo-spatial settings—but they each point to something important. In Singapore the nation-state within its self-imposed enclosure functions as an absolute. The nation is the terminal point of interest, not the global. Hence the question of internal spatial configurations is underplayed—what is important is that the activity is located and controlled within the island and not outside it, not how the activity is arranged in relation to others in Singapore—while the potential of a well organized and financed hub to orchestrate global flows is overplayed, as if these flows can be altogether abstracted from their local/national determinants. The exemplars that Singapore wants to emulate have advantages that no control system within the island can achieve: location on the Atlantic among a thick network of developed economies with front rank knowledge resources, or within the USA, which is overwhelming strong in all knowledge economy domains. The would-be centripetal strategy of inviting the world to come to Singapore on Singapore's terms, with all the global distances seen as equivalent, has limited purchase. It could only work if the hub was already hegemonic. Only the US could achieve such strategy at this time. Singapore is not the United States, nor is it China; and to enclose fewer than five million people is to shrink global identity towards zero.

The more effective global strategy for a small to medium power with advanced capacity would be to combine horizontal networking and a willingness to work with partners in their own domains as well as at home (that is, for Singapore as a whole to work in the manner of the national university); with a regional role that maximizes the potentials of 'adjacency.' The last suggests that Singapore's relationships with China and East Asia, India, Indonesia and its smaller neighbours are the main vectors of its future. As a regional hub embedded in the Asia-Pacific, not a de-territorialized local hub, it could maximize its global presence. But a larger regional strategy would require Singapore to embrace interests beyond the enclosure.

Other hubs

Singapore's Global Schoolhouse has left its mark on global imaginings. The hub strategy beckons as the pre-eminent means by which emerging nations can make their mark in the knowledge economy, drawing capital and talent and modernizing themselves at the same time. It is premised on desired foreign involvement. It is about smarts, so it makes the government look smart. Near to Singapore, Malaysia wants to be a hub and Hong Kong is also playing with the idea. There are many more. In early April 2009 authorities in the francophone island of Mauritius in the Indian Ocean announced that the carrying capacity of the University of Mauritius would be doubled, to 20,000 students, with the creation of a second campus. The Chief Executive of the State Land Development Company said that the new campus would be 'the most modern, and will meet the aspirations of the country to become the knowledge hub of the region.' The plan to transform Mauritius into 'a regional knowledge hub and a centre of higher learning' was part of the Tertiary Education Commission's strategic plan for the 2007–2011 period.[43] In practice this comes to no more than building the export of education from Mauritius. In emerging countries blueprints for hubs tend to underplay the R&D domain.

More weighty proposals for global hubs have emerged in the Gulf States. Like Singapore and unlike Mauritius, governments in the oil exporting nations can invest at scale, though their capacity to do so rises and falls with the price of oil. Large scale 'knowledge villages' have been created in Qatar, and at the two largest cities in the United Arab Emirates, Dubai and Abu Dhabi. Foreign providers have been invited in with offers they find difficult to refuse (see Table 5.2 below), supported by locally financed infrastructure, buildings and facilities. Compared to Singapore there is a greater reliance on the foreign providers and less on local k-economy capacity, less focus on research and development, and revenue projections are more dependant on the attractiveness of the hub to fee-paying international students. But being largely abstracted from the local setting—in fact the strategy is designed to secure a beach-head for modernization without directly confronting local tradition—the hubs in the Gulf cannot utilize 'adjacency' in their favour. In any case, Qatar and the Emirates do not offer the economic and cultural ambience of North America, Europe and East Asia; nor do they offer prospects of migration or the same range of business opportunities as Singapore. The hubs promise a safe environment to young students, and there is potential to build a market in Muslim countries, but it is unclear why other foreign students or scholars would want to travel to the Gulf State 'knowledge villages' unless there are overwhelming financial incentives to do so. Framed as financial businesses parallel to banking, missing the fuller potentials of knowledge in the open source ecology, the 'knowledge villages' are irretrievably parasitic on states and may not survive a protracted global recession. These are not cauldrons of creativity to be. The hubs in the Gulf are toys, education theme parks with a limited life.

Knowledge cities

The unwinding of the hub strategy suggests general conclusions. First, local strength is the heart of a hub. Location, identity and capacity matter. A pool of indigenous labour that is globally competitive in teaching, research and organization is a good start. It is unrealistic to expect the hub itself to supply the foundational pool of skills from expatriate labour sources, though these have a supplementary role. Second, knowledge hubs can succeed if they are located in cities with an established global role, especially if these are positioned in key world regions. Hubs cannot create a global role from nothing, like the 'knowledge villages' in the Gulf States, and those that try to do so will wither. The ideal place for an education or knowledge hub is a major city of economic and demographic passage, with attractive cultural resources. Here there is no substitute for a vibrant civil society. As Singapore has shown, there are limits to the extent to which this can be force-fed by government. Third, in the medium term, the direct economic returns from investment in the hub are likely to be modest.

Despite these constraints hubs can succeed. Regions and cities can secure advantages by concentrating, coordinating and modernizing their knowledge infrastructure, and involving selected foreign providers, provided these moves are matched by mobility in the outward direction. The payoffs in productivity and innovation will be optimized when the generation of knowledge is matched by the capacity of industry to absorb it. There remains the danger of the hub becoming locked into welfare dependence on state subsidies and the regulatory settings. Another danger of knowledge hubs and the associated R&D enclaves is that knowledge-intensive industries in manufacturing and services can become overly dependant on privileged access to the subsidies provided to higher education, rather than becoming globally effective.

An alternate strategy to the global hub is to build capacity in the form of a 'knowledge city' or 'knowledge region' with a global orientation. Most of the larger cities in the developed world are considering this approach. Only some nations apply serious resources to institution building along these lines but many more engage in the semiotics. At the outset of this period Harvey talked about 'the striving…for cities to forge a distinctive image and to create an atmosphere of place and tradition that will act as a lure for capital and for people 'of the right sort' (i.e. wealthy and influential).[44] The OECD encourages the development of regional knowledge economy strategies. The strand of that work focused on locally-oriented R&D seems misplaced because of the uncertain economic potentials of most SMEs and regionally-bound firms, and global leakages in research. However the strand focused on global cities is instructive. The OECD notes that for creative people both city livability and access to like-minded others are important. While low taxes encourage inward flows of financial capital, and entrepreneurship, people are often attracted to a good and stimulating environment with better services.[45] Whereas industrial economies needed expansive production sites and located industries on the edge of cities, 'post-industrial' knowledge activities benefit more from proximity to key services, transport and communications. This favours industry/university agglomerations at city centres in which cross-field and creativity/capital synergies can develop. In high-technology and scientific manufacturing, media, finance, cultural and fashion, 'there are advantages in both clustering and in global access to knowledge.'[46] Diverse knowledge workers concentrate, coming 'constantly into communication with each other in ways that help to unleash diverse innovative energies. Studies show that this process of communication is a critical factor in the generation of new ideas, sensitivities, and insights.'[47] Globally connected cities are already primary nodes in the evolution of the global. Knowledge city strategies amplify the effects. Global city strategies are less spectacular than global hub strategies and better integrated into existing capacity and activity. This form of global production, which mirrors the building of nodes in a network, is steadily transformative.

Beyond national boundaries

Beerkens defines globalization in higher education as 'a process in which basic social arrangements within and around the university become 'disembedded' from their national context due to the intensification of transnational flows of people, information and resources.'[48] Disembedding occurs when activity taking place in the global space and creative of that global space becomes sufficiently important to overshadow or displace activity in the national dimension, or weakens the regulatory capacity of national governments. When some institutions become more disembedded from national regulatory frameworks than others, a national system of higher education becomes a complex amalgam with varying degrees of national accountability. This also stretches the capacity of existing steering instruments.

There is potential disembedding in several areas. Many institutions seek an increasing proportion of their funds from outside the national jurisdiction, for example in the export market. In research a growing part of funding is accessible at international and supranational levels. Another set of examples relate to teaching programs that cross national boundaries. By operating either virtually or physically across national borders, institutions exceed the boundaries of their enabling national legislation while entering the jurisdiction of other nation states. Some institutions seek accreditation outside their originating national context[49] for several reasons: lack of accreditation opportunities at home; the use of international accreditation to secure advantage in the national dimension or to evade the requirements or prohibitions of national accreditation; and enhancing global recognition via accreditation by a reputable foreign accreditation body. National accreditation agencies also have motivations for exporting their services.[50] There is also a small group of would-be global accreditation agencies with a vested interest in expanding the role of global referencing in accreditation.

A further set of examples relates to research labour. Global people mobility appears to be increasing at the doctoral level, and probably also in post-doctoral employment and among the small but strategically significant group of leading disciplinary practitioners. Nevertheless, internationally-trained doctoral graduates enter national career systems and academic labour markets which in most countries have been slower to change. Musselin notes that in comparative studies of faculty labour markets in Germany, France and other European countries, comparing these also to the USA and UK, there are no signs of a tendency to Europeanization in academic recruitment and careers to parallel the evolving European research framework.[51] 'One of the most striking national patterns of each system is that academic labour markets, salaries, status, recruitment procedures, workloads, career patterns, and promotion rules tend to be very different from one country to another'[52] It is likely, however, that the mobility of leading researchers will have more transformative effects, segmenting national labour markets between a small group of the globally mobile and the rest. Governments and universities are under pressure to differentiate salaries previously held in an equal position across fields and institutions, and between individuals at the same level regardless of merit. The emerging alternative is two tier remuneration systems that will match the twin character of the profession: globally mobile/nationally bound profession.

Regionalization

Small-sized to medium-sized higher education systems, lacking the firepower of the US or China, have limited capacity to set the rules of global engagement, even using highly creative strategies like those of Singapore. This suggests that where feasible, regionalization of capacity and people mobility, particularly in research, is an attractive strategy. Physical proximity matters. But geography is not the only factor at work. There are three conditions for successful regional organization within the world setting: geographical proximity, cultural commonality, and political will. Cultural coherence across a region facilitates de-severing, and a distinctive cultural space also facilitates the creation of a regional enclosure. In the absence of political will, geography and culture are not enough. China, Korea, Japan and even North Vietnam share significant cultural elements and are adjacent geographically. There are unresolved historical and political tensions between China-Japan, Korea-Japan, China-Vietnam, and Vietnam-Japan, that stymie the potential for deep regional integration

In higher education and research the only zone that currently fulfils all three conditions for regionalization is Europe. The normative commitment to Europeanization is profound. It has two sets of roots. The first is the 75 years of self-destructive warfare, from the Franco-Prussian War and the turmoil of the Paris Commune, to Nazi Germany and the ruins left after World War II. The lesson of history has been deployed as the circuit-breaker and the foundation of regional imagining. France and Germany have comes to terms with their history. It is in the low countries where France and Germany meet; and in the Nordic countries, open to both cultures without losing their own project, that the commitment to Europeanization is most strong. The grasp of history provides the rationale for common identity. The second set of roots of the European project lies in global convergence. Europeanization is not simply a statement of mutual accord in a de-severed common space. It has a more active project in view, driven by desires for a United Europe to match the New World, which since 1945 and the American-financed Marshall Plan for reconstruction has overshadowed the European continent. The knowledge economy is seen as the key to achieving equal global status with the US. The shared idea animating the 2005 Lisbon declaration[53] is the hubris of Europe as the world's leading knowledge economy and hence (it is glibly assumed) the global leader per se. It seems that the world continues to be a place of terrors and threats and chosen peoples and the old imperial dreams are not altogether dead. It also seems ideas are everything and universities have the wit to lead bankers and business, and to anticipate the logic of capital accumulation without knowing about it. The nineteenth century world mission of the European nation has morphed into a collaborative project with competitive intent. The means of self assertion and global leadership are no longer settler farms and gunboats but research, education and industrial innovation. The well-springs are not just economic but cultural.

Nowhere is the momentum of Europeanization stronger than in the universities, where history is one of the technologies. The universities are the normative and practical heart of the imaginings of the European knowledge economy, and the universities are more than aware of the global weight of their American equivalents which powers the competitive challenge. And Europeanization benefits European higher education: partly because universities as institutions are unusually capable of international synchrony, partly because they have acquired a new sense of purpose. The contrast with Japan is instructive. Japan cannot contribute to a regional project in East Asia because it cannot bring itself to acknowledge its own military history. Japanese universities, which at the peak constitute a brilliant high research sector, now find themselves wavering between the old national autarky managed by an over-regulatory state; a poisoned regional legacy that remains uncorrected and turns the rising tide of universities in China, Korea and Taiwan China into a threat rather than an opportunity; and a half-glimpsed globalism that always remains out of reach. It seems that 'internationalization' in Japanese higher education is always a question that eludes definition, never an answer. By comparison many Northwestern European universities are vibrant, energized by the new investments, their pride in the common project, their continued diversity and the growing intersections with each other; though their weaker cousins in the South and East still have capacity-building to do. Only the British institutions remain largely indifferent to the momentous changes. They do not share the sense of mutual necessity. They nurse an older British global project, or imagine themselves into a global alliance of England and America that in the USA scarcely exists.[54]

The processes of Europeanization in education and research are much discussed in the research literature[55] and will not be reviewed in detail here. Europeanization consists of the Bologna alignment of the structures of national systems and qualifications, the creation of the European Higher Education Area (EHEA) and European Research Area, and the intensive mobility of students and staff that has developed in the wake of the Erasmus programs.[56] The formation of the European Research Area is the most extensive and perhaps least controversial aspect. It entails the partial integration of research budgets, a growing research collaboration across European borders, and measures to encourage doctoral and researcher mobility within

Europe. In decisions about research funding, there has been a partial transfer of activity and authority to the European level. The Bologna process is designed to establish a common structure of undergraduate and Masters degrees to assist student mobility within and from outside Europe. The structure is being implemented with varying degrees of speed and enthusiasm across European countries but overall can be accounted successful. Associated with the change to degree structures, approximately half of all institutions have adopted a European diploma supplement. This provides a common description of graduate qualifications that assists their portability. The Bologna process is also developing cooperation and system building in relation to nomenclature, equivalences, credentialing, credit transfer and quality assurance. In the Tuning project institutions across the region are developing a common set of curriculum descriptors, which again facilitates student mobility and also assists the dovetailing and mixing of academic programs across national boundaries. European higher education systems are also developing a common system of institutional classifications akin to the Carnegie classifications in the USA.[57] This is a crucial step in defining the European Higher Education Area as a regional space. It also transfers some authority over mission definition upwards to that regional space and so facilitates the longer term creation of a single multi-national and multi-lingual system with common systems and use of English.

Europeanization in the knowledge economy is both top down and bottom up. Much of it consists of voluntary institution-to-institution activity. Some of it requires the formal coordination of national systems in a chain of quasi-voluntary changes. A portion is shaped by formal regulation and law at both the national and regional levels. Though 'Brussels' is the universal butt there is a guarded acceptance of regulation. Europe is both Westphalian and post-Westphalian. It is imagined as a federal space of sovereign national governments, which when push comes to shove are still mindful of their own interests, but European trust, policies and systems have accumulated a growing weight. In Europe the knowledge economy has acquired a plural regulatory structure in which the nation-state is sustained and also partly disembedded at the same time. Regional identity and local/national identities are being reproduced together. At the same time each is changing with and responding to the other

What does the regional Europeanization process imply for the formation of the global dimension of action? Its primary importance lies in the formation of the region itself, an example of compelling long term significance. Its larger effects in the shaping of the global are restrained by a curious myopia of vision that might be the price of the European enclosure. The contrast with Singapore is helpful. Singapore sustains a centred, closed identity while keenly watching the world beyond it. It brings a matchless realism and foresight to bear on all its external dealings. The EHEA has to marshall not a centred but a multiple self. Its identity is defined as much by its outer boundary as by what its federated parts have in common. In turn that outer boundary, which like the whole project is self-created, serves to block a clear view of the world beyond. It seems that complex European synchrony demands the full attention of European higher education's thinkers and leaders; and also that in contrast with

Singapore, it is less vital to get the external world right. Certainly, the effective focus is largely inward. Documents generated out of the European project acknowledge higher education and research in the United States, which is the measuring stick, but they scarcely grasp the global well-springs of American power. The Lisbon process failed to situate American k-economy leadership in the larger context of the American role in the economy, technology, the media, entertainment and image making, not to mention the military sphere—as if displacing the leadership of American universities in the league tables could be achieved by investments in R&D alone, or that higher education determines the military and Hollywood. Aside from that caricature of the USA mobilized as the driver of the project, the EHEA's ambit of interest extends little further than North Africa, Turkey and the Middle East, the countries supplying the bulk of the half-welcomed migrants into Europe. Iran is on the border of vision. India, China and East Asia and Southeast Asia are simply too far away to become a preoccupation. European projects of engagement with Asia are peripheral to the real action. This is Roman Europe, the Mediterranean world and the nations to its north. Once again we see that vision is central to our imagining. The old visions, the old maps in our mind, can be resilient and retard the potential for new creations. Though in theory the capacity in cosmopolitan systems that has been developed in Europe could be applied in the global dimension for the benefit of all, the present process of European institution-building remains a reduced global project. [58] In contrast the American universities are more parochial, even insular in their national vision; but they are more adventurous beyond, and more clearly see the whole world as a single space.

Outside Europe, in higher education and research, the potential for regional developments is modest. The most promising signs are in South America, where the geo-spatial potentials are augmented by a shared Spanish/Portuguese heritage. Many South American nations have joined the European Tuning project; and Argentina, Brazil, Paraguay, and Uruguay have extended educational cooperation within MERCUSOR to other Latin nations. In Southeast Asia the Association of South East Asian Nations (ASEAN) federation, founded in 1967, sustains small scale collaborations in people movement and research projects, and there are gestures towards a Bologna-style integration of programs, but there is far to go; institutions in most countries are weak in research, and ASEAN is largely peripheral to domestic politics in Southeast Asia. The cultural stretch is a little further than Europe and the political will seems to be absent. In Africa the brake on regionalism is the weakness of states and consequently of higher education systems. The North American Free Trade Zone (NAFTA) has never been more than a partial free trade agreement; and at this point, universities in the USA, which resist the notion of a national system, see little to be gained in larger frameworks that would take in Mexico and Canada. Global hegemony can be exercised without regionalization.

Transnational education

Transnational education means the enrollment of students in a nation other than the home nation of the educational institution concerned.[59] The institution becomes the foreigner while the international student is at home; rather than, as in the case of education export on the soil of the provider nation, the international student acting the part of foreigner. Transnational education can be produced by distance education means (see the next section for discussion of e-universities) or by creating a branch campus. Branch campuses, the topic of this part of the chapter, come in two forms. The first is the stand-alone campus owned/rented and operated solely by the transnational institution. The second and more common model is collaboration with a local partner organization to provide education in the foreign country setting. All forms of transnational education take the production of education out of the national jurisdiction of the institution and into the national jurisdiction of another government. Because transnational institutions continue to be shaped, at least in their home country activities, by their own regulatory setting, once they move offshore they acquire an inescapable duality. It is harder for any one government to pin the university down but at the same time it must deal with both. This creates both new global freedoms and new unfreedoms generated by thicker regulation. Transnational education institutions do not negate or exceed the nation-state as such. But by freely operating across borders in the global setting, transnational institutions have rendered obsolete the notion of singular, unique and bounded territorial identity.

The viability of a branch campus does not depend on a prestige brand, though all else being equal that can help (and in particular cases, such as Singapore, is mandatory). Nor does viability depend on the existence of unmet demand. There are American providers in the Netherlands and Canada, and an Australian university offers teacher training in Ontario, Canada. One Australian university, Monash, adopted the strategic objective of building a stand-alone campus on every continent regardless of the state of development, though the plan only got as far as campuses in Australia, Asia (Malaysia) and Africa (South Africa) plus a conference centre in Europe (Italy), before the cost of the multinational extension became too great. For local governments the foreign branch campus can help to expand local capacity, in general or in a tailored area of priority; contribute to building an international hub; place competitive pressure on local institutions; or simply serve as an exemplar of standards or organizational norms. It also provides a means of transferring knowledge and skills directly into the local system, and some governments, such as China, have strict requirements concerning local partner presence. For local students the branch of the transnational institution may provide access to the foreign degree close to home and at a price cheaper than going aboard, in relation to both tuition and living costs, though without the benefit of language immersion in the export nation. It also provides the student with a route of passage into the parent campus on the basis of familiarity with language and curriculum and with the benefit of transferable credit. The capacity of branch campuses to lock onto other parts of international education provision in a networked institution alone can make them economically viable.

The number of branch campuses is growing rapidly. American institutions have followed their English speaking compatriots and are becoming dominant in numerical terms. Table 6.1 from Verbik and Merkley[60] is a list of stand-alone branch campuses by provider nation. This excludes franchising where the international university has little impact on the nature of provision. Despite the efforts of the researchers, the list is not fully comprehensive or current. For example, no institutions are listed for India, where international providers are active though officially unrecognized, and the table includes an Australian campus in Fiji that closed earlier. The institutions involved in branch campus activity range from fully commercial providers such as the University of Phoenix, to second sector public institutions, to the one third that are established research universities. In addition to the Australian providers Charles Sturt, Central Queensland, Curtin, Monash, Swinburne, James Cook, Monash, New South Wales, RMIT and Wollongong they include the University of Bologna (Argentina), Seoul National (Vietnam), the University of Nottingham (China and Malaysia), Johns Hopkins (China and Italy), Columbia (Jordan), Harvard Medical (Emirates) and the Chicago School of Business (UK). There are 14 such transnational institutions listed in the 'knowledge villages' in the Emirates, seven in Qatar, six in Singapore, and five in China. The full numbers are higher.

Table 6.1. Transnational branch campuses, by provider nation, 2006

PROVIDER NATION	INTERNATIONAL BRANCH CAMPUSES	LOCATIONS
USA	44	Qatar (5), China (4), Canada (3), Emirates (3), Jordan (2), Mexico (2), Netherlands (2), Singapore (2), UK (2), Czech Republic, Ecuador, France, Germany, Greece, Hungary, Israel, Italy, Jamaica, Japan, Panama, Poland, Puerto Rico, Switzerland, Thailand
Australia	10	Malaysia (3), Singapore (2), Canada, Emirates, Fiji, South Africa, Vietnam
India	5	Emirates (4), Singapore
UK	4	Emirates (2), China, Malaysia
Canada	3	Emirates (2), Qatar
Ireland	2	Malaysia, Pakistan
Netherlands	2	Qatar, South Africa
Pakistan	2	Emirates, Kenya
Philippines	2	Vietnam, Indonesia
Belgium	1	Emirates

(table continued on next page)

PROVIDER NATION	INTERNATIONAL BRANCH CAMPUSES	LOCATIONS
Chile	1	Ecuador
France	1	Singapore
Italy	1	Argentina
Korea	1	Vietnam
Sweden	1	Russia

Source: Berbik and Merkley, 2006, 25–30

There are many fine shadings between an overseas-controlled stand-alone campus and a franchised operation in which the international provider has a merely nominal role. Yet the differences between the polar types are important. The stand-alone campus requires major investment by the foreign provider and is unlikely to turn a profit in the near future. It is likely to be difficult to achieve and to negotiate with the national government on whose soil it is erected. On the other hand it enables a fuller level of quality control over the education provided, it allows the curriculum to be closely dovetailed with the provider country, and its creation provides an opportunity for a close engagement with the local system, though the last opportunity is not always taken. Franchising through a local partner is cheaper to provide and may generate an early surplus. On the other hand franchised campuses are prone to lack of control from home base, weak levels of equivalence with the home country degree, and from time to time the local partner collapses, a reputational risk. It can be difficult to achieve integration of curricula and assessment standards of the partner with those of the parent, unless twinning arrangements are in place, which tend to enforce a closer convergence.

Transnational education is more globally transformative than is onshore education export. It changes not just international students but to some extent also the provider institution, and often education in the nation in which provision is taking place. Though on the face of it transnational sites might seem classically imperial in form, staking a claim on foreign ground, their cultural meanings are different to onshore export. Transnational institutions must adjust their programs to meet local requirements, formal and informal. In order to operate they must meet registration, accreditation and quality assurance protocols. For example, foreign institutions operating in Malaysia provide core subjects in Islamic Studies and Malay. Transnational institutions must also adjust teaching to better fit with local educational traditions, language and cultural practice. They can no longer depend on the local cultural environment to homogenize the international students on their behalf. They themselves must adjust. The two parties, provider institution and international student, meet somewhere in the middle, in a hybrid zone. Transnational education fires experiments in synchrony. Sometimes the intercultural experience washes back to the home country and modifies the approach to teaching, for example assumptions about learning deficits, or it fosters bi-lingualism.[61] Mobile programs have a greater potential to break open the old enclosures than do mobile students.

Global e-universities

The delivery of educational programs through the Internet cuts out the nation of provision, the nation where program delivery occurs, and the processes of face-to-face teaching and learning. Located beyond effective regulation by any nation-state or multi-lateral process, it takes production straight into the formation of the global dimension. It opens prospects of a single global classroom, and a parallel universe of virtual institutions, in which all spatial passage is instantaneous, every de-severed distance is the same, and the common global language of English is both the agreed medium of instruction, and placed within everyone's reach. It also promises to simplify teaching, learning and administration: centrally delivered customizable curricula, assessment on line. In its first stages in the 1990s e-learning also offered to many cash strapped administrators the attractive prospect of dispensing with the cost and trouble of teachers, replacing them with a small number of communications specialists and pull-down menus with standard answers to learning problems, with everything organized from a small and mobile office: the staff room as call-centre. And because once the infrastructure was in place and the software was running the unit cost of each additional customer was negligible, there would be no need to build new classrooms as student numbers expand; it appeared that e-education would become more profitable as the network expanded. It would even be a license to print money; providing (small point) the virtual educational product would be attractive in the market. As the most radical of all spatial transformations in the knowledge economy, the e-U is also easy to imagine. Its forms are inherent in networked communication itself. At any given time the size of its commercial prospects is a simple proportion of the extent of de-severing that enters the imagination. This governs the outcome of the business calculations.

In many early imagining of e-learning the Internet had overcome the old need to situate and nuance programs in local, national and linguistic contexts. Once de-severing and homogenization at scale could be entertained, it became possible to imagine e-learning for hundreds of millions, even billions, with each new student unit generating largely cost-free revenues. 'Who will educate China?' asked the front page of *World Higher Education Reporter*, a newsletter on global trade in postsecondary education published by *University Business*, itself an outcome of the boom in e-learning, in September 2001.[62] On the policy side some believed e-Us could be the circuit breaker in the reproduction of educational under-development. If the communications infrastructure was in place, e-learning could meet the world's unmet demand for education of good quality at low unit cost, using public-private partnerships. This again offered e-learning business the prospect of vast new markets, this time in the creation of global public goods in nations that could never (it was asserted) meet the demands of educational modernization, and financing by the World Bank, the UN agencies and philanthropy. At the same time, the e-U format also held out the prospects of the formation of a new and lucrative global market in private positional goods. After all, young people all over the world were adopting the Internet in droves. Harvard on-line would be almost as good as Harvard au naturale. It seemed that venerable and powerful university brands were within everyone's reach. Rising business executives could access a Wharton degree at their desks during the working day. It all seemed too good to be true, and it was.

Many expected e-learning not to supplement or to augment or parallel but to displace conventional educational provision. Leading management theorist Peter Drucker boosted the emerging industry when he declared that within 30 years bricks-and-mortar universities would be replaced by virtual universities.[63] The corporate potentials of e-Us peaked in the dot.com equity boom of the late 1990s in the United States. Both universities and commercial interests moved in to command the emerging global market: the universities to regulate the value of their brands and slow their own expected displacement, or simply to hedge their bets; the e-learning and IT industries to seize control of the future and the rivers of cash to be. Much energy went into collaborations designed to enhance market penetration. Commercial players provided the business plan, the marketing and the communications expertise, which was often outsourced. The universities provided the brand. Columbia University's Fathom was developed in association with 14 other universities, including the London School of Economics plus libraries and museums. NYU On-line secured an investment of $22 million. Government money was also on the table. The US state of Maryland spent $40 million on the University of Maryland University College's distance education activities including UMUCOnline. State assistance was also provided by Virginia, Michigan and in the Western Governors project.[64] The UK government announced the UK e-University in February 2000 at a cost of £62 million over 2001–2004. It was conceived as a joint venture between UK institutions and a private sector expected to provide further investment, to provide degrees to a primarily global market largely via the Internet. The aim was to 'concentrate resources on a scale which can compete with leading US providers' (UK Secretary for Education). Awards would be provided by individual universities, not the UKeU. It was expected to recoup its public grant of £62 million by 2004. The enrolment target was 5600 students in the first year.[65]

Cardean University was based on Carnegie Mellon, Stanford, the business schools of Columbia and the University of Chicago, and the London School of Economics. The initial investment was $100 million. The intention was a high-quality Internet platform that would underpin ongoing student support. Cardean's business strategy depended on high volume sales of management education to senior and middle-level executives and managers worldwide. It targeted both the individual and corporate markets,[66] offering an MBA taught in six-week subjects and short programs of a few hours' duration. Cardean was in partnership with 'courseware developer' UNext which had responsibilities for course content, teaching and marketing. Teaching staff were not provided by the participating universities. In mid 2001 Cardean signed a training deal with General Motors, and UNext set up marketing offices in the Middle East and Korea with a branch in Singapore.[67] All systems go, it seemed.

But even as Peter Drucker was confidently predicting the new dawn the industry was imploding. In the 1999–2000 equity markets the dotcom and for-profit education bubbles burst. Online education initiatives were especially vulnerable because they had 'dramatically failed to deliver revenue.'[68] Investment analysts became sceptical. Meanwhile it was becoming clear there were high start-up costs for communications systems, web platforms for student administration and teaching, curriculum software and marketing. And student numbers were well below projections. One by one most of the e-Us were terminated. In late April 2004 The UK e-University effectively closed in April 2004: 900 students had enrolled in four years, compared to the target of 5600 after one year.[69] By September 2001 Cardean had laid off half its staff and run into accreditation problems. By 2004 its website was moribund.

A year later participation in tertiary education in China climbed past 20 per cent. It was now obvious *China* was going to educate China. And China was going to do so not in English with an on-line curriculum delivered from something approximating a call centre located in the USA, UK or Australia, but at home, in Putonghua, with real teachers in real classrooms.

No other space making strategy in the global knowledge economy has been attended by such high hopes, heavy investments or spectacular failure, all of it in half a decade. Why did the commercial e-Us fail? The first answer is that de-severing was taken too far. In that respect the weakness of the e-Us is the weakness of some of the proposals for global hubs. Global communications do not abolish locality and cultural specificity; people desire education and knowledge not simply because of its contents per se but because of the association between what they learn, where they learn and the rest of their life activities. The problem was not online learning itself, it lay in the assumptions attending its early global forms. Online tertiary education tailored to particular markets has been successful. As early as 2003 there were 350,000 students in mostly vocational e-learning programs in the American domestic market.[70] One was the University of Phoenix, the largest and fastest growing private university in the USA. Phoenix had built its standing as a commercial university prior to the e-learning boom and cemented it with television advertising. The Phoenix online mode was relatively teaching intensive and high cost, different to the early global e-U business models. At the same time, the viability of online learning in selected vocational programs does not translate into the potential to substitute for all forms of face-to-face teaching as Drucker imagined. Thus while most doctoral universities use online components in face-to-face programs, and parallel online delivery is widely used, no universities or commercial providers have yet developed an online mode strong enough to genuinely replace face-to-face doctoral university programs. Studies of student attitudes persistently show the great majority of students want organic interactions with teachers and other students via face-to-face delivery. The main exceptions are full time workers who need convenient access to part time learning, the Phoenix clients.

The second answer is that courseware is a public good; and while credentials are a potential private good the exchange value of online degrees in the labour markets is low. Online programs are handicapped by perceptions that the degree has less status than a face-to-face program, even when offered by leading brands such as New York University. There is limited room to develop commodity forms. The subsequent evolution of the knowledge economy has reflected this. The more important development than commercial delivery of e-learning has been non-proprietary open source models and systems.[71] These methods release the interactive potentials of online education more effectively than commercial learning systems. MIT placed its courseware on the Internet on an open source basis, enhancing MIT's global sway without diminishing the value of its onsite degrees. The parallel action of the Faculty of Arts and Science at Harvard, which in 2008 agreed to post its academic output on an open source basis,[72] reminds us that the public good character of knowledge sets limits on the business potential of Internet delivery. There is room for many forms of e-commerce in the global communicative dimension, but product development is always driven towards service specificity and niche networks. The 1990s e-Us imagined a global space populated by e-learning business websites. They vanished almost as quickly as they were created. The system architecture remains open. The contents of knowledge flows are again confirmed as public.

Re-inventing the global

The global e-Us promised to remake the global knowledge economy as a commercial space populated by virtual institutions. The grand project was stillborn when the parallel universe failed to colonize the existing one. At the same time other projects for re-setting the global dimension were also in process. The first, which locked onto worldwide policy systems and for a time seemed to gain considerable purchase in policy, was the worldwide process of national system reforms invoked by the World Trade Organization/General Agreement on Trade in Services (WTO-GATS). The second, which has proven more potent and whose effects are still working their way through the global knowledge economy—in fact we are probably in the early stages of this evolution—is the creation of university rankings, and other data-based global comparisons particularly in relation to research and publication.

WTO-GATS

The WTO-GATS negotiations were designed to create an open global trading regime in designated services sectors, including educational services. In seeking to open the policy settings governing national systems, and remake education as a commodity-producing sector so as to encourage enterprise and trade, including the entry of foreign providers, WTO-GATS also sought to close the global knowledge economy in principle to alternate practices associated with the product of educational services as national public goods. Nor did the potential for education to generate global public goods enter the framing of the WTO-GATS objectives and mechanisms. But the WTO-GATS process was not transformative.

The reform agenda developed out of successive rounds of global trade talks. It defined four aspects of cross-border educational provision: cross-border supply, for example online education; consumption abroad, for example students who cross borders to access education; commercial presence, for example transnational education; and movement of natural persons, for example temporary migration as a guest worker or education provider. Given the prima facie assumption underlying the process, that of an open trading regime, in the GATS round nations were expected to negotiate with each other to establish free trade in these areas, or adopt a general regulatory regime to the same end, registering their position with the WTO. At the same time the process offered them the option of exempting some or all parts of their education systems on grounds of 'national treatment.' The process was framed so that different sectors of education were distinguished. A nation could agree to create free trade in English-language programs, while maintaining national treatment for research universities. The prima facie bias in favour of trade deregulation meant that a separate case for exceptional treatment had to be made in each case. Even so, the process was unable to impose its global framing successfully on the national policy spaces. The exceptions soon proved to be the norm. Nations faithful to the process for the most part exempted their national education systems, maintaining the status quo, while others simply did not bother to fully participate.

The limitation of the WTO-GATS process from the beginning was that most national governments had little intrinsic interest in wholistically remaking education as a tradable commodity. Unlike other areas the subject of multi-lateral trade negotiations, such as agriculture and financial services, most of education is produced in non-commercial settings and not deployed for the direct creation of economic revenues. Further, all governments want to retain control of the national education and research sectors, which are seen as strategically significant to national competitiveness and development, and cultural identity. The exceptional case, where economic revenues are created at scale, is the export market in international education. But only a minority of countries engage in it and for them GATS made little difference. A handful of developing nations opened their doors to foreign for-profits. Most governments agreed to give cross-border online education a free hand in the national domain, thereby making a virtue out of necessity, for no one knew how to regulate it. That was it.

None of the major exporters agreed to fully open up its domestic education system to foreign providers by offering foreign entrants equal treatment in terms of regulation and subsidy. Here we find again the openness/closure paradox that often underlies strategies of global space making. Exporting institutions and national systems depend on the openness of the global setting to facilitate their strategic forays; and often express an in-principle desire for the global setting to be further opened up. But these same national or institutional forays are matched by forms of closure at home. The net benefits could be squandered if their own national citizens began to import from foreign transnational providers operating on home soil; and if their own educational insideness, their national heartland, was in play there might be other risks, the kind of risks that would arise in real estate markets if oil sheiks could buy and sell Lords cricket ground or the New York Stock Exchange. But the binary spatiality of the double standard works only in favour of the strong. The export nations weave and bluff to secure their one-sided advantages, modifications of global spatiality that suit their particular interest. In the global education export market, global openness is trumped by national particularism.

Global rankings

The second and more successful framing of the global dimension commenced in 2003 with the first Shanghai Jiao Tong University Institute of Higher Education world ranking of universities on the basis of research performance.[73] The process of ranking was conditioned by the visibility of each institution in the virtual environment, and the growing people movement and networking between them. But notwithstanding the globalization of the sector, and the role of *US News and World Report* ranking in the US system, the Shanghai initiative had a startling impact and triggered a proliferation of more global comparisons, of varying data quality. A major lacuna in the global comparisons has been data on comparative performance in teaching quality and/or student learning, aside from subjective data drawing on student evaluations of programs. However, in 2008 the OECD launched its Assessment of Higher Education Learning Outcomes (AHELO) project, which was designed to develop data on learning outcomes in two disciplines (engineering and economics), general skills such as problem solving and communication, and possibly the employment outcomes experienced by graduates.[74] It was expected that the evolution of these measures would take several years.

University rankings and other global performance measures have originated largely from outside nation-states, where there is a freer play of the global imagination: academic publishing; media and Internet-based communications; and the universities themselves. Those engaged in ranking sustain a global network which cuts across the global/national and public/private divides and has support from UNECSO and the OECD. But governments are quick to use the resulting data for their more restricted global strategies of national capacity building and promotion, applying those data in internal performance management regimes, the competitive allocation of funds and the identification of priorities for strategic development.

The effects of the new system of value in composing the global dimension were explored in Chapter 7 of our previous volume, *Creativity in the Global Knowledge Economy*. The creation of a performance-vectored global setting based on comparison—on one hand as a set of national higher education systems, on the other hand a set of individual higher education institutions—is of major importance in the history of the k-economy. Measures fitted for the computation, comparison and rank ordering of performance are readily translated into standards of value. The measures are based on status rather than money values but the former are equally capable of ordinal tasks. University and research rankings provide a means of sorting the producers of knowledge and of assigning values to the knowledge they produce. Not only do they confirm the status of research produced by the leading institutions, they enable research produced elsewhere to be assigned its place in the status hierarchy. They are a flexible tool in global space-making. Every participant in the global circuits of knowledge can map those circuits and position themselves and others within. They can identify like-minded institutions for cooperation, or differentiate themselves. This system of value-making lends itself to segmentation, boundaries and other mechanisms for regulating openness/closure and channelling mobility, especially mobility of persons. All students and all senior researchers want to work in highly ranked institutions. All students can identify where the prestige degrees are produced. The new hierarchy is both more transparent and comprehensive than the old informal hierarchy in which only a few top universities were household names. But it is also because university rankings lock into inherited perceptions of Oxbridge and the Ivy League that they have secured an unquestioned hold in the public culture and have done so worldwide. Work by Hazelkorn[75] shows that the new body of comparative information, especially institutional rankings and research output metrics, has been quickly installed in the perspectives, performance measurement systems and policy objectives of both national governments and higher education institutions; has entered the funding decisions of corporations, donors and philanthropists; and is feeding into student choices

Rankings have also quickened interest in institutional classifications, already established in North American and China and in process in Europe. Classifications provide a description of the k-world. They also create a form of hierarchy. In a codified division of labour between research universities and other kinds of institutions, the former look stronger. Because there is no rank ordering within each category, classifications also facilitate horizontal networks. Nevertheless the main effect of rankings is to generalize a culture of global comparison and hierarchy, distinct from commercial market valuation and the flatter relations in the open source sector, that confirms the traditional order of universities and nations. As such rankings constitute a blatant form of closure of the global knowledge economy and its broad potentials. Rankings also penalize all forms of diversity, whether of institutional mission, national culture or language of instruction, that fail to conform to the dominate template used in comparison, which is that of the comprehensive Anglo-American science university. This does not mean rankings have closed global space in any absolute sense. Global openness, disjuncture and contingency are irreducible. Creative ideas from strange places often but not always get through. Neither knowledge status nor knowledge content ever secure a final victory.

Global space making

We experience space and time as our own imaginative practices. Each of us has our own space and our own time. The harmonization of space-time is one of the constituents of society. Likewise change in the common experience of space-time opens up new potentials. Our means of communication, our ever-growing facility in knowledge creation, and perhaps our own deep desires, all seem to be propelling towards a closer spatiality and 'thicker,' more compelling connections across borders. Nowhere is this more apparent than in the institutions of the knowledge economy, where the strategic potentials for national education and research systems, and individual universities and actors, have expanded in novel ways. The global dimension of the knowledge economy is itself in a continuous process of creation.

These geo-spatial global strategies of universities and governments in the knowledge economy can be understood as acts of imagination, acts of production and acts of regulation.

Acts of imagination

In the knowledge economy four kinds of imagining of the global space have emerged. As we have seen, two of these are explicit. Two we can draw out from the strategies discussed.

The only one of these four visualizations of the global dimension officially endorsed by governments is the WTO-GATS imaginary of the global trading space. This is a neo-classical economic imaginary; one that pre-dates the global era, though the global-part integration of finance and trade has encouraged the visualization. The second and more influential imaginary is that of the comparison and rankings world, the global space of performance comparisons and hierarchy in the value of knowledge and knowledge producing institutions. This has roots in the old knowledge hierarchies, the administration of science and the performative cultures fostered by the new public management, but the synthesis is new and could only have occurred in an era of communicative globalization and convergence of institutions. The other imaginings of the global space have also been powerful in forming behaviour. The third is the networking-based imagining of the world of linkages, partnerships, consortia and hubs. While networks have long-standing origins in social science, today's network-based imaginary is a product of the era of communicative globalization, synthesized from the ideas of Manuel Castells about the information society, the actor network theorists and others. The fourth imagining of the global is that of the universe of networked virtual institutions grounded in the configuration of the Internet, the visualization with parallels in science fiction that underpinned the idea of a world populated by e-Us that would begin to displace bricks and mortar institutions of teaching and research. Again, this is an imaginary that could have arisen and touched human actions only in the wake of communicative globalization.

Acts of production

Global space making has created a vast new territory of opportunities for action, beyond national higher education systems. It is like an empty continent lying beyond the nations that are now being explored and peopled. To what extent have these new potentials become manifest in new forms of production in the knowledge economy: new ways of organizing material outputs, and new kinds of products, or new emphases in production? The more important changes are yet to come. But some changes in production can be detected.

In research and knowledge we have the burgeoning volume of knowledge as measured by the traffic on the web, though this is scarcely the outcome of deliberate strategy. We can speculate that there is a shift in emphasis to basic research, as distinct from commercializable research, and this is supported in government as well as in the university executive. Data on science papers and citations play a central role in research performance measures. The main part of the codified scientific output is in basic research. In teaching programs, the main global development has been the emergence and spread of the commodity form of international education, which has been the product of deliberate government strategies. Another important change has been the proliferation of joint production in the networked environment; not just student and staff exchange, but cross-border cooperation through jointly organized teaching and learning programs, twinning arrangements and jointly-badged degrees that involve an increasing number of institutions. The last trend in degree programs matches the growth in international collaborations in research.[76] At the level of system organization, Europe has achieved the first large scale cross-border integration of degree structures, nomenclature and graduate certification. Globally we have seen the emergence of a new kind output: comparative rankings and performance data.

Acts of regulation

A key aspect of the nation-building period from the seventeenth century onwards in Europe was the state's monopoly in the organization of space, from which much else followed: the planning state that squared and circled and criss-crossed and counted its way across the national map, the ideological state that coloured the map according to the beliefs of its leaders, the state of husbandry for whom the population was a resource to be managed and developed, the pastoral state that cared for all and only all inside the magic line. The essence of this power was the nation-state's control by military force over a bordered geographical territory. This monopoly has been fragmented by global communications across borders (states can no longer control the minds of their citizens unless they eliminate those citizens altogether), by global de-severing, by virtual forms of space, and by the freedom of all kinds of agents—public and private, business and bureaucracy, creative and civil organizations and loosely networked friendship groups—to imagine and devise spatial forms of association bounded only by their own chosen forms of rule. Geography still matters. States still patrol their physical borders. But this has become a part of the geo-spatial picture rather than its final point of termination. Meanwhile we have a growing global dimension of action but no global state. In a still Hobbesian world of separated, territorially-defined zones with no intrinsic or lasting obligation to each other or to the common global good, the nation remains the site of much of the political economy and most of the politics. To that extent the nation state remains powerful in making the global, though it no longer sets the horizon of the global. At the same time global governance is under-developed. There are structures for multi-lateral discussion but most international moves in the sphere of regulation depend on voluntary cooperation. This is no bad thing in principle but it can be frustratingly slow, it can fly apart under pressure, and it tends to postpone issues and leave gaps in areas of policy where actions in one nation affect others. The machinery of international law is limited. Financial coordination is voluntary and can be stymied by disagreements. In higher education and research common protocols in areas such as intellectual property, people mobility, and recognition and quality assurance evolve piece by piece and cover only some kinds of activity and some nations rather than all nations.

This patchy map of governance affects and is affected by global space forming strategies in three ways. One effect is that the limitations of regulation and control have opened a larger space for new initiatives and for the agency of higher education and research institutions. Globalization offers a sense of growing up and steering one's own trajectory beyond the limits of pastoralism. It must be added that in practice the fuller benefits of these freedoms have been mostly confined to universities with a substantial presence in research. Not only is research more global than other activities, it nurtures resources and sensibilities of crucial value in this environment. The uneven spread of global capacity means that higher education in many nations, and in some zones in all nations, remains largely excluded from the opportunities of the knowledge economy (see Chapter 7), not because of a lack of talent or because people in those institutions are unwilling to communicate or cooperate, but because they lack resources or because the systems conspire deliberately or not to close them out. The brute facts of uneven distribution retard global creation and are a principal issue for governance in the next phase.

The second effect is that in this process of growing up some universities have become further disembedded from nation-states. Disembedding is advanced by all processes involving cross-border networking—and as we have seen there is little in the knowledge economy that does not—and also by forms of production such as transnational campuses and the virtual delivery of programs. It is also advanced by the non-government regulation of global comparisons, rankings and performance measures in which the horizon is not national but global. At the same time, through other strategies the nation-state has stepped back into the processes of global space making. It does so through capacity building policies, through the education export industry whose objective is to augment national exports and foreign relations, and through the more advanced and globally active mutation of national capacity building in the formation of would-be global hubs, and sometimes also knowledge cities, though the latter are often pursued by civic and sub-national regional authorities rather than nations. The WTO-GATS process was an attempt to sustain the regulatory role of the nation-state in the ordering of the knowledge economy while providing a necessary modernization through a set of instruments for coordinating the regulation of global matters. But it failed, and this reflects not simply weak political will but the impossibility of regulating the global knowledge economy while leaving unchanged the present role of nation-states, and without global government. On balance we can say that the nation-state is partly displaced from the ordering of the global knowledge economy, where research universities have a proactive freedom that is irreducible unless they cease to house autonomous research and scholarship and learning (that genie cannot be put back in the bottle), but the nation-state remains a major player and its own inventiveness has not been exhausted. Perhaps nations will themselves become more fluid across borders and less territorially bound in their authority and powers.

The third effect is that in the outreaching of the knowledge economy, with its jagged and not always predictable moves beyond the boundaries of every enclosure old and new, forms of governance are being established that in some respects are post-national in form. In that respect developments in the global knowledge economy might have a larger importance in shaping future systems of governance and world society. The knowledge economy has advanced the scope for direct and unregulated human association; and has also brought a broad range of semi-government institutions, civil organizations, professional networks, media and communications and others into a more prominent role. Europeanization is often the most advanced laboratory for this kind of development. For example, a distinctive feature of the Bologna process is the extent to which it combines inter-state negotiations with collaboration at the level of sub-systems, individual institutions, particular regulatory agencies such as those handling quality assurance and professional training; and the spontaneous outcomes of staff and student mixing across borders. Necessarily states now find themselves having to work with and through this lattice of agents, and to some extent the ideas driving government are coming from outside the central bureau more often than before. This does not mean that the centering moments in which states bring it all together have gone, but it means that the pathway to those centering moments has become more complex (though the resources along the way are richer) and the level of performance expected of states has risen, especially the capacity to draw on a wide set of data and people, and manage international negotiations.

Successes and failures

Examining the four global imaginings that have shaped strategy making, it is apparent two of them have a superior purchase on the global creations of universities and governments (and probably also on the practices of other k-economy actors largely outside this chapter, such as commercial entrepreneurs in R&D, business corporations that use science, philanthropists who finance knowledge creation, and creative artists). These two superior imaginings are the global as networked social relations, and the global as performance comparisons and rankings.

Networks are integral to almost all imaginings of the global. They are congruent with the forms of communication and mobility of information and ideas, and the 'flat' character of open source knowledge. In the absence of an intrinsic boundary or enclosure of global space, it becomes more necessary to focus on the relations or bindings as a means of imagining and organizing sets of practical actors or 'fields' in Bourdieu's sense. The reach of performance comparison, rankings and hierarchies of value is narrower, specific to the knowledge economy and its higher education and research institutions. There the hierarchical vision, arbitrary and problematic as it is, has secured great influence on practical thought, in the manner that distasteful strategic imperatives (such as the need to use force to defend ourselves) become compulsory in war. The normative implications of these two imaginaries differ. Network imaginaries gently enjoin us to connect. They encourage openness and work against closure. These effects are moderate. Rankings and measurement of performance are tougher, creating firm binaries (big/small, strong/weak, winner/loser) readily used to create exclusions. Rankings push us hard towards differentiation. But neither global imagining is normative in relation to the institutional, political, or ideological maps. Both have a flexible utility in description, in the ordering of observations, that confers a broad intellectual and practical role. Both are capable of many permutations and reflexive self-transformation. Network models are constant changing social science tools. Better rankings systems such as that of Shanghai Jiao Tong are engaged in a continuing collective conversation about techniques and effects.

It is significant that global networks and global rankings taken together, the horizontal and the vertical, provide us with a full set of vectors of social organization. Flat networks and ordering hierarchies are mixed in varying ways in different sites. Together they provide the conceptual resources for visualizing internal relations in an organization, relations between organizations, and those relations understood as a field in Bourdieu's sense (see Chapter 7). Note that a system of comprehensive classification of institutions of higher education in a field has the potential to feed into both the horizontal and vertical imagining of organizations in the knowledge economy. Classifications organize ranking so that institutions of like mission are compared with each other; and also inform universities looking for like-minded partners.

So what then of the less successful global imaginings? Both are the product of mainstream economics and, more specifically, business management thought. The new public management has proved flexible, inventive and comprehensive as a body of practical ideas. It has a central place in the evolution of organizations across the world. Yet business management thought has yet to evolve a satisfactory imagining of the global. The WTO-GATS vision lacks purchase, because commercial production is largely marginal to education and especially research, given the public good nature of knowledge. The market imaginary is influential in relation to the relatively narrow range of activities in which commercial trade is important, notably full fee international education. It misses the majority of the global dealings of universities, which are nearer to the forms of the gift and status economies, or open source knowledge relations which are scarcely an economy at all. Pivoting on a binarism between what it includes/excludes, more ideological than are network and rankings models, the WTO-GATS imagining cannot provide a comprehensive description of global activity. The universe of virtual institutions suffers from similar limitations. It imposes a duality between what it includes, the virtual domain, and what it excludes, which is everything else. The issue on which the imagining is silent is the relation between the virtual and other worlds. The only possible conclusion it suggests is 'we are the future, the rest is the past, we will replace it.' This ideological line of reasoning confers on the imagining a bounded, inflexible, stand-alone character. It was this that underpinned Drucker's mistaken prediction and the spectacular rise and fall of the e-Us. The outcome suggests there is a vacancy for imaginings of the virtual domain that can situate that domain more effectively alongside the non virtual.

The strategies reviewed in this chapter all draw on varying ways on the four imaginings. Capacity building strategies are often situated in a comparative framework and informed by rankings data. Connectivity is primarily about networking. Decisions about regionalization, partnerships, consortia and global hub design are also informed by rankings and classifications, as they require the full horizontal/vertical picture of the field. (Networking in theory is largely horizontal but in practice networking often involves a strong element of the vertical as well.) Transnational education strategies draw comfort from the WTO-GATS vision and gain from both network imaginings and rankings. Education export strategies also benefit from the policy and ideological space making that is inherent in the GATS process, and dovetail with a rankings view of the world. Reciprocally, rankings affect activity in the export market.

We can also isolate elements of global imagining that are common to several strategies. And here again we have clues that help to explain the successes and failures of global creation.

First, the imagining of flat networked relations, which is continually posed by the structures of global communication itself, continually locks into our practices and modifies both the competition dynamics of economic markets and NPM quasi-markets and the hierachical ordering of status in the rankings world. The practices of flat networking, which are inclusive and meritocratic, dominate open source knowledge exchange, but their impact extends further than this. For example, the cross-border dealings of universities and university leaders are mostly practised in terms of flat networks. Here traditional academic collegiality seems to have morphed into something more inclusive and meritocratic. Thus an ethical duality runs through global networks. Their politeness regimes are soaked in openness and equality, partly masking the constant struggles for local and global status and the projects of enclosure. And the most successful universities are very good at both kinds of ethical practice.

Second, in the global knowledge economy there is an almost universal commitment to openness and mobility as positive qualities. They are integral to thinking globally, it seems. This is the public good sea in which all global fish swim. But in practice many projects are designed to close off segments of the global for the benefit of nation or institution, or are framed to firmly enclosure the self (Singapore, American domestic education) or the networked association (Europe), while demanding free mobility abroad (all export nations). As we have seen, the oscillation between openness and closure repeatedly runs through global moves. In general we can say this is a necessary antinomy. Without closure a global strategy has no definition or purchase in history. Without openness there can be no scope for new global creations. But this oscillation between openness and closure can take more than one form. Sometimes these are helpful, sometimes not. We have seen that to exercise maximum global effectiveness, agents need to be both open and bounded. But this is true of the internal (self) and the external (global) domains of thought and action. It is widely understood by global actors that it is necessary to be open and engaged, to learn continually and to be responsive—while also being strategically centred and relentless in carrying through the chosen courses of action—in the external, global domain. But the same combination of qualities, the same openness/boundedness, is also essential for the self. Here the key is to sustain a self-enclosure that is sufficiently porous and flexible to maximize the capacity to engage, respond and evolve. A more fixed form of identity, a less reflexive self, will tend over time to reduce the scope for global creation. For example if the dyad of open/bound becomes correlated to the dyad of external/internal, then global potential is reduced. This appears to have been the case with the Singapore hub strategy, and some others, that are externally flexible in action but have more difficulty in remaking their own project over time.

A third element common to nearly all strategic thinking and global creation is the de-severing of distance. Here we have a vital insight into the successes and failures of strategy.

There is no question that confidence in the reduction of distance is the key element in universities opening up the global. De-severing and the ease of synchrony it creates are the living, beating heart of the voluntary networks central to most activity in the knowledge economy. De-severing suggests the hub strategies. It enables Europeanization. It is integral to transnational developments, to global research collaboration and open source knowledge and to virtual learning. De-severing is also where it can all go wrong. The too easy assumption that all distances had been rendered equivalent—that the virtual distances are the same as the geographical and cultural distances, and so low teaching intensity e-Us would build a market of millions in China just like that—doomed the e-Us even before the first prospectus had been issued. The assumption that a 'knowledge village,' an education theme park, can be erected in the desert on the edge of Gulf State cities, disembedded from all forms of local context, and connect effectively with students and universities from all over the world is the product of the same hubris. Likewise transnational education fails when the franchised institution loses contact with the parent. De-severing is also where problems of university rankings can start. To treat all institutions as equivalent, as members of a homogeneous space of comparison, is to cut off the potential for contextual and historical explanation of the varying performance of institutions and of nations. The source of the error is absolute de-severing. This creates an identity between the 'here' and there.' There is no distance, no journey, no problem of cultural difference anymore. Absolute disembedding means no locality, no context, no embeddedness, no identity. But activities in the knowledge economy are *always* locally embedded (though often more than one locality is involved). In the global knowledge economy 'place,' the 'here-and-now' in the words of Hegel, is closer to other places but it is as real and present as ever. The best executive and policy strategies gain their practical purchase from a close understanding of exactly that. Again we see that the capacity to sustain a reflexive, evolving self, which is also the capacity to manage a living breathing *place* in the global setting, is a vital component of successful global creation.

Global creation

Remarkable organizational initiatives have emerged in the global dimension of the knowledge economy. These initiatives are related to, and distinct from, the parallel innovations in public administration and business. The best of these global creations should be given their due. If not quite the theory of relativity or the *Goldberg Variations*, some of the strategic initiatives reviewed in this chapter are as creative as scientific research, or scholarship, or art. If we were to look for an analogy for these space forming strategies in art, we might say 'cubism,' where old perceptions of space and its constituents were reworked, freeing us for more agile actions. In helping to form the global dimension of the knowledge economy and remap the social, these global creations have a vast reach across human affairs. Institution making and network building are rarely as visible as city buildings or bridges, but they are often more important.

The most successful strategies tend to be the ones that generate the most imitators (though bad ideas can also spawn quickly until the model finally falls over, like the e-Us and some of the hubs). The daring originality that underpinned the creation of the most productive global strategies is hidden under the subsequent mimetic mass. It must be said that by no means all of the global strategies now being used by universities and governments are novel departures. For example, national capacity building has a long history, though aspects like communications are specific to the global. But consider the radicalism of certain global space making strategies at the moment that they were new. Consider the first transnational campuses in Southeast Asia, pioneering a model of multiple cross-cultural provision, with the potential for cosmopolitan effects in educational practice in both the home country and the country of provision, and a move that has been decisive in puncturing the absolute regulatory authority of nation-states and freeing universities and colleges to range across the global space. This model could yet be decisive in releasing the export nations from the old imperial hubris, the Eurocentric notion of cultural superiority that still runs through much of the export industry at home. Consider the Singapore Schoolhouse and the more outward looking engagements of the National University of Singapore. No other nation has so fully grasped the nature and potential of the global setting, or indeed, contributed as much to framing the global knowledge economy as a space for executive strategy than has Singapore. Consider the Shanghai Jiao Tong rankings group, which decided to do it properly, using publicly available data that could not be manipulated by the universities affected, and so gained the authority to shape the field of performance comparison and the global knowledge hierarchy. And so a top ten university from China put the American universities in their (leading) places, and in doing so, showed us not simply that higher education in China is rising to greatness, but that the nations of Asia are already global partners in shaping world society. Consider the new form of dual identity and governance that has evolved in Europe, the novel mix of regulation with an advanced voluntarism that works, and the fecund excitement and the wave of innovation that Europeanization has opened up.

'The best of times and the worst of times,' said Charles Dickens of the French Revolution that coincided with Mozart's death. Perhaps this aphorism is endlessly repeated because it is the signature of modernity, in which we hunger for expanding potentials that we see with an ever growing clarity, and never seem to reach, and so we never stop creating. Certainly it is the sign of our time. 'The world is on fire' said the Buddha (who might have been the first modernist) in one of his sermons; and there is no mistaking that we live in a time of danger in which the fire has come. We change or we die. It may be also that we live in a time of protean creation in which we can make our condition together in a galaxy of new and shining stars, using all of the different wisdoms now made transparent to us. This is what global space-time offers. We are very fortunate in the new freedoms that it brings. The world has opened up. Perhaps we are not so far from the promises and perils of Vienna in the 1780s, except that we have more communicative resources, and for the first time we can see to the ends of the earth. But we have yet to show we can nurture talents like Wolfgang Amadeus Mozart and engage with what they do. Though it is early days in the knowledge economy, it is clear much of the future will be made there. It is impossible to forecast the next generation of global creation, but we know it will be the best and the worst and it will be more extraordinary than ever.

Endnotes

1. Beerkens, 2004; Marginson and van der Wende, 2006.
2. Clark, 1998; Marginson & Considine, 2000.
3. Kerr, 2001.
4. Marginson & Considine, 2000. See also Chapter 1.
5. Marginson, 2008b; OECD, 2008b.
6. See among others the discussion in Arendt, 1998.
7. Heidegger, 2002, 75.
8. Heidegger, 2002, xiii.
9. SJTUIHE, 2009.
10. Harvey, 1990, 271.
11. Schulz, 1960; Denison, 1962.
12. van der Wende, 2008.
13. OECD, 2008a.
14. See Chapter 6 and also Marginson, 2009a.

15. Li et al., 2008, 11.

16. Beerkens, 2004.

17. Between 2004 and 2009 the author conducted empirical case studies of the global activities of 15 research universities in 14 different countries. All but one of these institutions mentioned active links with NUS. At more than half of these universities, leaders singled out NUS for special praise for the quality of its global programs and the level of engagement.

18. OECD, 2008a.

19. Reserve Bank of Australia, 2008.

20. DEEWR, 2009.

21. Verbik and Lasanowski, 2007.

22. Bashir, 2007, 19.

23. Marginson, 2007a.

24. Marginson, 2007b.

25. OECD, 2004.

26. Harvey, 1990, 252.

27. See for example the collection by Ninnes and Hellsten, 2005; Marginson, 2009b.

28. Marginson, et al., forthcoming.

29. Sidhu, 2009, 129.

30. *ibid*, 128.

31. *ibid*, 131.

32. *ibid*, 129.

33. *ibid*, 130.

34. *ibid*, 132–133.

35. Florida, 2002.

36. Kong, et al., 2006, 177–181; Sidhu, 2009, 130.

37. CWTS, 2009. Normalization by field means that the different field citation practices (e.g. research literature in medicine cites more often then engineering) are evened out.

38. Sidhu, 2009, 132.

39. *ibid*, 133.

40. Arguably China has made a parallel error by investing too high a proportion of its advancing R&D budget in the state enterprises with too little in the universities where most of the basic research takes place.

41. Kong, et al., 2006, 137.

42. Sidhu, 2009, 137.

43. University World News, 2009.

44. Harvey, 1990, 295.

45. OECD, 2007a, 20 and 41.

46. OECD, 2007a, 60.

47. OECD, 2007b, 295.

48. Beerkens, 2004. See also Held et al., 1999.

49. Altbach, 2003; OECD, 2004.

50. Eaton, 2003.

51. Musselin, 2004, 72.

52. Musselin, 2005, 135.

53. EC, 2007.

54. A London headline reporting early battles in the second Gulf War spoke to this sense of England's continuing claim to greatness, which has now been displaced from trade and bayonets to finance and the knowledge economy: 'British brains and American muscle break through.'

55. See for example van der Wende, 2008; de Wit, 2008; Kehm et al., 2009; van Vught, 2009.

56. de Wit, 2008.

57. Bartelse and van Vught, 2007; van Vught, 2009.

58. Marginson, 2009c.

59. Verbik and Merkley, 2006; Ziguras and McBurnie, 2007.

60. Verbik and Merkley, 2006.

61. Marginson and Eijkman, 2007.

62. Borton, 2001.

63. Drucker, 2000.

64. Ryan and Stedman 2002, pp. 11 and 17.

65. Maslen, 2004.

66. Hirsch, 2001.

67. Ryan and Stedman, 2002, 10–11; WHER, 2001.

68. Ryan and Stedman, 2002, 3.

69. Maslen, 2004.

70. *ibid.*

71. OECD, 2005, 134–135.

72. The motion passed by the Harvard Faculty in February 2008 read: 'Each Faculty member grants to the President and Fellows of Harvard College permission to make available his or her scholarly articles and to exercise copyright in those articles.' This granted to the Provost's office at Harvard the necessary authority to make all scholarly work produced by the Faculty available to the public in an open access repository. In a parallel initiative the US Congress decided to mandate open access to National Institute of Health funded research beginning on 7 April 2008. The bill requires deposit of manuscripts in PubMed Central immediately upon acceptance by a peer-reviewed journal.

73. SJTUIHE, 2009.

74. OECD, 2008b.

75. Hazelkorn, 2008.

76. NSB, 2009.

References

Altbach, P. (2003). American accreditation of foreign universities: Colonialism in action. *International Higher Education*, 32, 5–7.

Bartelse, J. and van Vught, F. (2007). Institutional profiles: Towards a typology of higher education institutions in Europe. *IAU Horizons*, 12 (2–3), pp. 9–11.

Bashir, S. (2007). *Trends in International Trade in Higher Education: Implications and Options for Developing Countries*. Education Working Paper Series, Number 6. Washington: The World Bank.

Beerkens, H. J. J. G. (2004). *Global Opportunities and Institutional Embeddedness: Higher Education Consortia in Europe and Southeast Asia*. Center for Higher Education Policy Studies, University of Twente. Accessed on 10 February 2006 at http://www.utwente.nl/cheps/documenten/thesisbeerkens.pdf

Borton, J. (2001). A home-grown education industry pursues 'digital China.' *World Higher Education Reporter*, 24 September, 1. University Business: New York.

Centre for Science and Technology Studies Leiden University, CWTS (2007), *The Leiden Ranking 2008*. Accessed on 3 May 2009 at: http://www.cwts.nl/ranking/LeidenRankingWebSite.html

Clark, B. (1998). *Creating Entrepreneurial Universities: Organizational Pathways of Transformation*. Oxford: Pergamon.

Dennison, E. (1962). *The Sources of Economic Growth in the United States and the Alternatives Before Us*. New York: Committee for Economic Development.

Department of Education, Employment and Workplace Relations, DEEWR (DEST) (2009). *Selected Higher Education Statistics*. Accessed 10 January 2009 at: http://www.dest.gov.au/sectors/higher_education/publications_resources/profiles/students_2005_selected_higher_education_statistics.htm.

Drucker, P. (2000). Webucation. *Forbes*, 15 May.

Eaton, J. (2003). The international role of U.S. recognized accrediting organizations. *International Higher Education*, 31, 10–12.

European Commission, EC (2007). *Lisbon Declaration. Europe's Universities Beyond 2010: Diversity with a Common Purpose*. Accessed 30 April 2009 at: http://www.eua.be/fileadmin/user_upload/files/Lisbon_Convention/Lisbon_Declaration.pdf

Florida, R. (2002). *The Rise of the Creative Class*. New York: Basic Books.

Harvey, D. (1990). *The Condition of Post-modernity*. Cambridge: Blackwell.

Hazelkorn, E. (2008). Learning to live with league tables and ranking: The experience of institutional leaders. *Higher Education Policy*, 21, pp. 193–215.

Heidegger, M. (2002). *The Essence of Human Freedom: An introduction to philosophy*. Transl. by T. Sadler. London: Continuum,

Held, D., A. McLew, D. Goldblatt & J. Perraton (1999). *Global Transformations: Politics, Economics and Culture*. Stanford: Stanford University Press.

Kehm, B., Huisman, J. and Stensaker, B. (Eds.) (2009). *The European Higher Education Area: Perspective on a Moving Target*. Rotterdam: Sense Publishers.

Kong, L., Gibson, C., Khoo, L. and Semple, A. (2006). Knowledges of the creative economy: Towards a relational geography of diffusion and adaptation in Asia, *Asia Pacific Viewpoint* 47 (2), pp. 173–194.

Li, Yao, Whalley, John, Zhang, Shunming and Zhao, Xiliang (2008). *The Higher Educational Transformation of China and its Global Implications*. NBER Working Paper No. 13849. Cambridge: National Bureau of Economic Research.

Marginson, S. (2007a). The new higher education landscape: Public and private goods, in global/national/local settings. In S. Marginson (Ed.) *Prospects of Higher Education: Globalisation, Market Competition, Public Goods and the Future of the University*, pp. 29–77. Rotterdam: Sense Publishers.

Marginson, S. (2007b). Global position and position-taking: the case of Australia. *Journal of Studies in International Education*, 11 (1), 5–32

Marginson, S. (2009a). University rankings and the knowledge economy. In M. Peters, P. Murphy and S. Marginson (eds.) *Creativity and the Global Knowledge Economy*, 185–216. New York: Peter Lang.

Marginson, S. (2009b). Sojourning students and creative cosmopolitans. In M. Peters, P. Murphy and S. Marginson (eds.) *Creativity and the Global Knowledge Economy*, 217–255. New York: Peter Lang.

Marginson, S (2009c). The external dimension: Positioning the European higher education area in the global higher education world. In B. Kehm, J. Huisman, J. and B. Stensaker (Eds.) (2009). *The European Higher Education Area: Perspective on a Moving Target*, 297–321. Rotterdam: Sense Publishers.

Marginson, S. and Considine, M. (2000). *The Enterprise University: Power, Governance and Reinvention in Australia*. Cambridge: Cambridge University Press.

Marginson, S. & Eijkman, H. (2007). *International Education: Financial and organizational impacts in Australian Universities*. Report prepared for the Monash Institute for the Study of Global Movements. Melbourne: Monash University. Accessed 5 August 2007 at: http://www.cshe. unimelb.edu.au/people/staff_pages/Marginson/Marginson.html

Marginson, S. and van der Wende (2007). *Globalisation and Higher Education*. Education Working Paper Number 8, Organisation for Economic Cooperation and Development. Paris: OECD, 6 July (2007). Accessed 9 July 2007 at: http://www.oecd.org/dataoecd/33/12/38918635.pdf

Maslen, G. (2004). E-Universities struggling to find students. *Campus Review*, 5–11 May, 5.

Musselin, C. (2004). Towards a European academic labour market? Some lessons drawn from empirical studies on academic mobility, *Higher Education*, 48, pp. 55–78.

Musselin, C. (2005). European academic labour markets in transition, *Higher Education*, 49, pp. 135–154.

National Science Board, NSB (2009). *Science and Engineering Indicators*. Accessed on 8 March at: http://www.nsf.gov/statistics/seind04/

Ninnes, P. and Hellsten, M. (eds.) (2005). *Internationalizing Higher Education: Critical Explorations of Pedagogy and Policy*, 141–158. Dordrecht: Springer.

Organisation for Economic Cooperation and Development, OECD (2004). *Internationalisation and Trade in Higher Education*. Paris, OECD.

Organisation for Economic Cooperation and Development, OECD (2005), *E-learning in Tertiary Education: Where Do We Stand?* Paris: OECD

Organisation for Economic Cooperation and Development, OECD (2007a). *Higher Education and Regions: Globally Competitive, Locally Engaged*. Paris: OECD.

Organisation for Economic Cooperation and Development, OECD (2007b). *Competitive Cities in the Global Economy*. Paris: OECD.

Organisation for Economic Cooperation and Devlopment, OECD (2008a). *Education at a Glance: OECD Indicators*. Paris: OECD.

Organisation for Economic Cooperation and Development, OECD (2008b). *Roadmap for the OECD Assessment of Higher Education Learning Outcomes (AHELO) Feasibility Study*. IMHE Governing Board, Document Number JT03248577. Paris: OECD.

Reserve Bank of Australia (2008). Australia's exports of education services. *Reserve Bank Bulletin*, June.

Ryan, Y. and Stedman, L. (2002): *The Business of Borderless Education 2001 Update. Evaluations and Investigations Programme*. Canberra: DEEWR.

Schultz, T. (1960). Capital formation by education. *Journal of Political Economy*, 68 (6), 571–583.

Shanghai Jiao Tong University Institute of Higher Education, SJTUIHE (2009). *Academic Ranking of World Universities*. Accessed 23 March 2009 at: http://ed.sjtu.edu.cn/ranking.htm

Sidhu, R. (2009). The 'brand name' research university goes global. *Higher Education*, 57, 125–140.

University World News (2009). Mauritius: Country aims to become 'knowledge hub.' Accessed 5 April 2009 at: http://www.universityworldnews.com/article.php?story=20090402213110403

van der Wende, M. (2008). Rankings and classifications in higher education: A European perspective. In J. Smart (Ed.) *Higher Education: Handbook of Theory and Research*. Dordrecht: Springer.

van Vught, F. (Ed.) (2009). *Mapping the Higher Education Landscape: Towards a European Classification of Higher Education*, Heidelberg: Springer.

Verbik, L. and Merkley, C. (2006). *The International Branch Campus—Models and Trends*. London: Observatory on Borderless Higher Education (OBHE).

Verbik, L. and Lasanowski, V. (2007). *International Student Mobility: Patterns and trends*. Report, The Observatory on Borderless Education. Accessed 21 March 2008 at: www.obhe.ac.uk [password protected]

de Wit, H. (2008). International student circulation in the context of the Bologna Process and the Lisbon Strategy, in H. de Wit, P. Agarwal, M. Elmahdy Said, M. T. Sehoole & M. Sirozi (Eds.), *The Dynamics of International Student Circulation in a Global Market*, pp. 167–198. Rotterdam: Sense Publishers.

World Higher Education Reporter, WHER (2001). UNext plans 'global footprint,' 25 June. New York, University Business.

Ziguras, C. & McBurnie, G. (2006). *Transnational Education: Issues and Trends in Off-shore Higher Education*. London: Routledge

CHAPTER 7

Higher Education as a Global Field

◻ Simon Marginson

World-wide higher education

We can understand worldwide higher education as a relational environment that is simultaneously global, national and local.[1] Institutions such as universities, and the individual agents that study and work within them, live their lives in all three of these often overlapping dimensions, more or less simultaneously. This relational environment of worldwide higher education takes in many and diverse organizational players: international agencies such as the World Bank and the Organization for Economic Cooperation and Development (OECD) that affect educational provision and its activities and mentalities, national and local governments and systems of higher education and of research, individual universities and other institutions, academic disciplines, professions, e-learning companies and other commercial interests, and many more. It intersects with other relational environments, for example in the economy and labour force, the polity and the arts.

Most of the activity within the worldwide higher education environment continues to be nation-bound. Nevertheless, as discussed in the previous chapter, a distinctive global dimension is growing in importance. This global dimension is a relational space that intersects with each national system, while being also in some sense external to them all. The growing weight of the global dimension of higher education has many historical roots. In this period it derives above all from worldwide roll-out of instantaneous messaging and complex data transfer, and the growth and cheapening of air travel. These material changes in technology, and the practices that they have made possible, have come to constitute more intensively and extensively networked inter-subjective global communities. In this context the cross-border dealings of research-intensive universities, and the cross-border relations between governments in higher education matters, have come to constitute something more than a mass of bilateral connections. In higher education, as in other spheres of life, we can identify *global systems* that are characterized by recurring and distributed commonalities, points of concentration (nodes), rhythms and modes of movement.

Above all there is the globalization of knowledge itself as a single world system. This is one of the key elements that constitute the material practices of what is often called the 'global knowledge economy.' Research and scholarship have become predominantly (though by no means exclusively) global in orientation. This is truer of scientific research and of work in the scientistic social sciences such as economics, demography, psychology and quantitative sociology, than of the humanities and the humanistic social sciences. It now extends also to mainstream business studies, which is surprisingly homogenized across the world, and has become dominated by universities and texts from the Atlantic countries. There is a single mainstream system of English language publication of research knowledge, a system that tends to marginalize work in other languages rather than absorbing it.

Similarly, in the governance of higher education, there is an emerging common approach to recognition and quality assurance, for example the Washington Accords in Engineering. The Bologna accord facilitates partial integration and convergence in degree structures and research organization in Europe, though so far, this level of intensive cross-border negotiation is yet to be replicated in other regions.

Any theorization of the world-wide global higher education space and within it, the global dimension of higher education, must account for two elements. The first is the pattern of flows and networks across borders. Using Arjun Appadurai's terminology,[2] global flows include the flows of people (students, administrators, academic faculty), or ethnoscapes; flows of media and messages, information and knowledge, or mediascapes; flows of norms, ideas and policies, or ideoscapes; flows of material and social technologies, or technoscapes; and flows of finance capital and economic resources, or financescapes. These global flows constitute lines of communication and lines of effect that are relatively visible. In many (though by no means all) respects they are open to numerical measurement. But equally important is a second, less explicit element: the worldwide patterns of *difference* that channel, limit and interpret global flows. There is horizontal diversity in the form of the different languages, pedagogy, scholarship, and organizational systems and cultures found in higher education systems and governments around the world. These various kinds of horizontal diversity have the potential to block, to retard, to change, to nuance and to alter the direction of patterns of flow. There is also vertical diversity in the form of competitive differentiation, ranking and hierarchies; binary systems of inclusion and exclusion, and the patterns of unequal holdings of resources and capabilities.

Global higher education is not a level playing field. It is shaped by inequality and hierarchy.

Yet structural explanations are never enough to satisfy us by themselves: more so when the terrain under examination is the fast evolving global terrain with its notorious indeterminacy, unpredictability and its sharp variations according to velocity, location and culture. Structural explanations are limited by an inbuilt tendency to contain factors of contingency within the pre-given structure, which thereby closes the horizon of possibility. Thus a description of structure all too readily becomes read as a description of lines of determination. More specifically, structural explanations underplay human agency and creativity. Structural explanations are useful in laying out the coordinates, the lines of passage, which guide the navigation of human agents. But they collapse when those same agents suddenly change course or re-imagine the map altogether. Where structural theorists acknowledge the role of agency (and many are impelled to do so, if only to provide an escape from the structures they describe) the agency they introduce is external to the structure they have defined and so undermines the whole problematic. Analysis becomes riven by the binary of voluntarist agency/determined agency. The account of freedom is incoherent. A situated, relational democracy appears as fraudulent, or beyond reach.

The chapter

This chapter is concerned with mapping the global dimension of higher education and research in terms of relations of power, incorporating the freedom, the self-determination of human agents, in order to contribute to understandings of global transformations[3] in and through higher education.[4] Noting Appadurai's theorization of global flows,[5] the main discussion concerns the dynamics of global relations. Here Pierre Bourdieu's notion of fields of power[6] is supplemented by Antonio Gramsci's notion of hegemony.[7] Gramsci opens more space for agency. Though this is not a primarily empirical paper, references are made to data from the OECD,[8] the World Bank[9] and other sources to illustrate the conceptual discussion and identify possible markers for observation. The final section pushes beyond Bourdieu's structure-dominated theorization. Drawing again on Appadurai and Amartya Sen,[10] it expands on agency in the global dimension and suggests a more rounded global ontology.

Scapes and domains

Global flows in higher education are exceptionally dynamic and uneven. In the decade from 1995 to 2004, the number of students enrolled outside their country of citizenship rose from 1.3 to 2.7 million.[11] Cross-border research collaborations and university partnerships are also growing rapidly. Manuel Castells explains the inbuilt expansionary dynamic of networks and the flows that they carry. When networks expand the cost grows in a linear fashion but the benefits grow exponentially because of the greater number of connections. Correspondingly, 'the penalty for being outside the network increases.'[12] Networked flows clump around nodal cities in North America, UK, Europe and East Asia. Meanwhile, a large part of the world remains outside not just the Internet but electricity.

For Appadurai the global dimension is a space for new imaginings and the construction and self-construction of identity. As noted, emphasizing mobility, plurality 'and in general, agency,' he describes 'a new global cultural economy…a complex, overlapping, disjunctive order,'[13] with 'interactions of a new order and intensity'[14] in which human agents generate global cultural flows and flows generate and transform agents. Diasporic populations use media, communications and return travel to make hybrid identities within more malleable configurations of locality, breaking the monopoly of nation-states over modernization.[15] Ethnoscapes, mediascapes, technoscapes, financescapes and ideoscapes are the 'building blocks' for the construction of newly imagined worlds.[16] While Appadurai's flows/scapes are structural, their form is not exactly a linear positivist's dream. The scapes are fluid, irregular, uneven, overlapping, disjunctive, asynchronous, temporary and contingent. They are structural forms unusually accessible to agency. As such the scapes are a brilliant explanatory device which has advanced our understanding of both the global dimension and the structure/agency problem. Still, they are not the only possible structural explanation and they do they do not exhaust the ontology of the global.

As noted also there are lacunae in Appadurai. Writing in 1996, he was too quick to dismiss the longer term prospects of the nation-state and the continued salience of 'Americanization' in the making of the global dimension. He was right to argue that globalization is not necessarily Americanization, wrong to imply it could never be so. Extending that point, the global is not simply a single open space in which the scapes are played out, and it is accessible to forms of closure (however temporary and incomplete) more firmly bordered than the scapes. The scapes coexist with structures less fluid, flexible and ambiguous in character which will be here called 'domains.' The global dimension takes in zones of practice in the activities of law, governmental regulation and finance. These domains are not reducible to the global as a whole, nor do they take the form of scapes. Grounded in traditions and institutions, they are more regular, stable and tightly bordered than scapes. Nevertheless, these global domains are less stable (and seem to be bigger) than they once were, and they have been infused with a greater element of dynamism and unpredictability by the scapes. One such global domain is that of higher education and the associated research. It is continually subject to partial destabilization by the flows of people, ideas, policies and capital, while also drawing much of its definition and momentum from them.

How then might we understand this domain of higher education and research? The functions that distinguish higher education and the associated research from other social domains are the credentialing of knowledge-intensive labour, and the production and authoritative codification and circulation of the great bulk of basic research. Global higher education is a bounded domain that includes institutions with cross-border activities in these areas, while excluding other institutions. Though this domain is frayed at the edges by diploma mills, corporate 'universities' and cross-border e-learning, and there are many connections with other social formations—the boundedness and distinctiveness of the domain are irreducible. The dual of inclusion/exclusion that shapes outer and inner relations is one of the keys to the domain. This suggests Bourdieu. He terms such domains as 'fields of power.'

Bourdieu and the global field

Bourdieu develops 'the notion of a field, understood as a space, that is, an ensemble of positions in a relationship of mutual exclusion.'[17] A field of power is a social universe with its own laws of functioning. It enjoys a variable degree of autonomy, defined by its ability to reject external determinants and obey only its own specific logic. The notion of field is explored in *Distinction* (1984), applied to French universities in *Homo Academicus* (1988), and deepened in *The Field of Cultural Production* (1993).[18] Rajani Naidoo uses Bourdieu's theorization of higher education as a field to analyze the differentiation of higher education institutions in South Africa. She notes also that Bourdieu's argument was developed in the context of a relatively stable compact between higher education, society and nation-state[19]; and also that Bourdieu has little to say about the structuring and content of knowledge.

Can Bourdieu assist us in our imaginings of global higher education, given that he is nation-bound when old national certainties have dissolved, and that knowledge formation, which he tends to under-emphasize, is both primary to universities and one function of universities that is quintessentially global? Yes. Bourdieu does not provide a conclusive blueprint for understanding the domain of global higher education. But his particular explanation of the dynamics of higher education as a field of power is suggestive, including his interpolation of agency as 'positioned' and 'position-taking,' his tenacious attempt to install a logic of action as the continual interplay of other determination/self-determination within structured boundaries.

Polarity of the field

Bourdieu argues that the field of cultural production is structured by an opposition between the elite sub-field of restricted production, and the sub-field of large scale mass production tending towards commercial production.[20] Each sub-field has a distinct principle of hierarchization. In the mass or 'popular' institutions it involves economic capital and market demand and is heteronomous; though from time to time institutions renew themselves by adapting ideas from the elite sector. In the elite sub-field outputs are scarce, driving up their value. Among elite universities the dominant principle of hierarchization, cultural status, is autonomous and specific to the field. Between the two sub-fields lie a range of intermediate institutions that combine the opposing principles of legitimacy in varying degrees and states of ambiguity.

Table 7.1. Peaks of the global knowledge economy: the top 30 universities as measured by research performance, 2007

	UNIVERSITY	SJTU POINTS	NATION
1	Harvard U	100.0	USA
2	Stanford U	73.7	USA
3	U California, Berkeley	71.9	USA
4	U Cambridge	71.6	UK
5	Massachusetts IT	70.0	USA
6	California IT ('Caltech')	66.4	USA
7	Columbia U	63.2	USA
8	Princeton U	59.5	USA
9	U Chicago	58.4	USA
10	U Oxford	56.4	UK
11	Yale U	55.9	USA
12	Cornell U	54.3	USA
13	U California, Los Angeles	52.6	USA
14	U California, San Diego	50.4	USA
15	U Pennsylvania	49.0	USA
16	U Washington (Seattle)	48.2	USA
17	U Wisconsin-Madison	48.0	USA
18	U California, San Francisco	46.8	USA
19	Johns Hopkins U	46.1	USA
20	Tokyo U	45.9	Japan
21	U Michigan, Ann Arbor	44.0	USA
22	Kyoto U	43.1	Japan
23	Imperial College, London	43.0	UK
23	U Toronto	43.0	Canada
25	U College London	42.8	UK
26	U Illinois—Urbana-Champaign	42.7	USA

(table continued on next page)

	UNIVERSITY	SJTU POINTS	NATION
27	Swiss Fed Instit of Technology, Zurich	39.9	Switzerland
28	U Washington (St Louis)	39.7	USA
29	Northwestern U	38.2	USA
30	New York U	38.0	USA
30	Rockefeller U	38.0	USA

Source: Shanghai Jiao Tong University Institute of Higher Education (SJTUIHE), 2007

Bourdieu's polarity helps to explain the shaping of relations of power within national systems, where heteronomy is determined by governments, market forces, and by both operating together. The polar contrast in South Africa between more autonomous white English-language universities focused on products for the intellectual field and more heteronomous black universities and white Afrikaans-medium universities,[21] is replicated in the differentiation of the Australian system where the polarity falls between the more autonomous and selective 'sandstone' universities that see themselves as global research players, and the more heteronomous technical and regionally focused institutions.[22] Many other examples could be cited. Far from making a universal journey from elite to mass higher education as Martin Trow argues,[23] national systems typically contain both kinds of institution simultaneously, or sustain the Bourdieuian polarity inside single institutions. However, the point here is that the same polarity is apparent in the global field.

In the global sub-field of restricted production we find Harvard, Stanford, Yale, MIT, Princeton, Berkeley, Oxford, Cambridge, and other Anglo-American universities that are household names in the world's educated circles. These institutions provide an unequivocal career advantage everywhere: places are prized by research students and academic faculty, and selectivity is enhanced by modest first degree intakes. Concentrating knowledge power to themselves by housing many of the world's leading researchers, characteristically autonomous, their agency freedom is further strengthened by the globalization of knowledge and their pre-eminence on the web and in global university rankings. *The Economist* has christened them the 'Global Super-league.'[24] Given the role of English-language research in constituting status in higher education, research performance as measured by the Shanghai Jiao Tong University (SJTU) provides a proxy indicator of status (Table 7.1).[25] How far down the rankings the 'super-league' extends is unclear, but it is apparent that elite universities from outside the USA and UK in general enjoy a lesser global eminence.

In the opposite sub-field we find the tertiary education institutions that are solely focused on revenues and market share. This includes not only for-profit vocational universities such as the University of Phoenix, which is now doing business in a dozen

Figure 7.1. The polar field of global higher education, after Bourdieu

(Horizontal axis maps autonomy/heteronomy. Vertical axis maps degree of global engagement. Numbers signify order of status in global field)

AUTONOMOUS SUB-FIELD of elite research* universities, prestige- not profit-driven *Notes* 1. autonomy relative to *global* field 2. elite teaching-only liberal arts colleges feed into category 1	1 The 'Global Super-league': Much of American doctoral sector and a few high prestige universities in UK. Prestige derived from stellar research reputation and global power of degrees [Harvard U, Cambridge etc.]	2b Elite non U.S. national research universities with strong cross-border roles: Prestige-driven non-profit research universities at national level. Global presence in research; cross-border students, some on for-profit basis [U Sydney, U of Warwick]	4b Teaching-focused export universities: Lesser status non-profit universities, commercial players in global market: lower cost/quality foreign education at scale. May have minor research role [Oxford Brookes, Central Queensland U]	3 Elite and globally focused for-profits: Prestigious fully for-profit institutions operating globally, largely teaching focused with some research. National exclusivity and global power creates autonomy vis a vis 6. Very small group. [Indian IITs & IMs]	6 Lesser prestige teaching only global for-profits: Fully commercial operators actively building export markets, low cost mass production, no research [U Phoenix, DeVry, various global e-U's, etc.]	HETERONOMOUS SUB-FIELD of institutions providing commercial vocational cross-border education (includes for-profits & revenue-driven units of non-profits)
	2a Less globally engaged American doctoral universities Global prestige and some research, marginal foreign engagement and cross-border students [some U.S. state universities]	4a Nationally-bound elite research universities: Prestige providers in one nation. Research intensive, varying global research roles. Inward looking. Nationally competitive with segment 2b, not 1. [U Buenos Aires, many in Europe and Japan]	5 Teaching-focused national universities Largely teaching focused institutions, marginally global in research and/or cross-border teaching [most Malaysian public universities, some Canadian community colleges, etc.]		8 For-profits with minor global functions: Commercial operators focused on local market with some cross-border students. [some private industry training in Australia]	
			7 Non-profits without global agendas: teaching-focused, local demand mission, no cross-border role. Largest group, e.g. in importing nations		9 For-profits without global agendas: local degree mills, no cross-border role. Many in some nations[Brazil, Philippines]	

countries, but also in their global teaching at least, many British and Australian non-profit universities that provide international education on a commercial basis.

A range of institutions occupy intermediate positions in the global field (Figure 7.1). Some universities assume and elite position in the national field and compete in the global research stakes while also building high volume concentrations of full fee-paying international students (category 2b). Beneath that group are ostensibly teaching-research universities for whom the research mission is decisively subordinated to cross-border revenues (category 4b). They vary in the extent to which they practise global research and the status-building mission. Some national research universities position themselves as elite institutions within their own borders, but lack the research mass and global attraction powers of the Super-league and, without a presence in the commercial market for students, are nationally confined (category 4a).

Outside the global field are institutions solely national and local (categories 7 and 9). Nations and institutions do not experience the global dimension in common. Cross-border flows of people, knowledge and ideas and capital confront heterogeneous national cultural traditions and a sharp differentiation of resources and capacities. For example non English-speaking universities, and those lacking scientific infrastructure start from behind in the research race. The global power of the sub-field of restricted production rests on the exclusion of most institutions and nations from the global field and the subordination of the rest.

Bourdieu's field of power that differentiates and includes/excludes is closer to the global dynamics of higher education than the neo-liberal imaginary of a universal market. As a vertical hierarchy the global field in Figure 7.1 looks like this (Table 7.2):

Table 7.2. Global segmentation of higher education institutions

THE GLOBAL FIELD OF HIGHER EDUCATION

1	Global Super-league' of leading US and UK research universities
2a	Lesser globally engaged American doctoral universities
2b	National elite research-intensive universities with role in education exports
3	Elite and globally focused commercial institutions (small group, e.g. in India)
4a	Nationally-bound elite research universities with no significant export role
4b	Teaching-focused export universities with a foothold in research
5	Teaching-focused national universities
6	Lesser prestige teaching-only globally active commercial institutions
6	For-profits with minor global-functions

Outside the global field

7	Non-profits without global agendas
9	For-profits without global agendas

However in some respects in global higher education the polarity between the two principles of hierarchization differs from that described by Bourdieu in *Homo Academicus* (1988) and *The Field of Cultural Production* (1993). Anglo-American universities do not follow the French division between high intellectual schools and those preparing the business elite. In Anglo-American leading universities the two functions are combined, increasing their weight and integrating them closer with those institutions and agents that are the primary nodes in the networks of economic and political power. Further, these elite universities, particularly the US Ivy League, are not just status dominant but *economically* dominant in relation to the mass producers. The super-league command extraordinary resources; for example the much cited Harvard endowment, and the commercial presence of American research universities in bioscience. Nevertheless Bourdieu's notion that the logic of economic market competition is inversely related to, and exclusive of, the logic of a status competition—or in other words, the more autonomous a university, the less commercial it is in temper—does apply to the dynamics of the US and UK Super-league. Though they are unambiguously wealthy in terms of their measurable income, assets and apparent brand power, Ivy League institutions do not expand willy-nilly in the manner of a capitalist business. Their lodestone is not revenues *per se* but socio-cultural power. Their authority derives not from their equity price or their market share, but their domestic student selectivity and their global dominance of knowledge formation. Money is more a means than an end; though one of the wellsprings of the power of the super-league universities lies in the fact that culturally speaking, these are institutions (like leading government agencies) in which the constituents of economic value and the terms of market exchange are themselves accessible to influence.

Where the super-league institutions run commercial sub-operations of their own, the tension between Bourdieu's two principles of hierarchization becomes absorbed within the institution. This tension plays out within their research activities, which are alternately fundamental and commercial; the two being mixed together almost irretrievably in bioscience;[26] and in the cultural differences between arts and disciplinary science at one end of the university and business studies at the other.

Position and position-taking

Within Bourdieu's field of power, agents compete for resources, status or other objects of interest. Here he describes a reciprocal but rather lop-sided interaction between the prior positions where agents are located (the social structuring of agency) and the position-taking strategies that the agents select. 'Every position-taking is defined in relation to the *space of possibles* which is objectively realized as a *problematic* in the form of the actual or potential position-takings corresponding to the different positions; and it receives its distinctive *value* from its negative relationship with the coexistent position-takings to which it is objectively related.'[27] Position-taking is the 'space of creative works.'[28] But this is not an open-ended free-wheeling creativity. The range of possible strategies is relatively narrow. Only some position-takings are possible, identified by agents as they respond to changes in the settings and moves of others in the competition game. Agents have a number of possible 'trajectories,' meaning the succession of positions occupied by the same agent over time, and employ semi-instinctual 'strategies' to achieve these trajectories. Agents respond in terms of their 'habitus,' their acquired mix of beliefs and capabilities, and in particular their 'disposition' which mediates the relationship between position and position-takings.[29]

Bourdieu talks about a 'homology' between the space of position-takings and the space of positions. There are no Appadurian disjunctures here, nothing is so left to chance, and at bottom the space of positions always seems to come before that of position-taking; structure is prior to agency. Nevertheless, from time to time Bourdieu attempts to open the structure of positions to determination by the agents, as well as *vice versa*. 'Although position helps to shape dispositions, the latter, in so far as they are the product of independent conditions, have an existence and an efficacy of their own and can help shape positions,' he declares.[30] Usefully, he argues that this scope for the self-determination of agents, what he calls 'the scope allowed for dispositions,' is variable, being shaped by the autonomy of the field in relation to other fields, by the position of the agent in the field, and by the extent to which the position is a novel and emerging one, or path-dependency has been established.[31] This suggests relatively novel field structures are less determined, and determining. In turn, this helps to explain how the global field of higher education is more open than are most national fields.

Bourdieu's description of a position-taking that is largely fashioned by position is consistent with much of the evidence we have concerning the decision making behaviour of university executives as they strive to maintain and improve relative advantage in relation to other institutions.[32] As will be discussed further below, there are some empirical data that Bourdieu does not explain, and there remain questions about how much room is left for self-determining agency. Bourdieu also fails to distinguish hierarchy per se from overwhelming power within a field such as higher education. This latter, 'structural' issue is now considered before returning to the question of agency. Here Bourdieu's argument about field, position, and position-taking can be supplemented by Antonio Gramsci's notion of *egemonia* (hegemony).

Gramsci and hegemony

Gramsci contrasts and also couples two different regimes of power. The first is domination or coercion by the open state machine, the 'State-as-force.'[33] Second, there is hegemony which is secured primarily through civil society, including education. Hegemony is 'the "spontaneous" consent given by the great masses of the population to the general direction imposed on social life by the dominant fundamental group.'[34] It is a social construction in the realms of intellectual reason and popular culture, in which, as Gwyn Williams puts it, 'a certain way of life and thought is dominant, in which one concept of reality is diffused throughout society in all its institutional and private manifestations.'[35] In this argument, civil institutions like universities are analytically distinct from the state (political society) but are intertwined with it. There are parallels with Foucault's distinction between government as political sovereignty, and government as the conduct of conduct permeating all aspects of life.[36] Like Foucault, Gramsci also emphasizes that these two regimes of power constitute mutually dependent strategies. 'One might say that state = political society + civil society, in other words hegemony protected by the armour of coercion.'[37] Rule by consent is ultimately underpinned by rule by force. Once secured, hegemony opens the tactical possibility of the episodic imposition of direct controls.

Tradition is an active, shaping force in making hegemony. As Raymond Williams puts it, hegemonic institutions sustain a 'deliberately selective and connective process which offers a historical and cultural ratification of a contemporary order.'[38] Certain meanings and practices are selected into the common tradition, while other meanings and practices become neglected or excluded. Thus elite universities secure their claim as privileged manufacturers of hegemonic tradition, a role which is distinct from that of other universities, by populating themselves with the recognized symbols of venerable power: baroque stonework, roman numerals, ivy-clad gothic buildings.

Does Gramsci see hegemony—with its grounding as he describes it, in particular localities, city states and nations—as operational in the global dimension? Yes.

> Every relationship of 'hegemony' is necessarily an educational relationship and occurs not only within a nation, between the various forces of which a nation is composed, but in the international and worldwide field, between the complexes of national and continental civilizations.'[39]

In one respect, however, Gramsci's theorization has dated. He saw the USA as lagging behind because it 'has not yet created a conception of the world or a group of great intellectuals to lead the people within the ambit of civil society.'[40] If that statement was true in the high time of Gramsci's activism in the 1920s, it is no longer the case. It is American, not European, universities that now lead global civil society and install 'a conception of the world' consistent with American economic, political and military power. More to the point, Gramsci remarks that hegemony can vary in the degree of integration it facilitates. Though hegemony mostly presupposes that account is taken of the interests and tendencies of the groups over which it is exercised, there is the hegemony of the Italian *Risorgimento*, which does not feel the need to secure concordance between its interests and those of the dominated groups or engage with their specificities such as languages and ways of life: 'they wished to "dominate" and not to "lead." '[41] This argument is more contemporary, more indicative of the forms of American hegemony in higher education and university research.

American hegemony in the universities

The instrumental strength of the United States in higher education is massive compared to that of all other nations. The USA has the third largest population in the world, the largest GDP, and a GDP per head over $40,000 USD. The next com-

Table 7.3. United States' GDP, GDP per head, spending on tertiary education, and leading researchers and research universities, compared to the next ten OECD nations on spending and five largest nations

	POPULATION 2005	GDP IN PPP TERMS 2005	GDP PER CAPITA PPP 2005	PROPORTION OF GDP ON TERTIARY EDUCATION 2005	SPENDING ON TERTIARY EDUCATION PPP (EST.) 2003/2005	THOMSON-ISI 'HₗCₗ' RESEARCHERS 2007	RESEARCH UNIVERSITIES IN SHANGHAI JIAO TONG UNIVERSITY RANKING 2008		
	MILLIONS	BILLION $USD	$USD	%	BILLION $USD		TOP 20	TOP 100	TOP 500
USA	296.5	12,409.5	41,854	2.9	360	3837	17	54	159
Japan	128.0	3943.8	30,811	1.3	51	246	1	4	31
South Korea	48.3	1056.1	21,868	2.6	27	3	0	0	8
Germany	82.5	2417.5	29,309	1.1	27	243	0	6	40
France	60.7	1829.6	30,120	1.4	26	157	0	3	23
Canada	32.3	1061.2	32,885	2.4	25	175	0	4	21
UK	60.2	1926.8	32,007	1.1	21	444	2	11	42
Italy	57.5	1667.8	29,019	0.9	15	75	0	0	22
Mexico	103.1	1052.4	10,209	1.3	14	14	0	0	1
Spain	43.4	1133.5	26,125	1.2	14	18	0	0	9
Australia	20.3	643.0	31,642	1.5	10	105	0	3	15
China *	1311.4	8787.2	6701	n.a.	n.a.	18	0	0	23
India **	1095.6	3815.6	3483	0.7	27	11	0	0	2
Brazil	186.4	1627.3	8730	0.8	13	4	0	0	6
Russia	143.2	1559.9	10,897	0.7	11	5	0	1	2
Indonesia **	221.6	847.4	3842	0.3	3	0	0	0	0

PPP = Purchasing Power Parity n.a. = data not available includes Hong Kong, excludes seven universities from Taiwan*

*** proportion of GDP spent on tertiary education is 2004 for India and Indonesia. Spending on tertiary education estimated using 2005 GDP data and 2003 proportion of GDP allocated to tertiary education*

Sources: World Bank (2007), OECD (2006), Thomson-ISI (2007), SJTUIHE (2007)

petitor in terms of the size, wealth and scope of the material underpinnings of higher education is Japan. Japan has less than half the population and one third of the GDP of the USA and a *per capita* income of just over $30,000.[42] The USA also spends the highest proportion of its GDP on tertiary education, 2.9 per cent in 2003.[43] Applying this proportion to the 2005 GDP, this amounted to approximately $360 billion USD in 2005 in Purchasing Power Parity (domestic price spending) terms. The next largest spender was Japan at $51 billion.[44] In other words *the United States invested seven times as much on tertiary education in material terms as does the next nation.* It is not surprising that the USA had 17 of the world's top 20 research universities and 84 of the top 200 as measured by the Shanghai Jiao Tong University in 2006[45] (Table 7.3).

This overwhelming concentration of resources explains little in itself, but it is a condition for many things. How is the US hegemony in higher education manifest? Hegemony is not a top-down relationship in the manner of a military command. It works by osmosis, in the day-to-day accumulation of messages, money, people, and publications; in networks dominated by American institutions that channel and limit global flows, forming and controlling not just research, scholarly, managerial, and policy agendas but the very idea of a university in this era. It facilitates and is facilitated by American global geo-strategic mobility, that apparent freedom to go anywhere and freely intervene in other national sites while maintaining territorial control of the homeland. Of many possible illustrations, this chapter will briefly discuss research concentration and mediascapes, the passages of knowledge, the role of the English language in the global communicative environment, the gravitational role of the USA in determining the concentration and directions of ethnoscapes, and the Americanized templates (ideoscapes) of higher education that seem to be shaping the imaginings of higher education systems and university 'quality' everywhere else.

Knowledge power above all is determined by research concentrations, the production and flow of knowledge and the language of use. First, consider the patterns of publication and citation. In 2005 US scientists and social scientists published 205,320 papers in major journals compared to 55,471 in Japan, the UK 45,572, Germany 44,145, China 41,596 and India 14,608. Figure 7.2 has details. In Indonesia, the world's fourth most populous nation, there were 207 papers in 2001. Not much knowledge flows back from Indonesia to the USA.[46]

The direction of global knowledge flows can be traced more precisely in citations. In 2001 the USA produced less than a third of the articles but accounted for 44 per cent of citations in the scientific literature. In 2007 US research institutions employed 3837 of the Thomson-ISI 'HiCi' researchers that influence performance in the Shanghai Jiao Tong University rankings, compared to 444 in the UK, Japan 246, Germany 243, China 18, India 11 and Indonesia zero. Among American universities Harvard alone has 160 HiCi researchers, Stanford 135 and UC Berkeley 82. There are 44 at Cambridge and 29 at Oxford.[47]

In 2008 Leiden University in the Netherlands announced a new ranking system based on its own bibliometric indicators, using various rankings of institutions for the 2003–2007 period. One of these rankings was by number of scientific publications,

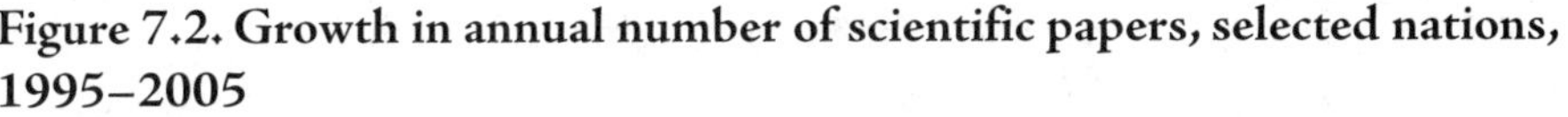

Figure 7.2. Growth in annual number of scientific papers, selected nations, 1995–2005

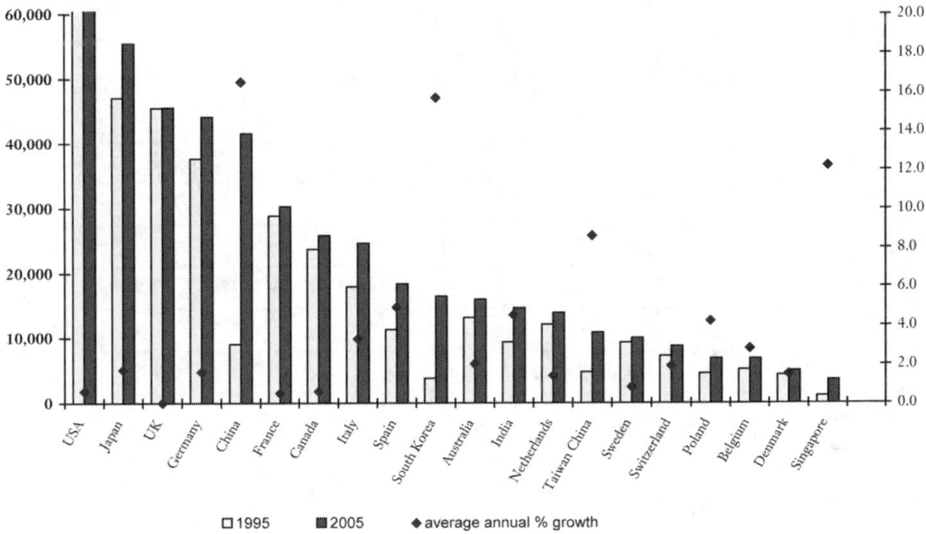

Note: USA total papers 193,337 in 1995 and 205,320 in 2005. Source: NSB, 2008.

modified by citations per publication, modified by normalization for academic field, that is, controlled for different rates of citation in disciplines (Leiden calls this the 'brute force' indicator because it rewards large institutions for size; this is a good proxy for presence in the knowledge economy). Another was citations per publication, modified for academic field, which the Leiden group calls its 'crown' indicator. This does not reward size and is the closest we can get to a comparative measure of the relative quality of university publications.[48] In the table for the 'brute force' indicator, Harvard *more than doubles* the modified publication volume of the next university, the University of California at Los Angeles. US universities constitute 28 of the first 40. In relation to the Leiden 'crown' indicator, *US universities hold the world's first 36 places*. Next is Cambridge university in the UK at 37. US researchers are very strong in the core discipline groups. In 2008 European nations aside from the UK housed 88 of the top discipline groups as measured by the Shanghai Jiao Tong University Institute of Higher Education. The UK had 50, the USA had 308. There were just ten in China, nine of these in engineering.[49] Table 7.4 has details.

American universities also connect more effectively than do universities in the rest of the world. Webometrics ranks the communications power of universities in the k-economy. It records the number of webpages, external hits, 'rich pages' such as pdfs and word documents attached to websites, and publication and citation counts in Google Scholar. The last constitutes 50 per cent of the index. Thus there is a strong element within the ranking derived from the formal publication world but it also picks up elements in the open source domain. Nevertheless, the same institutions that

Table 7.4 University discipline groups in the world top 100, by nation, Shanghai Jiao Tong rankings, 2008

	PHYSICAL SCIENCES	ENGINEERING	LIFE SCIENCES	MEDICINE	SOCIAL SCIENCES	TOTAL
USA	59	49	62	61	77	308
UK	9	7	11	12	11	50
Canada	2	6	5	6	7	26
Germany	7	1	6	6	0	20
Japan	7	7	3	2	0	19
Netherlands	1	3	2	5	4	15
Switzerland	3	2	4	2	0	11
Australia	1	3	4	3	1	10
Israel	4	2	2	2	0	10
China	0	9	0	0	1	10
Sweden	2	3	2	2	0	9
France	5	2	1	1	0	9
Belgium	0	2	3	2	1	8
Italy	2	3	0	1	0	6
Denmark	2	1	1	1	1	6
South Korea	1	3	0	0	0	4
Singapore	1	2	0	0	1	4
others	1	2	1	3	1	8

Source: SJTUIHE, 2008

dominate formal science also tend to lead informal academic publication. Communicative capacity is even more concentrated than research capacity. Being an English-speaking country appears more of an advantage in webometrics than the Shanghai Jiao Tong. The US universities in the first 23 places are led by MIT, Stanford and Harvard.[50]

We should note, however, tendencies to pluralization of research capacity. From 1995 to 2005 the annual number of scientific papers produced in China rose from 9061 to 41,596. Between 1995 and 2005 China's annual output of papers rose by 16.5

per cent per annum. The annual rate of growth in South Korea was 15.7 per cent, in Singapore 12.2 per cent, and Taiwan China 8.6 per cent.[51] In 2003 Singapore invested 2.24 per cent of GDP on R&D, a higher figure than Canada.[52] As with outputs so with inputs. Between 2000–2005 R&D investment in China rose by 18.5 per cent per year. Between 1996 and 2005 China's investment in R&D as a proportion of GDP rose from 0.57 to 1.35 per cent.[53] In 2006 China became the world's number two R&D spender. Significant shifts in research capacity shares are taking place. Nevertheless, the USA has a very long lead in research.

Second, there is American (or Anglo-American) supremacy in academic language. Gramsci remarks that in hegemonic projects 'great importance is assumed by the general question of language, that is, the question of collectively attaining a single cultural "climate."'[54] Bourdieu puts it more sharply. Establishing a canon is an act of 'symbolic violence' that occludes the norms it displaces and the underlying power relations which sustain it.'[55] Certain practices become legitimated as 'naturally' superior and made especially superior to those who do not participate.[56] In terms of patterns of recognition and authority at least, creativity that is expressed in English has come to appear superior to creativity expressed in other languages. The first language of one sixth of the world, English has become the sole global language of research, in the process marginalizing the earlier cross-border roles of Latin, German, French and Russian. It also has a growing importance in Masters programs offered in universities outside the English-speaking world in Europe and Asia, dominates the managerial literature, and as Castells notes it dominates the contents of the Internet. Universities in each world region have partial linkages with universities in other regions but they normally link to universities in the USA. The American institutions operate as the global hub structuring the communicative field.[57]

Third, as noted in the previous chapter, US universities are extraordinary global attractors of creative talent, and this plays a key role in reproducing their global hegemony. Compared to the procedures governing academic careers and appointments in most Western European and East and Southeast Asian nations, especially the appointment of foreigners, American higher education institutions are open and flexible. They also provide greatly superior scholarship opportunities and post-doctoral fellowships, and compared to most national systems, superior job opportunities and salaries. An average of half the foreign doctoral graduates stay on in the USA. The US is also the main site for short term academic visits, and this can encourage later career migration. Though the openness of the US researcher labour market is stymied from time to time by prejudicial immigration policies, security monitoring and visa delays, notably in the wake of 11 September 2001, it is more than mere words. Foreign entrants into the American research system often outperform locals. In a study for the OECD Guellec and Cervantes note that 'the foreign born and foreign educated are disproportionately represented among individuals making an exceptional contribution to science and engineering in the United States...18.1 per cent of recipients of highly cited patents (the top 3.5 per cent over the period 1980–91) are foreign born' compared to the expected 11.8 per cent.[58] The USA has become the world graduate school and main destination for creative researchers and scholars everywhere else so as to accumulate knowledge power.

The orientation of international education in the USA is different to that of the other English-speaking countries. As in Japan and Germany international education is as much as a branch of foreign policy as a facet of policy on universities. Foreign student entry into the doctoral universities is heavily subsidized. American universities focus not so much on generating revenues from foreign students as on attracting the best people into the USA. In the universities foreign doctoral talents are utilized as research assistants and teaching assistants. After graduation they are often recruited to faculty positions, especially in engineering and technologies where the American universities could not function without foreign recruits. In other words, the US deploys global people flows in higher education so as to boost the hegemonic knowledge power of the USA, rather than to accumulate capital within a commercial education market. No doubt American doctoral universities would make much more money from international education if they behaved like universities in the UK, Australia and New Zealand. In Australia, which has built education into its third largest export industry, a dozen universities enroll more than 8000 international students, with over 16,000 at Monash, Curtin and RMIT Universities.[59] In the USA the doctoral university with the largest complement, the University of Southern California, enrols less than 7000.

In its global operations the doctoral segment of the American higher education sector has firmly positioned itself in Bourdieu's sub-field of restricted production, as against the sub-field of mass or commercial production (Figure 7.1). This has consequences for universities and research systems everywhere else. Diasporas are increasingly mobile and multiple in their choice of place, and in the case of people from countries such as Korea and Taiwan China, a significant proportion of those graduating with American PhDs and staying to work in the United States will return home during their future careers, some more than once. Many analysts talk about 'brain circulation' rather than 'brain drain.' But the brutal fact is that for most nations the net flow of creative higher education talent *does* constitute a brain drain, and in net terms this brain drain is problematic because it continually erodes the capacity of universities and the national innovation system. For example Germany, despite its relatively strong research-intensive universities and scientific research institutes, is losing many doctoral students to the USA and also some to the UK. At the same time its own capacity to attract foreign faculty and doctoral students has diminished. Berning remarks that while German research universities are seen as uniformly good, there is a lack of highest prestige in the US-style 'centres of excellence':

> German study courses and degrees have lost part of their former international reputation. This is mainly due to the worldwide expansion and adoption of the Anglo-American HE system, its courses and degrees, but not to a lack of scientific quality in Germany. The consequence is a loss of foreign students from countries close to Germany but now following the Anglo-American mainstream (e.g. East Asia, Turkey). The loss of foreign students may cause a loss of young scientists from abroad too.[60]

But in the USA 'brain circulation' is 'brain gain' and it is an unambiguous virtue.

Fourth, there is the primarily American content of the norms of good practice in university and system organization. These norms derive originally from the New Public Management (NPM) in public enterprise, which began life as a British invention but in its higher education guise it has become infused with American contents. As discussed in chapter 5, for the last two decades the NPM, formidably supported around the world by the finance sector and government economic agencies, has provided the main narrative of transformation of higher education. There are two NPM norms of ideal practice, ideologized via a selective reading of American practices:

- The high status not for-profit private research-intensive university: focused on research and graduate education, student selective, high tuition and high aid, receiving significant income from donations, and competing with similar institutions for the best students and staff (that is, an idealized Ivy League university)
- The for-profit vocational institution, broad-based training in business studies and possibly also technologies, health and education: commercial, expansionary, spare and efficient, no academic frills like research, 'customer'-focused using performance management of staff and quality assurance (that is, the University of Phoenix on a good day).

It is striking that these two Americanizing ideoscapes, which are those of the enterprising, modernized research-intensive university and the for-profit vocational training institution, embody in NPM form the two sub-fields that are identified by Bourdieu. In other words the NPM has earmarked each Bourdieuian sub-field for organization as a specific national and global market. Here we find that the exercise of global hegemony extends not simply to normalization of a single ideal type of university but to the continuing reconstitution of the global field as a whole. In discussing the modernizing process of 'de-severing,' the bringing of remote places into proximity that is inherent in communicative globalization (Chapter 1), and also in imperial outreach, Heidegger noted that de-severing typically entails 'directionality.'[61] The bringing-close is in a direction taken in advance, towards a particular 'region.' De-severance and directionality together constitute the regional form of spatiality. In higher education and knowledge the 'region' is the real-imagined realm of American culture.

Yet these idealized American models of higher education confront a set of very diverse higher education systems and institutions, including the Latin American participatory national universities that take in a large slice of economic, social, political and cultural life, such as the University of Buenos Aires and UNAM in Mexico; the German *Fachhochschulen* and high quality vocational sectors in Finland and Switzerland; and the research institutes in France and Germany. Inescapably, these other types and systems are being marginalized by the twin NPM ideoscapes. The process of marginalization is made explicit in worldwide university rankings, which again normalize the student selective, science-based, research intensive university, and tend also to favour English language nations because English is the language of research. The *Times* Higher university rankings promotes a handful of institutions with industry in their mission, but specialist institutions and non-research intensive tertiary education sectors are excluded.[62] Whether intended for the purpose or not, like research publication the annual global university rankings have become a technology for securing hegemony.

Open and bounded

Although American research-intensive universities are not organized as a national system and are unusually open to foreign personnel, American exceptionalism sustains a firm boundary with the rest of the higher education world and American institutions exhibit a remarkable cultural coherence in dealings with it. To be both open and bounded is a powerful condition.[63] Openness is expressed in the free mobility of talent into the USA and the outward flows of American knowledge, a gift than no one can refuse. Boundedness is sustained by American-dominated English language research and publishing and above all by the abiding sense of national superiority. Heidegger called it 'a way of Being in space which we call "insideness"…an entity which is itself extended is closed around by the extended boundaries of something that is likewise extended.' US universities are extended everywhere into the world while enclosed by their own national-imperial identity.

This is the hegemony of the *Risorgimento*. For the most part, rather than engaging closely with non-American institutions, learning their languages of use and helping with capability building, US universities benignly ignore them, leaving them to evolve towards US templates according to their capacity and 'merit.' Scholars outside the USA are under-cited and in some American university circles simply unnoticed. The worldwide Carnegie survey of the academic profession found that over 90 per cent of scholars from other nations believed it necessary to read foreign books and journals but 62 per cent of Americans agreed. This was much the smallest level among developed nations.[64] For many if not most American university eyes the world outside is on the periphery of vision, at least until its scholars take a place within the US on American terms. But for the remainder of the higher education world, the great American universities loom large and central in the landscape.

American hegemony in higher education and university research plays out alongside the parallel and overlapping American domination of communications and creative industries, including the contents of film, television and hand held media. US hegemony in the knowledge economy is equivalent in scale to US hegemony in affective inter-subjectivity; if there is a world-mind it is heavily Americanized in all its functions, though it must be said that the extent of domination falls short of the US supremacy in military capacity. Perhaps a case could also be made for the notion of an Anglo-American hegemony in higher education, given the centrality of the English language to higher education and research, and the global importance of the leading UK research universities, especially Cambridge and Oxford. But the middling UK universities have much less cross-border clout than their US counterparts. It must be said that if there is an Anglo-American hegemony the UK is a very junior partner.

Is there a way out? How solid are these hegemonic power relations in global higher education? It is evident that the domain of university creativity is uneven, with its pre-set agendas, its overwhelming presences, its exclusions and silences, its peaks and troughs that derive from more than just fluctuations in the intrinsic intellectual power of the work. It is always destined to be so. But is this particular pattern inevitable? This takes us to questions of global agency and ontology.

Agency in the global field

From time to time university and research leaders engage in off-the-wall innovations that are not fully explained by prior positions and conditions, especially in the global field: for example the first branch campuses of education exporters that were established in importing nations; the global schoolhouse strategy developed by the government of Singapore; and the MIT open courseware initiative. Here the limits of Bourdieu's theorization of agency are apparent and these limits have implications also for his theorization of the field of power and especially its translation into the global dimension. The problem is not simply that the changes in the global setting, the emergence of a worldwide communicative system, and one system of published research, have transformed the map of positions and the position-taking options. Bourdieu himself would make that point, while continuing to defend his system. The problem is his attenuated notion of the potentials of agency and self-transformation.

One difficulty is that Bourdieu universalizes competition. There can be no respite from the relentless war of all against all which continually eats into our conditions of possibility. Yet inter-subjective relations in global higher education are often cooperative. A further problem is that Bourdieu's pre-structuring of agency and conscious imagining leaves insufficient scope not just for the changeability of identities and the possibilities of self-transformation but for the multiplicity and shifting locational determinacy of identities in the global setting. Sen notes that people mostly invest in more than one field and more than one identity and this multiplicity is particularly characteristic of the open global setting,[65] in which not just agency but the map of positions are continually made and remade by strategic actions.

Another and fundamental difficulty is that Bourdieu sees agency freedom, self-determining identity, as ultimately bound *a priori* by a stratification of class power lodged in the unconscious. First, *Distinction* (1984) talks about an opposition between 'the tastes of luxury (or freedom) and the tastes of necessity.'[66] In other words, the potential for self-determination is confined to freedom from material necessity.[67] There are a number of problems in this. Those who exercise self-determination are defined as those free of necessity, only the wealthy are free, and the path to freedom must be simultaneously a journey to material enrichment. We are back in the economic determinism which he wants to evade. Second, for Bourdieu 'strategy' is not based on conscious imagining and deciding so much as learned dispositions, the habitus. The habitus has been absorbed through the skin in the course of inheritance and experience and it is only dimly accessible to the conscious mind if accessible at all. He imagines that the range and limits of the possible position-taking strategies, which are structured so as to be congruent to the social position of each agent, have been burned into the mind of each agent and conditions her/his every action. While Bourdieu wavers on the point, sometimes seeming to provide more space for voluntary action than at other times, the main thrust of his argument is that agents move instinctively in response to the changing possibilities as the struggle shifts. For example: 'because position-takings arise quasi-mechanically—that is, almost independently of the agents' consciousnesses and wills—from the relationship between positions, they take relatively invariant forms.'[68] Though he notes that conscious lucidity is possible, nevertheless, 'lucidity is always partial and is, once again, a matter of position and trajectory within the field.' Game over.[69]

This reifies not just human reflexivity but the painstaking reciprocity between structure and agency on which Bourdieu's argument turns. He is trapped on the structure side of the dual. If the scope for action is so confined by limitations to our inner mental horizons, installed by a *prior* materiality, this locks up self-determination itself. Self-determination *is* conditioned by resources and historical relations of power. It is essential to understand these conditions. But they do not close the list of possibilities. History suggests that freedom is conditioned also by agency itself, by the imagination and the capacity of agents to work on their own limits. Gramsci, with his emphasis on the will and individual initiative, was aware of this. In sum, when we consider the domain of worldwide higher education and its global dimension, we find that Bourdieu has left insufficient space for the play of the conscious imagination in the global strategy making of universities, research clusters and scholarly groups.

Amartya Sen finds that freedom as self-determination has two principal components: 'agency freedom' and 'freedom as power.'[70] Agency freedom is where identity is located, the imagination is gathered and the will is formed. Freedom as power is, roughly speaking, positive freedom, including the resource capacity to realize one's goals. Sen distinguishes both forms of freedom from negative freedom, the freedom from coercion foundational to Hayek[71] and the neo-liberalism that is foundational to the techniques of the NPM. Negative freedom is one condition of self-determination but it is less important than freedom as power, and it is presupposed by freedom as power. Sen argues that the range of choices available is an important element of freedom, again in contrast to Hayek for whom the range of choice is not important and what matters is the absence of coercion.[72] Sen also emphasizes that the extent of freedom should be distinguished from resources and other means to freedom. That is, two agents with the same resources and same negative freedom may have a different freedom to achieve. For example, in the worldwide higher education environment, one agent may imagine a new strategy than can be pursued. Another agent, operating in much the same material circumstances, may not. When resources are held constant the primary source of variations in self-determination is agency freedom. Here the range of choices can be expanded, in the first instance by thought. Thus to the long list of elements that might differentiate freedom to achieve in global higher education, including the level of GDP, the volume of financial investment in higher education, research capacity, language of use, the volume and intensity of cross-border engagements, and so on, another quality is crucial. It is the creative *imagination* of governments, universities, disciplines, groupings and individuals.

Global ontology

Appadurai is alert to precisely this set of possibilities, envisioning the global as a zone of new imaginings and emphasizing its uncertainty. Each scape has its own logic and intersects with and conditions the other scapes in unpredictable ways. 'The suffix -scape allows us to point to the fluid, irregular shapes of these landscapes.'[73] This challenges not only Bourdieu's attenuated notion of agency but also his more robust notion of fields. As Bourdieu defines it, the domain of higher education requires not just self-identity and a certain insularity, but boundedness and predictability.

The global dimension of higher education is in continuous formation, the map of positions is continually being reworked. Novel positions are emerging. Why the greater ontological openness in the global setting? Some reasons have already been suggested. One is the recency of global higher education, the raw unsettled character of the field. Another factor is the growth, extension, reciprocity, dynamism, instability and contingency of global flows. As the fluid moving metaphor of 'flows' suggests, flows continually generate change even as they themselves are changing. These effects are conditioned by permeable national borders, transient global networks and the flaky borders of the global field, lacunae in the governmental regulation of cross-border relations and the room for spontaneous association this creates. Above all there are the expanded potentials for agency freedom that are created by global transformations in space and time. More multiple locations. Faster passage between them. Instantaneous, expanded, intensified, multi-associating communications. Variously articulated spheres of action. It all loosens relations of power.

Yet Appadurai's suggestive reading of flows, scapes and disjuncture does not provide us with more than one part of the picture of the global. It is unhelpful to consider the global as a single space open and volatile, containing the whole of human action, as he appears to suggest. To summarize, the global dimension is just one dimension of action, one identifiable space where human strategies are played out, albeit one that is suffused with unpredictability in the manner of Appadurai's scapes. The global space sits alongside the national and local spaces and connects with them at many points. As noted, working across all three of these relatively open spaces—local, national and global—we find more bounded and predictable domains such as law, government, finance, and higher education and knowledge. These domains of practice have their own global aspect or dimension as has been analyzed here in relation to higher education, and these domains of practice intersect with Appadurai's global scapes. But they are not reducible to the global (still less to the national) 'as a whole.' The point rather is that in this more global era, domains such as higher education and research knowledge are both bigger and less stable than they once were, and infused with greater dynamism and unpredictability by the scapes.

Within such domains, Bourdieu's notions of field of power and position-taking retain the larger part of their potency. The key move, though, is to open the boundaries of the field as Bourdieu describes it, to tolerate the coexistence of structure and contingency; of borderness on one hand, and porousness and uncompletion on the other. This opens the way for the fuller play of agency and creative imagination.

If the global space is immersed in the multiple and unpredictable with an ever-growing scope for imagining, this places a question mark alongside American hegemony. Hegemony is a bold effort to impose form on flux, to stop time and centre control in particular sites. How could any such project ever be anything but provisional? How could it not fail 'in the long run'? That does not mean that US university hegemomy is ephemeral or incapable of domination into the foreseeable future, only that the project must be continually made and remade as Gramsci saw until its capacity for renewal is finally undermined, fragmented or exhausted.

Appadurai's argument in *Modernity at Large*[74] would suggest that this kind of hegemonic relationship can be routinely subverted from below, via hybrid academic forms that are created by diasporic communities in the spaces left by American exceptionalism and isolationism. People movement, where the US fosters openness, readily generates complex identities and the lines of force, passage and effect can flip over as conditions change. Organizational models are nested in historical conditions and open to local making and variation. In teaching there is plurality of languages of use, including the heterogeneous 'Englishes,' especially in Africa and Asia, hybrid responses to tenacious cultural traditions. However, and despite the fluidity of intellectual discourse, it seems that there is rather less scope for hybridity in the shaping of authoritative research and knowledge. It is here, above all, that elite status and global power in higher education are secured. Here a tight binary logic of inclusion/exclusion assigns worldwide academic labour to one of two categories: part of the global research circuit that uses the dominant language and publishes in the recognised outlets, or 'not global,' outside the hegemonic circuit, the bearer of knowledge obsolete or meaningless and doomed to be invisible. Will this hold? The closure of research rests on the larger openness of mobility and scapes, a vast potential for imaginings. More concretely, there is cultural pluralization in the rise of China and other Asian science powers—China doubled its investment in R&D as a share of GDP from 1995 to 2005—and the potential of Putonghua, Spanish and Arabic as global languages.

This expanded and more open global ontology is experienced differentially. Some have more freedoms of action than others. Bourdieu's point is that autonomy, capacity and scope for strategy are concentrated in the high academic sub-field. Here an individual institutional break with the main patterns of hegemony can be telling, but few risk losing their place in the sun. Bourdieu's point about concentration is broadly right but it is not the end of the story. There is no doubt that the creative potential of agency is scattered unevenly but some of it is distributed beyond the diffuse boundaries of elite institutions. All structures are open to change including hegemonic structures. Especially in the global field, any structural dynamic must be considered partial, relativized by the other parts of the field, provisional and in continuous transformation. There is no closure. One element always at play in the field and a primary source of this ontological openness is the imagination and will of agents.

Endnotes

1. Marginson and Rhoades, 2002; Valimaa, 2004.
2. Appadurai, 1996.
3. Held et al., 1999.
4. The work has been informed by case studies of the cross-border practices of individual research-intensive national universities in the Asia-Pacific, the Americas and Western Europe. See for example Marginson and Sawir, 2006.
5. Appadurai, 1996.
6. Bourdieu, 1984; Bourdieu, 1988; Bourdieu, 1993; Bourdieu, 1996.
7. Gramsci, 1971.
8. OECD, 2006.
9. World Bank, 2007.
10. For example Sen, 1985; Sen, 1992.
11. OECD, 2006, 287.
12. Castells, 2000, 71.
13. Appadurai, 1996, 32.
14. *ibid*, p. 27.
15. *ibid*, p. 10.
16. *ibid*, p. 33.
17. Bourdieu, 1996, 232.
18. See also Bourdieu, 1996 and others.
19. Naidoo, 2004, 468–469.
20. Bourdieu, 1993, 38–39.
21. Naidoo, 2004, 461.
22. Marginson and Considine, 2000, 175–232.
23. Trow, 1974.
24. *The Economist*, 2005.
25. The Shanghai Jiao Tong University Institute of Higher Education (SJTUIHE) measures of research performance include publication and citation in leading journals, the number of highly cited researchers, and the location of the education and employment of winners of Nobel Prizes and field medals in mathematics. SJTUIHE, 2007.
26. Bok, 2003.
27. Bourdieu, 1993, 30. Emphasis in original.
28. *ibid*, 39.
29. *ibid*, 30.

30. *ibid*, p. 61.

31. *ibid*, p. 72.

32. For example Marginson and Considine, 2000, 68–95.

33. Gramsci, 1971, 56.

34. *ibid*, 12.

35. Williams, 1960.

36. Foucault, 1991.

37. Gramsci, 1971, 10.

38. Williams, 1977, 116.

39. Gramsci, 1971, 350.

40. Gramsci, 1971, 272.

41. *ibid*, 104–105.

42. World Bank, 2007.

43. OECD, 2007.

44. China may now exceed this figure, but comparable expenditure data are not available.

45. SJTUIHE, 2007.

46. National Science Board, NSB, 2009.

47. Thomson-ISI, 2007.

48. Compared with the Jiao Tong ranking, the Leiden CWTS has dispensed with Nobel indicators, counts of leading researchers and a composite indicator based on arbitrary weightings. CWTS, 2009.

49. However, there is a lag of up to a decade between changes in relative research outputs and change in rankings position, due to measurement-related factors.

50. Webometrics, 2009.

51. NSB, 2008.

52. World Bank, 2007.

53. World Bank, 2007.

54. Gramsci, 1971, 349.

55. Bourdieu, 1993, 20.

56. *ibid*, 24.

57. Castells, 2001.

58. Guellec and Cervantes, 2002, 98.

59. Marginson, 2007a.

60. Berning, 2004, 177.

61. Heidegger, 1962, 143–145.

62. Marginson, 2007b.

63. I am indebted to Peter Murphy for this formulation.

64. Altbach, 2005, 148–149.

65. Sen, 1999, 120.

66. Bourdieu, 1984, 177.

67. In *Freedom* (1988) Zyggy Bauman makes a similar argument.

68. Bourdieu, 1993, 59.

69. *ibid*, 72.

70. Sen, 1985. In later work 'freedom as power' is re-christened as 'effective freedom'—Sen, 1992.

71. Hayek, 1960.

72. Sen, 1992, 63.

73. Appadurai, 1996, 33.

74. Appadurai, 1996.

References

Altbach, P. (2005). Academic challenges: The American professoriate in comparative perspective. In: A. Welch (ed.) *The Professoriate: Portrait of a Profession*. Springer: Dordrecht.

Appadurai, A. (1996). *Modernity at Large: Cultural Dimensions of Globalization*. Minneapolis: University of Minnesota Press.

Bauman, Z. (1988). *Freedom*. Milton Keynes: Open University Press.

Berning, E. (2004). Petrified structures and still little autonomy and flexibility: Country report Germany. In J. Enders and E. de Weert (ed). *The International Attractiveness of the Academic Workplace in Europe*. Frankfurt: Herausgeber und Bestelladresse.

Bok, D. (2003). *Universities in the Marketplace: The commercialization of Higher Education*. Princeton: Princeton University Press.

Bourdieu, P. (1984). *Distinction: A Social Critique of the Judgment of Taste*. London: Routledge and Kegan Paul

Bourdieu, P. (1988) *Homo Academicus*. Cambridge: Polity.

Bourdieu, P. (1993). *The Field of Cultural Production*. New York: Columbia University Press.

Bourdieu, P. (1996). *The State Nobility*. Cambridge: Polity.

Castells, M. (2000). *The Rise of the Network Society*, 2nd Edition. Oxford: Blackwell.

Castells, M. (2001). *The Internet Galaxy*. Oxford: Oxford University Press.

The Economist (2005). The brains business, 8 September.

Foucault, M. (1991). Governmentality. In: G. Burchell, C. Gordon and P. Miller (eds.) *The Foucault Effect: Studies in Governmentality*, 87–104. London: Harvester Wheatsheaf.

Gramsci, A. (1971). *Selections from the Prison Notebooks*. New York: International Publishers.

Guellec, D. and Cervantes, M. (2002). International mobility of highly skilled workers: From statistical analysis to policy formulation. In OECD, *International Mobility of the Highly Skilled*. Paris: OECD.

Hayek, F. (1960). *The Constitution of Liberty*. London: Routledge and Kegan Paul.

Heidegger, M. (1962). *Being and Time*. Transl. by J. Macquarie & E. Robinson. New York: Harper and Row.

Held, D., McGlew, A., Goldblatt, D., and Perraton, J. (1999). *Global Transformations*. Stanford: Stanford University Press.

Marginson, S. (2007a). Global position and position-taking: the case of Australia. *Journal of Studies in International Education*, 11 (1), 5–32

Marginson, S. (2007b). Global university rankings. In S. Marginson (Ed.) *Prospects of Higher Education: Globalisation, Market Competition, Public Goods and the Future of the University*, 79–100. Rotterdam: Sense Publishers.

Marginson, S. and Considine, M. (2000), *The Enterprise University: Power, Governance and Reinvention in Australia*. Cambridge: Cambridge University Press.

Marginson, S. and Rhoades, G. (2002). Beyond national states, markets, and systems of higher education: a glonacal agency heuristic. *Higher Education*, 43, 281–309.

Marginson, S. and Sawir, E. (2006). University leaders' strategies in the global environment: A comparative study of Universitas Indonesia and the Australian National University. *Higher Education*, 52, 343–373.

Naidoo, R. (2004). Fields and institutional strategy: Bourdieu on the relationship between higher education, inequality and society. *British Journal of Sociology of Education*, 25 (4), 468–469.

National Science Board, NSB (2009). *Science and Engineering Indicators*. Accessed 1 March 2009 at: http://www.nsf.gov/statistics/seind04/

OECD (2006). *Education at a Glance*. Paris: OECD.

Sen, A. (1985). Well-being, agency and freedom: The Dewey lectures 1984. *The Journal of Philosophy*, 82 (4), 169–221

Sen, A. (1992). *Inequality Reexamined*. Cambridge: Harvard University Press.

Sen, A. (1999). Global justice: Beyond international equity. In I. Kaul, I. Grunberg and M. Stern (Eds.) *Global Public Goods: International Cooperation in the 21st century*. New York: Oxford University Press.

Shanghai Jiao Tong University Institute of Higher Education, SJTUIHE (2007). *Academic Ranking of World Universities*. Accessed 1 January 2008 *at*: http://ed.sjtu.edu.cn/ranking.htm

Thomson Publishing/Institute for Scientific Information, Thomson-ISI (2007). Data on highly cited researchers. ISIHighlyCited.com. Accessed 24 March 2007 at:http://isihighlycited.com/

Trow. M. (1974). Problems in the transition from elite to mass higher education, in *Policies for Higher Education*, from the General Report on the Conference on Future Structures of Post-Secondary Education. Paris: OECD.

Valimaa, J. (2004). Nationalisation, localisation and globalisation in Finnish higher education, *Higher Education*, 48, 27–54.

Webometrics (2009). *Ranking Web of World Universities* (title of website). Accessed 21 March at: http://www.webometrics.info/

Williams, G. (1960). The concept of 'egemonia' in the thought of Antonio Gramsci: Some notes on interpretation. *Journal of the History of Ideas*, 21 (4), 586–599.

Williams, R. (1977). *Marxism and Literature*. Oxford: Oxford University Press.

World Bank (2007). World Bank data and statistics. Accessed 1 December 2008 at: http://www.worldbank.org/data

The Rise of Global Science and the Emerging Political Economy of International Research Collaborations[1]

◻ Michael A. Peters

'Truth…and utility are the very same things,'
Francis Bacon, *New Organon*, I, Aphorism 124.

Introduction

Increasingly, emphasis has fallen on the economics and productivity of science in both firms and institutions of higher education, as policy-makers and politicians seek to foster innovation and to draw strong links between scientific performance and emerging economic structures (Crespi and Geuna, 2004, 2005). In these science policy discussions the accent often falls on measuring scientific productivity, on 'intellectual property' and the codification of knowledge, and on research collaboration, partnership and cooperation in regional, national and international contexts. Investment in science, engineering and technology has received strong attention from governments as the basis of the 'knowledge economy' and most governments now look to their international science policy strategy to emphasise national competitive advantage and to encourage research collaboration on global science projects.

Indeed, it is the age of *global science*, but not primarily in the sense of 'universal knowledge' which has characterised the liberal metanarrative of 'free' science since its early development, where scientific findings or results are open to peer review, public scrutiny and, in principle, reproducible by others following the same procedures.[2] It is the age of global science but not necessarily in the sense of 'international' collaboration (part of the same liberal metanarrative) as, say, the incipient norms of free exchange of ideas, free inquiry and collaboration developed during the so-called 'scientific revolution' and period of classical science, when 'scientists,'[3] particularly within Europe, travelled to meet one another and to share their ideas. This was the period when learned societies were established and the first journals flourished with the growth of publishing during the seventeenth and eighteenth centuries helping both to generate the international exchange of theories, concepts, methods and discoveries, and to aid the processes of research collaboration. This (older) liberal metanarrative of science now has been submerged by official narratives based on an economic logic linking science to national purpose, economic policy, and national science policy priorities. In the era of 'post-normal' science (Funtowicz & Ravetz, 1992), where globalised corporate science dominates the horizon and scientific 'outputs' differ from the traditional peer reviewed published scientific paper, quality assurance replaces 'truth' as the new regulative ideal. In contemporary science policy regimes outputs often take the form of patents, unpublished consultancy, 'gray literature' or are covered by legal arrangement and 'lawyer-client confidentiality.' As a result there are expressed concerns with the fate of scientific publishing. The rise of digitized publications have led to a counterrevolution in scholarly publishing where actual sales are recast into licenses and commercial publishers are taking advantage of the growth of open archives (Guédon, 2001). The Select Committee on Science and Technology in the United Kingdom Parliament (2003), for example, has urged the adoption of a new government strategy to address the problem of increasing journal prices imposed by commercial publishers, recommending 'that all UK higher education institutions establish institutional repositories on which their published output can be stored and from which it can be read, free of charge, online.'[4]

Global science as a term to describe the emerging *geography of scientific knowledge and collaboration* as an aspect of globalization and its new interconnectedness within a globalized world is a distinctly new phenomenon, although judging by scholarly criteria global science still reflects a strong Western control and bias and is still heavily nationalistic and seen as a vital part of national culture and state economic policy. In modern Baconian statecraft, science belongs to a knowledge economy and is the source of innovation and growth in productivity. To a large extent the developing infrastructure of global science is an outgrowth of earlier historical conditions, particularly, the industrial-military research complex established during the two world wars and extended through nuclear escalation and the space race of the Cold War, and the incipient infrastructure provided by 'colonial science' of the European expansionist era (arguably the *first* globalization of science). On one reading the term global science reflects an extension of the 'old' liberal (as opposed the market-driven neoliberal) ideology of 'universal free knowledge' based on exchange and peer review that developed with the emergence of the modern research university in the nineteenth century. Yet it is also clear that it also smacks of 'imperial science'—science in the service of the empire—strongly motivated Francis Bacon's new philosophy and the views of the founders of the Royal Society in the seventeenth century during the early institutionalization of British science. At the same time the emergence of 'global science' also reflects new global exigencies, new global problems and an enhanced global network of science communicative practice.

Today big science projects require massive state and intergovernmental funding support in an era of intense international competition for knowledge assets, which has forced governments and institutions to collaborate with one another on certain issues. Global science in the form of international science agencies also recognises the need for cooperation on a number of pressing common global issues that run across borders, such as global warming and other ecological problems, AIDS/HIV, other global diseases and virus outbreaks, natural species extinction, preservation of biomass features and so on. This chapter provides a first attempt to theorize international research collaboration in the emerging age of global science. It adopts an historical perspective and an implicit sociological history of modern science (Rehbock, 2001; Teich, 1996). It begins by examining three 'moments' in the history of science—classical science, colonial science, and 'big' science. These are three illustrative moments in an extended chronology of science that might register other episodes such as 'industrial science,' 'Cold War science,' and the rise of multinational corporate science, without implying anything too profound about the temporal logic of the development of science or narratives of the emergence of world science that might be crafted from these dates, events and discoveries.

In this chapter I adopt an explicit history of science that rests on a chronology to a large extent driven by scientific-technical innovation based on emerging scientific methodologies and technologies. It is a history that is, therefore, materialist and centred on the emergence of *scientific practices* but is not technologically deterministic. For example, in this regard we might talk of methodologies in the 16th and 17th centuries including the emergence of systematic observation, classification, systematisation, systematic experimentation and quantification, and the formulation of laws of nature. By contrast, we can mention the systematic collection and detailed description of new fauna, flora, and the exploitation of new world 'resources,' including the development of principled scientific sampling (and the first systematic ethnographies) during the expansionist era of colonial science (e.g., Chambers & Gillespie, 2000). Given the space we could also elaborate the technical break-throughs of steam, electric power and microelectronics and their relationship to new scientific developments in the period of industrial science. We might also detail the developments of modern physics and, in particular, the advent of nuclear and particle physics and the emergence of the industrial-science-military complex that developed during the two world wars (Greenhill, 2000). It would be important also to chronicle the technical developments of Cold War science that briefly saw the emergence of a science-public relationship in the atomic scientists' movement before anticommunist ideology, loyalty tests and surveillance destroyed it (Wang, 2002). In turn, we might document the developments in the computerization and mathematicization of communication that helped to enable international research collaboration in the era of 'big' science. Any attempt to work programmatically with these 'moments' needs also to consider the rise of multinational science contemporaneous with the rise of global science and with the advent of globalization (Dickson, 1999; Tudge, 2004).[5]

This historiographical reconstruction is Heideggerian in inspiration in that it frames the question of history of science in terms of successive eras that metaphysically determine 'what is' (e.g., Glazebrook, 2000; see also Busch, 2000). These periods serve as ontological templates but against Heidegger I argue that science and technology are constituted through and by social, economic and political forces. I do entertain with Heidegger a reversal of the standard historiography of science. In terms of the received view technology is something that stands in a subsidiary, instrumental, and temporal relation with modern science. Modern physical science begins in the seventeenth century, historically it is seen as achieving a kind of take-off by 1750, and its institutionalisation through learned societies, royal societies and universities also dates from that period. 'Machinic technology,' by contrast, chronologically speaking, begins in the eighteenth century and is pictured essentially as the "handmaiden" to science: it is regarded as an application of "pure" science or applied science.

Heidegger, however, reverses the chronological order of the received view. He distinguishes technology in its various manifestations from its essence, which is not technological and describes this essence by returning to the Greek concept of *techne*, which relates to the activities and skills of the artisan. The essence of technology, Heidegger maintains, is a *poiesis* or "bringing forth" which is grounded in revealing (*aletheia*). As he says: "The essence of modern technology shows itself in what we call Enframing…It is the way in which the real reveals itself as standing-reserve" (Heidegger, 1977: 23). This has been referred to as a "productionist metaphysics" because the concept of "standing reserve" refers to resources which are stored in anticipation of consumption. For Heidegger the essence of technology is part of the broader project of understanding the relation of this mode of objectifying experience to the tradition of Western metaphysics, which means that the question concerning technology cannot be thought apart from the critique of Western metaphysics.[6]

This is to tell a story (admittedly highly truncated and abridged)—to craft a narrative—about the emergence of global science that de-emphasizes the traditional historical picture that highlights Western origins for I would want to elaborate the sources of pre-classical or ancient science by discussing cultural exchange and hybridisation among Phoenician, Egyptian, Arabian, Chinese, Indian rather than solely in terms of the Ancient Greeks, and to adopt an historical framework that emphasizes the connection of scientific development to other political, economic and social forces (such as colonialism and the Cold War). Of course, it is not possible to elaborate all of these concerns in one paper. My concern here is to suggest an alternative reading and merely to suggest another sketch, another history, in programmatic terms, that allows us to investigate the rise of *global science* as a relatively new phenomenon and the emerging politics of international research collaborations.

The chapter, thus, does not deal directly with universities but rather focuses on the history of science and research networks from a sociological viewpoint that takes questions in political economy as significant in understanding both past and present science formations and especially the current emerging geography of science. One commentator described this chapter as a 'chronotopology,' a term I like very much because is emphasizes both the temporal and the spatial dimensions. The chapter, then, serves to provide a context and historical reach, as well as raising some questions about universities in the rise of global science and the leading role European scientists are playing in this new global configuration. The chapter focuses primarily on the natural sciences, although it is not meant to imply that the same kinds of arguments cannot be advanced with regard to the social sciences.[7]

The social sciences also played a crucial role in the service of empire and one can also document the changes in the typology of the social sciences in relation to the 'industrial' and 'Cold War' periodizations. The positive social sciences entertained a strong interdependence and symbiosis with developing forms of industrial and welfare capitalism as clearly evidenced by the growth of Tayloristic management science, industrial psychology, and welfare-oriented sociology and social work. The rise of political economy (later, politics and economics), geography, cartography, anthropology, psychology and sociology (among others) as disciplines oriented to the state, as well as the rise of statistics (state-istics), provided the political and economic framework within which the contribution of the natural sciences and its role in the service of empire was theorized. This was certainly true of the early accounts provided by Thomas Hobbes of the problem of social and political order and the need for science. While the institutionalization of the social sciences was slower and often followed developments in the natural sciences (including, the formalization and mathematicization of method) it is impossible and undesirable to separate off the social sciences from the natural sciences in the processes of historical and disciplinary formation. The rise of global social science, however, is another story and takes different forms to natural science yet it is also open to similar historiographical treatment.[8]

A contemporary feature of this interdependence can be seen in the transformed relations between social science and natural science after Kuhn's (1970) *The Structure of Scientific Revolutions* that led to historical and cultural studies of science (e.g., Bloor, 1971; Fuller, 1993), the displacement of the 'enchantment of science,' and the ensuing 'science wars' that were sparked by the Sokal affair (Sokal, 1996; Sokal & Bricmont, 1998).

Three 'moments' in the rise of global science

Most theories of globalization—including Marxist, modernization, dependency, world systems, and commodity-chain theories—do not speak to the issue of the *globaliza-*

tion of science, even although officially the 'free exchange' of knowledge among scientists has been the overwhelming orientation of universities well before the term 'globalization' was first coined. Global science has its modern origins in 'colonial science' when academic infrastructures for knowledge traffic was first laid down, although there was also a strong but highly circumscribed tradition of scientific cooperation among European countries during the Enlightenment. In this section I chart three historical 'moments' of the rise of global science beginning with the scientific revolution and age of classical science, moving to colonial science and to the emergence of 'big' science in the late twentieth century.[9] In each case I will provide only the briefest of profiles, as each of these moments in the history of science has a massive and growing literature devoted to it. Each moment is treated externally rather than internally; it is a sociological and political history of science rather than a philosophy of science that I am attempting for this provides the important political economy of international research collaborations. The emphasis falls on the *geography of science*—an aspect of science largely ignored in the literature. These historical interpretations, then, are merely illustrative and evocative.

First sketch: Classical science

The life of science in its recognizable modern form dates from the Royal Society, which was preceded by the Philosophical College. A group of scientists in London, including Robert Moray, Robert Boyle, John Wilkins, John Wallis, John Evelyn, Christopher Wren and William Petty, began holding regular meetings in 1645. They were inspired by induction and experimental science, the ethos of which had been explored by Francis Bacon (1561–1626) a generation earlier in utopian works like, *The Advancement of Learning* (1605) *Novum Organum* (1620), *The New Atlantis* (1626). The two salient aspects of Bacon's new philosophy of nature, both its experimentalism based on induction and its pragmatism committed to the extension of human power through the exploitation of natural phenomenon, were derived from the traditions of alchemy, natural magic and religion (Henry, 2002). As Lord Chancellor Bacon was first to discuss the organisation and bureaucracy of modern science based on a new 'administration of learning' he set out in the *Advancement of Learning* and *New Organon*. His ideas were highly influential championed by Newton, popularised by the Royal Society—and figuring centrally in Thomas Sprat's *The History of the Royal Society* (1667)—and celebrated by the *philosophes* of the French Enlightenment.

While Bacon, the Renaissance man, travelled little outside England, members of the Royal Society established in 1660 had strong contacts in Europe and travelled to meet other scientists. The 'European tour' was then fashionable for the upper classes and Boyle, for instance, spent part of his education in Lyons and Florence, and was in the city in 1642 when Galileo died. Learning Greek, Latin, French and Italian enabled English scientists to read the works of Copernicus, Kepler, Mersenne Galileo, Gilbert, Descartes, Pascal, Cavalieri, Roberval, Torricelli, and many others.

To take one notable example, Voltaire (1694–1778) took refuge in London in 1726 for two years after being exiled from Paris and in his letters later wrote of English tolerance and freedom of speech. He wrote of the changed scene in London in comparison with Paris and compared Descartes and Newton (Letter XIV: On Descartes and Newton). He also commented directly on Bacon's 'new philosophy' in *Novum Scientiarum Organum*—regarding him as the 'father of experimental philosophy,' and wrote of Locke, Newton's 'attraction,' optics and geometry, as well as the Royal Society of which he observes:

> The English had an Academy of Sciences many years before us, but then it is not under such prudent regulations as ours, the only reason of which very possibly is, because it was founded before the Academy of Paris; for had it been founded after, it would very probably have adopted some of the sage laws of the former and improved upon others.

And he goes on to compare the Royal Society with the Academy in the following terms:

> A seat in the Academy at Paris is a small but secure fortune to a geometrician or a chemist; but this is so far from being the case at London, that the several members of the Royal Society are at a continual, though indeed small expense. Any man in England who declares himself a lover of the mathematics and natural philosophy, and expresses an inclination to be a member of the Royal Society, is immediately elected into it. But in France it is not enough that a man who aspires to the honour of being a member of the Academy, and of receiving the royal stipend, has a love for the sciences; he must at the same time be deeply skilled in them; and is obliged to dispute the seat with competitors who are so much the more formidable as they are fired by a principle of glory, by interest, by the difficulty itself, and by that inflexibility of mind which is generally found in those who devote themselves to that pertinacious study, the mathematics.[10]

The development of learned societies in Europe[11]—from the establishment of Compagnie du Gai Sçavoir in 1323—were contemporaneous with the establishment of the early medieval universities at Bologna, Paris, Padua, St Andrews, Oxford, Cambridge, and Glasgow in the eleventh, twelve and thirteenth centuries. Both learned societies and universities slowly developed the norms of cooperation and textual conventions in scholarly activities that were inherited by the modern research university in the early nineteenth century, beginning with the establishment of the University of Berlin in 1810.

The Academy of Science, modelled on the Royal Society, was founded in Paris in 1666 and similar societies were established in Dublin (1683), St. Petersburg (1725), Stockholm (1739), and Edinburgh (1783). Learned societies, in particular, were responsible for publication of scientific findings and issued the first academic journals that institutionalised the norms of scholarships including ownership of an idea and priority of discovery, as well as societal recognition and membership of a scientific community. A model of scientific communication gradually became established as printing and publishing industries developed and helped to shape the scientific analytical method through rationalising research methods, sharing theories and methods among scientists from different countries, and gradually establishing an international 'scientific community.' By 1700 there were already 30 journals and by 1800 hundreds of scientific journals existed (see Meadows, 1980)

Henry Oldenburg, the Secretary of the Royal Society, issued the first edition of *Philosophical Transactions* in 1665. The Royal Society was based in London, first in Gresham College and later in Crane Court, and remained very much a local and English phenomenon, although seventeenth century British science, epitomised by Newton, was based on the works of his European predecessors and, therefore, presupposed the transport and geographical spread of scientific ideas in the form of books and by other published means such as journals. The learned societies represented a new form of cooperation that bypassed politics and religion and established norms for independent inquiry, collaborative research and discussion, and methods for replication and verification.

The *Philosophical Transactions of the Royal Society* was the first serial publication of a learned society. As Fjällbrant (1997) notes:

> It was a medium for publication of new observations and original experiments in science, mostly carried out by the Fellows of the Society. This was a monthly publication of scientific material, together with book reviews and with space for discussions between people holding differing scientific opinions. The *Philosophical Transactions of the Royal Society*, provided a model for subsequent publications of scientific academies throughout Europe. It was translated into French—*Transactions philosophique de la Societé royale de Londres*—from 1731 to 1744. The *Histoire de l' Académie royale des sciences*, Paris (1666–1699) is one example of a publication modelled on the *Philosophical Transactions*.

Journals of the learned societies contained reviews of scientific work and reprints, especially in translation. Fjällbrant (1997) argues 'The learned societies were concerned with spread and diffusion of scientific knowledge' and indicates significantly that scientific journals were also published by private 'commercial' interests:

> The *Giornale de' Letterati* which was modelled on *Journal des Sçavans* , was published in Rome from 1668 to 1681. In contrast the *Acta Erutditorum* first published in Leipzig in 1682, editor Otto Mencke, followed the pattern of the *Philosophical Transactions of the Royal Society*. The *Acta Eruditorum* contained many papers by Leibnitz on his work on the calculus. There was a slow growth in the publication of scientific journals in the eighteenth century with some five new titles published between 1700 and 1750, followed by a more rapid growth in the second half of the century, with some seventy new titles including such well known titles as *Annales de Chimie (et de Physique)*, 1790; *Annalen der Physik*, 1799. The oldest Swedish technical journal is *Daedalus Hyperboreus* by Swedenborg, 1716–1718. The journal *Jernkontorets annaler* was first published in 1817 and *Tidskrift för teknologie och tillämpad naturlära* was published in Gothenburg 18591866.

Journals were supplemented by letters (important in pre-journal days), newspapers, books and scientific anagrams.

These developments in the institutionalisation of science simultaneously were part and parcel of the first wave of colonial expansion and conquest by the European powers. For example, the botanist Joseph Banks (1743–1820), in the second generation of the Royal Society, and as its longest serving president (1778–1820), travelled to Newfoundland and Labrador in 1776 to collect samples and was made a member of the Royal Society the same year. Two years later he accompanied Captain Cook on his expedition to Tahiti organised by the Royal Society to observe the transit of Venus and later visited and made observations in South America, New Zealand, Australia, and Iceland. He founded the Royal Horticultural Society, became Superintendant of the Royal Botanical Gardens at Kew and a member of the Board of Longitude, and was a member of both the Trade and Coin Committees of the Privy Council.[12]

On the first HMS *Endeavour* journey in 1768 (to 1770) Banks identified and documented around 1,400 plants and more than 1,000 animals previously unknown to European science. Banks' specimen collection accounted for some 110 new genera and 1,300 new species. In his capacity as scientist-botanist and director of Kew Gardens, Banks made use of his plant specimens that he had brought back from various parts of the empire. Banks helped organise the *Bounty* voyage of William Bligh, in part to obtain Tahitian breadfruit and establish it as a food source in the West Indies. (In 1779 and 1785 he recommended establishing colonies on the east coast of Australia.) He maintained a strong correspondence with Benjamin Franklin and was one of the first vice-presidents of the Linnean Society founded in 1800 after Carl Linneaus, the great Swedish naturalist who developed a system of classification based on a binomial system that Banks used to classify his specimens.

Both Linneaus and Banks brought back specimens for the benefit of their national economies, placing science at the very centre of trade and politics and forging an interdependent relationship between scientific inquiry and the state that still endures (see Gascoigne 1994, 1998). Unquestionably, this is the basis of national science institutions, the establishment and integration of national science systems, and later the development of science policy—public good science—as an indispensable aspect of the modern state.

Second sketch: Colonial science

Questions of hegemony in science cannot be separated from the history of 'colonial science,' 'science and empire' or 'imperial science.' Indeed, as many scholars have pointed out in the burgeoning literature on colonial science that has developed rapidly since the mid 1980s, the rise of modern science is inextricably intertwined with the story of European colonial expansion since the later 15th century and took specific cultural forms in the first and second waves depending on territories, the colonizer-colonized relationship, and a myriad of other relevant factors. Indeed, the origins of global science, it might be argued, had its origins in imperial science, where science contributed to colonial development and administration, not only to facilitate the exploitation of native natural resources but also to administer local populations. The early infrastructures for the emergence of global science, for its incipient knowledge systems in taxonomic classifications, its field-testing in local sites, its data-gathering activities, and for its educational base, importation of ideas and spurious ideologies (based on 'race' and gender), and for its means and methods of exchange and eventual recruitment of scientific personnel.

There is now a massive and growing literature on 'colonial science,' which is not easy to summarize given its many different threads since it was established as a field in the 1980s.[13] Cultural studies of science question its value-neutral stance. Harding (2003), for instance, provides the feminist critique along these lines, in an argument that in many respects parallels the cultural critique:

> The method of western modern sciences was supposed to generate value-neutral, objective, disinterested facts about nature's order. Yet feminist analyses have shown how these methods and facts have been permeated by gendered values and interests. To be sure, this is so to different degrees and in different ways for different sciences. Nevertheless, standard ways of conceptualizing and practicing scientific method appear to leave research incapable of achieving cultural neutrality in principle, not just in practice. Moreover, gender analyses have shown how in at least some research contexts cultural neutrality is undesirable; culture is also productive of knowledge, not just an obstacle to it. Which people get to do science can influence what we will know about the world.

Goonatilake (1995) talks of global science in terms of three registers that starts from this critique: *Viewing science without eurocentric blinkers* explains how science was active in the ancient world outside Europe; *Examples of mining for contemporary science* identifies medicine, mathematics and psychology as areas where ancient science might contribute; *More imaginative explorations* suggests how ancient science could contribute to future technology.

Recent studies have focussed on 'scientific' readings of the colonial experience and emphasized environment, ecology, diseases and medical topography as major categories of inquiry into the 'objective' nature of science and its power relations to colonial expansion.[14] These studies are not of a piece and should not be interpreted straightforwardly as an attack on the objectivity of science or its efficacy, although they do indicate that the origins and development of global science certainly has its roots in colonial science, and that cultural and institutional contexts help shape the constitution of knowledge.

Building on these studies Warwick Anderson in a provocative paper talks of 'Postcolonial Technoscience'[15] suggesting that,

> A postcolonial perspective suggests fresh ways to study the changing political economies of capitalism and science, the mutual reorganisation of the global and the local, the increasing transnational traffic of people, practices, technologies, and contemporary contests over 'intellectual property. The term 'postcolonial' thus refers both to new configurations of technoscience and to the critical modes of analysis that identify them. We hope that a closer engagement of science studies with postcolonial studies will allow us to question technoscience differently, find more heterogeneous sources, and reveal more fully the patterns of local transactions that give rise to global, or universalist, claims.

His essay is an exploration of 'the turbulence and uncertainty of contemporary global flows of knowledge and practice.' It is clear that 'colonial science' studies and cultural studies of science have provided strong historical evidence of the role of science in the service of empire—not only its contribution to the exploration, navigation and the mapping of the 'new world' but also the economic exploitation of the biota and governance of its peoples.

Third sketch: Emergence of 'big science' and European collaboration

The term 'big science' actually dates back to the late 1950s when it was used to herald the transition from individual to team research and development. The term was employed to refer to large scale and instrument-expensive, mainly government-funded projects in basic science (high-energy physics), space research and military science, and also the shifts in science policy and funding after WWII.[16] Derek J. de Solla (1963) in *Little Science, Big Science* applied publications analysis to the system of science communication providing the first systematic approach to the structure of modern science, helping to establish bibliometrics and scientometrics that later became essential in the evaluation of the productivity of scientific research.[17]

In conceptualising 'big science' the OECD Global Science Forum[18] puts it this way:

> Big Science is global. Research and development in medicine, technology, engineering, chemistry, biology and physics have long since overrun national borders, in part because no single government has the time, money or indeed skills that such work demands. Projects, from the International Space Station to building particle colliders and light sources, or semi-conductor research: all thrive on global co-operation. It was not always so. Governments, scientists and investors have often been wary of each other, with co-operation tending to take place on an ad hoc basis.

The OECD puts an emphasis on 'Big Science' and adduces a resources-based reason as the imperative driving global co-operation. Yet global science per se does not reduce simply to 'big science,' even although it may account for genuine attempts to build international cooperation and adopt a strategic approach to collaborative partnerships at the extra-national level.

Bilateral and regional science and technology relations, of course, go back a long way, relatively speaking. In the early 1950s the European Laboratory for Particle Physics (CERN) in Geneva was the result of cooperation among European governments which now has member scientists from both European and non-European countries. The European Science Foundation[19] was established in 1974 and established a scientific network in the early 1980s for the coordination of European science based in various subject group areas such as Physical and Engineering Sciences and Life, Environmental and Earth Sciences. In the early 1990s the ESF also set up research linkages with Asia and APEC established protocols for scientific cooperation amongst its members.[20] Scientists, sponsored by world organizations like UNESCO and FAO, have set up global research programs, based on obvious cross-border exigencies. Earth scientists, in particular, have been instrumental in establishing international research programs dealing with the dynamics of the earth system such as the Global Climatic Observation System,[21] the Global Ocean Observation System[22] and the Global Terrestrial Observation System.[23]

Yet these recent examples of extra-national scientific collaboration do not take account of the many smaller institutional exchanges and partnerships, the development of university consortia for across-the-board cooperation, or firm and firm/university partnerships. Nor does it take account of the increasingly increasingly multinational driven corporate corporate nature of international research by world conglomerates like Monsanto and other biotech companies or the large pharmaceutical or drug companies. Some of these partnership arrangements and examples of multinational science probably fit better into theories of globalization than traditional university-based collaborations.

The emergence of global science, thus, can be seen to conform to both the global business model based on the market and the science model based on free exchange of give and take. The development economist, Amartya Sen (2002), for instance, makes the following contrast essential to understanding the different kinds of associations needed for development:

> Contrast the sharing that underpins science with the transactional nature of market relations. The market mechanism is not only an important social institution, it is also an organisational ideology. Its success—perceived as well as real—can help stifle independent thinking about interactive relations of other kinds, including that of give and take. The gaps it leaves are worth filling since sharing is not only crucial to science, it is also central to development.

Not only does he contrast science with the market but he argues for a position that views science as a global tradition, avoiding the 'anti-Western' globalization sentiments as well as Western chauvinism and a proprietary approach to 'Western science,' explaining Western science drew on a world heritage (e.g., the mathematics of Al-Khwarizmi). Yet Sen does not contemplate the rise of global science or the complex ways in which global science proceeds on mixed models integrating both traditional 'science sharing' (as he calls it) and market relations, especially evident in the emerging international regime of 'intellectual property' rights through the WTO. In a sense he avoids the difficult question of scientific hegemony based on private and cultural ownership of scientific discoveries, inventions, and insights (see e.g., Tudge, 2004).

Global science and research collaboration

It is clear that the age of global science has arrived. This is manifested not only in the growth of multinational corporate science but also mandated in administrative and organisational structures that are both regional and rhetorically 'global.' For instance, Euroscience was founded in 1997 to 'provide an open forum for debate on science and technology; strengthen the links between science and society; contribute to the creation of an integrated space for science and technology in Europe; influence science and technology policies.'[24] Framework 6 for funding of science in Europe is approximately 16.27 billion Euros, an increase of 17% over the previous Framework V. This funding programme constitutes an estimated 5% of the research budget of EU countries overall and yet is seen to play a crucial role in structuring European research by defining the aims of European science and funding collaborative activity among scientists in Europe. Of the seven programme areas biotechnology and information technology account for well over 40% of total funding, with the rest shared by nuclear energy, nanotechnology, aeronautics, food safety, and sustainable development and global change (see also Simons & Featherstone, 2000).

At the same time, U.S. science policy and science advocacy now cluster around the buzz words 'bioinformatics,' 'Bose condensates,' 'genomics,' 'nanotechnology,' 'supersymmetries,' and 'wavelets' with increases in the science budget, the reorganization of science councils under Clinton and an increasing politicization of domestic science issues under Bush (Bromley & Lubell, 2003).

Meanwhile, administrators like Bruce M. Alberts, president of the National Academy of Sciences, called for a 'global science.' Alberts (2003: 26) writes:

> A major aim of the National Academy of Sciences (NAS) is to strengthen the ties between scientists and their institutions around the world. Our goal is to create a scientific network that becomes a central element in the interactions between nations, increasing the level of rationality in international discourse while enhancing the influence of scientists everywhere in the decision making processes of their own governments.

It is clear that the communications technologies are crucial to the strategy for enhanced collaboration. Alberts indicates that 'Electronic communication networks make possible a new kind of worm science' and he emphasizes 'that we are only at the very beginning of the communications revolution' promising greater commercialization with attendant benefits for the developing world (p.27). He also mentions that the National Research Council (the operating arm of NAS and the National Academy of Engineering) will attempt to prepare an international science road map to help the State Department.

An NSB report 'Toward a More Effective Role for the U.S. Government in International Science and Engineering,' as Paula Park reports (2002: 8) 'encourages agencies to evaluate whether new immigration and intellectual property policies and regulations will affect international science cooperation' and emphasizes, quoting Eamon Kelly, chairman of the NSB that 'the future of the developing countries rests on their ability to adapt to a culture of science and technology in the 21st century.'

Further Hal Cohen (2003) also indicates that scientists themselves are organizing global structures. The International Council of Scientific Unions created in 1931 has been recently renamed the International Council for Science which has established several programmes, including one in biology (1964–1974). Current programmes include the International Geosphere-Biosphere Programme and the World Climate Research Programme (following the Kyoto Protocol).

The OECD going back the late 1980s tried to establish a set of guidelines covering all aspects of international relations in science (Dickson, 1987: 743) which included a focus on 'the extent to which each country should contribute to the world's basic research effort and the conditions under which foreign research workers are permitted to attend scientific meetings.' Much of the initiative under the Reagan administration emphasized the policing and protection of intellectual property rights within GATS and, later, WTO protocols.

Within these emerging structures of global science collaboration takes many different forms. Increasingly, under neoliberalism it presupposes a competitive relationship which is the main form of collaboration, for instance, between Europe and the US. This normally revolves around the shared investment of personnel and resources and is directed at cutting edge science and technology. Increasingly, also public-private partnerships take on an international dimension especially in relation to aeronautics and space research. Over and above these international forms there are collaborative relationships that are not premised on competitive criteria but rather takes on forms of 'cooperation' or 'assistance' that fall within traditional development aid categories.

There is a third category, perhaps, other than non-competitive and market collaboration which is implied in Alberts (2003) and has been a feature of U.S. science policy since the 1960s is the relation between expertise and governance. This form draws networks back to their funding bases and organizational homes in universities and laboratories, and raises interesting questions concerning the reorganisation of the university in a shift from knowledge to expertise.[25]

In discussing developments of the emerging world knowledge system and, in particular, the structures of international research collaboration it is necessary to locate the merging systems within the historical context, a context that reveals the politics and competitive nature of collaboration and the leading position of the U.S.-Europe constellation. In the age of knowledge capitalism where knowledge increasingly is seen to be the basis of national competitive advantage, the emphasis has fallen on the policing and reinforcement of intellectual property rights regimes and on forms of knowledge hoarding, especially with the growth of multinational science and the privatization of science funding regimes. While there are encouraging signs that both India and China (especially, related to foodstuffs, information science and the production of microchips, and recently space research) are developing more of a competitive science base their science sectors pale into insignificance when compared to the West. Some concern has been expressed recently by Western governments, especially in the U.S., of the increasing outsourcing of R&D functions, especially the training of technicians and scientists who work for much less money and also willing on contract without the normal employment benefits of Western scientists. There are some forms of global science and associated forms of international collaboration that have been established or are being established that take on the more traditional liberal justifications of science and emphasize its status as a global public good (see e.g., Stiglitz, 1999).

Be that as is may, it is clear that there are a diversity of forms, that they have emerged out of existing infrastructures and histories that strongly reflect politics, not merely the arms industry and its relation to the industrial-military research complex but also past colonial origins and the continuing nature of many of the colonial relationships in forms that develop new 'neo-imperial' forms based around trading agreements or work against this hegemony to establish science as part of the basis of global social democracy harnessed in the service of global civil society and based on the needs of the world's population.

Universities encourage both competitive and non-competitive forms of international collaboration, but increasingly with the historic downturn in state funding of higher education in the U.S. and the development of nearly 200 science research parks[26] nationwide, with an emphasis on venture capital funding of spin-off companies, patents of university discoveries, and the attraction of leading multinationals on campus, the latter is giving way to the former as institutions struggle to diversify their funding bases. A major question is whether the funds accrued from competitive forms of collaboration will be used to help support and subsidise non-competitive forms of collaborative activity, and, therefore, whether the university can subscribe to twin legitimating discourses that embrace social justice goals as well as accommodating for-profit motives. Yet it may well be that technology-dependent 'sharable goods' as one form of social production and exchange (see Benkler, 2004), alongside the state and the market, will emerge as a third mode of organising economic production, bringing in its wake changes in the material conditions of production of the networked information economy that encourage non-propriety forms of academic production and facilitate international research collaboration.

Endnotes

1. I would like to thank Nicholas Burbules, Martin Lawn and anonymous reviewers for useful comments on the structure and contents of an earlier version of this paper.

2. 'Truths' established through these scientific norms have, thus, always been considered universal or so some positivist philosophers of science maintain—and there is *some* sense to this claim although its content is notoriously difficult to unpack. The problem of truth of scientific knowledge in this respect is especially difficult to fathom given the competing accounts of truth and their (different) role within the sciences (natural and social). The easy philosophical examples tend to abstract individual statements from their theory contexts; yet the 'truth' of theories in science is more complex as scholars like Popper, Lakatos and Feyerabend have demonstrated, suggesting that it serves as a regulative ideal. I do not want to deny 'truth' of scientific knowledge or its 'universality' yet at the same time I want to emphasise that questions of truth and validity should not obscure that the institutionalization of science has strongly reflected patterns of national, corporate and multinational interests.

3. I have put the word scientist in inverted commas because the term was not used until relatively recently, after the institutionalization of natural philosophy and the professionalization of science. Most 'scientists' in the period of the institutionalization of science were often wealthy gentleman amateurs, like Joseph Banks, for instance, who became president of the Royal Society nearly 120 years after its establishment. On biographies of Fellows of the RS see http://www.royalsoc.ac.uk/page.asp?id=1679 (accessed December 24, 2005) and for a broader account of

'antebellum American science' see, e.g., Clark Elliot's review and bibliography at http://home. earthlink.net/~claelliott/index.html (accessed December 24, 2005).

4. Lyotard (1984) raised similar questions a generation ago. See my *Education and the Postmodern Condition* (Peters, 1996) and, more recently, *Building Knowledge Cultures* (Peters & Besley, 2006).

5. This is a hugely under-researched field (history of multinational science), which is seemingly ignored in the globalization literature. A good starting point is http://multinationalmonitor. org/links/scat1.php?cat_id=3 and the list of resources 'The Impacts of Multinational Corporations' at http://www.lib.berkeley.edu/BUSI/pdfs/multiCorp.pdf#search='IMPACTS %20OF%20MULTINATIONAL%20CORPORATIONS%3A' (both accessed 10 Nov. 2005).

6. Much more could be said here about history and historiography of science, a discourse which would need to include reference to Kuhn's (1962) distinction between 'normal' and 'revolutionary' science but also the assumptions underlying the historical context of Kuhn's own writings at Harvard during the Cold War (see Fuller, 2000).

7. The Editor remarked: [The social] "'sciences' have been very important for building the nation state, leading to the consequences you describe. See for example: Wagner, P. & Wittrock, B. (1991). 'States, Institutions, and Discourses: A Comparative Perspective on the Structuration of the Social Sciences,' in P. Wagner, B. Wittrock & R. Whitley (Ed.), *Discourses on Society. The Shaping of the Social Science Disciplines* (pp. 331–357, Dordrecht: Kluwer). Or Peter Wagner's (2001) *A History and Theory of the Social Sciences* (Sage). I am not sure whether this area of research would alter your argument but it is necessary to it."

8. In *Les mots et les choses—une archéologie des sciences humaines* (1966) (trans. *The Order of Things: An Archaeology of the Human Sciences*) Foucault develops the claim that all periods of history possessed certain underlying conditions of truth constituting what was acceptable as 'scientific' discourse in the human sciences. He argued that these conditions of discourse changed over time, in major and relatively sudden shifts, or epistemes. While Foucault never applied this model to the natural sciences scholars like Rouse (1987) have attempted to do so.

9. There is a story to be told of the 'globalisation' of science in the Ancient world, not only of the Ancient Near East of Babylon and Egypt, and Greco-Roman culture, but also Byzantium, the Islamic World, China and India; and, the exchanges and 'transport' of ideas between these worlds that often mirrored trade patterns. For some resources see The Internet History of Science Sourcebook at http://www.fordham.edu/halsall/science/sciencesbook.html (accessed 21 June, 2005).

10. For the full set of Voltaire's letters on the English, including those mentioned in the text, see http://www.fordham.edu/halsall/mod/1778voltaire-lettres.html (accessed 21st June, 2005).

11. See http://www.scholarly-societies.org/1599andearlier.html (accessed 11/6/05).

12. Some of his paper are available in digitised form on the web site of the National Library of Australia at http://nla.gov.au/nla.ms-ms9 (accessed 21 June 2005). See also The Papers of Sir Joseph Banks by the State Library of New South Wales at http://www.sl.nsw.gov.au/banks/ (accessed 21 June 2005).

13. See, for instance, Goonatilake (1984, 1995), Nandy (1988), Petitjean, et al (1992), Watson-Verran, & Turnbull (1995), Harding (1993, 1998, 2003). The Sciences and Empires mail list as an 'unmoderated' list was established and is operated by the Sciences et Empires Groupe, a Commission of the International Congress of the History of Science. The group was founded at an international meeting held at UNESCO in Paris in April, 1990 under the theme 'Sciences and Empires: European Expansion and Scientific Development of Asia, Africa, America and Oceania,'and includes Patrick Petitjean, Catherine Jami, Anne Marie Moulin, Kapil Raj,

Deepak Kumar, Venni Krishna, Roland Waast, Mic Worboys, and Silvia Figueiroa, as members. See also the bibliography by Pratik Chakrabarti 'Knowledge, Science and Empire' at http://www.history.ox.ac.uk/hsmt/courses_reading/advanced_papers/biblios/knowledge_science_empire.pdf (accessed 21 June 2005).

14. This literature is also huge and I can only indicate some of the relevant studies: Crosby (1986, 2004), Madhav & Guha (1995), Grove (1997), Arnold (1988, 1993), Harrison (1994, 1997), Bewell (1999).

15. See his paper at http://sts.nthu.edu.tw/~tsts/W-paper/Poco_Techno_Final_ms%5B1%5DWarwick.htm Social Studies of Science, 32, 5–6: 643–658 (accessed 21 June 2005).

16. For an introduction to the literature on changes to sciences after WWII see, for instance, Alexei Kojevnikov's course at http://www.aip.org/history/syllabi/postwar.htm (accessed December 20, 2005).

17. Price's studies were continued in two directions: Eugene Garfield (1970, 1972) developed more sophisticated measures of quality using citations, and Jerome R. Ravetz (1996) observed that the processes of peer review are 'informal,' not themselves normally submitted to open scrutiny and review, and open to a variety of abuses, including bias and plagiarism. Bibliometric indicators based on the SCI while having limitations, nevertheless, are probably the best indicators of world science output. A recent UNESCO Institute for Statistics (UIS) report states: 'In 2000, the SCI included a total of 584,982 papers, representing a 57.5% increase from 1981, when 371,346 papers were published worldwide. Authors with addresses in developed countries wrote 87.9% of the papers in 2000, a decrease from 93.6% in 1981. Developing countries, on the other hand, saw a steady increase in their share of scientific production: from 7.5% of world papers in 1981 to 17.1% in 2000.' North America has lost its 1996 lead, producing 36.8% of papers in 2000, with most gains in the EU and Asia (particularly Japan). Significantly, the report also mentions that international collaborations in the 20 years from 1981 has also increased: 'The proportion of publications from authors in developed countries co-signed with authors in other countries has risen more than three times from 6.0% to 20.4% between 1981 and 2000, and in developing countries the share of collaborative papers doubled from 15.1% to 30.8%.' See the pdf report: http://www.uis.unesco.org/file_download.php?URL_ID=6313&filename=11285 455005BulletinNo2EN.pdf&filetype=application%2Fpdf&filesize=81825&name=BulletinN o2EN.pdf&location=user-S/ (accessed December 25, 2005).

18. The OECD Global Science Forum started as the 'Megascience Forum' in 1992, focusing on Big Science projects (ultra high-energy neutrinos electron accelerator facilities, nuclear physics and global biodiversity) and was expanded as the Global Science Forum in 1999 with the aim of addressing more basic issues (e.g., short-pulse lasers, neuro-informatics, outer space airwaves). See OECD Observer at http://www.oecdobserver.org/news/fullstory.php/aid/1019/ Global_science.html (accessed 26/5/05). On OECD best practices for establishing scientific cooperation and managing large-scale projects see http://www.oecd.org/department/0,2688, en_2649_34319_1_1_1_1_1,00.html (accessed 26/5/05).

19. See the ESF website at http://www.esf.org (accessed 25/5/05).

20. See the ASEM Science and Technology Ministers' Meeting, on which some of this pare is based, at http://europa.eu.int/comm/external_relations/asem/min_other_meeting/sc_tech_ comque.htm and also *Connecting Asia Pacific and Europe (CAPE)* 1998 at http://www.dante. net/cape/-cape.html (accessed 25/5/05).

21. See http://www.epa.gov/geoss/ (accessed 25/5/05).

22. See http://ioc.unesco.org/goos/ (accessed 25/5/05).

23. See http://www.fao.org/gtos/ (accessed 25/5/05).

24. See http://www.euroscience.org/about.htm. See also the European Science Foundation at http://www.esf.org/ (both accessed 10th Nov., 2005).

25. I am indebted to Martin Lawn for making this observation to me almost in these words.

26. See The Association of University Research Parks' website at http://www.aurp.net/ (accessed December 26, 2005).

References

Alberts, B. M. (1998) 'Toward a global science,' *Issues in Science and Technology*, Summer, 14, 4: 25–28.

Arnold, D. & Guha, R. (1996) (Eds.): *Nature, Culture, Imperialism*, Delhi: Oxford University Press.

Arnold, David (1988) (Ed.) *Imperial Medicine and Indigenous Societies*, Manchester: Manchester University Press.

Arnold, David (1993) *Colonizing the Body: State Medicine and Epidemic Disease in Nineteenth-Century India*, Berkeley: University of California Press.

Benkler, Y. (2004) 'Sharing Nicely: On Shareable Goods and the Emergence of Sharing as a Modality of Economic Production,' *The Yale Law Journal* (114): 273–358. Also at: http://www.yalelaw-journal.org/pdf/114-2/Benkler_FINAL_YLJ114-2.pdf (accessed December 27, 2005).

Bewell, Alan (1999) *Romanticism and Colonial Disease*. Baltimore and London: The Johns Hopkins University Press.

Bloor, D. (1991) *Knowledge and Social Imagery*, Chicago: University of Chicago Press.

Bricmont, J. & Sokal, A. D. (1998) *Fashionable Nonsense: Post-modern Intellectuals' Abuse of Science*, New York: Picador.

Bromley, A.D. & Lubell. M.S. (2003) 'Science's growing political strength,' Issues in Science and Technology, Summer, 19, 4:13–16.

Busch, P. (2000) 'Nietzsche's Political Critique of Modern Science,' *Perspectives on Political Science*, Fall, 29, 4: 197–210.

Chambers, D. W. & Gillespie, R. (2000) 'Locality in the history of science: colonial science, techno-science, and indigenous knowledge' *Osiris*, Annual: 221–242.

Cohen, H. (2003) 'ICSU: International Council for Science,' *The Scientist*, April 21, 17, 8: 14–15.

Crespi, G. and Geuna, A. (2004) *The Productivity of Science: an International Analysis*, SPRU.

Crespi, G. and Geuna, A. (2005) *Modelling and Measuring Scientific Production: Results for a Panel of OECD Countries*, SPRU.

Crosby, A. (1986) *The Columbian Exchange: Biological and Cultural Consequences of 1492*, Cambridge; New York: Cambridge University Press.

Crosby, A. (2004) *Ecological Imperialism: The Biological Expansion of Europe, 900—1900*, Cambridge: Cambridge University Press.

Dickson, D. (1987) 'OECD to set rules for international science,' *Science*, Nov 6, 238 4828: 743–744.

Dickson, D. (1999) 'Open house or closed shop?' *UNESCO Courier*, May: 25–27.

Fuller, S. (1993) *Philosophy, Rhetoric and the End of Knowledge: The Coming of Science and Technology Studies*, Madison: University of Wisconsin Press.

Fuller, S. (2000) *Thomas Kuhn: A Philosophical History for our Times*, Chicago: University of Chicago Press.

Funtowicz, S. O. & Ravetz, J. R. (1992) 'Three Types of Risk Assessment and the Emergence of Post-Normal Science.' In: Krimsky S, Golding (eds), *Social Theories of Risk*, Westport CT:Greenwood: 251–273.

Gadgil, M. & Guha, R. (1995) *Ecology and Equity : The Use and Abuse of Nature in Contemporary India*, London, Routledge.

Garfield, E. (1970) 'Citation Indexing for Studying Science,' *Nature*, (227): 669–671.

Garfield, E. (1972) 'Citation Analysis as a Tool in Journal Evaluation,' *Science*, (178): 471–479.

Gascoigne, J. (1994) *Banks and the English Enlightenment: Useful Knowledge and Polite Culture.*

Gascoigne, J. (1998) *Science in the Service of Empire: Joseph Banks, the British State and the Uses of Science in the Age of Revolution* Cambridge: Cambridge University Press.

Glazebrook, T. (2000) *Heidegger's Philosophy of Science*, New York: Fordham University Press.

Goonatilake, S. (1984) *Aborted Discovery: Science and Creativity in the Third World*, London, Zed.

Goonatilake, S. (1995) *Toward a global science: mining civilizational knowledge*, New Delhi: Vistaar Publications.

Greenhill, K.M. (2000) 'American Science Policy Since World War II,' *Polity*, Summer, 32, 4: 633–645.

Grove, R. (1997) *Ecology, Climate, and Empire: Colonialism and Global Environmental History*, Cambridge: White Horse Press.

Grove, R. (1995) *Green Imperialism: Colonial Expansion, Tropical Island Edens and the Origins of Environmentalism, 1600–1860*, Cambridge & New York: Cambridge University Press.

Guédon, J-C. (2001) 'In Oldenburg's Long Shadow: Librarians, Research Scientists, Publishers, and the Control of Scientific Publishing' available at: http://www.arl.org/arl/proceedings/138/ guedon.html#v (accessed December 26, 2005).

Harding, S. (1993) (Ed.) *The 'Racial' Economy of Science*, Indianapolis: Indiana University Press.

Harding, S. (1998) *Is Science Multicultural?* Bloomington: Indiana University Press.

Harding, S. (2003) 'Science and Technology in a Multicultural and Postcolonial World: Gender Issues,' http://www.unb.br/ih/his/gefem/labrys3/web/fran/sandra2.htm (accessed 27/5/05).

Harrison, M. (1999) *Climates and Constitutions: Health, Race, Environment and British Imperialism in India 1600–1850,*

Heidegger, Martin (1977) *The Question Concerning Technology*, trans. W. Lovitt, New York: Harper and Row.

Henry, J. (2002) *Knowledge is Power: How Magic, the Government and an Apocalyptic Vision inspired Francis Bacon to create Modern Science*, Cambridge: Icon Books.

Kuhn, T. (1962) *The Structure of Scientific Revolutions*, Chicago: University of Chicago Press.

Kuhn, T. S. (1970) *The Structure of Scientific Revolutions*, 2d.ed. Chicago: University of Chicago Press.

Lyotard, J-F. (1984) The *Postmodern Condition: A Report on Knowledge*. Manchester: Manchester University Press.

Marrison, M. (1994) *Public Health in British India: Anglo-Indian Preventive Medicine, 1857–1914*, Cambridge: Cambridge University Press.

Nandy, A. (1998) (Ed.) Science, Hegemony, and Violence: A Requiem for Modernity, New York: Oxford University Press. Also see the web site at http://www.unu.edu/unupress/unupbooks/ uu05se/uu05se00.htm (accessed 27/5/05).

Nustad, K. G., and Ole J. S. (2000) 'The Instrumentalisation of Development Knowledge,' *Banking on Knowledge: The Genesis of the Global Development Network*. Ed. Diane Stone, New York: Routledge.

Park, P. (2002) 'Toward a United Nations of science: US science board calls for more than international collaboration funding' *The Scientist*, May 13, 16, 10: 8–10.

Parpart, J. L. (1995) 'Deconstructing the Development "Expert": Gender, Development, and "Vulnerable Groups" ', *Feminism, Postmodernism, Development*. Ed. Marianne H. Merchand and Jane L. Parpart, New York: Routledge.

Peters, M.A. & Besley, T. (2006) *Building Knowledge Cultures*. Boulder: Rowman & Littlefield.

Peters, M.A. (1996) (Ed.) *Education and the Postmodern Condition*. Foreword by J-F. Lyotard, Westport, CT, and London: Bergin & Garvey.

Petitjean, P. et al, (1992) Science and Empires: Historical Studies about Scientific Development and European Expansion, Dordrecht: Kluwer.

de Solla, P.D.J. (1963). *Little Science, Big Science*. New York and London: Columbia University Press.

Ravetz, J. R. (1996) *Scientific Knowledge and its Social Problems, with a New Introduction by the Author.* New Brunswick, N.J.: Transaction Publishers. (Orig. 1971).

Rehbock, P. I. (2001) 'Globalizing the History of Science,' *Journal of World History*, Spring, 12, 1: 183–193.

Rouse, J. (1987) *Knowledge and Power: Toward a Political Philosophy of Science*. Ithaca, New York, Cornell University Press.

Select Committee on Science and Technology (UK) (2003) *Scientific Publishing*, at http://www.publications.parliament.uk/pa/cm200304/cmselect/cmsctech/399/39902.htm (accessed December 26, 2005).

Sen, A. (2002) 'The science of give and take,' *New Scientist*, April 27: v174 i2340, pp. 51–54.

Simons, K. & Featherstone, C. (2000) 'Science in Europe,' *Science*, Nov 10, 290 5494: 1099.

Sokal, A. D. (1996) 'Transgresing the Boundaries,' *Social Text* (14): 217–252.

Stiglitz, J. (1999) 'Knowledge as a Global Public Good,' World Bank, at http://www.worldbank.org/knowledge/chiefecon/articles/undpk2/index.htm (accessed December 26, 2005).

Takeshita, C. (2001) 'Bioprospecting and Its Discontents: Indigenous Resistances as Legitimate Politics,' *Alternatives* 26: 259–282.

Teich, M. (1996) 'The 20th-century Scientific-Technical Revolution,' *History Today*, Nov., 46, 11: 27–34.

Tudge, C. (2004) 'The honesty of science is being compromised at every turn': can we still rely on what scientists tell us? Alas, no. Their conferences and papers are sponsored by industry, their bad results are concealed, their jobs are threatened if they step out of line,' *New Statesman*, April 26, 133: 29–32.

Wang, J. (2002) 'Scientists and the problem of the public in cold war America, 1945–1960,' *Osiris*, Annual : 323–49.

Watson-Verran, H., and Turnbull, D. (1995) 'Science and Other Indigenous Knowledge Systems,' *Handbook of Science and Technology Studies*, Ed.s S. Jasanoff, G. E. Markle, J. C. Peterson & T. Pinch, Thousand Oaks: Sage.

CHAPTER 9

The Virtues of Openness in Higher Education

Towards an Open Science Economy: Science and Knowledge as Global Public Goods

◻ Michael A. Peters

Introduction

One aspect of the crisis of neoliberal globalization that has emerged as a positive trend is the growth and significance of open source models of knowledge, science, and education. Indeed, the emerging political economy of openness seems to offer a social mode of production that rests on the economics of file-sharing and promotes new architectures of participation and collaboration. Open models of innovation in the world global digital economy have been increasing adopted by world governments, international agencies and multinationals as well as leading educational institutions. MIT adopted OpenCourseWare (OCW) in 2001 and Harvard University's Faculty of Arts and Sciences adopted a policy that requires faculty members to allow the university to make their scholarly articles available free online in 2008. The new policy makes Harvard the first university in the United States to mandate open access to its faculty members' research publications and marks the beginning of a new era that will encourage other U.S. universities to do the same.

These broad initiatives in open source, open access and open publishing are part of emerging knowledge ecologies that will determine the future of educational resources and scholarly publishing challenging commercial publishing business models and raising broader and deeper questions about content development processes as well as questions of resourcing and sustainability. The new digital technologies promise changes in creation, production and consumption of scholarly resources including the development of new formats allowing integrated electronic research and publishing environments that will enable real-time dissemination and dynamically-updated content as well as alternative distribution models including institutional repositories, pre-print servers, and open access journals, that will broaden access, reduce costs, and enable open sharing of content.

This marks the emergence of global science and knowledge as a global public good that rests on an ethic of participation and collaboration based on the co-production and co-design of knowledge goods and services. This chapter introduces the term techno-political economy to provide an account of the rapidly developing global movement of openness in higher education, detailing an analysis based on the politics, economics and technology of openness.

The techno-political economy of openness

For the purposes of this paper I define the techno-political economy of openness in terms of three elements; the politics of openness, the economics of openness, and the technologies of openness. These are overlapping and historically related. For analytical purposes I shall treat them separately. To this, of course, we might also add a psychology of openness or openness as a psychological variable that since the early 1930s in trait theory stood for an openness to experience: and appreciation for art, a thirst for adventure, a toleration of diversity and unusual ideas, a willingness to try new things, and above all, imagination and curiosity.

The politics of openness

Openness is a contested political value. The overriding conception of openness that prevailed since the end of WWII has been a liberal culture of modernity promoted equally strongly though differently by Hayek and Popper. These Cold War warriors between them forged a conception that emerged as the single most dominant view. Popper promoted a view of the Open Society which was really a defense of liberal democracy and an attack upon the historicism of Plato, Hegel, and Marx. In the *Open Society and Its Enemies* Popper (1945), driven by state phobia and fear of totalitarianism, was anxious to point to the failure of Marxism against fascism. Earlier in *The Logic of Scientific Discovery* he had developed an open epistemology that he called critical rationalism that was based on what he called 'falsification,' which was an attack on the essentialism of conceptual analysis and the logical atomism of the early

Wittgenstein and Russell, a wider critique of logical empiricism and a solution to the problem of induction. There was more than an analogy between his model of science and his conception of the open society: the magical or tribal or collectivist society was called the closed society, and the society in which individuals are confronted with personal decisions, the open society. Popper was not the first to theorize the open society. The French philosopher Henri Bergson in *Two Sources of Morality and Religion* contrasts 'closed morality' as static religion with 'open morality' as dynamic religion. The latter is in Bergson's terms universal (includes everyone) and aims at peace and it is based on 'creative emotions'—the emotions create representation (rather than vice versa).

Friedrich von Hayek wrote the liberal classic *Road to Serfdom* in 1944 and *Constitution of Liberty*, his magnum opus, in 1960. He had been invited by Lionel Robbins to join the LSE in 1931, leaving for the University of Chicago in 1950, where he joined the Committee on Social Thought. He was a relentless critic of collectivism and the demand economy advocating catallaxy—'self-organizing system of voluntary co-operation'—and institutions of spontaneous order. In short, Hayek was a defender of the Open Market, and he established the Mt Pelerin Society in 1947, of which Popper was an early member. The Mt Pelerin Society was an institution that defended political and economic liberalism as the open market society. In the statement of aims written in 1947 the founding members wrote:

> The central values of civilization are in danger. Over large stretches of the earth's surface the essential conditions of human dignity and freedom have already disappeared. In others they are under constant menace from the development of current tendencies of policy. The position of the individual and the voluntary group are progressively undermined by extensions of arbitrary power. Even that most precious possession of Western Man, freedom of thought and expression, is threatened by the spread of creeds which, claiming the privilege of tolerance when in the position of a minority, seek only to establish a position of power in which they can suppress and obliterate all views but their own.

> The group holds that these developments have been fostered by the growth of a view of history which denies all absolute moral standards and by the growth of theories which question the desirability of the rule of law. It holds further that they have been fostered by a decline of belief in private property and the competitive market; for without the diffused power and initiative associated with these institutions it is difficult to imagine a society in which freedom may be effectively preserved.

In the present day, George Soros has become the faithful disciple of the Popper-Hayek 'open market society' conception. Soros studied under Popper at LSE and he established the Open Society Institute in 1994 (named after Popper's work). The Open Society Institute (OSI), advertises itself as 'a private operating and grant making foundation, aims to shape public policy to promote democratic governance, human rights, and economic, legal, and social reform.' It was responsible for the highly influential Budapest Open Access Initiative (2001) and Soros has written a number of works that draw on the concept of the open society including *Europe as a Prototype for a Global Open Society* (2006), *Open Society: Reforming Global Capitalism* (2000), and *Opening the Soviet System* (1990).

Largely independent of the Popper-Hayek legacy is the movement of open government which is seen to epitomize democratic practice and has been developed through the architecture of freedom of information legislation. With its roots in Enlightenment thought of constitution of civil society and in democratic *practice* the movement of open government is linked to freedom of speech, freedom of the press, and other freedoms that have become basis for constitutional law and its strongly associated with passage of freedom of information law in US (1966), Denmark & Norway (1970), France & Holland (1978), Australia, Canada, NZ (1982), UK (2000), Japan & Mexico (2002), and Germany (2005). In Open Government the norms of openness address transparency, accountability, official secrets, public trust. More recently, Open Government has become strongly reinforced through open source governance, that is, the application of open source to democratic principles encouraging citizen participation in legislative process. Open source governance advocates the application of models of open source and open content to democratic principles in order to enable any interested citizen to add to the creation of policy, fostering forms of direct e-government and participation in the political process. Here is an example of an existing movement that is recuperated into the emerging architectures of Web 2.0 technologies. Indeed, Government 2.0 is the attempt to apply the social networking and integration advantages to the practices of government.

Open morality, dynamic religion

Technologies of openness

There is a complicated history of technologies of openness that I can only sketch in the briefest of detail here. I begin with the Macy Cybernetic group conferences and the development of the concept of the open systems in the Cold War period. The inaugural Macy Conference was entitled 'Feedback Mechanisms and Circular Causal Systems in Biological and Social Systems.' In the opening session von Neumann presented an overview of the state of the art in digital computers and Lorente de Nó did the same for neurophysiology. From the beginning a philosophical perspective was adopted that brought scientists from different disciplinary backgrounds together: Wiener talked about automatic mechanisms for self-regulation; McCulloch showed how simulated neural networks can emulate the calculus of propositional logic; Bateson presented his anthropological field work of the 1930s distinguishing between 'learning' and 'learning to learn'; while Wiener and von Neumann claimed that their theories and models would be of utility in economics and political science. The topics of the 10 Macy conferences beginning in 1946 discussed the applicability of the logic machine model to both brain and computer, human and social communication, analogies between organisms and machines, cybernetics machines, information theory and general epistemology.[1] It was in this general context that Claude Shannon developed his mathematical theory of communication published in 1948.[2] Shannon wrote:

> The fundamental problem of communication is that of reproducing at one point either exactly or approximately a message selected at another point. Frequently the messages have *meaning;* that is they refer to or are correlated according to some system with certain physical or conceptual entities. These semantic aspects of communication are irrelevant to the engineering problem. The significant aspect is that the actual message is one *selected from a set* of possible messages. The system must be designed to operate for each possible selection, not just the one which will actually be chosen since this is unknown at the time of design.

Shannon's mathematical model provided a basis for information theory and his early work on the electrical application of Boolean algebra enabled the invention of the digital computer (an invention Shannon is credited with) as well as the mathematics for packet switching as a basis for the digital era. We had to wait until 1992 for the development of the Internet although there were many networks trialed through DARPA to ARPANET and established in the late 1960s. From these models a variety of public networks developed and TCP/IP (internet protocols) provided a means of unifying them in the mid 1970s. These developed as regional networks and gradually transitioned toward the Internet during the 1980s. The shift from PC to Internet as platform was a critical step before the development of so-called Web 2.0 technologies, a term coined by Tim O'Reilly in 2005 and best summarized by his meme map below.[3]

Figure 9.1. Web 2.0 Meme Map

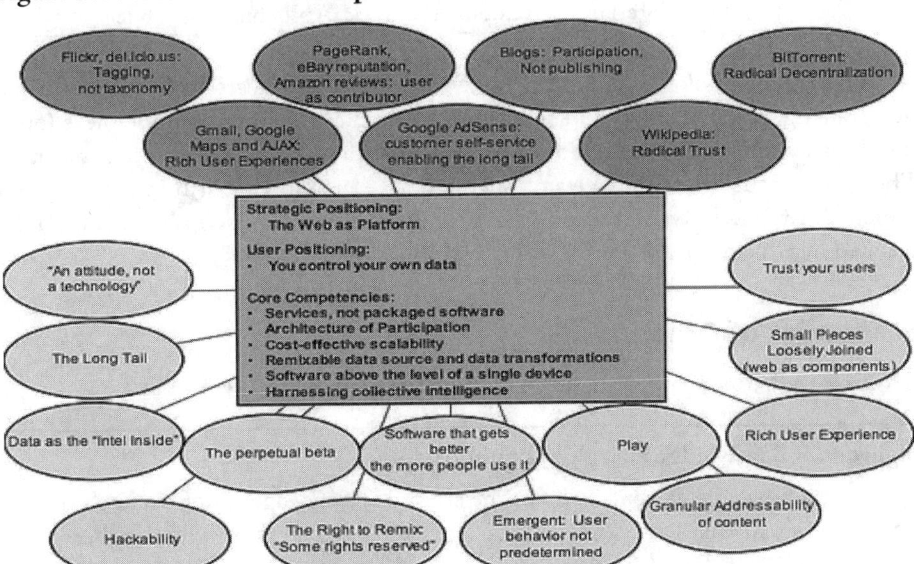

Web 2.0 technologies are the technologies of openness: they provide new architectures of participation and collaboration; they promote social media-social networking; they develop through wiki-collaborations based on 'collective intelligence' and 'the wisdom of the crowd.' O'Reilly outlines Web 2.0 in terms of 'web as platform' ('If Netscape was the standard bearer for Web 1.0, Google is most certainly the standard bearer for Web 2.0, if only because their respective IPOs were defining events for each era'); 'Harnessing Collective Intelligence,' ('*Network effects from user contributions are the key to market dominance in the Web 2.0 era*'); 'Data is the Next Intel Inside' ('we expect the rise of proprietary databases to result in a Free Data movement within the next decade'); 'End of the Software Release Cycle' ('*Users must be treated as co-developers*'); 'Lightweight Programming Models' ('*lightweight programming models...allow for loosely coupled systems*'); 'Software Above the Level of a Single Device' ('What applications become possible when our phones and our cars are not consuming data but reporting it?'); 'Rich User Experiences.' He summarizes the core competencies of Web 2.0 as:

Figure 9.2 Core competencies of Web 2.0

- Services, not packaged software, with cost-effective scalability
- Control over unique, hard-to-recreate data sources that get richer as more people use them
- Trusting users as co-developers
- Harnessing collective intelligence
- Leveraging the long tail through customer self-service
- Software above the level of a single device
- Lightweight user interfaces, development models, AND business models

Web 2.0 technologies enhance creativity and communications, secure information sharing, collaboration, and functionality of the web based on openness (open standards, open platforms), innovation, and evolution of web-culture communities. The applications of technologies of openness to education are still in their infancy (Peters & Britez, 2008) and the logic of new open systems outstrips that of our educational institutions built for the industrial age.

Economics of Openness

Knowledge as a global public good has the following features:

Figure 9.3. Knowledge as a global public good

- Knowledge is *non-rivalrous*: the stock of knowledge is not depleted by use and in this sense knowledge is not consumable; sharing with others, use, reuse, and modification may indeed add rather than deplete value;

- Knowledge is *barely excludable*: it is difficult to exclude users and to force them to become buyers; it is difficult, if not impossible, to restrict distribution of goods that can be reproduced with no or little cost;

- Knowledge is *not transparent*; knowledge requires some experience of it before one discovers whether it is worthwhile, relevant, or suited to a particular purpose.

Knowledge at the ideation or immaterial stage considered as pure ideas operates expansively to defy the law of scarcity. Digital information goods, in so far as they approximate pure thought, also defy the law of scarcity. Information goods, especially in digital forms, can be copied cheaply, so there is little or no cost in adding new users. Information and knowledge goods typically have an experiential and participatory element that increasingly requires the active co-production of the reader/writer, listener, and viewer. Digital information goods can be transported, broadcast or shared at low cost which may approach free transmission across bulk communication networks. Since digital information can be copied exactly and easily shared, it is never consumed. As Perry Barlow (1994), the lyricist for the Grateful Dead, put it in an insightful early paper: 'Information is an activity'; 'Information is a verb, not a noun; it is experienced not possessed; it has to move; it is conveyed by propagation, not distribution'; 'Information is a life form'; 'Information wants to be free; it replicates into the cracks of possibility; it wants to change; it is perishable.'

Globalization and the virtues of openness in higher education

Openness has emerged as an alternative mode of social production based on the growing and overlapping complexities of open source, open access and open archiving and open publishing. It has become a leading source of innovation in the world global digital economy. It is clear that the Free Software and 'open source' movements constitute a radical non-propertarian alternative to traditional methods of text production and distribution. This alternative non-proprietary method of cultural exchange threatens traditional models and the legal and institutional means used to restrict creativity, innovation and the free exchange of ideas. In terms of a model of communication there has been a gradual shift from content to code in the openness, access, use, reuse and modification reflecting a radical personalization that has made these open characteristics and principles increasingly the basis of the cultural sphere. So open source and open access has been developed and applied in open publishing, open archiving, and open music constituting the hallmarks of 'open culture.' For some theorists, such as law professors Yochai Benkler (Yale) and Larry Lessig (Stanford), this symbolizes a new mode of social production and a form of cultural formation that represents an alternative to capitalist forms of globalization. As a number of economists have remarked, this marks the emergence of global science and knowledge as a global public good that rest on an ethic of participation and collaboration based on the co-production and co-design of knowledge goods and services.

As one author expresses the point:

> The present decade can be called the 'open' decade (open source, open systems, open standards, open archives, open everything) just as the 1990s were called the 'electronic' decade (e-text, e-learning, e-commerce, e-governance) (Materu, 2004)

And yet it is more than just a 'decade' that follows the electronic innovations of the 1990s; it is a change of philosophy and ethos, a set of interrelated and complex changes that transforms markets and the mode of production, ushering in a new collection of values based on openness, the ethic of participation and peer-to-peer collaboration.

New forms of freedom are occurring in the fundamental shift from an underlying metaphysics of production—a 'productionist' metaphysics—to a metaphysics of consumption as use, reuse and modification. New logics and different patterns of cultural consumption are appearing in the areas of new media where symbolic analysis becomes a habitual and daily activity. It is now a truism to argue that information is the vital element in a 'new' politics and economy that links space, knowledge and capital in networked practices. Freedom is an essential ingredient in this equation if these network practices develop or transform themselves into knowledge cultures.

The specific politics and eco-cybernetic rationalities that accompany an informational global capitalism comprised of new multinational edutainment agglomerations are clearly capable of colonizing the emergent ecology of public info-social networks and preventing the development of knowledge cultures based on non-proprietary modes of knowledge production and exchange.

Complexity as an approach to knowledge and knowledge systems now recognizes both the development of global systems architectures in (tele)communications and information with the development of open knowledge production systems that increasingly rest not only on the establishment of new and better platforms (sometimes called Web 2.0), the semantic web, new search algorithms and processes of digitization. Social processes and policies that foster *openness* as an overriding value as evidenced in the growth of open source, open access and open education and their convergences that characterize global knowledge communities that transcend borders of the nation-state. Openness seems also to suggest political transparency and the norms of open inquiry, indeed, even democracy itself as both the basis of the logic of inquiry and the dissemination of its results.

The role of nonmarket and nonproprietary production promotes the emergence of a new information environment and networked economy that both depends upon and encourages great individual freedom, democratic participation, collaboration and interactivity. This 'promises to enable social production and exchange to play a much larger role, alongside property- and market-based production, than they ever have in modern democracies' (Benkler, 2006, 3). Peer production of information, knowledge, and culture enabled by the emergence of free and open-source software permits the expansion of the social model production beyond software platform into every domain of information and cultural production.

Open knowledge production is based upon an incremental, decentralized (and asynchronous), and collaborative development process that transcends the traditional proprietary market model. Commons-based peer production is based on free cooperation, not on the selling of one's labor in exchange of a wage, nor motivated primarily by profit or for the exchange value of the resulting product; it is managed through new modes of peer governance rather than traditional organizational hierarchies and it is an innovative application of copyright which creates an information commons and transcends the limitations attached to both the private (for-profit) and public (state-based) property forms. (See, for instance, Michel Bauwens' P2P Foundation work at the P2P Foundation at http://p2pfoundation.net/3._P2P_in_the_Economic_Sphere).

As the Ithaka Report *University Publishing in a Digital Age* (2008) reveals, these broad initiatives in open source, open access, open publishing and open archiving are part of emerging knowledge ecologies that will determine the future of educational resources and scholarly publishing challenging commercial publishing business models and raising broader and deeper questions about content development processes as well as questions of resourcing and sustainability. The new digital technologies promise changes in creation, production and consumption of scholarly resources including the development of new formats allowing integrated electronic research and publishing environments that will enable real-time dissemination and dynamically-updated content as well as alternative distribution models including institutional repositories, pre-print servers, open access journals that will broaden access, reduce costs, and enable open sharing of content.

On February 14, 2008 Harvard University's Faculty of Arts and Sciences adopted a policy that requires faculty members to allow the university to make their scholarly articles available free online. The new policy makes Harvard the first university in the United States to mandate open access to its faculty members' research publications and marks the beginning of a new era that will encourage other US universities to do the same. Open access means 'putting peer-reviewed scientific and scholarly literature on the internet, making it available free of charge and free of most copyright and licensing restrictions, and removing the barriers to serious research.' As Lila Guterman reports in *The Chronicle of Higher Education* News Blog

> Stuart M. Shieber, a professor of computer science at Harvard who proposed the new policy, said after the vote in a news release that the decision "should be a very powerful message to the academic community that we want and should have more control over how our work is used and disseminated (http://chronicle.com/news/article/3943/harvard-faculty-adopts-open-access-requirement).

Open access has transformed the world of scholarship and since the early 2000s with major OA statements starting with Budapest in 2002 movement has picked up momentum and developed a clear political ethos. Harvard's adoption of the new policy follows hard on the heels of open access mandates passed within months of each other—the National Institutes of Health (NIH) and the European Research Council (ERC). As one blogger remarked: 'open archiving of peer-reviewed journal literature [is] now on an irreversible course of expansion' not only as U.S. universities follow Harvard's lead but also as open archiving makes available learning material to anyone, including students and faculty from developing and transition countries. Harvard's adoption of the open archiving mandate is similar in scope to the step taken by MIT to adopt OpenCourseWare (OCW) in 2001. These initiatives are part of new strategies to establish knowledge cultures that will determine the future of scholarly publishing, the form and content of educational resources, and therefore also the future of innovation, science and research in the digital global economy.

Towards an open science economy

The emerging political economy of global science is a significant factor influencing development of national systems of innovation and economic, social and cultural development, with the rise of multinational actors and a new mix of corporate, private/public and community involvement. It is only since the 1960s with the development of research evaluation and increasing sophistication of bibliometrics that it has been possible to map the emerging economy of global science, at least on a comparative national and continental basis. In 2000 the SCI included a total of 584,982 papers, representing a 57.5 per cent increase from 1981, when 371,346 papers were published worldwide. Authors from developed countries wrote 87.9 per cent of the papers in 2000, a decrease from 93.6 per cent in 1981. Developing countries saw a steady increase in their share of scientific production: from 7.5 per cent of world papers in 1981 to 17.1 per cent in 2000. North America lost the lead it had in 1996, and in 2000 produced 36.8 per cent of the world total, a decrease from 41.4 per cent in 1981(UNESCO, 2005). The countries occupying the top eight places in the science citation rank order produced about 84.5 per cent of the top 1 per cent most cited publications between 1993 and 2001. The next nine countries produced 13 per cent, and the final group share 2.5 per cent. There is a stark disparity between the first and second divisions in the scientific impact of nations (King, 2004).

The current science system has moved through several eras: the small science era with the institutionalization of science after the establishment of the Royal Society in the 17th century (Boyle's "invisible college"); the professionalization of science in the 18th century (Curie, Pasteur, Volta); development of the disciplines in the 19th century with the separation of science fields, technology, physics and biology; the rise of scientific nationalism based on industrialization in the 20th century (the 'big science' of D. Solla Price); and the emergence of the era of global science in the 21st century (Wagner, 2007; Peters, 2007). The US science system also moved through various phases in the modern period that can be briefly summarized (based on Mirowski's & Sent, 2002):

In 2006 the total expenditure for R&D conducted in the U.S. was about $340B in current dollars. Of this total, basic research accounts for about 18 per cent ($62B), applied research about 22 per cent ($75B), and development about 60 per cent ($204B). Federal funding is the primary source of basic research support in the U.S. (over 59 per cent in 2006), of which about 56 per cent is carried out by academic institutions. Federal obligations for academic research (both basic and applied) and especially in the current support for National Institutes of Health (NIH) (whose budget had previously doubled between the years 1998 to 2003) declined in real terms between 2004 and 2005 and are expected to have declined further in 2006 and 2007.[4]

Figure 9.4. Development phases of the U.S. science system

- The Protoindustrial Science regime

- The Cold War regime

- Vannevar Bush established NDRC, then OSRD in 1941 (with James Conant, Karl T. Compton, Frank B. Jewitt), and finally NSF in 1950 (to cement ties between academic, industry, and military); *Science, The Endless Frontier* (1945) with emphases on freedom of inquiry, the war against disease, science and public welfare, renewal of talent, science reconversion and NSF (http://www.nsf.gov/about/history/vbush1945.htm)

- The Globalized Privatization regime

- Shifts in science funding, end of 'big science' based on physics as model (cancelation of superconductor '93), move from funding of only elite institutions, shrinking budgets, breakdown of scientific nationalism, collapse of soviet science system, c ollapse of nation security imperative up until 9/11

- New Models of Open Science—a new regime?

In the emergent science system five forces are structuring the 21st century (open) science system: networks; emergence; circulation; stickiness (place); and distribution (virtual) (Wagner, 2007).

The decline of the U.S. economy relative to those of the rest of the world is facilitating the strengthening of science elsewhere. An evolving multi-polar world economy is leading to multiple centers of science—the United States, the European Union, Japan, China, Russia and possibly India. The increasing wealth of several of these societies is enabling them to lure back many younger scientists trained abroad in the world's leading institutions. In particular, China is moving towards an integrated system of national innovation replacing state control with more enabling frameworks and focusing on improving the university and research systems. It is also stepping up the internationalization of research with collaborative networks across Europe, Japan and the U.S. The predictions are that by the end of 2020 China will achieve more science and technological breakthroughs of great world influence, qualifying it to join the ranks of the world's most innovative countries. Some think that in twenty years global science will be driven by Indian scientists, with new interfaces in science and new rules, where new countries can contribute on an equal footing.

One thing that is clear is the emergence of a globalized science system with the increasing globalization of research, science, engineering and technology. The growth of China, India and South Korea are changing the atlas of the world scientific knowledge system.

International research collaboration is becoming an important source of national comparative advantage, and nations see the importance of tracking and analyzing global knowledge flows and transfers to determine national and regional collaborations. Increasingly, national science administrations use information technologies and bibliometrics in facilitating cross-border knowledge flows and also in analyzing citations, co-authorship, and collaborations, and focus on the development of new metrics systems including webometrics for the measurement of research impacts, growth and distributions. What is even more marked is the increasing significance of new social networking and social media for Web 2.0 science and open-access publishing.

In this new 'open science economy' there is significant advantages of smallness both with the shift to international collaborative research and virtual organization of global science teams. Teams produce more papers and receive more citations (see Wuchty et al., 2007). Big science has built in irreversible constraints including bureaucratic, fragmented communication difficulties, organization rigidities. Now science policy experts argue that excellence in science requires nimble, autonomous organizations—qualities more likely to be found in small research settings. Enhanced performance takes place through the creation of several dozen small research organizations in interdisciplinary domains or in emerging fields. Small, flexible, specialized teams are seen to be the answer. Dozens of scientists who made significant advances did so in organizations with fewer than 50 full-time researchers. In the past decade Nobel prizes have been awarded to scientists for work done in relatively small settings: Günter Blobel (physiology or medicine), Ahmed Zewail (chemistry), Paul Greengard (physiology or medicine), Andrew Fire (physiology or medicine), Roderick MacKinnon (chemistry), and Gerhard Ertl (chemistry) (see Hollingsworth, et al., 2008). Many economists draw attention to the development of small, flexible, specialized teams in regional centers ('clustering').

Alongside nation science systems an increasingly complex transnational science is occurring. New research partnerships that are no longer solely state and university-oriented are emerging. There is also spectacular growth of corporate multinational research especially in new materials, biotechnology (genetics), pharmaceutics, information technology—growth of private science with shifts in funding regimes from public to private, state to global, and big science to applied science, science to technology and technology transfer. In this context a new role exists for humanities, performing arts and social sciences as 'soft' sciences and technologies concerned with new international values, legalities, global civic cultures, knowledge measurement, management and PR—the so-called 'soft' programing architectures that encourage new forms of technology-led education on the basis of new architectures of participation and collaboration. There is also an emergence of global science and research organization and cultures—extra-national organizations, NGOs, UN, UNESCO, ESF and other international science-based organizations.

New models of open science are rapidly developing based on mode 2.0 with greater interdisciplinarity and 'flattening' of geocentric science centers and knowledge flows toward global teams. Correspondingly there is a reversal from close conduit peer review to open source public scrutiny and increased use of open source data analysis, management of large data bases, and sharing (bioinformatics). Science publishing has undergone a sea-change with 'changes in creation, production and consumption of scholarly resources—'creation of new formats made possible by digital technologies, ultimately allowing scholars to work in deeply integrated electronic research and publishing environments that will enable real-time dissemination, collaboration, dynamically-updated content, and usage of new media' and 'alternative distribution models (institutional repositories, pre-print servers, open access journals) have also arisen with the aim to broaden access, reduce costs, and enable open sharing of content' (Ithaka Report, 2007, p. 4).[5] The new models of open science are to some extent in opposition or conflict with expanded protection of IP. Open source initiatives have facilitated the development of new models of production and innovation. The public and nonprofit sectors have called for alternative approaches dedicated to public knowledge redistribution and dissemination. Now distributed peer-to-peer knowledge systems rival the scope and quality of similar products produced by proprietary efforts where speed of diffusion of open source projects is an obvious advantage. The successful projects occur in both software and open source biology. Open access science has focused on making peer-reviewed online research and scholarship freely accessible to a broader population (including digitized back issues). Open science demonstrates an "exemplar of a compound of 'private-collective' model of innovation" that contains elements of both proprietary and public models of knowledge production (Von Hippel & von Krogh, 2003). Rhoten & Powell (2007) asks 'does the expansion of a patenting culture undermine the norms of open science? Does the intensification of patenting accelerate or retard the development of basic and commercial research?'

As *Scientific American* (2008) acknowledges, the emergence of Science 2.0

> generally refers to new practices of scientists who post raw experimental results, nascent theories, claims of discovery and draft papers on the Web for others to see and comment on. Proponents say these "open access" practices make scientific progress more collaborative and therefore more productive. Critics say scientists who put preliminary findings online risk having others copy or exploit the work to gain credit or even patents. Despite pros and cons, Science 2.0 sites are beginning to proliferate; one notable example is the OpenWetWare project started by biological engineers at the Massachusetts Institute of Technology.

Waldrop (2008) demonstrates that rich text, highly interactive, user generated and socially active Internet (Web 2.0) has seen linear models of knowledge production giving way to more diffuse open ended and serendipitous knowledge processes

Open science economy plays a complementary role with corporate and transnational science and implies strong role for governments. Increasingly, portal-based knowledge environments and global science gateways support collaborative science (Schuchardt et al., 2007; see, for instance, Science.gov & Science.world). Cybermashups of very large data sets let users explore, analyze, and comprehend the science behind the information being streamed (Leigh & Brown, 2008). The World Wide Web has revolutionized how researchers from various disciplines collaborate over long distances especially in the Life Sciences, where interdisciplinary approaches are becoming increasingly powerful as a driver of both integration and discovery (with regard to data access, data quality, identity, and provenance) (Sagotsky et al., 2008). National science review and assessment to focus on formative role in developing distributed knowledge systems based on quality journal suites in disciplinary clusters with an ever finer mesh of in-built indicators. Meanwhile, economists argue that open source software can be an engine of economic growth (see Garzarelli et al., 2008; Etzkowitz, 1997; 2003; 2008; David, 2003) and clearly the notion of open science economy is one of the leading sectors of the knowledge economy. The recent *Science in the 21st Century* conference[6] sees the relationships between science, society, and information technology as an increasingly complex triangle:

Figure 9.5. Science, Society and Information Technology

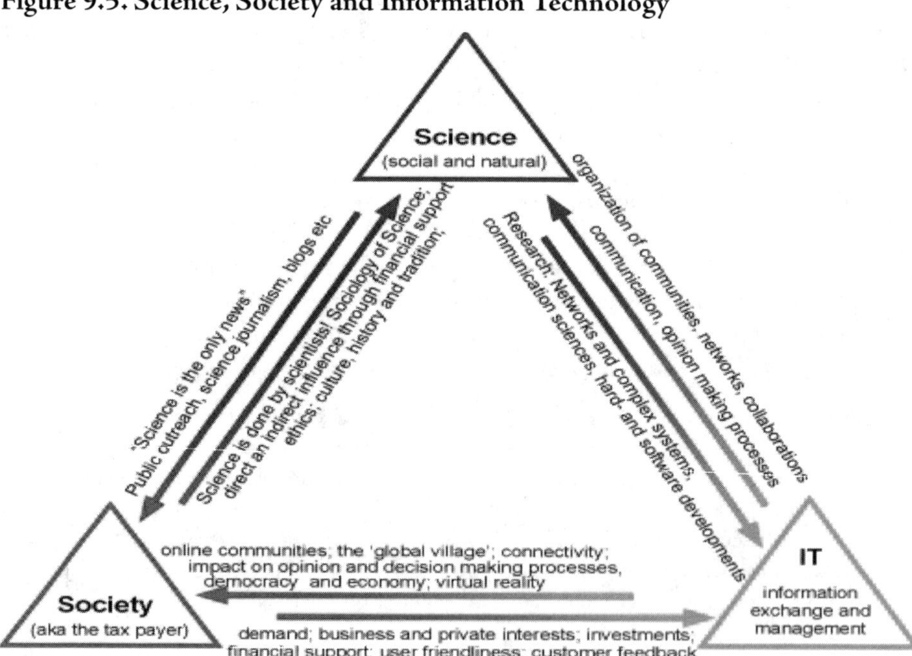

Source: http://www.science21stcentury.org/ittriangle.html

One of the invited speakers at the conference, which was organized by Sabine Hossenfelder and Michael Nielsen at the Perimeter Institute for Theoretical Physics, Cameron Neylon, puts up an economic case for open science in this way:[7]

Science in the open or How I learned to stop worrying and love the blog

Vast sums of money, probably of the order of \$US200 billion, are spent annually by national government agencies and charities on scientific research. Yet despite the sums invested and despite the requirement to demonstrate 'Economic Impact' rising up the political agenda very little critical analysis is made of the efficiency of scientific research in generating its desired outputs. A large proportion of all scientific research is never made public and the vast majority is not made available to other scientists in a timely manner.

The thesis of the 'Open Science Movement' is that by making data, results, and protocols freely available to the research community for use and re-use a step change in the efficiency of science practice can be achieved and there is a growing interest in some sectors of the academic research community in adopting more 'open' approaches to research practice. These range from publishing in the open access literature, through research discussions on message boards to discussing the details of their research on blogs. The logical extreme of these approaches is 'Open Notebook Science'; a term coined by Jean-Claude Bradley to describe making the researcher's laboratory notebook freely available online. It is even possible to carry out the preparation of a research grant in public. While the application of Open Science approaches remains limited in academic research they nonetheless raise serious questions about the value of the current academic reward structure, and the future of both research publication and peer review, in their current form. Responses to the advocacy of 'Open Science' therefore, understandably, run the gamut from fanatical support, through amused tolerance, to derision and, in some cases, extreme hostility.

The question of 'open science' and its underlying logic is a topic that has been pursued by Paul David (2003)[8] and is also being developed at the school level.[9] Today, in the Obama era increasingly we can speak of the historical moment of open science, the open science economy and the virtues of openness in higher education based science and knowledge as global public goods.

Endnotes

1. I based my account on the Summary of the Macy Conferences at http://www.asc-cybernetics.org/foundations/history/MacySummary.htm#Part2.

2. See http://cm.bell-labs.com/cm/ms/what/shannonday/shannon1948.pdf

3. See http://www.oreillynet.com/pub/a/oreilly/tim/news/2005/09/30/what-is-web-20.html

4. National Science Board, Research and Development: Essential Foundations for U.S. Competitiveness in a Global Economy. A Companion to Science and Engineering Indicators, 2008 http://www.nsf.gov/statistics/nsb0803/start.htm

5. See, for instance the *Journal of Visualized Experiments* at http://www.jove.com/.

6. See the list of abstracts at the conference 'Science in the 21st Century: Science, Society and Information Technology' at http://www.science21stcentury.org/index.html.

7. Cameron Neylon also runs a blog called 'Science in the Open': An openwetware blog on the challenges of open and connected science, at http://blog.openwetware.org/scienceinthe open/.

8. See also his video presentation 'The Historical Origins and Economic Logic of "Open Science"' at http://videolectures.net/cern_david_openscience/.

9. See Project Open Science, an EU funded project, at http://www.otevrena-veda.cz/ov/index. php?p=o_projektu&site=ov_en.

References

Allen, G. (2004, April 13). Bioinformatics: New technology models for research, education, and service. *Research Bulletin*, Educause Center for Applied Research.

Bell, D. (1973). *The Coming of the Post-Industrial Society*. New York: Basic Books.

Bellaver, R., & Lusa, J. (Eds.). Knowledge management strategy and technology. Boston, Artech House Publishers.

Bush, V. (1945, 1990). *Science- the Endless Frontier: A Report to the President on a Program for Postwar Scientific Research*. Washington, D. C.: National Science Foundation.

Cooke, P. (2005). Regionally asymmetric knowledge capabilities and open innovation. Exploring 'globalisation 2'- a new model of industry organisation. *Research Policy*, 34, 1128–1149.

David, Paul (2003) The Economic Logic of "Open Science" and the Balance between Private Property Rights and the Public Domain in Scientific Data and Information: A Primer, at siepr.stanford. edu/Papers/pdf/02–30.pdf.

Edvquist, O. (2004). Layered science and science policies. *Minerva*, 41, 207–221.

Etzkowitz, H. (1997). The entrepreneurial university and the emergence of democratic corporatism. In H. Etzkowitz, & L. Leydesdorff, L, (Eds.), *Universities and the Global Knowledge Economy: A Triple Helix of University-Industry-Government Relations*. (pp. 141–154). London: Continuum.

Etzkowitz, H. (2003). Innovation in innovation: the triple helix of university-industry-government relations. *Social Science Information*. 42(3), 293–337.

Etzkowitz, H. (2008). *The Triple Helix: University- Industry-Government Innovation in Action*. London: Routledge.

Etzkowitz, H., Carvalho de Mello, J. S., & Almeida, M. (2005). Towards "meta-innovation" in Brazil: the evolution of the incubator and the emergence of a triple helix. *Research Policy*, 34, 411–424.

Garvey, R. & Williamson, W. (2002). *Beyond Knowledge Management: Dialogue, Creativity, and the Corporate Curriculum*. Essex, England: Pearson Education Limited.

Garvin, D. (1993). Building learning organizations. *Harvard Business Review*, 71(4), 78–91.

Garzarelli, G., Yasmina R. L. & Bjørn T. (2008) Open Source Software and Economic Growth: A Classical Division of Labor Perspective, *Information Technology for Development*, Vol. 14 (2) 116–135.

Gibbons, M., Nowotny, H., Limonges, C., Trow, M., Schwartzman, S. & Scott, P. (1994). The new production of knowledge. Beverly Hills, CA: Sage.

Gibson, F. (2008). Do scientists really believe in open science? Accessed online October 14, 2008 at http://peanutbutter.wordpress.com/2007/06/26/do-scientists-really-believe-in-open-science/

Gilbert, W. (1991). Towards a paradigm shift in biology. *Nature*, 349, 99.

Gray, B. (1989). *Collaborating: Finding Common Ground for Multiple Problems.* San Francisco: Jossey-Bass.

Hollingsworth, J. R., Karl H. Müller, K. H., & Hollingsworth, E. J. (2008). China: the end of the science superpowers. *Nature* 454(7203): 412–415.

Ithaka Harbors, Inc. (2007). University publishing in a digital age. Accessed online October 14, 2008 at http://www.ithaka.org/strategic-services/university-publishing

Jones, B. F., Wuchty, S., and Uzzi B. (2008). Multi-University Research Teams: Shifting Impact, Geography, and Stratification in Science. Published online 9 October 2008 [DOI: 10.1126/science.1158357] (in Science Express Reports)

King, D. A. (2004) 'The scientific impact of nations: What different countries get for their research spending,' *Nature,* Vol 430 , 15 July: 311–316, at www.nature.com/nature.

Kremic, T. (2003). Technology transfer: A contextual approach. *Journal of Technology Transfer,* 28, 149–158.

National Science Board, Research and Development: Essential Foundations for U.S. Competitiveness in a Global Economy. A Companion to Science and Engineering Indicators, 2008 http://www.nsf.gov/statistics/nsb0803/start.htm

National Science Board, Research and Development: Essential Foundations for U.S. Competitiveness in a Global Economy. A Companion to Science and Engineering Indicators, 2008 http://www.nsf.gov/statistics/nsb0803/start.htm.

Schuchardt, K., Pancerella, C., Rahn, L.A., Didier, B, Kodeboyina, D., Leahy, D., Myers, J.D., Oluwole, O.O., Pitz, W., Ruscic, B., Song, J., Von Laszewski, G., Yang, C. (2007). Portal-based knowledge environment for collaborative science. *Concurrency Computation Practice and Experience* 19 (12), 1703–1716

UNESCO (2005) 'What do bibliometric indicators tell us about world scientific output?' *UIS Bulletin on Science and Technology Statistics* Issue No. 2, September.

Waldrop, M. M. (2008). Science 2.0. *Scientific American,* 298 (5). Accessed online October 18, 2008 at http://www.sciam.com/article.cfm?id=science-2-point-0-great-new-tool-or-great-risk.

Wessner, C. (2007). *Innovation Policies for the 21st Century.* Washington, D. C.: National Academy Press.

Wuchty, S., B. F. Jones, B. F., & Uzzi, B. (2007). The Increasing Dominance of Teams in Production of Knowledge, *Science,* 316, 1036–1039.

CHAPTER 10

Cultural Exchange, Study Abroad and Discourse of the Other

◻ Michael A. Peters And Shivali Tukeo

Introduction

Student mobility and international institutional collaborations are connected to the expansion of study abroad programs that have, by now, become prominent features of the US higher educational experience. Institutionalization of study abroad is often advanced on two grounds: preparing students for a global workforce and offering them cultural knowledge. These goals are echoed in the annual *Open Doors* report (2007) that claims a dramatic yearly increase (8.5 per cent) in the number of students studying abroad, and signals that the growth is indicative of an overall shift in higher learning. Study abroad programs exhibit a great deal of variety in terms of their duration, learning emphasis and the extent of institutional involvement from host countries. Yet, common elements emerging from the claims of success of these programs often point out that the encounters with other cultures have learning potential and study abroad experiences, at the very least, make students "less biased" towards cultures other than their own. Underpinned in these claims are some of the interesting assumptions about other cultures, academic-cultural exchange and models of cultural learning. Innovations in transportation and communication technologies have made international travel an important component of US higher education. Simply put, travel-based models of learning have given students an opportunity to learn by reciprocity, participation and engagement with people as opposed to relying exclusively on the mediation of textbooks and expert knowledge.

We can tentatively identity seven major models that provide a basis for cultural exchange and study abroad. The liberal model is based on assumptions of liberal anthropology and the neoliberal model tends to take both forms of the consumer model (discussed below) and the competency model. The intercultural model about which we say little is based upon a psychological model in communications theory. The postcolonial model is in part a reaction to and response to both the liberal and neoliberal models. And the hospitality model based on the work of Derrida that we explore in the second half of the paper is a model that makes ethics first philosophy in the study of cultures.

Models of Cultural Exchange and Study Abroad

1. The liberal model of cultural exchange
2. The intercultural model
3. The neoliberal model
4. The competency-based model
5. The consumer model
6. The postcolonial model
7. The hospitality model

This chapter begins by briefly examining the expansion of study abroad programs in the US and mentions three strategic papers by Mell Bolen (2001), Nadine Dolby (2007) and Maria Mendoza (nd) as current examples of what we call the postcolonial model designed to critique the worst features of (neo)imperialism. In the next section of the chapter we examine the discourse of the Other, beginning with first contact and the myth of the 'noble savage' by reference to Montaigne's famous essay. We believe that this critical genealogy is necessary because it provides the framing for liberal anthropology, ethnography, politics and the multicultural society. It also reminds us of how deeply embedded are the assumptions of the discourse of the Other and the complex ways that they informed cultural exchange and also colonial administration and education. In the final section we investigate the work of the French philosopher Jacques Derrida and especially his Paris seminar on the notion and practice of hospitality as a model that provides an ethics for cultural exchange and study abroad, and an ethical basis for understanding modern cosmopolitanism. In the last section of the chapter entitled 'Culture goes to school' we review the footprint of modern study abroad and raise some questions about its conceptualizations. The chapter ends with a brief conclusion that profiles our rethinking of cultural exchange as a basis for study abroad.

Study abroad in the US context

Expansion of study abroad programs occurred in the US in part because of the growing institutional support for internationalization. The increase in the number of students studying abroad can be attributed to a series of initiatives including the federal financial aid for study abroad (1992), President Clinton's executive memorandum (2000), the Abraham Lincoln Study Abroad Fellowship Program (2003) and the establishment of Forum of Education Abroad (Institute of International Education, 2005). Despite the sizable scholarship in transnationalization of higher education, study abroad and cultural exchange has not received much theoretical attention. Research on study abroad has largely focused on learning outcomes and attitudinal changes in the students involved (Ingraham & Peterson, 2004; Sutton & Robins, 2004; Chieffo & Griffiths, 2004). Our focus in this paper is more aligned toward the social and philosophical connections between study abroad, cultural exchange and internationalization of higher education. To that end, the following three papers are particularly useful starting points. Mell Bolen's (2001) articulation of study abroad in terms of the contemporary consumer practices, Nadine Dolby's (2007) examination of national identity in the context of international travel, and Maria Mendoza's (nd) analysis of study abroad as an opportunity to break down the orientalist assumptions. Bolen's essay 'Consumerism and U.S. Study Abroad' sets up a context for study abroad within the larger social transitions of US higher education. Institutionalization of study abroad is coterminous with the shift in higher education that brought to the fore connection between consumerism and education. The explicit repositioning of education as an asset has in turn strengthened the involvement of markets in education. In these circumstances, the promotion of study abroad programs was developed with the following two-fold logic: the extension of higher education beyond national borders and the facilitation of mass-produced experiences of consumption and travel for youth. Curiously, the scholarly inquiry into the aspects of culture did not attract much institutional support until 'culture' was rearticulated in order to fit within the terms of tourism, travel and the desirability of international experience.

Dolby's empirical work 'Reflections on Nation: American Undergraduates and Education Abroad' engages with the possibilities of political transformation in study abroad by looking at the intended and unintended consequences of travel and social interactions. As the study reveals, travel and communication with people outside US serve as useful points of entry in rethinking one's sense of national pride and identity. This has become especially clear in the wake of the resurgence of US patriotism since September 11. Dolby's interviews with undergraduate students confirm that direct participation in the non-US communities offers students alternative perspectives on US politics, often to their surprise. Like Dolby, Maria Mendoza sees possibilities of change through study abroad. Her paper 'Cultural Exchange as a Challenge to Orientalism' pays attention to the implicit components of cultural encounters including reciprocity, empathy and cultural awareness. In its true spirits, cultural exchange can be an effective antidote to the orientalist constructions of non-western cultures as exotic, irrational and inferior. The three views on study abroad presented above draw attention to the links between the components of cultural exchange, academic models of cultural learning and practices of cultural negotiation. Learning through travels and interactions has for long been valued to be good and transformative. From Peace Corps to GlobalExchange and from Heritage Tours to Relief Programs, the understood meaning of cultural exchange denotes a wide range of practices. Even when the objective of travel is not overtly educational, the direct involvement of participants is considered to be educative. Reciprocity and fair intentions are central to the experiences of cultural exchange. At the very least, encounters with other cultures help create greater awareness about the host culture, and they can lead toward creating a renewed awareness of one's own culture.

Through their ideas and practices, study abroad programs rehearse the well-defined and age-old assumptions about cultural exchange. For instance, culture is seen as an embodiment of place, language, customs, arts and food among others. And cultural competence is understood to involve the necessary acquisition of cultural traits. In much the same way, study abroad relies on the notions such as cultural literacy, cross-cultural communication and cultural competence. In this paper we look at study abroad and its complex deployments. In particular, the history of cultural exchange and its connections to imperialism, discursive constructions of the cultural Other, and the institutionalization of liberal multiculturalism occupy focal points. Situating 'the first contact' and the myth of the noble savage in what can be called the history of ethnography, the next section examines Michael de Montaigne's text 'Of Cannibals.' Examining Montaigne is useful in order to see the early forms of the doctrine of cultural relativism that later spilled over in the production of ideas about morality, normativity and superiority of the west. This thread is further developed in the next section that maps out the concepts of hospitality and gift as they relate to the acts of travel and exchange. In their contemporary political garb these concepts translate into the political conflicts around immigration, citizenship and identity. We then turn our attention to education, looking at the culture question therein. The subsequent discussion views study abroad as an extension of liberal multiculturalism.

The discourse of the other: First contact and the myth of the noble savage

Everything is good in leaving the hands of the Creator of Things;
everything degenerates in the hands of man.
—Jean-Jacques Rousseau, Emile

Ethnography in the service of anthropology once looked out at clearly
defined others, defined as primitive, or tribal, or non-Western,
or pre-literate, or nonhistorical—the list, if extended, soon becomes
incoherent. Now ethnography encounters others in relation to itself,
while seeing itself as other.
—James Clifford, Introduction: Partial Truths, Writing Culture, p. 23

'Of Cannibals' is a set of reflections by Michel de Montaigne penned and published in 1580, many years after his meeting in Rouen in 1562 with a cannibal who had been brought to France by the French explorer Villegagnon. This piece which exemplifies the genre of the essay form which Montaigne established is justly famous in the history of ethnography. Montaigne, for instance, was hailed by Claude Lévi-Strauss as the father of the human sciences and the pioneer of 'cultural relativism' insofar as that term represents the central operating premise of ethnography, an approach to the appreciation of cultural diversity and a serious challenge to Western ethnocentrism and assumptions of cognitive superiority. The modern version of cultural relativism retrieved from Montaigne at least in the French tradition was central also to Franz Boas's and Ruth Benedict's opposition to the racist models of cultural evolution emerging in the nineteenth century that invented a spurious 'science' based on a teleology of human development representing European societies as the pinnacle while relegating indigenous cultures as 'primitive' beginnings. For better or for worse epistemologically speaking, the doctrine of cultural relativism became the official ideology of UNESCO following WWII, largely as a result of two pieces commissioned by the UNESCO from Lévi-Strauss, *Race et histoire* (Lévi-Strauss 1971 [1952]) and 'Race et culture' (Lévi-Strauss 1979 [1971]).

It is instructive to return briefly to Montaigne's essay to reexamine one of the origins of the myth of the 'noble savage' and the form of cultural relativism it encouraged. It becomes clear that Montaigne is writing about a place that the French naval officer and explorer, Nicolas Durand de Villegaignon called 'Antarctique France' meaning present day Brazil. With a couple of ships and six hundred soldiers and colonists Villegaignon invaded Rio de Janeiro to establish a Huguenot stronghold to escape Catholic persecution in Europe. Montaigne writes in a famous passage:

> ...I do not find that there is anything barbaric or savage about this nation, according to what I've been told, unless we are to call barbarism whatever differs from our own customs. Indeed, we seem to have no other standard of truth and reason than the opinions and customs of our own country. These nations seem to me, then, barbaric in that they have been little refashioned by the human mind and are still quite close to their original naiveté. They are still ruled by natural laws, only slightly corrupted by ours. They are in such a state of purity that I am sometimes saddened by the thought that we did not discover them earlier, when there were people who would have known how to judge them better than we.

Noting (falsely, as it turns out) that they have 'no commerce,' 'no knowledge of letters,' 'no knowledge of numbers,' no concept of property, 'no occupations,' and 'no respect for any relationship except ordinary family ones' Montaigne goes on to describe 'their wars' against neighboring tribes and the custom of cannibalism—'having slashed him [the enemy] to death' 'they roast him and eat him together, sending portions to their absent friends.' Montaigne then remarks 'They do this, not as is supposed, for nourishment as did the ancient Scythians; it represents instead an extreme form of vengeance.' And he offers the following account and makes an unfavorable comparison with his own alleged 'civilized' society:

I consider it more barbarous to eat a man alive than to eat him dead; to tear by rack and torture a body still full of feeling, to roast it by degrees, and then give it to be trampled and eaten by dogs and swine—a practice which we have not only read about but seen within recent memory, not between ancient enemies, but between neighbors and fellow citizens and, what is worse, under the cloak of piety and religion—than to roast and eat a man after he is dead.

In Montaigne's essay we get one of the first expressions of the myth of the 'noble savage' that shaped accounts of the Other. Montaigne's essay also influenced authors such as Shakespeare who contributed to European Romanticism that equated 'natural' with 'good' and celebrated a kind of benign Nature (and human nature) in contrast to a corrupted civilized self, a doctrine that comes to fruition and receives full treatment by Rousseau. In *A Discourse on the Origin and Basis of Inequality Among Men* (1754) and *The Social Contract* (1762) Rousseau elaborates a theory of 'natural man' that held that man when in a state of nature was good. Men in a state of nature do not know good and evil, but their independence, along with 'the peacefulness of their passions, and their ignorance of vice,' keep them from doing ill (*A Discourse*, 71–73). Against Hobbes, he asserts an account of natural man as virtuous and, quoting Locke, he argues '*There can be no injury, where there is no property.*' Inequality is the outgrowth of enlarged desires that only comes into play with the concept of property. Rousseau pits instinct and appetite of natural existence against justice and reason of civil society, contrasting natural liberty with civil liberty, and individual strength against the general will. Man is only created as a moral and social being once natural liberty is destroyed and there is the need to establish civil liberty conceived as the rule of right over power.

Early contact with the Other not only shapes the myth of the noble savage but also develops a fully fledged and highly influential political theory about the origins of morality, power, and civil society. Montaigne's highly idealized characterization of the natives of the New World, without the trappings of modern civilization, rescues the Biblical account of human nature after the Fall and develops a doctrine of 'naturalism' that associates 'natural' (read 'uncivilized') with a kind of unfettered 'true' natural virtue based on 'Nature' itself—a concept so important to Romanticism not only for its fecundity and its vigor but also as the source of creativity.

These 'early' accounts were preceded by first contact stories not with 'savages' but with peoples from the East—Chinese, Indian, 'Tartar'—generally in the form of travel narratives of traders. Marco Polo's father and uncle, Niccolò and Maffeo, traded with the East (Constantinople and the Black Sea) in the mid thirteenth century and he himself allegedly made his journey to Cathay in 1271 with his father and uncle-spending seventeen years in China in the service of the Khan. Marco Polo in his Prologue emphasizes 'the diversities of the sundry regions of the World' and in Chapter VI how 'the Great Kaa asked all about the manners of the Christians' sending the two Polo brothers to the Pope as an envoy and returning to the court of 'the Great Kaa.' But the Polos were not the first to travel overland to China. The Radhanites, medieval Jewish merchants, established an extensive trading network in the early Middle

Ages (approx. 600–1000 CE) and mediated trade between Christian and Muslims, and Persians, before them, conducted trade between Europe and East Asia.

Indeed, the whole myth of first contact with non-European others was fabricated around certain strategic texts like Polo's that fictionalized and romanticized aspects of these encounters defying an easy classification but recording general admiration for the ancient civilizations of China and India. The first reported encounter with indigenous cultures and tribal others in Europe was largely postponed until the Enlightenment philosophies steeped in classical and Biblical sources fictionalized the myth of the noble savage, imbuing it with a theological and utopian overlay of Garden of Eden or Golden Age that picked up a new set of nuances with the 'discovery' of the Pacific ('South Sea') Islands popularized in novels like *Oroonoko; or, The Royal Slave* (1688), *Robinson Crusoe* (1719), in Montesquieu's (1712) hilarious and bleak *Persian Letters*, in Chateaubriand's and Cooper's novels, and later by Robert Louis Stevenson's and Paul Gauguin's accounts of the Pacific. Modern anthropology and in particular ethnography was to echo this fictionalized and philosophically mediated history. As Stephen A. Tyler (1986), writes in 'Post-Modern Ethnography'

> The history of ethnographic writing chronicles a cumulative sequence of different attitudes toward the other that implicate different uses of ethnography. In the eighteenth century, the dominant mode was 'ethnography as allegory,' centering around the key concept of utopianism in which the 'noble savage' played his ennobling role as therapeutic image. In the nineteenth century, the 'savage' was no longer noble; she was 'fallen,' in the continuing biblical allegory, or a figure of therapeutic irony—a minatory Satanic finger, or an instance of the primordial 'primitive,' a 'living fossil' signifying past imperfection healed by time in the emerging evolutionary allegory. In the twentieth century, the 'savage' was no longer even 'primitive.' She was only 'data' and 'evidence,' the critical disapproving instance in the positivist rhetoric of political liberalism. Later, in structuralist and semioticist revival of a formal pattern of collocated signs totally robbed of therapeutic signification. Now, in addition to these each of which, or some combination of them, still feeds the imagination of some ethnographer somewhere, she has become the instrument of the ethnographer's 'experience,' the ethnographer having become the focus of 'difference' in a perverse version of the romanticism that has always been in ethnography, no matter how desperately repressed and marginalized by the objective impulses of seeker for pure data. As in the utopianism of the eighteenth century, the other is the means of the author's alienation from his own sick culture, but the savage of the twentieth century is sick too; neutered, like the rest of us, by the dark forces of the 'world system,' It has lost the healing art (pp. 127–8).

Here Tyler expertly pulls apart the fictionalized elements that insinuated themselves into ethnography through earlier first contact discourse. In essence Tyler is also unraveling the orientalist assumptions that underpin a Christian view of nature and the 'savage,' demonstrating the way in which these 'signs' found their way into the practice of ethnography and the ethnographer's imagination, creating a precolonial subject, and then also providing a basis for aspects of colonial administration by analyzing the conditions of 'civilization' including the necessity of education in the metropolitan language and culture as a prerequisite for participation in the modern world.

Hospitality, the gift and the politics of friendship

Hospitality is culture itself and not simply one ethic amongst others.
Insofar as it has to do with the ethos, that is, the residence,
one's at-home, the familiar place of dwelling, as much as the manner
of being there, the manner in which we relate to ourselves and to others,
to others as our own or as foreigners, ethics is hospitality;
ethics is entirely coextensive with the experience of hospitality,
whichever way one expands or limits that.
—Jacques Derrida, On Cosmopolitanism and Forgiveness,
pp. 16–17.

One of the most promising approaches to understanding the ethical issues at stake in current notions and practices of cultural exchange that inform study abroad and internationalization is that provided by the philosopher Jacques Derrida whose seminar on the theme of hospitality at the Ecole des Hautes Etudes en Sciences Sociales in Paris in 1996 develops a set of related concepts tying hospitality to 'friendship,' 'forgiveness' and 'the gift.' His seminar, now a kind of pedagogical institution, also maps the development of his thought in a series of related texts. At the same time, the seminar on hospitality provides a context for raising a range of related questions concerning national and ethnic identity, citizenship, and immigration all in close proximity to the Other and the welcoming of the Other. Derrida's network of concepts produces a novel ethical space in which to revisit the Kantian liberal notion of cosmopolitanism within the context of globalization and to raise fresh questions about our openness to the Other—also about segregation, separation, and exclusion as instruments of 'othering.' Derrida's late philosophy of hospitality, although not easy to read or understand, promises an approach suited to understanding the discourse of the Other and many of the underlying ethical issues that trouble existing practices and justifications of study abroad and internationalization of higher education.

Derrida's understanding of 'hospitality' is colored by the uniqueness of his own personal experience as a French Jew born into a family that had lived in Algeria for many years. David Carroll, a colleague at the University of California at Irvine, in memoriam describes Derrida's uncomfortable identity caught between Arab Algerian and French colonialist communities and excluded by Vichy government by the fact of his Jewishness:

Jacques Derrida was born in El-Biar, Algeria on July 15, 1930 into a family that had lived in Algeria for centuries before its conquest and colonization by the French. His grandparents had become French citizens in 1870, when the *Crémieux Decree* granted citizenship to the Jewish population of Algeria, who, like its Arab and Berber inhabitants, had until then been considered French subjects with limited civil and legal rights. Jacques described more than once the effect on him of arriving at school one day at the age of 12 to be told that he could no longer attend classes. He had been excluded from the French public school system because of the severe *Numerus Clausus* imposed on Jewish students after the Vichy collaborationist government rescinded citizenship for all Algerian Jews. He was able to return to school a year after the arrival of Allied troops in North Africa, but never forgot how it felt to be a victim of discrimination, deprived of basic civil rights, and treated as an unwanted foreigner in his own land; to realize, as he put it, that he was a citizen of no country at all. (*http://www.universityofcalifornia.edu/senate/inmemoriam/ JacquesDerrida.htm*)

In a recent paper Carroll (2006) inspired by Derrida's remarks on his 'remains' of Algeria, what remains in his identity and work, he considers Derrida's experience as an 'other,' connecting it to his view of the arbitrariness and accidental nature of citizenship and its relation to systematic exclusions of certain peoples. He begins by referring to Derrida's own reflections on his loss of citizenship in *Monolingualism of the Other* that is important to cite in this context:

A supposedly 'ethnic' or 'religious' group that finds itself one day deprived, as a group, of citizenship by a state that, with the brutality of a unilateral decision, withdraws it without asking for their opinion, and *without the said group gaining back any other citizenship. No other.* Now I have experienced that. Along with others, I lost then recovered my French citizenship. I lost it for years without having any other. None at all, you see [...]. And then, one day, 'one fine day,' without once again having requested anything, and still too young to know it with a properly political knowledge, I found my aforementioned citizenship again. The state, to which I had never spoken, had returned it to me [...]. The withdrawal of French citizenship from the Jews of Algeria, with everything that followed, was the work of the French alone. They decided it all by themselves, in their heads; they must have been dreaming about it all along; they implemented it all by themselves. I was very young at that time, and I certainly did not understand very well [...] what citizenship and the loss of citizenship *mean.* (*Monolingualism of the Other* (15–16, trans. modified [34–35])

Carroll (2006: 908) comments:

What is 'learned' from the loss of citizenship, without ever understanding exactly what is meant by the term, is the precarious, arbitrary, artificial nature of citizenship and national identity, that they are not in any sense "natural." What is experienced are the destructive effects of exclusion, of being put in the place of the other, the outsider who is declared by law not to be in his proper place even in the place where he has always been, the indigenous alien who is not granted the same basic rights as others who inhabit the same place. It is to learn what it is to be 'hostage' to others in one's own home, in this case, hostage to the French in one's native land [*pays*]. This is something, Derrida admits, that always remained with him.

Influenced by Levinas and the priority he accords to ethics and to an absolute form of hospitality that exists prior to politics, Derrida forges an ethics as responsibility to the Other based on a series of possible and impossible aporias—hospitality, the gift, forgiveness, mourning—that in themselves transcend and avoid the common assumption in liberal accounts 'that responsibility is to be associated with behavior that accords with general principles capable of justification in the public realm' (Reynolds, 2006 *http://www.iep.utm.edu/d/derrida.htm#H6*). Reynolds' discussion of Derrida's approach to the Other is both insightful and instructive not only in terms of elaborating 'responsibility to the other' and the injunction of Abrahamic principle of 'radical singularity' before God but also an account of the 'wholly Other/Messianic' that taps the Judaic tradition and points to 'the *messianic* structure of existence is open to the coming of an entirely ungraspable and unknown other' as well as 'the concrete, historical *messianisms* are open to the coming of a specific other of known character-istics.' (ibid.).

'Hospitality,' for Derrida, thus, has a rich religio-philosophical significance and complexity that motivates his pedagogy in the seminar and his writings of the last decade. Gil Anidjar (2001) in 'A Note on Hospitality' suggests:

> The thread of hospitality—here explicitly linked to forgiveness and friendship, to humor and transcendence—can be followed in Derrida's work since at least *Writing and Difference*, most notably, though not exclusively, in his readings of Levinas. It has emerged in a more explicit fashion in *Politics of Friendship, Adieu to Emmanuel Levinas,* and recently in *Of Hospitality* (which includes two earlier sessions of Derrida's seminar on hospitality). But who or what is the subject of hospitality? To one reading of this question, the French lan-guage provides a disarmingly and qualitatively simple answer: the *hôte*. In French, the hote is both the one who gives, *donne,* and the one who received *reçoit,* hospitality. As Derrida argues, however, this distinction finds its condition in the aporetic laws of hospitality that prior to either, give both *hôtes* the possibility and the impossibility of the gift of hospital-ity. (356)

He concludes that Derrida's neologism *hostipitalité* 'raises in a radically new way the question of the subject of hospitality.' It is to be located in an aporia, a puzzle or paradox that harnesses an impossible reconciliation between two contradictory imper-atives: the imperative to welcome the Other in an absolute or unconditional sense before the knowledge or recognition that comes with names or understanding iden-tity and the imperative to welcome someone in particular, someone who might pose a threat to us or even to whom we might refuse entry to our home. Derrida himself expresses unconditional hospitality

> But pure or unconditioned hospitality does not consist in such an invitation ('I invite you, I welcome you into my home, on the condition that you adapt to the laws and norms of my territory, according to my language, tradition, memory, and so on'). Pure and uncon-ditional hospitality, hospitality itself, opens or is in advance open to someone who is nei-ther expected nor invited, to whomever arrives as an absolutely foreign visitor, as a new arrival, nonidentifiable and unforeseeable, in short, wholly other. (*Philosophy in a Time of Terror*, p. 17)

In 'Hostipitality' Derrida investigates a reading of Kant's cosmopolitanism given in the third article of *Perpetual Peace* which stipulates "Cosmopolitan Right shall be limited to Conditions of Universal Hospitality." As Derrida explains:

> In this context hospitality [Hospitalität (Wirtbarkeit)] means the right of a stranger [bedeutet das Recht eines Fremdlings] not to be treated with hostility [en ennemi] when he arrives on someone else's territory [seiner Ankunft auf der Boden eines andern wegen von diesem nicht feindselig behandelt zu werden].

And he goes on to argue:

> Two words are underlined by Kant in this title: "cosmopolitan right" [Weltbürgerrecht: the right of world citizens]—we are thus in the space of right, not of morality and politics or anything else but of a right determined in its relation to citizenship, the state, the subject of the state, even if it is a world state—it is a question therefore of an international right; the other underlined word is "hospitality" [der allgemeinen Hospitalität, universal hospitality]. It is a question therefore of defining the conditions of a cosmopolitan right, of a right the terms of which would be established by a treaty between states, by a kind of UN charter before the fact, and one of these conditions would be what Kant calls universal hospitality, die allgemeine Hospitalität. (p. 3)

Yet this liberal cosmopolitan right will not suffice. In order to truly resolve all conflict and otherness one has to welcome the Other unconditionally, that is without prior knowledge of the Other or without a name, indeed, without documents such as a passport. This unconditionality implies a total openness—of house, of being, of culture—to the Other, an ethical relation that is transgressive in its overcoming of conditions either religious as in the Judeo-Christian understanding of hospitality, or political as in Kant's reference to citizenship and the state. Derrida is in direct, conscious, and acknowledged opposition to the anthropological and ethnological tradition. And it is a tradition that he, in the last analysis, is forced to debate on the terrain of pure semantics: archaic exchange is indeed, as Mauss, Boas, and Malinowski described it, but the generic name 'gift' is completely misapplied. It does not translate the reality of the primitive gesture, but the moralizing intention of the author (the 'liberal socialism' of Mauss opposed to Marxism and mercantilism, wishing to reinject generosity in times dominated by egoism and individualism). It also presupposes the 'invention' (or at least the overestimation) of the *hau* (the spirit of the object given) as a 'causal non-causal factor' of the gift (it is at this point that Derrida repeats the critique that Levi-Strauss had already made).

Culture goes to school:
Education and the dilemmas of culture

Being a central organizing force for numerous academic disciplines, 'culture' is deployed regularly to understand and interpret human experiences. Even as culture is believed to embed a host of social relationships, they do not exhaust the many usages and meanings of the term. From assumptions about knowledge, habits and capabilities to that of law and art, the ever-expanding reach of culture involves social and material practices including everyday moments of talk and text.[1] A common treatment of culture has often been associated with orders, actions and interactions. In this formulation, culture is seen as an ordering device that provides a frame to code, classify and make sense of human experiences. Even as they differ radically in their practices, the articulations such as counter-culture, sub-culture, popular culture etc. are responses to the functions of culture. Seeing culture as an ordering device, however, opens up two major problems. First, such a prescription accords culture an existential autonomy. The foundational status of culture can lead to forging a simplistic and misplaced causal relationship between individual's behavior and her culture. Second, the thesis of autonomy makes a clear separation between culture and its material organization. The autonomy and neutrality of culture is called into question by neo-Marxists who argue against thinking of culture as an entity "in itself" and state that contrary to the claims of their natural origins, cultural attributes are often staged (Held, 1980:78). Marcuse (1964) sees bourgeois culture containing two necessary parts: material culture consisting of social and economic practices including work, family, education and leisure among others, and intellectual culture involving values of science, humanities and the autonomous arts. Recognizing that the bourgeois culture is plugged into the larger capitalist system, Marcuse famously asserts that culture serves to maintain harmonizing illusions. In different contexts, Adorno & Horkheimer (1979) formulate a concept of culture industry that they see functioning like a factory leading people to become passive, content consumers. Culture, in this view takes focus away from the genuine rapture of creativity and freedom.

Culture shares an uneasy and tenuous relationship with education. Among the many dilemmas, some of the urgent questions revolve around the degree of cultural content in curriculum, instruction and educational environments. How much culture is desirable in schools? Whose culture? What aspects of culture? These questions hint at a much more complex terrain of negotiations between competing values such as creating democratic civic sense in schools despite the dangers of social reproduction of dominant cultures, and promoting the ideals of freedom and pluralism against the administrative wisdom of setting feasible solutions. Historically, education assumed the role of citizenship formation that was orchestrated by putting in place several measures to make people more akin to each other. Single language instruction, the pledge of allegiance and school uniforms were some of the ways in which schools attempted to create their own culture involving order, norms, rewards and punishment. To a large extent, schools mirrored the social arrangements and roles culture performed therein. Thus, the norm-setting functions of culture were picked up by schools as they employed the 'culture-as container' model. Invested in the neutrality of culture, the container model was normative, integrationist and drew on the method of transmission of culture/knowledge—from the old to young, teacher to student and the initiated to the novice. Some of the pluralistic models went beyond the integrationist or assimilatory visions of culture in schools. The main difference lies in the ways they address the non-dominant/minority cultures in schools. Ranging from tolerance, inclusion, diversity and acceptance, the pluralist models of schooling involve representations and degrees of participation of some non-dominant cultures. The academic emergence of area studies/non-western studies and the social celebration of non-dominant cultures such as Cinco de Mayo or the Chinese New Year have been some of the manifestations of pluralist models. While these models are liberal, they define and accommodate non-normative cultures in terms of the dominant culture. In practice, the customary celebration of minority cultures often showcases them to be static on the one hand and hinges on exoticizing them on the other. The largely symbolic inclusion of minority cultures does not redefine the meaning of diversity; neither does it provide a sustainable engagement with culture.

In recent years, the scholarship on difference and identity formation has drawn attention to the limits of articulating non-dominant cultures in terms of their symbolic representation without addressing the complex issues of power involved in education. Reasserting a much-needed rethinking of the relationship between culture and education, the scholarship emerging across disciplines has paid serious attention to the multiple nodes of identity and practices of identifying—including but not limited to—dialects, creoles, hybrids, body art, cross-dressing and trans-gendering.[2] At the minimum, these efforts have been able to bring about a change in what was previously understood to be an adequate response to tackling culture. And the shift from integration, accommodation to that of recognizing difference, has, more than anything, brought to fore the contested and complex sphere of culture in academic spaces. Theorizing the discourse of difference, scholars have deployed the notion of border, especially in analyzing immigrant and working class experiences, dissident sexualities, and experiences of women of color, among others. In as much as the metaphors of border-zones and border-subjects draw attention to difference, they also indicate that borders are permeable. It is possible for individuals to operate in multiple cultural spheres and belong to them all. Education based on difference can offer learning opportunities by opening up spaces that are usually considered to be "controversial"; it can structure education around empathy, solidarity and non-hegemonic visions of life. In practice, difference presents a range of challenges for educators. As Burbules (1997) cautions, "…certain differences are not simply neutral, but imbued with power differentials that divide us; and because differences can reveal incommensurabilities that stand beyond the limit of language and our ability to understand."

The ambivalence of practicing difference is markedly clear in the discourse of liberal multiculturalism that recognizes non-dominant cultures, but nonetheless exhibits a clear affirmation of the limits of such recognition. Multicultural education shares several of the pluralistic elements including diversity, inclusion, tolerance and acceptance; it has also put in place institutionalized support including cultural houses, faith-based centers and area studies.[3] The short span of institutional life of multiculturalism is a testament to the tensions between progressive resistance politics, largely articulated by students, and its eventual appropriation into an apolitical discourse. Be it the mass student protests for racial justice in colleges, or the uprising against

Vietnam and Iraq occupations, or the service workers and graduate employees strikes on various campuses, the oppositional resistance has attempted to redefine the hierarchical academic cultures.[4] Remaining on the safer side, however, multiculturalism has engaged the question of culture in academy by positing that all cultural groups have unique sets of beliefs and logics that are interpretable within the group. In his spirited piece "Multiculturalism kills me!" Vijay Prashad (2007) sums up the agenda, "More diversity, less racism. That's the received wisdom. Diversity and tolerance are part of an ensemble of concepts that form the heart of liberal multiculturalism."

Despite strong financial support and widespread acceptance, liberal multiculturalism has not been able to engage with culture substantively. At the outset two major problems can be identified with current practices of multiculturalism. First, the treatment of culture through texts and social events has led to forms of cultural consumption and cultural tourism in which students are at free will to take a tour of a culture of their choice. Speaking about multiculturalism-as-tourism model, Julie Drew (1997:301) states, "Students learnt to 'tour' the Chinese experience, the Latina experience, the lesbian experience. The act of tourism erases the notions of heterogeneity and difference within groups—groups that are marked as others by the very inclusion. Tourism does not compel students to negotiate or dialogue, but rather sit back and be entertained/educated." Second, the rhetoric of multiculturalism centering on cultural celebrations is being used increasingly to hurl insidious forms of racism against minority students. The resurgence of "theme parties" bordering on stereotypes, caricatures and racism under the pretext of fun and, ironically, cultural respect presents a case in point.

The footprints of modern study abroad can be unmistakably traced back to the history of travel, cultural exchange and liberal multiculturalism. In as much as institutional multiculturalism continues to invest in culture without engaging with relations of power or questions of reinvention, it stands the risk of reducing culture to cultural artifacts. The social history of multiculturalism—from its initial connections to student activism to the subsequent institutionalization—is a fascinating cultural phenomenon in itself that is shaped by identity politics, internationalization of higher education and commodification of culture. At the outset, an inquiry into study abroad needs to pay attention to the idea of place, since it is central to the project. How does place become a special object of learning and exchange? What places hold currency in the economy of study abroad? In line with the purpose of study abroad, the newer international destinations are undergoing change in order to get connected to the larger system of institutional mobility and networks. While previous destinations for study abroad concentrated in Europe and Australia, the recent locales include China, India and the Philippines, which reflects the integration of these countries in the global economy. Following Mendoza and Dolby, we believe that it is possible to construct humanistic, reflexive and critical study abroad by exploring the logics of place and culture. For instance, even as an unintended outcome, a study tour to the developing world can start off reflections about the politics of resources. Particularly fitting to the present circumstances in the US would be an exchange focusing on the misrepresentations of Islam. As Dolby (2007: 152) observes, "Although courses in political science may teach students the theories of empire, the experience of constantly being questioned and probed about American foreign policy while abroad had a more lasting impact on students."

Conclusion

Culture is as much about inventing as it is about preserving; about discontinuity as much as about continuation; about novelty as much as about transcendence of norm; about the unique as much as about the regular; about change as much as about monotony or reproduction; about the unexpected as much as about the predictable...." (Bauman, 1999, p. xiv).

Traveling to distant shores in order to understand other cultures was once a possibility available to a chosen few including anthropologists, religious and political leaders and the elite. Foregrounded in the logics of interconnectivity and transnationalization of education, culture has become more pronounced in the contemporary curricula. Institutionalization of study abroad can be seen as the new social life in education. It is embedded within the intensification of information and electronic communication on the one hand, and it is an enhanced articulation of the liberal multiculturalism on the other.

In this chapter we have argued for rethinking of cultural exchange by paying attention to its conceptual ancestry involving the history of ethnography and understanding its relevance to think about citizenship, difference and institutional makeup. Documenting the cannibal Other has implications for how the other is essentialized, toured or turned into an ahistorical spectacle. For education, this merits a renewed attention to power and a dislodgement of the continued practice of affixing non-dominant cultures as add-on. A critique of the promotion of selective, non-conflicting aspects of culture would be instructive in thinking about study abroad. There exists a need to develop a critical theory of cultural exchange that would engage with a broad range of scholarship including cultural studies, progressive education and critical geography among others. In much the same way, the theory will need to take a cue from culture-jamming practices of numerous kinds that have been able to invert the bureaucracies of hierarchical culture in order to open up humanistic, civic engagements.

Endnotes

1. A host of definitions of culture rest on its durability, all-inclusive scope and its role in norm-setting. The much cited formulation by Edward B. Tylor (1924 [1871], in his treatise *Primitive Culture* and the more recent definition put forth by UNESCO are two cases in point. Tylor writes, "Culture or civilization, taken in its wide ethnographic sense, is that complex whole which includes knowledge, belief, art, morals, law, custom, and any other capabilities and habits acquired by man as a member of society." (p.5). A century later, UNSECO's description of

culture entails " a set of distinctive spiritual, material, intellectual and emotional features of society or a social group, and that it encompasses, in addition to art and literature, lifestyle, ways of living together, value systems, traditions and beliefs." [UNESCO, 2002]

2. Difference and identity have been engaged on multiple levels, addressing a range of issues from citizenship and media to political action and coalition building (Young, 1997, 2002; Woodward, 1997; Castles, 2000; Darder & Torres, 2004).

3. Institutionalization of area studies makes for an interesting genealogy. Emerged in post world war II US context, the area studies truly came of age during the cold war years as centers for national security before being accommodated into multicultural education. Territorialization of knowledge took new shapes in the 1990s in the wake of intensified economic processes. This historic shift can be seen in David Ludden's paper (1997) 'The Territoriality of Knowledge and the History of Area Studies.'

4. Joy Ann Williamson's social biography "Black Power on Campus: The University of Illinois, 1965–1975" looks at the politics of defiance against the academic power elite. Interestingly, Vietnam and Iraq uprisings on college campuses and their role in re-conceptualizing academic spaces have not received much scholarly attention.

References

Adorno, T. & Horkheimer, M. (1979) *Dialectic of Enlightenment*. London: Verso.

Anidjar, Gil. (2001) 'A Note on Hospitality' in J. Derrida (Ed.), *Acts of Religion*. New York: London.

Bauman, Z. (1999) *Culture as Praxis*. London: Sage .

Behn, Aphra(1688) *Oroonoko; or, The Royal Slave* at http://www.pinkmonkey.com/dl/library1/book0222.pdf.

Bolen, M. (2001). Consumerism and U.S. study abroad. *Journal of Studies in International Education*, 5(3), 182–200.

Burbules, N. (1997). A Grammar of Difference. Some Ways of Rethinking and Diversity of Educational Topics. *Australian Education Researcher*, 24(1), 97–116. http://faculty.ed.uiuc.edu/burbules/papers/difference.html

Carroll, D. (2006) 'Remains' of Algeria: Justice, Hospitality, Politics.*MLN*,121 (4) September 2006 (French Issue), pp. 808–827.

Chieffo, L. & Griffiths, L. (2004) Large-Scale Assessment of Student Attitudes after a Short-Term Study Abroad Program. *Frontiers: The Interdisciplinary Journal of Study Abroad*, 10(4) 165–177.

Clifford, J. (1986) *Writing Culture: The Poetics and Politics of Ethnography*. Berkeley & Los Angeles: University of California Press.

Darder, A. & Torres, R. (2004) *After Race: Racism After Multiculturalism*. New York: NYU Press.

Defoe, D. (1719) *Robinson Crusoe*. London: W. Taylor, at http://www.pierre-marteau.com/editions/1719-robinson-crusoe.html.

Derrida,J. (1997a) *Adieu a Emmanuel Levinas*. Paris: Galilee.

Derrida, J. (1997b) *The Politics of Friendship*. (G. Collins Tr.) London: Verso.

Derrida, J. (1998) Monolingualism of the other: or the prothesis of origin (P. Menash, Tr.) Stanford, Stanford University Press.

Derrida, J., & Dufourmantelle, A. (2000) *Of Hospitality* (R. Bowlby, Trans.). Stanford, CA: Stanford University Press. (Original work published in 1997).

Derrida, J. (2000) Hospitality. (B. Stocker & F. Morlock Tr.) *Angelaki, Journal of the Theoretical humanities,* 5, 3 December: 3–18

Derrida, J. (2001) *On Cosmopolitanism and Forgiveness.* London: Routledge.

Derrida, J. & Roudinesco, E. (2004) *For What Tomorrow…*(J. Fort, Trans.) Stanford, CA: Stanford University Press. (Original work published in 2001).

Derrida, J. (2005) The Principle of Hospitality [An interview with Dominique Dhombres]. *Le Monde,* December 2, 1997. Translated by Ashley Thompson, *Parallax,* 2005, vol. 11, no. 1, 6–9.

Dolby, N. (2007). Reflections on Nation: American Undergraduates and Education Abroad. *Journal of Studies in International Education,* 11(2), 141–156.

Drew, J. (1999) Cultural Tourism and the Commodified other: Reclaiming Difference in Multicultural Classroom. *The Review of Education/Pedagogy/Cultural Studies,* 2–3, 297–309.

Eriksen, T.H (2001) 'Between universalism and relativism: A critique of the UNESCO concepts of culture.' In Jane Cowan, Marie-Bénédicte Dembour & Richard Wilson (Eds)., *Culture and Rights: Anthropological Perspectives,* pp. 127–48. Cambridge University Press. Copy at http://folk.uio.no/geirthe/UNESCO.html

Gillespie, S. (2003). Toward "Genuine Reciprocity": Reconceptualizing International Liberal Education in the Era of Globalization. *Liberal Education,* 89(1), 6–15.

Held, D. (1980). *Introduction to Critical Theory: Horkheimer to Habermas.* Berkeley & Los Angeles: University of California Press.

Hoffman, D.(1996). Culture and Self in Multicultural Education: Reflections on Discourse, Text, and Practice. *American Educational Research Journal,* 33(3), 545–569.

Ingraham, E. & Peterson, D. (2004) Assessing the Impact of Study Abroad on Student Learning at Michigan State University. *Frontiers: The Interdisciplinary Journal of Study Abroad,* 10(4) 165–177.

Institute of International Education. (2005). *Open doors 2005.* New York: Author.

Kordvani, A. (2006) Hospitality, Politics of Mobility, and the Movement of Service Suppliers under the Gats. *Melbourne Journal of International Law,* 7(1), 74–103.

Lévi-Strauss, C. (1961 [1952]) Race et histoire. Paris: Denoël.

Lévi-Strauss, C. (1979 [1971]) "Race et histoire," in Raymond Bellour & Catherine Clément (Eds)., Claude Lévi-Strauss, pp. 427—462. Paris: Gallimard (originally published in *Revue internationale des sciences sociales,* 23(4).

Ludden, D. (1997) 1997) 'The territoriality of Knowledge and the History of Area Studies,' Retrieved on April 14, 2008, from http://www.sas.upenn.edu/~dludden/areast1.htm

Marcuse, H. (1964) *One-Dimensional Man: Studies in the Ideology of Advanced Industrial Society.* Boston: Beacon Press.

Mendoza, M. (nd). *Cultural Exchange as a Challenge to Orientalism.* Retrieved on April 12, 2008, from htttp://www.faf.org/aboutfaf/pdf/MM_Challenge per cent20to per cent20Orientalism. pdf

Montaigne, de M. (1580) *On Cannibals* (P. Brians, Tr.) at http://www.wsu.edu:8080/~wldciv/world_civ_reader/world_civ_reader_2/montaigne.html

Montesquieu (1712) *Persian Letters,* at http://web.wm.edu/history/rbsche/plp/?svr=www.

Open doors (2007) *Report on International Educational Exchange.* Retrievd on April 12, 2008 from http://www.opendoors.iienetwork.org/

Parekh, B. (2000) *Rethinking Multiculturalism: Cultural Diversity and Political Theory.* London: Macmillan.

Prashad, V. (2007) Multiculturalism Kills me! *ZNet*. Retrieved on April 12, 2008. http://www.zmag.org/sustainers/content/2007–04/26prashad.cfm

Reynolds, J. (2006) Jacques Derrida (1930–2004). *Internet Encyclopedia of Philosophy*. Retrieved April 12, 2008 from *http://www.iep.utm.edu/d/derrida.htm#H6*

Rousseau, J. (1754) A Discourse on a Subject Proposed by the Academy of Dijon: What Is the Origin of Inequality Among Men, and Is It Authorised by Natural Law? Translated by G. D. H. Cole at *http://www.constitution.org/jjr/ineq.htm.*

Rousseau, J. (1979) *Emile, or on education* (A. Bloom, Tr.) Basic Books. (Original work was published in 1762) at http://www.ilt.columbia.edu/pedagogies/rousseau/Contents2.html.

Rousseau, J. (1754) *A Discourse on the Origin and Basis of Inequality Among Men* at http://www.constitution.org/jjr/ineq.htm.

Sutton, R. & Rubin, D. (2004). The GLOSSARI Project: Initial Findings from a System-Wide Research Initiative on Study Abroad Learning Outcomes. *Frontiers: The Interdisciplinary Journal of Study Abroad*, 10 (4), 65–82.

Tylor, E.B. (1958/1871) *Primitive Culture*, 2 vols. New York: Harper.

Tyler, S. (1986) Post-Modern Ethnography: From Document of the Occult to Occult Document. In J. Clifford (Ed.), *Writing Culture : The poetics and Politics of Ethnography*. Berkeley: University of California Press.

UNESCO (2002) Universal Delcaration on Cultural Diversity. Retrieved on April 14, 2008 from http://www.unesco.org/education/imld_2002/unversal_decla.shtml

Vaughan, A.T. & Vaughan, V.M (1992) *Shakespeare's Caliban*. Cambridge: Cambridge University Press.

Williamson, J. A (2003) *Black Power on Campus: The University of Illinois, 1965–1975*. Urbana, IL: University of Illinois Press.

Woodward, K. (1997) *Identity and Difference: Culture, Media and Identities*. Thousand Oaks/New Delhi: Sage Publications.

Young, I.M. (2000) *Inclusion and Democracy*. New York: Oxford University Press.

Young, I.M. (1997) *Intersecting Voices: Dilemmas of Gender, Political Philosophy, and Policy*. Princeton, NJ: Princeton University Press.

Zlomislic, M.(2004) Conflict, Tolerance and Hospitality, *The Philosopher*, Volume LXXXXII, No. 2, at http://www.the-philosopher.co.uk/conflict.htm

About the Authors

Simon Marginson is Professor of Higher Education at the University of Melbourne, Australia, where he works in that University's Centre for the Study of Higher Education. He was elected as Fellow of the Academy of Social Sciences, Australia in 2000, designated an Australian Research Council Australian Professorial Fellow in 2002, and has held continuous Australian Research Council project funding since 1995. During an academic career dating from 1993 he has developed work on, successively, higher education and education policy, comparative and international education, studies of globalization, and the knowledge economy and creativity. He is a member of the boards of the *Journal of South East Asian Education*, the *Journal of Education and Work, Higher Education, Higher Education Quarterly, Thesis Eleven*, the *ASHE Reader on Comparative Education, Critical Studies in Education, Higher Education Policy, Asia-Pacific Journal of Education* and the *Journal of Higher Education* and edited the *Australian Journal of Education* from 1995–2000. His academic awards include the Outstanding Publications Award of the American Educational Research Association Division J, for 2001 (with Mark Considine) and the George Z. F. Bereday award for the best journal article of 2001, Comparative and International Education Society, in 2002 (with Marcela Mollis, University of Buenos Aires). He has published eight sole authored or jointly authored books, 51 chapters, 73 refereed journal articles, 20 review essays and reviews, and numerous other journal articles as well as media commentary, policy monographs, government reports and contributions to policy debate. His books include *Markets in Education* (1997), *The Enterprise University: Power, Governance and Reinvention in Australia* (2000), *Prospects of Higher Education: Globalization, Market Competition, Public Goods and the Future of the*

University (2007), *Creativity in the Global Knowledge Economy* (with Michael Peters and Peter Murphy, 2009) and *International Student Security* (with Chris Nyland, Erlenawati Sawir and Helen Forbes-Mewett, forthcoming). He is active in scholarly circles throughout the world, particularly in the Asia-Pacific, Europe, and North America and Mexico; has provided advice on higher education and globalization for the governments of Australia, Malaysia, Hong Kong, Vietnam and New Zealand, is frequently called on to provide papers in relation to university comparison and ranking, and has completed several policy papers for the OECD including two chapters on *Higher Education and Globalization* (with Marijk van der Wende, forthcoming), and the 2007–2008 thematic review of tertiary education in the Netherlands. Four of his books have been published in China and a fifth book on higher education and globalization is presently being translated for publication by Peking University Press.

Peter Murphy is associate professor of communications at Monash University, Australia. He is co-author of *Creativity and the Global Knowledge Economy* (Peter Lang, 2009) and *Dialectic of Romanticism: A Critique of Modernism* (Continuum, 2004), author of *Civic Justice: From Greek Antiquity to the Modern World* (Prometheus/Humanity Books, 2001), co-editor of *Agon, Logos, Polis* (Franz Steiner, 2000) and *The Left in Search of a Center* (University of Illinois Press, 1996), and editor of a special issue of *South Atlantic Quarterly* on friendship (Duke University Press, 1998). His body of work includes more than seventy journal articles and chapters in edited collections. He has been research fellow and visiting professor of philosophy in the Graduate Faculty of the New School for Social Research in New York City; visiting scholar in the Hellenic language and literatures programme at the Ohio State University; visiting scholar at Panteion University in Athens, Greece; visiting professor in political science at Baylor University, Texas; director of the master of communications programme at Victoria University of Wellington, New Zealand; visiting research fellow in philosophy at Ateneo de Manila University in the Philippines; and visiting professor in communications and media studies at Seoul National University, South Korea, and in the Department of Arts and Cultural Studies at the University of Copenhagen, Denmark. He is coordinating editor of the international critical theory and historical sociology journal *Thesis Eleven: Critical Theory and Historical Sociology* (Sage), and from 1998 to 2001 worked in senior editorial roles for Australia's most successful Internet start-up company, Looksmart.

Michael A. Peters is Professor of Education in the Department of Educational Policy Studies at the University of Illinois at Urbana-Champaign and holds a position as Adjunct Professor at the Royal Melbourne Institute of Technology (School of Art). He held joint professorial positions at the Universities of Auckland (NZ) and Glasgow (UK). He was elected Academic Vice-President of the New Zealand Association of University Teachers and elected an inaugural Fellow of the New Zealand Academy of Humanities. He is the executive editor of *Educational*

Philosophy and Theory (Wiley-Blackwell) and editor of two international ejournals, *Policy Futures in Education* and *E-Learning* (Symposium). His interests focus broadly on education, philosophy, and social theory and he has written some forty books and many academic papers, including most recently: *Creativity and the Global Knowledge Economy* (Peter Lang, 2009) with Simon Marginson and Peter Murphy; *Showing and Doing: Wittgenstein as a Pedagogical Philosopher* (Paradigm, 2008) with Nick Burbules and Paul Smeyers; *Global Knowledge Cultures* (Sense) with Cushla Kapitzke; *Subjectivity and Truth: Foucault, Education, and The Culture of Self* (Peter Lang, 2008) with Tina Besley; *Why Foucault? New Directions in Educational Research* (Peter Lang, 2007) with Tina Besley; *Knowledge Economy, Development and the Future of the University* (Sense, 2007); and *Building Knowledge Cultures: Educational and Development in the Age of Knowledge Capitalism* (Rowman & Littlefield, 2006), with Tina Besley.

Shivali Tukeo is a doctoral candidate in the department of Educational Policy Studies, University of Illinois at Urbana Champaign and she has been working with the Global Studies in Education program for over four years. Her doctoral research focuses on the connections between social networks, transnational advocacy groups, and educational policy production. Other areas of her research interests include International Education, Social Movements, and South Asian politics.

Index